MODERN DATA WAREHOUSING, MINING, AND VISUALIZATION

George M. Marakas

Kelley School of Business
Indiana University

Upper Saddle River, New Jersey 07458

This book is dedicated to all who seek to answer the unanswered. Good luck on your adventures!

Library of Congress Cataloging-in-Publication Data

Marakas, George M.
    Modern data warehousing, mining, and visualization : core concepts / George M. Marakas.
        p.   cm.
    ISBN 0-13-101459-5
    1. Data warehousing. 2. Data mining. 3. Visualization—Data processing. I. Title.

QA76.9.D37 M37 2002
658.4′038′0285574—dc21

2002034556

Executive Editor: Bob Horan
Publisher: Natalie Anderson
Project Manager: Kyle Hannon
Editorial Assistant: Maat Van Uitert
Media Project Manager: Joan Waxman
Senior Marketing Manager: Sharon Turkovich
Marketing Assistant: Scott Patterson
Managing Editor (Production): John Roberts
Production Editor: Kelly Warsak
Production Assistant: Joe DeProspero

Permissions Coordinator: Suzanne Grappi
Associate Director, Manufacturing: Vincent Scelta
Production Manager: Arnold Vila
Manufacturing Buyer: Michelle Klein
Cover Design: Bruce Kenselaar
Cover Illustration: Getty Images, Inc.
Full-Service Project Management and Composition: BookMasters, Inc.
Project Manager: Jennifer Welsch, BookMasters, Inc.
Printer/Binder: RR Donnelley & Sons Company

Credits and acknowledgments borrowed from other sources and reproduced, with permission, in this textbook appear on appropriate page within text.

Microsoft Excel, Solver, and Windows are registered trademarks of Microsoft Corporation in the United States and other countries. Screen shots and icons reprinted with permission from Microsoft Corporation. This book is not sponsored or endorsed by or affiliated with Microsoft Corporation.

Pearson Education LTD.
Pearson Education Australia PTY, Limited
Pearson Education Singapore, Pte. Ltd
Pearson Education North Asia Ltd
Pearson Education, Canada, Ltd
Pearson Educación de Mexico, S.A. de C.V.
Pearson Education–Japan
Pearson Education Malaysia, Pte. Ltd

10 9 8 7 6 5 4 3 2 1
ISBN 0-13-101459-5

CONTENTS

PREFACE

CONCEPT AND PURPOSE

This text provides a foundation for teaching the basic concepts of data mining, warehousing, and visualization. The contents emphasize both technical and managerial issues and the implication of these modern emerging technologies on those issues.

I find it somewhat counterintuitive that the primary goal of the business school is to develop a thorough understanding of these emerging technologies from a user's perspective, yet the texts available to teach the subject to students in business schools tend to be written from a designer's perspective. In response, this text places strong emphasis on helping the student thoroughly understand the value of data warehouses and their associated technologies. The content focuses on a distinctly "real-world" orientation that emphasizes application and implementation over design and development in all topic areas. Managers of tomorrow need to understand data warehouse design, but they also must possess the skills necessary relate to the effective and strategic application of these technologies to advance the quality of problem identification and the associated solutions. Taking a multidisciplinary user/manager approach, this text looks at data warehousing technologies necessary to support the business processes of the twenty-first century.

In short, this book was motivated by my belief in the importance of preparing our future managers to be conversant with and capable of deploying data warehouse, mining, and visualization technologies. Application and understanding of use are, and will continue to be, more important to our managers of today and tomorrow than design.

WHO SHOULD USE THIS BOOK

This book is directed to business school students who aspire to a career in management with a firm that is a significant user of technology or is a member of a technology-driven industry — in others words, all students in business school. The primary course targets for this text are upper-level undergraduate or graduate information systems (IS) or operations and decision technologies (ODT) electives. These types of courses are regularly offered at 4-year universities as well as many community colleges. Ideally, students should have completed an introductory MIS program and possibly a semester of both systems analysis and design and database concepts before moving on to a focus on data warehousing. In addition, the further students are in their business curriculum, the more relevant the data mining and visualization coverage in the text becomes. In addition to being directed to students, many of the chapters in this text offer a good reference for practitioners in the course of their daily managerial activities.

ELEMENTS OF PEDAGOGY

The text makes appropriate use of many traditional pedagogical features commonly found in top business school curricula. The writing style is intended to strike a useful balance between a professional and conversational approach. The text uses graphics and examples of each concept introduced. Each chapter contains an introductory minicase highlighting the concepts introduced in that chapter. The end-of-chapter structure contains a summary of the key concepts introduced, review questions and problems, and references and additional support readings. A brief description of each of the pedagogical features of the text is listed here.

CHAPTER LEARNING OBJECTIVES

A statement of learning objectives for each chapter is presented in both performance and behavioral terms. In other words, the objectives state what the student should be capable of doing and understanding as a result of reading the chapter.

CHAPTER MINICASES

The minicases are all derived from actual situations and were selected to allow the student a point of reference for the material about to be presented in the chapter. In addition, each minicase makes specific reference to each of the key players in the scenario so that additional investigation using a variety of research tools could be conducted by either an individual student or a student team to further explore the situation presented.

FIGURES AND TABLES

Clear, carefully designed figures and tables can aid in the student's understanding of the material. Wherever possible, the diagrams contained in each chapter are not only referenced in the body of the text, but are positioned in such a way that they serve as a repeated visual reference for the textual discussion.

NARRATIVE VIGNETTES

To further the explanation of some of the concepts associated with the process of making a decision, the technique of narrative vignette is employed. Here, a situation using a fictitious cast of characters is presented to allow the student not only to see how the particular technique under discussion is applied but also to relate it to a set of circumstances or a context in which it might be considered relevant or applicable.

DATA MINING AND DATA VISUALIZATION EXERCISES

Of particular value to this first edition is the bundling of Megaputer's PolyAnalyst and TextAnalyst data mining and visualization software applications. This software suite represents the leading edge in data mining and visualization applications and is being distributed exclusively with this textbook. To purchase a commercial version of this software would cost more than $10,000. The version included with the text is fully enabled but has a time-out built into it such that the software will only be available for use by the student during the semester in which they are studying with this text. Included with the Megaputer applications is access to several actual datasets to be used in both the tutorials for the application and for many of the Megaputer exercises included at the end of relevant chapters.

IMPORTANT NOTE: The software bundled with this text is intended for use only in conjunction with adoption or purchase of this text. Following the installation and registration process, the software will be fully functional for a period of 6 months from the date of the installation. The software cannot be copied to another machine or reinstalled without purchasing an additional software license.

KEY CONCEPTS

Immediately following each chapter summary is an outline of the key concepts presented in the order of their appearance in the chapter. This section can aid the student in reviewing the material contained in the chapter in preparation for class discussion or examination.

QUESTIONS FOR REVIEW

Each chapter contains a list of 10 to 20 questions intended to support student retention and understanding of the material contained in the chapter. Each question is phrased in such a manner that a detailed and precise answer can be readily found in the chapter. Sample responses to each question are provided in the instructor materials supplied with adoption of the text.

FURTHER DISCUSSION

Several questions at the end of each chapter expand upon the material presented to allow the student to engage in a richer thought process and discussion than would occur using the review questions. Each of the discussion questions can be used to engage students in an open class discussion and many of them can be easily expanded into individual or team miniprojects.

NOTE TO THE INSTRUCTOR

COMPANION WEBSITE (WWW.PRENHALL.COM/MARAKAS)

The instructor support materials contain a number of useful support elements and materials. PowerPoint files, intended for use in preparing class lectures, are provided for each chapter. The review questions found in the text are also posted online so students can conveniently e-mail their answers directly to their professors.

Access to the instructor's section of the Web site requires a valid user ID and password. You simply need to register yourself as the instructor of the course by going to the Web site and completing the initial instructor registration process. Upon completion of the process, your registration request will be forwarded to your sales representative for validation. If you have any problems with your authorization, please contact your Prentice Hall sales representative. Once you are granted access to the instructor's section of the Web site, you will be able to download the Instructor's Manual and Test Item File for the text.

MEGAPUTER POLYANALYST AND TEXTANALYST SOFTWARE

Also note that the Megaputer software bundled with this text is designed to be installed on one machine only and, upon completion of the installation and registration process, will operate for a period of 6 months from the date of installation. Sample copies of the software for review can be obtained from your Prentice Hall representative.

CHAPTER DESCRIPTIONS

CHAPTER 1—INTRODUCTION TO DATA MINING, WAREHOUSING, AND VISUALIZATION

Logically enough, we begin at the beginning. This first chapter outlines the scope of the coverage for each of the three technologies of interest and lays a foundation for a more detailed study of each. In addition, a brief history of each of the technologies is presented so that the evolution and velocity of these powerful new business tools can be better realized.

CHAPTER 2—THE DATA WAREHOUSE

A detailed focus on the modern data warehouse is contained in Chapter 2. In this chapter, we explain the goal of the data warehouse and its associated characteristics. In addition, definitions and examples of the various data warehouse configurations are presented along with a detailed coverage of the role of metadata in the design and implementation of a successful data warehouse.

CHAPTER 3—DATA MINING AND DATA VISUALIZATION

Extending the concepts introduced in Chapters 1 and 2, this chapter looks at the realm of data mining and complex pattern extraction. The concept of online analytical processing (OLAP) and its variations are introduced. In addition, the chapter contains a discussion of the techniques used to mine data, their current limitations, and their application in data visualization contexts.

The second portion of this chapter focuses on data visualization and data mining analysis. To date, this book is the only text available on these subjects that includes a real, commercially available data mining and data visualization software package and integrates it into the content and pedagogy.

CHAPTER 4—MACHINES THAT CAN LEARN

The newest members of the world of artificial intelligence and data mining are the focus of this chapter. The concepts of decision trees, fuzzy logic, and linguistic ambiguity are introduced in detail as a precursor to a discussion of artificial neural networks and genetic algorithms. These analytical approaches are commonly employed in a typical data mining environment. Appended to Chapter 4 is an overview of a popular software application within this realm. In addition, a mathematical derivation of the most popular artificial neural network learning algorithm is also provided.

CHAPTER 5—EXECUTIVE INFORMATION SYSTEMS

This chapter turns our attention to one of the most often implemented interfaces in a modern data warehouse environment—the executive information system (EIS). Here, we look at the domain of the executive and the application of various enabling technologies to the development and application of an EIS. Coverage includes a definition of EIS technology, a brief history of its evolution, the unique characteristics of executive-level decisions and decision makers, as well as issues related to the successful introduction of an EIS into an organizational environment.

CHAPTER 6—DESIGNING AND BUILDING THE DATA WAREHOUSE

Chapter 6 delves deeper into the processes, procedures, tools, and techniques commonly found in conjunction with the development of an organizational data warehouse. This material allows students to better understand the unique challenges associated with this new and powerful approach to data storage.

CHAPTER 7—THE FUTURE OF DATA MINING, WAREHOUSING, AND VISUALIZATION

In this final chapter, we explore some of the trends and predicted future applications for data warehousing, mining, and visualization. Challenges to the advancement of these technologies into new realms are also discussed.

ACKNOWLEDGMENTS

Having lived through several textbook writing experiences, I am still learning a great deal and stumbling on occasion. Without the constant help of a number of people correcting my mistakes, answering my questions, contributing to the vast amount of required labor, and reassuring me in times of self-doubt, I do not believe this book would exist. What follows is a heartfelt expression of my deepest gratitude and dedication to those people who were instrumental in the development of this project.

First and foremost, I wish to thank my biggest supporters, my parents, George and Joan Marakas. I know I will always have at least two avid readers of my work as long as you are alive. Thank you.

To my daughter, Stephanie, who is about to embark on her own career as an educator. Always remember that I am proud of you and that I love you. If you give your energy and love to your students as you have to me, you will change the world for the better.

To my best everything, Debra Herbenick. Thank you, LB, for touching feet, hands, and heart. Your devotion to me is forever embedded in this book.

To my army of assistants—Yu-Ting "Caisy" Hung, Ji-Tsung "Ben" Wu, Han-Chieh "Harry" Jiang, Yu-Lin "Emily" Lin, and Nate Stout—all who invested endless hours of their lives in the creation of all my textbook projects and the supporting Web sites. You will be a part of all books I write, and whatever contribution they make, forever.

To my mentors, Dan Robey and Joyce Elam. In giving of yourself to teach me, you taught me how to teach others. Without your wisdom and guidance I would be lost.

To Bob Horan, David Alexander, Kyle Hannon, Sharon Turkovich, Kelly Warsak, Beth Spencer, JoAnn DeLuca, and the rest of the gang from Prentice Hall. Your combined contagious energy and excitement gave me the courage to write my first textbook and to successfully move on to many more.

To the newest members of this family, Sergei Ananyan and Brian Moore from Megaputer Corporation. Your enthusiasm and hard work made this text better and made the learning experience for all students who experience it much richer indeed.

In closing this rather lengthy, but quite necessary, acknowledgment, I would be remiss if I failed to thank my good friends and colleagues Brad Wheeler, Steven Hornik, Richard Johnson, and Deric Rush. Each of you, in your own unique way, gave me energy with your friendship and comfort with your faith.

Finally, my sincere appreciation and thanks goes out to all my students who attended my classes and assisted me in my development of ideas, examples, explanations, and content. You are my true motivation, and I will always remember you.

ABOUT THE AUTHOR

George M. Marakas is an Associate Professor of Information Systems and the BAT Faculty Fellow in Global IT Strategy at the Kelley School of Business at Indiana University in Bloomington. His teaching expertise includes systems analysis and design, technology-assisted decision making, managing IS resources, behavioral IS research methods, and data visualization and decision support. In addition, Marakas is an active researcher in the area of systems analysis methods, data mining and visualization, creativity enhancement, conceptual data modeling, and computer self-efficacy. Dr. Marakas is a world-renown author of textbooks. Including this text, he has written *Systems Analysis and Design: An Active Approach* and *Decision Support Systems in the 21st Century*, Second Edition, both published by Prentice Hall.

Marakas received his doctorate in Information Systems from Florida International University in Miami and his MBA from Colorado State University. Prior to his academic career, he enjoyed a highly successful career in the banking and real estate industries. His corporate experience includes senior management positions with Continental Illinois National Bank and the FDIC. In addition, Marakas served as president and CEO for CMC Group, Inc., a major RTC management contractor in Miami, for 3 years.

During his tenure at the University of Maryland and now at Indiana University, Marakas distinguished himself both through his research and in the classroom. He received numerous national teaching awards, and his research has appeared in the top journals in his field.

Beyond his academic endeavors, Marakas is also an active consultant and serves as an advisor to a number of organizations including the Central Intelligence Agency, the Department of the Treasury, the Department of Defense, British-American Tobacco, Xavier University, Citibank Asia-Pacific, Nokia Corporation, Eli Lilly Corporation, and United Information Systems, among many others. His consulting and executive education activities, spanning five continents, are concentrated primarily on e-commerce strategy, workflow reengineering, CASE tool integration, and global IT strategy formation. He is a Novell Certified Network Engineer and has been involved in the corporate beta testing program for Microsoft Corporation since 1990. Marakas is also an active member of a number of professional IS organizations, an avid golfer, a second-degree black belt in Tae Kwon Do, a PADI-certified divemaster, and a member of Pi Kappa Alpha fraternity.

1
INTRODUCTION TO DATA MINING, WAREHOUSING, AND VISUALIZATION

Learning Objectives

◆ Explain the purpose and motivation for developing a data warehouse.

◆ Understand the differences between an operational data store and an organizational data store.

◆ Understand the position of the data warehouse within the technology infrastructure of the organization.

◆ Understand the relationship between the data warehouse and the business data mart.

◆ Become familiar with what a data warehouse can and cannot do for the organization.

◆ Understand the roots of data mining.

◆ Become familiar with the sequence of events associated with a typical data mining project.

◆ Understand the concept of correlation.

◆ Become familiar with the history and application of data visualization techniques as they relate to the modern data warehouse.

THE BUILDING OF THE INSURECO DIMENSIONAL DATA WAREHOUSE

Insurance is an important and growing sector of the data warehousing (DW) market. Insurance companies generate several complicated transactions that must be analyzed in many different ways. Until recently, it was not practical to consider storing hundreds of millions—or even billions—of transactions for online access. However, with the advent of powerful processors and sophisticated database query software, large complicated databases can now be used for data warehousing. At the same time, the insurance industry is under incredible pressure to reduce costs. Costs in this business come almost entirely from claims or "losses," as the insurance industry more accurately describes them.

InsureCo is a major insurance company with annual revenues of more than $2 billion that offers automobile, homeowner's, and personal property insurance to about two million customers. InsureCo's challenge was to construct a corporate data warehouse capable of analyzing all claims across all its lines of business, some of which had histories stretching back more than 15 years.

The first step toward reaching this goal was the gathering of information via interviews with prospective end users in claims analysis, claims processing, field operations, fraud and security management, finance, and marketing. From each group of users came descriptions of what they did in a typical day, how they measured the success of what they did, and how they thought they could understand their businesses better.

Three major themes emerged from the interviews that would profoundly affect the final data warehouse design. First, to understand their claims in detail, users needed to see every possible transaction. This precluded presenting summary data only. Many end-user analyses required the slicing and dicing of the huge pool of transactions.

Second, users needed to view the business in monthly intervals. Claims needed to be grouped by month and compared at month's end to other months of the same year or to months in previous years. This conflicted with the need to store every transaction, as it was impractical to roll up complex sequences of transactions just to get monthly premiums and monthly claims payments.

Third, the design needed to accommodate the heterogeneous nature of InsureCo's lines of business. The facts recorded for an automobile accident claim are different than those recorded for a homeowner's fire loss claim or for a burglary claim.

These data conflicts arise in many different industries and are familiar themes for data warehouse designers. The conflict between the detailed transaction view and the monthly snapshot view almost always requires that the designer provide for both kinds of tables in the data warehouse.

The solution for InsureCo was to first tackle the transaction and monthly snapshot views of the business by carefully dimensionalizing the base-level claims processing transactions. Every claims-processing transaction was able to fit into the star join schema shown in Figure 1-1. This structure is characteristic of transaction-level data warehouse schemas.

This transaction-level star join schema provided an extremely powerful way for InsureCo to analyze claims. The numbers of claimants, the timing of claims, the timing of payments made, and the involvement of third parties, such as witnesses and lawyers, were all easily derived from this view of the data. Strangely, it was somewhat difficult to derive "claim-to-date" measures, such as monthly snapshots, because of the need to crawl through every detailed transaction from the beginning of history. The solution was to add a monthly snapshot version of the data to InsureCo's data warehouse. The monthly snapshot removed some of the dimensions while adding more facts. Monthly snapshot tables were very flexible because interesting summaries could be added as facts, almost at will.

After dispensing with the first big representation problem, InsureCo faced the problem of how to deal with their heterogeneous products. This problem directly impacted the monthly snapshot fact table, in which they wanted to store additional monthly summary measures specific to each line of business. These additional measures included automobile coverage, homeowner's fire coverage, and personal article loss coverage. After reviewing the information derived during the early interviews with the various insurance specialists in each line of business, the designers realized that there were at

DATA MINING MINICASE

(continued)

least 10 custom facts for each line of business. Logically, the fact table design could be extended to include the custom facts for each line of business, but physically the challenge was daunting.

The solution to this problem was to create a design that could accommodate the core facts while simultaneously allowing for repetition or redundancy where necessary. This concept is sometimes difficult for database designers to accept, but in this case it proved to be very important. In large databases, it is very dangerous to access more than one fact table at a time. It is far better, as was done in this case, to repeat a little of the data in order to confine user queries to single fact tables.

InsureCo's data warehouse is a classic example of a large data warehouse that has to accommodate the conflicting needs for detailed transaction history, high-level monthly summaries, company-wide views, and individual lines of business. Using standard data warehouse design techniques, including transaction views and monthly snapshot views, as well as heterogeneous product schemas, the designers were able to develop an effective design that addresses InsureCo's needs. The age of the data warehouse is here, and the competitive advantage associated with its use is one of the long-term keys to success at InsureCo.

FIGURE 1-1   InsureCo's Star Join Schema

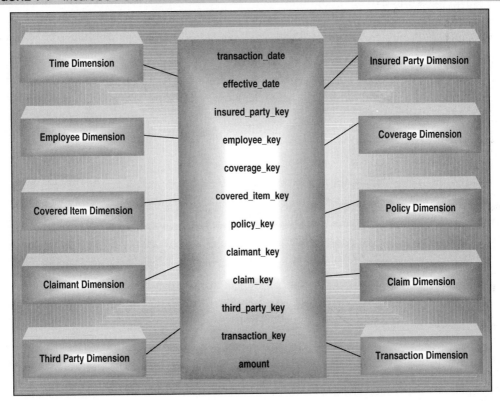

INTRODUCTION

The never-ending cycle of data generation followed by the increased need to store that data has been a challenge faced by information systems professionals for decades. Despite successes in recent years in the area of large-scale database design, we are still challenged by the difficulties associated with "unlocking" the data we need and removing it from the cavernous databases in which it resides. In addition, we are becoming increasingly aware of the hidden treasure trove of new knowledge quietly residing in our data and face considerable frustration when we attempt to get at it. This constant cycle of data generation, storage, and difficulty in retrieval and analysis has resulted in the development of new and powerful tools to assist us in meeting this challenge.

This text is about these new and powerful tools: the *data warehouse, data mining*, and *data visualization*. This trio of weapons that can be used to unlock the secrets contained within our vast data stores is rapidly becoming the de facto standard for realizing competitive advantage in any data-driven industry or environment. In this text, we will explore the basic concepts of each tool, the advantages associated with their successful deployment, and the challenges faced in their realization.

Before we begin, it is important to note that no text of this size and scope can cover the details of data warehousing, mining, and visualization in their totality. Literally volumes have been generated about each of these three subjects, and the general consensus amongst the experts is that we are only beginning to scratch the surface of understanding. Nonetheless, we do know some things about these powerful organizational tools, and we will share with you what we know in this book. By understanding the core concepts associated with each of the three related tools, you can immediately begin to make use of these weapons while simultaneously contributing to the development of our further understanding of them.

One last note is in order. Despite the title of the text, *Modern Data Warehousing, Mining, and Visualization: Core Concepts,* we must take certain liberties with the order in which we conduct our investigation of these tools. As such, we will begin our exploration with the "center of gravity" for the trio—*the data warehouse.* Once we have a grasp of the data warehouse, our understanding of the power and applicability of the remaining two tools will come much easier and more quickly.

1.1: THE MODERN DATA WAREHOUSE

The journey of a thousand miles begins with a single step.
    —OLD CHINESE PROVERB

Perfection is spelled P-A-R-A-L-Y-S-I-S.
    —WINSTON CHURCHILL, 1942

All explorations must begin with a definition of that which we seek to explore. As you will see, the two quotations at the beginning of this section could have easily been directed toward explaining the vast challenges facing the design and deployment of the modern data warehouse.

These quotations, however, only allude to the challenges. They fall short of clearly defining our object of interest. As such, we should dive right in by stating exactly what we are exploring:

> A data warehouse is a copy of transaction data specifically structured for querying, analysis, and reporting.

From this definition, we can begin to build a mental picture of exactly what a data warehouse is. First, it is a database containing a copy of transaction data. This suggests that the organizational data warehouse and the various transaction-processing systems and databases within the organization are two separate and distinct entities. Further, because the data warehouse contains a copy of transaction data rather than the actual record generated by the original transaction, the data warehouse data is not subject to update or change once it is committed to the data warehouse. This suggests the data in a data warehouse is static and, once entered, remains unaltered in any shape or form. This further suggests that data warehouses generally do not get smaller, but rather have a propensity to grow to enormous proportions.

Proceeding further in decomposing our definition, we see that this copy of transaction data is specifically structured. This suggests that the data committed to the data warehouse, while originating from live transactional data, is somehow transformed to conform to a specific structure such that transactional data from a variety of sources can reside in the data warehouse using this specified structure.

In the transactional world, the data for identifying a unique customer can be represented in a database using an infinite number of labels—CUSTOMERNO, CUSTNO, CUST_ID, C_ID, CUSTOMER, and so forth. Further, the structure of the data contained in a given transactional database field can be unique to that database—$1,760.82, 1760.82, 1,760.82, 176082, and so forth.

In the world of the data warehouse, however, these myriad structures must be accounted for and transformed into a specific structure that will facilitate the formation of queries and further analysis. In the modern data warehouse, all customers, from all sources, will be referred to by a single method. You can imagine the complexity of this transformation by simply considering the typical number of transactional databases in a large organization and the literally infinite number of ways in which each data element in each database can be represented.

Finally, our definition tells us what the purpose of the data warehouse is—querying, analysis, and reporting. The data warehouse becomes a central repository for all organizational data deemed useful for the exploration of new relationships, trends, and hidden values. It serves as the common point of focus for all members of the organization seeking to advance their knowledge of their business.

Our definition also serves to contribute to the formation of our understanding of a data warehouse by virtue of what it does not say. Notice that while we are bound by a specific structure, we are free to determine what that specific structure looks like. Because of this, the form of the stored data has nothing to do with whether something is a data warehouse. A data warehouse can be normalized or denormalized. It can include a relational database, multidimensional database, flat file, hierarchical database, or an object database.

Looking further at what our definition leaves unsaid, we find no specific group of individuals serving as the beneficiary of the organization data warehouse. Data warehousing is not necessarily for the needs of decision makers or for use in the decision-making process. Of course, you are free to define every data warehouse user as a decision maker and all activities as decision-making processes, but, generally speaking, data warehouses are most often used for quite mundane, nondecision-making purposes rather than for making decisions with wide-ranging effects (so-called "strategic" decisions). In fact, you will see that most data warehouses are used for post-decision monitoring of the effects of decisions (or, as some people might say, for "operational" issues). Note that this is not saying that using data warehousing in the decision-making process is not a wonderful, potentially high-return effort. Rather, it suggests that while the trade press, vendors, and many industry experts trumpet the role of data warehousing vis-à-vis decision making, this is, in reality, very much an area with which we really do not have a clear understanding.

You may be thinking that, given our earlier definition, the nebulous nature of a data warehouse makes it impossible to study it in any organized manner. This is true in some cases, but if we simply break our exploration down to its component elements, the task becomes far more tenable. The first place to focus our attention, then, is on the specific structure of a data warehouse. Although no single structure is used for the design of a data warehouse, all data warehouses have a specific and well-defined structure. There are just many different kinds of these specific and well-defined structures.

1.2: DATA WAREHOUSE ROLES AND STRUCTURES

To understand the different data warehouse structures and the reasons for them, we will begin by examining the various roles of the data warehouse within the organization. The data warehouse, as shown in Figure 1-2, serves as both the target of data acquisition and the source for data delivery.

This rather generalized perspective of the data warehouse allows us to categorize the role of the data warehouse into the following primary functions:

- The data warehouse is a *direct reflection of the various business rules of the enterprise*— not just of a specific function or business unit—as they apply to strategic decision-support information. This characteristic requires resiliency to easily accommodate changes to the business rules that include new data elements, shifts in hierarchical relationships, or changes to relationships between existing entities.
- The data warehouse is also *the collection point for the integrated, subject-oriented strategic information* that is handled during the data acquisition process. This characteristic calls for a data modeling and design technique that supports *subject orientation* and provides the flexibility to integrate data from additional sources over time.
- It is the *historical store of strategic information,* with the history relating to either the data or its relationships or both. This characteristic calls for a data modeling and design technique that easily supports the incorporation of *history.*
- It is the *source of information that is subsequently delivered to the data marts.* The data marts in question may be used for exploration, data mining, managed queries, or online analytical processing. This requires the model to provide unbiased data that can subsequently be filtered to meet specific objectives. It further requires the model to support *summarized and aggregated data.*
- It is the *source of stable data* regardless of how the processes may change. This requires a data model that is not influenced by the operational processes creating the data.

In Chapter 2, we will dive deep into the characteristics and specific structures of the modern data warehouse. For now, we need to stay focused on the basic concepts and how they work

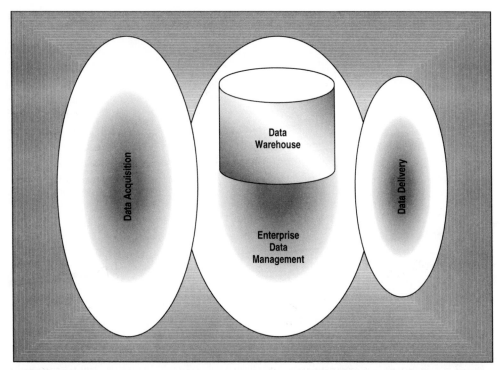

FIGURE 1-2   Position of the Data Warehouse Within the Organization

together. Probably the most important of the basic concepts and clearly one of the most important derivative structures of the data warehouse is the *data mart*.

DATA MARTS

The data mart (DM) is nothing more than a smaller, more focused data warehouse. In many cases, organizations find it useful to create data marts for specific business units that have equally specific data analysis needs. Although the larger data warehouse could support those needs, the enormous bulk of data contained within a typical data warehouse could reduce the efficiency of a consistently focused data analysis effort. As shown in Figure 1-3, the data mart established for a specific online analytical effort is both the target of data delivery and the direct source of data accessed by end users associated with that data mart.

The data mart serves the following primary functions:

- In contrast to the larger data warehouse, the data mart is a reflection of the business rules of a *specific function or business unit*—not the enterprise—as they apply to strategic decision-support information. The business rules reflected by the data mart need to be consistent with the enterprise rules, but are commonly tailored to the unique business capabilities addressed by the data mart.
- Unlike the data warehouse, the data mart obtains its data from a relatively stable, cleansed, and integrated source—the organizational data warehouse. As such, the data mart does not need to cleanse or integrate the incoming data.

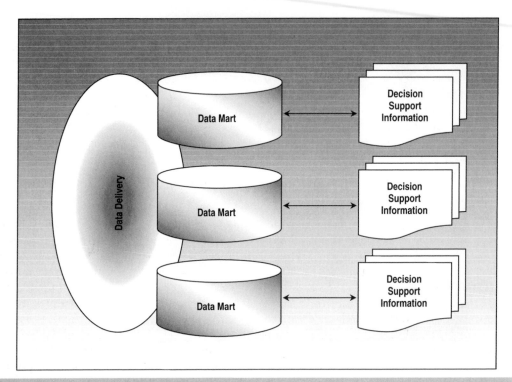

FIGURE 1-3   Position of the Data Mart Within the Organization

- The data mart is a set of tables designed for direct access by users who need to analyze data according to a set of predefined parameters (i.e., dimensions). This characteristic requires a structure that supports *easy, intuitive analysis* across parameters and hierarchies within those parameters.
- It is a set of tables that is designed for *aggregation*. The fact table may contain detailed data, but most of the queries will view this data by the business constraints that form the dimensions. For example, the data mart may contain sales transaction data, and the user query will be for a summary of sales transactions by a time period, product line, and store. This characteristic requires a structure that supports *easy, intuitive data aggregation* across appropriate parameters (i.e., business constraints or dimensions).
- Finally, the data mart is typically not a data source for traditional statistical analyses needed for exploration or data mining. Omission of this requirement permits the data to be collected along predefined, known relationships.

We will explore the relationship between the data warehouse and its associated data marts in greater detail in Chapter 2. For now, think of data marts as miniwarehouses.

1.3: WHAT CAN A DATA WAREHOUSE DO?

So now that we have a cursory idea of what a data warehouse is, the real questions of importance are, what can it do and what are the benefits of having one?

IMMEDIATE INFORMATION DELIVERY

Data warehouses shrink the length of time between when common business events occur and when management is alerted to those events. For example, in many organizations, sales reports are printed once a month—normally within a week after the end of each month. Thus, the June sales reports are delivered no later than the first week in July. Although useful, this forces management into making decisions on a historical basis; recent history to be sure, but history nonetheless. With a data warehouse, those same reports can be made available on a daily basis. Given this data delivery time compression, business decision makers can exploit opportunities that they would otherwise miss.

DATA INTEGRATION FROM ACROSS AND EVEN OUTSIDE THE ORGANIZATION

Think of the various databases within a typical organization as pieces of a large puzzle. If all we are interested in is the piece itself, then the single database will provide us with the necessary information. If, however, we are interested in the picture provided by the entire puzzle, we have to find a way to assemble all of the pieces. To provide a complete picture, data warehouses typically combine data from multiple sources, such as a company's order entry, payables, materials planning, sales, and warranty systems. Thus, with a data warehouse, it becomes possible to track all facets of the interactions a company has with each customer—from that customer's first inquiry, through the terms of their purchase, all the way through any warranty or service interactions. This makes it possible for managers to have answers to questions such as, "Is there a correlation between where a customer buys our product and the amount typically spent in supporting that customer?" In Chapter 3, we will see several examples of exactly how such a question might be answered and what actions can be taken as a result of that answer.

FUTURE VISION FROM HISTORICAL TRENDS

Effective business analysis frequently includes trend and seasonality analysis. To support this, warehouses typically contain multiple years of data. In the following chapters, we will explore many techniques for analyzing and drawing conclusions from the vast store of historical data contained within the data warehouse.

TOOLS FOR LOOKING AT DATA IN NEW WAYS

Beyond the long-standing paper report, a data warehouse provides its users with tools for looking at and manipulating data in many different ways. Oftentimes, a color-coded map speaks volumes over a simple paper report. An interactive table that allows the user to drill down into detail data with the click of a mouse can answer questions that might otherwise take months to answer using a more traditional approach.

FREEDOM FROM IS DEPARTMENT RESOURCE LIMITATIONS

One of the problems with information systems is that they usually require computer experts to use them. When a report is needed, the requesting manager calls the IS department. IS then assigns a programmer to write a program to produce the report. The report can be created in a few days or, in extreme cases, it may take over a year. With the advent of the data warehouse, end users create most of their queries and reports themselves. Thus, if a manager needs a special (ad hoc) report for a meeting in half an hour, the manager can easily create that report without the help of the IS department or the departmental computer guru.

WHAT DOES ALL THIS MEAN TO MY DAILY TASKS?

Although it is easy to understand the various capabilities of the data warehouse (and we only identified a few of them), translating those capabilities into daily actions requires a bit more thought. How will having a data warehouse make your job easier and improve your performance? If you make decisions that affect the performance of your organization and, potentially, its competitive position in the marketplace, then the answer to this question is easy.

On a daily basis, organizations turn to their data warehouses to answer a limitless variety of questions. A brief listing of data warehouse applications can be found in Table 1-1.

NOTHING IS FREE

Although the benefits of having a data warehouse are vast, they do come with a cost. Most notably, the cost of designing the data model and implementing the data warehouse can be substantial. In addition, the data warehouse has ongoing costs that stem from the daily transfer, cleansing, and storage of new data entering the warehouse environment. Finally, there are costs

TABLE 1-1   Examples of Common Data Warehouse Applications

Sales Analysis

- Determine real-time product sales to make vital pricing and distribution decisions.
- Analyze historical product sales to determine success or failure attributes.
- Evaluate successful products and determine key success factors.
- Use corporate data to understand the margin as well as the revenue implications of a decision.
- Rapidly identify preferred customer segments based on revenue and margin.
- Quickly isolate past preferred customers who no longer buy.
- Identify daily what product is in the manufacturing and distribution pipeline.
- Instantly determine which salespeople are performing, on both a revenue and margin basis, and which are behind.

Financial Analysis

- Compare actual to budgets on an annual, monthly, and month-to-date basis.
- Review past cash flow trends and forecast future needs.
- Identify and analyze key expense generators.
- Instantly generate a current set of key financial ratios and indicators.
- Receive near-real-time, interactive financial statements.

Human Resource Analysis

- Evaluate trends in benefit program use.
- Identify the wage and benefits costs to determine company-wide variation.
- Review compliance levels for EEOC and other regulated activities.

Other Areas
- Warehouses have also been applied to areas such as logistics, inventory, purchasing, detailed transaction analysis, and load balancing.

associated with adding new data sources to the data warehouse as end-user needs evolve and mature. Although the accurate calculation of these costs is not beyond the skills or understanding of the IS professionals and their colleagues in accounting, several unique characteristics concerning the cost estimation of a data warehouse must be taken into consideration.

To begin, many companies make the mistake of trying to simply put a value on their data warehouse. The reality is that the value of the warehouse is a result of the new and changed business processes that it enables. Thus, in developing a warehouse, it is extremely important to envision who is going to use the warehouse, how they will use it, and why using it will improve upon the current process. It is not unusual for well-considered and well-designed warehouses to generate first-year returns on investment (ROI) of 100 to 400 percent. As with any other capital investment in the organization, the value of the new business processes can be determined by comparing their costs with their expected benefits. The important point is that the value of the data warehouse lies not with its cost, but with its ability to return those costs many times over via improved business processes and new information leading to competitive advantage in the marketplace. Table 1-2 briefly outlines this comparative value approach.

IS THERE ANYTHING A DATA WAREHOUSE CANNOT DO?

Data warehouses do have limitations. Remember that data warehouses gather and report data that already exists. Therefore, a data warehouse cannot create more data. If an organization wishes to analyze its customers by zip code but addresses are not captured by the company's systems, a data warehouse will not solve the problem unless some method is found to gather this address data. In addition, if an organization's data is "dirty," in that current systems are not recording the correct information or the necessary optional fields, the data warehouse will not be able to correct that data. The warehouse is useful in identifying where data problems exist, but corrections to those problems must be made in the systems that capture the data.

TABLE 1-2   Comparison of Typical DW Costs and Benefits

Costs

- Hardware, software, development personnel, and consultant costs.
- Operational costs like ongoing systems maintenance.

Benefits

Added Revenue
- Will the new (business objective) process generate new customers? (What is the estimated value?)
- Will the new (business objective) process increase the buying propensity of existing customers? (By how much?)
- Is the new process necessary to ensure that the competition doesn't offer a demanded service that you can't match?

Reduced Costs
- What costs of current systems will be eliminated?
- Is the new process intended to make some operation more efficient? If so, how and what is the dollar value?

1.4: THE COST OF WAREHOUSING DATA

Anyone who chooses to live within his means suffers from a lack of imagination.
—LINEAL STANDEE, 1967

Solvency is entirely a matter of temperament and not of income.
—LOGAN PEARSALL SMITH, 1931

The costs associated with the data warehouse environment begin with the separation of costs into two primary categories: (1) *recurring, ongoing costs* and (2) *one-time initial costs.* The initial costs can be further categorized into *hardware* and *software* costs. In addition, we can categorize all costs into *capital costs* (costs associated with acquisition of the warehouse) and *operational costs* (costs associated with running and maintaining the data warehouse). Using this categorization method, the costs associated with a data warehouse can be represented in matrix form, as shown in Table 1-3.

VARIABLE COSTS

Generally speaking, the costs of a data warehouse are highly variable. One organization builds a large data warehouse for a large amount of money. Another organization builds a large data warehouse for a significantly smaller amount of money. Ironically, the organization that spends

TABLE 1-3 Various Expenditures Associated with Building and Deploying a DW

	Recurring Costs	*One-Time Costs*	
		Hardware	*Software*
Capital Expenditures	• Hardware maintenance • Software maintenance • Terminal analysis • Middleware	• Disk • CPU • Network • Terminal analysis	• DBMS • Terminal analysis • Middleware • Network • Log utility • Processing • Metadata • Infrastructure
Operational Expenditures	• Ongoing refreshment • Integration transformation • Data model maintenance • Record identification maintenance • Metadata infrastructure maintenance • Archival of data • Data aging within the DW	• Integration/transformation processing specification • Metadata infrastructure population • System of record definition • Data dictionary language definition • Network transfer definition • CASE/Repository interface • Initial data warehouse population • Data model definition • Database design definition	

Source: Adapted from Inmon, 2000. "The Data Warehouse Budget." www.billinmon.com/library/library_frame.html

significantly less money for their data warehouse is usually much happier with their data warehouse than the organization that spent much more money. Table 1-4 lists some of the various factors that contribute to the cost of and satisfaction with a data warehouse.

If an organization does not understand these basic issues, then the costs of the warehouse will rise at an alarming rate, along with the overall dissatisfaction on the part of the end users with the warehouse. The first and most important key to managing the costs of the data warehouse is to understand the architecture of the warehouse and the environment that surrounds it.

COST JUSTIFICATION

As with most capital expenditures, a variety of approaches can be used to determine the cost justification of the data warehouse initiative. The easiest and most straightforward way to address cost justification is to simply say that the data warehouse greatly reduces the cost of getting information into the hands of the user—across the board—for the whole organization. With a data warehouse, the cost of getting information shrinks dramatically for everyone, every time there is a need to access information of any kind. In other words, data warehousing dramatically reduces the cost of accessing the information owned by the organization.

INFORMATION WHERE THERE IS NO DATA WAREHOUSE

In order to understand how data warehousing reduces the cost of accessing information, consider the classical environment shown in Figure 1-4.

As shown in Figure 1-4, an environment consists of various source systems (in reality, literally thousands), usually called the *legacy environment*. These source systems provide the data needed by the end user. In most cases, these legacy systems are *transaction processing systems* (TPS) that reflect various business requirements. The need for information from these legacy systems is represented as the desire for a report or a screen. In order to fulfill that need, legacy systems are accessed, information is gathered, and that information is fed into the report or screen. This simple scenario is descriptive of most organizations prior to their decision to build a data warehouse.

INFORMATION WHERE THERE IS A DATA WAREHOUSE

The storage and retrieval of information is different when a data warehouse is involved. Consider the scenario depicted in Figure 1-5.

TABLE 1-4 Various Factors Which Contribute to Both Cost and Satisfaction with a DW

- Does the organization understand that with the large volumes of data found in a data warehouse the mass of the data should not be placed on high performance disk storage?
- Does the organization understand that building a central architected data warehouse surrounded by data marts is the best long-term approach?
- Does the organization understand that the data warehouse must be built in small fast iterations of development rather than in a single large "big bang" approach?
- Does the organization understand that for serious amounts of exploration a separate structure called an *exploration warehouse* is required?
- Does the organization understand that for true OLTP response time a separate structure called an *organizational data store* (*ODS*) is required?

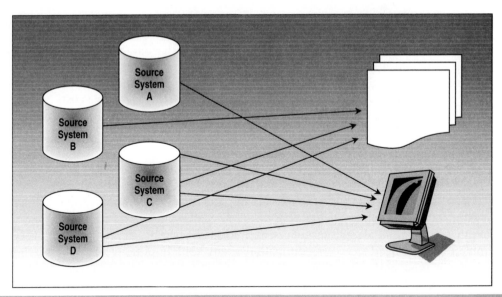

FIGURE 1-4 Typical Multidatabase Report and Screen Generation

FIGURE 1-5 Typical Data Warehouse Environment

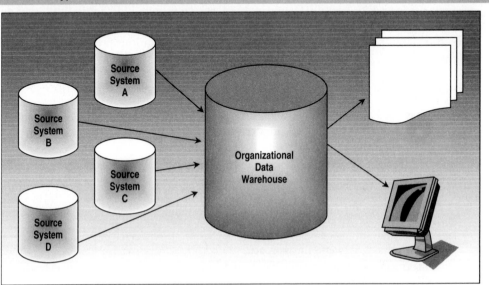

TABLE 1-5   Necessary Steps to Produce a Report in a Typical Legacy Environment

- The data needed for the desired reports or screens is located in the legacy source systems.
- Once located, the data is gathered. This means accessing the data across a wide variety of database technologies, such as IMS, IDMS, VSAM, ADABAS, Oracle, DB2, etc.
- Once the data is gathered it must be converted or integrated. This means reconciling keys, internal encoding values, reference tables, data structures, operating systems, etc.
- Upon successful conversion, if there are multiple sources of data, the data must be merged, and the report or screen can then be produced.

Note that the scenarios in Figures 1-4 and 1-5 are exactly the same except for the presence of a data warehouse. The data warehouse sits between the legacy applications and the report. The legacy applications feed the data warehouse, and the data warehouse feeds the report or screen.

THE COST DIFFERENTIAL

In order to understand the cost differential between the scenarios in Figures 1-4 and 1-5, consider the work that has to be done in order to produce a report. Table 1-5 outlines the work that must be done to produce a report when there is no data warehouse.

Depending on the state of the legacy environment, how many legacy applications must be accessed, and the size and complexity of the report, the time required to produce the report from the legacy environment may range from 2 or 3 months to 2 or 3 years, and the cost may range from anywhere between $100,000 to $2 or $3 million. In fact, the cost of getting information from the legacy environment is so high that many organizations simply give up in frustration.

Now consider the costs and activities required to get the same report from the data warehouse environment. This scenario is described in Table 1-6.

The first four steps performed in Figure 1-4 are also necessary in Figure 1-5. In Figure 1-4, the preparation steps are done to produce the report. In Figure 1-5, those same steps are conducted to produce the data warehouse. In fact, the only real difference between the scenarios depicted in the two figures is that the report is issued from the data warehouse in Figure 1-5 instead of being directly issued from legacy systems as in Figure 1-4.

The costs of locating, gathering, converting, integrating, and merging are the same in both scenarios. Therefore, why is there any savings at all when the same activities must be done regardless of whether a data warehouse exists or not?

TABLE 1-6   Necessary Steps to Produce a Report in a Typical DW Environment

- The data needed for the desired reports or screens is located in the legacy source systems.
- Once located, the data is gathered in preparation for movement into the DW. This means accessing the data across a wide variety of database technologies, such as IMS, IDMS, VSAM, ADABAS, Oracle, DB2, etc.
- Once the data is gathered it must be converted or integrated as it moves to its new home in the DW. This means reconciling keys, internal encoding values, reference tables, data structures, operating systems, etc.
- Merge the data into the existing data within the data warehouse.
- Produce the desired reports or screens.

MULTIPLE REPORTS

The answer to the cost-savings question lies with the fact that if only one report had to be created, then there would be no measurable cost savings realized by creating a data warehouse. However, the reality is that no organization operates on a single report. Rather, the typical situation is that organizations operate on thousands of reports and hundreds of screens.

The cost of *each* report and *each* screen is very high when the source of the data is the legacy environment. Now consider the costs of reporting when there is a data warehouse. Once gathered into a data warehouse, the data is available for as many reports and/or screens as the data within the data warehouse can support.

The gathering of data into the data warehouse is a one-time only cost. With a data warehouse, data has to be located, gathered, integrated, and merged only once. However, in the absence of a data warehouse, these tasks must be done for every report. That is where the tremendous cost savings occur and the cost justification is made for a data warehouse.

FARMERS AND EXPLORERS

Beyond the reduced transaction costs associated with reporting and screen generation, another aspect of the cost justification of a data warehouse should be explored: *For whom in the corporation is the data warehouse justified in the first place?* In order to answer that question, consider that the corporation has two very different kinds of users—we will call them *farmers* and *explorers*.

A *farmer* is someone who knows what they want before they set out to find it. As such, a farmer's actions are highly predictable. A farmer submits small queries but seldom finds huge nuggets of information. Occasionally, however, a farmer finds small flakes of gold. If a farmer were a basketball player, the farmer would hit a lot of short jump shots and layups, seldom miss from the free throw line, but only infrequently hit three pointers or other tough shots.

In contrast, an *explorer* behaves quite differently from a farmer. An explorer is the original "out of the box" corporate thinker. Very unpredictable in their actions, an explorer may go months without submitting a query and then submit 10 queries in a week. In addition, an explorer generally submits very large queries and often finds nothing. From time to time, however, an explorer finds a priceless nugget of corporate wisdom that has been long overlooked. If an explorer were a basketball player, the explorer would hit a great proportion of three pointers and spectacular dunks. Correspondingly, the explorer would also regularly miss free throws and simple plays.

FARMERS, EXPLORERS, AND COST JUSTIFICATION

The issue of data warehouse cost justification is very germane to both farmers and explorers. However, the cost justification for a data warehouse is almost always done on the basis of the results obtained by farmers, not explorers. The predictability of the farmer makes it much easier to determine the scope and structure of the data warehouse. Conversely, basing a cost justification for a data warehouse on the work of explorers is much less predictable and is generally considered a very risky and unadvised approach to data warehouse design and costing.

Why is it that cost justification for a data warehouse is not done for explorers? The answer is that with explorers, you never know what you are going to come up with. If by some chance you conduct a search and achieve a spectacular result, then management will feel good about sponsoring the data warehouse. In contrast, if you conduct a search and come up with nothing, then management will probably be unwilling to pay for the data warehouse. In addition, at the outset of an exploration activity, you never know what you are going to come up with. The chances are excellent that as an explorer, you will not strike gold on the first time out.

Management generally does not like to back what they perceive to be a losing proposition. Therefore, when it comes to cost justification for the data warehouse, it needs to be done on the basis of the expectations for farmers, not explorers. Of course, some organizations are very sophisticated and understand the risks from an explorer's perspective. In this case, a data warehouse may be justified on the basis of the expectations of explorers. However, the more normal case is that it is very risky to try to use the results of explorers as a basis for the data warehouse.

DATA MARTS AND THE DATA WAREHOUSE

Another issue relevant to the cost justification of the data warehouse is that of whether the organization should build a data warehouse or a data mart. In order to better understand the issues surrounding this decision, it is first necessary to understand what a data warehouse is, what a data mart is, and how they differ.

Earlier in this chapter, we stated that a data mart is nothing more than a smaller, more content-focused data warehouse. More to the point, a data mart is a representation of a particular departmental structure.

Typical departments having a data mart are the finance department, the sales department, the marketing department, the accounting department, and so forth. The data in a data mart is designed for optimal access by the different users of the data mart. The data warehouse is structurally different from a data mart in that the data warehouse must serve the needs of the entire corporation, not just a few departments. The data warehouse is a truly corporate structure, serving many different needs. Figure 1-6 shows the positioning of the data marts within the larger data warehouse.

Figure 1-6 indicates that the data warehouse feeds data to the organizational data marts. In turn, the data warehouse is fed its data from the legacy applications. Despite their obvious similarities, data marts and data warehouses have a number of fundamental differences, some of which are illustrated in Figure 1-7.

A data warehouse contains corporate data, granular data, and normalized data. The normalization of the data in the data warehouse allows the data in the warehouse to serve a wide variety of purposes. In contrast, the data in the data mart is both summarized and very denormalized. The data mart data serves the needs of a specific department or user constituency, not the entire organization.

Appendix A contains a simple set of formulas for calculating the impact of a data warehouse on an organization's access to information and for determining whether the data warehouse or the data mart should be built first (or even at all).

1.5: FOUNDATIONS OF DATA MINING

If data warehousing is the hot topic in modern organizations, data mining is one of the hottest topics in data warehousing. Virtually every organization that has embraced the concept of a data warehouse believes that data mining is part of its future and that its future is directly linked to the investment the organization has already made in the data warehouse.

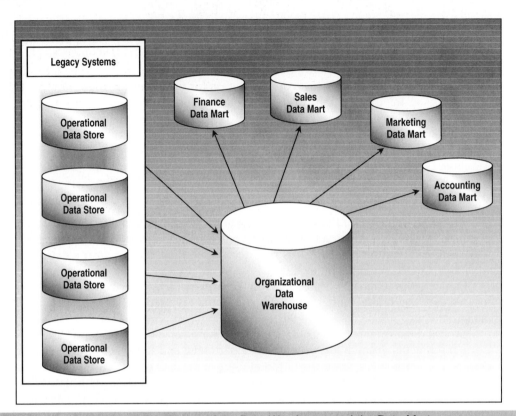

FIGURE 1-6   Architectural Positioning of the Data Warehouse and the Data Marts

Data mining is the process of using raw data to infer important business relationships. Once the business relationships have been discovered, they can then be used for business advantage. A data warehouse has uses other than data mining. However, the fullest use of a data warehouse must include data mining.

Despite this general consensus of the value of data mining, a great deal of confusion exists as to just exactly what data mining is. Is data mining simply a fancy name for data analysis? Does it require special tools and special knowledge in order to do it? The answers to both questions are "yes" and "no."

In this section, we will define the main categories of data mining and get a "big picture" perspective of its value to the organization. In Chapters 3 and 4, we will drill down into the depths of data mining techniques and explore the myriad of applications and complex tasks that can routinely be performed through an understanding of data mining techniques.

However, first we need to see the big picture:

- Data mining is a collection of powerful data analysis techniques intended to assist in analyzing extremely large datasets. Properly applied, data mining can reveal hidden relationships and information buried within the organizational data warehouse.
- There is no one data mining approach, but rather a set of techniques that often can be used in combination with each other to extract the most insight from a set of data.

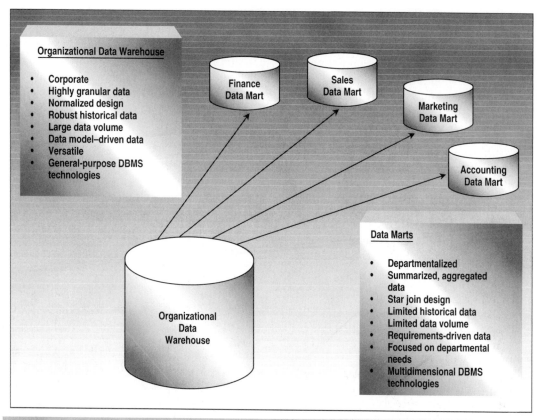

FIGURE 1-7   Fundamental Differences Between a Data Mart and a Data Warehouse

Before we venture further into our examination of data mining, it might prove useful to take a trip into the past and explore the roots of modern-day data mining techniques and applications.

1.6: THE ROOTS OF DATA MINING

Despite the seemingly recent emergence of data mining, the approach has a rich tradition of research and practice dating back over 30 years. In the early 1960s, data mining was referred to as *statistical analysis*. During this period, the pioneers of statistical analysis were SAS, SPSS, and IBM. Even today, all three of these companies are very active in the data mining field and have highly respected product offerings based on their years of experience. Originally, statistical analysis consisted of classical statistical routines such as *correlation, regression, chi-square,* and *cross tabulation.* Although most modern data mining packages still offer these classical approaches, data mining has moved far beyond these first-generation statistical measures to more insightful and powerful approaches that assist in explaining or predicting "what is going on in the data."

By the late 1980s, classical statistical analysis was augmented by a more powerful set of techniques with names such as fuzzy logic, heuristic reasoning, and neural networks. This was the heyday of artificial intelligence (AI). In Chapter 4, we will explore these powerful and highly useful contributions from the world of artificial intelligence.

Into the new millennium, we are rapidly learning how to apply the best approaches from classical statistical analysis, neural networks, decision trees, market basket analysis, and other powerful techniques and use them in a much more compelling and effective way. The arrival of the data warehouse was the necessary ingredient that has made data mining real and viable.

A GENERAL APPROACH

Although all data mining endeavors are unique to their respective analyst and problem under study, each possesses a certain set of commonalities with regard to the process steps necessary to achieve a successful outcome. The diagram in Figure 1-8 is not a methodology, per se. Instead, the diagram represents a more generic approach to data mining.

Infrastructure Preparation

The first step in data mining is the identification and preparation of the infrastructure. It is in the infrastructure that the actual data mining activity will occur. The infrastructure contains (at a minimum):

- A hardware platform
- Database Management System (DBMS) platform
- One or more tools for data mining

In almost every case, the hardware platform is a separate platform than that which originally contained the data. Said differently, it is unusual to perform data mining on the same platform as the operational environment. To be done properly, data must be removed from its host environment and prepared before it can be properly mined.

Removing data from the host environment is merely the first step in preparing the data mining infrastructure. In order for data mining to be done efficiently, the data itself needs to have undergone a thorough analysis, and in most cases the data must be *scrubbed*. The scrubbing of the data entails integrating the data, as the operational data will often have come from multiple sources. In addition, a metadata dictionary that sits above the data to be mined must also be constructed. Metadata is simply data about the data: Where it came from, how old is it, how it was captured, what units it represents, etc. Unless there is only a small amount of data to be mined (which is almost never the case), the metadata dictionary sits above the data to be mined and serves as a roadmap as to what is and is not contained in the data. The metadata contains such useful information as:

- What data is contained in the data to be mined
- The source of the data
- How the data has been integrated
- The frequency of refreshment

We will explore the concept of metadata in more detail in Chapter 2.

Granularity

One of the biggest issues associated with the creation of a data mining infrastructure is that of the *granularity* of the data. Granularity refers to the size of the unit represented by the data. Think of granularity in terms of different sizes of grains of sand. Very fine, powdery sand would be referred to as having a very fine granularity. In contrast, small pebbles would represent a unit of fairly coarse granularity. The finer the level of granularity, the greater the chance is that

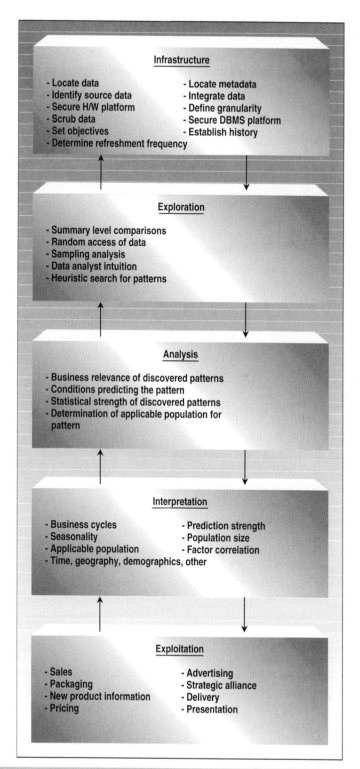

FIGURE 1-8   General Approach to Data Mining

unusual and never before noticed relationships of data will be discovered. However, the finer the level of granularity, the more units of data there will be, and the greater the storage requirements become. In many cases, important relationships become hidden behind the sheer volume of data. Therefore, refining the level of granularity can greatly help in discovering important relationships.

A very important trade-off is made between the very fine level of detail that is possible and the need to manage volumes of data. Making this trade-off properly is one of the reasons why data mining is often more of an art than a science.

Exploration
Once the infrastructure has been established, the first steps in data exploration can commence. Data exploration can be approached in many different ways. Some of the approaches to the discovery of important relationships include:

- Analyzing summary data and "sniffing out" unusual occurrences and patterns
- Sampling data and analyzing the samples to discover patterns that have not been detected before
- Taking advantage of the intuition and experience of the experienced DSS analyst
- Conducting simple random accesses to the data
- Heuristically searching for patterns

Analysis
Once a set of patterns has been discovered, each "discovered" pattern must be analyzed. Some patterns will not be statistically strong, whereas others may display high statistical strength (i.e., *significance*). The stronger a pattern, the better the chance that pattern will form a fruitful basis for exploitation. On the other hand, if a pattern is not strong today, but its strength is increasing over time, the pattern may be of great interest because it may be a clue as to changes in the environment and a key to anticipating changes in the marketplace.

When looking at discovered patterns, strength is not the only thing that needs to be considered. A second consideration is whether the pattern potentially represents a *false positive*. A false positive is a correlation between two or more variables that is statistically significant but completely random and meaningless. Given the large number of occurrences of data and the large number of variables, it is inevitable that there will be some number of false positive correlations of data when conducting deep exploration data mining.

A third consideration is whether a valid correlation of variables has any business significance. It is entirely possible that there will be a valid correlation between two variables that is not a false positive but for which there is no real business significance. In these cases, although a valid discovery has been made, no direct use for this new knowledge exists. This does not mean, however, that it will never be of relevance, just not in the current business environment.

Interpretation
Once the patterns have been discovered and analyzed, the next step is to interpret them. Without interpretation, the patterns that have been discovered are fairly useless. In order to interpret the patterns, it is necessary to combine technical and business expertise. Some considerations in interpreting the patterns include:

- The larger business cycles of the business
- The seasonality of the business
- The population to which the pattern is applicable
- The strength of the pattern and the ability to use the pattern as a basis for future behavior

- The size of the population the pattern applies to
- Other important external correlations to the pattern, such as:

Time of week, day, month, year, etc.
Geography, where the pattern can be applied
Demographics, the group of people to which the pattern can be applicable

Once the pattern has been discovered and the interpretation has been made, the last phase of the data mining process can take place.

Exploitation

Exploitation of a discovered pattern is both a business and a technical activity. The easiest way that a discovered pattern can be exploited is to use the pattern as a predictor of future behavior. Once the behavior pattern is determined for a segment of the population served by a company, the pattern can be used as a basis for prediction. Once the population is identified and the conditions under which the behavior will predictably occur are defined, the business is now in a position to exploit the information. An organization can exploit new patterns in the data in a number of ways, including:

- Specific sales offers
- Packaging products to appeal to the predicted audience
- Introducing new products
- Pricing products in an unusual way
- Advertising to appeal to the predicted audience
- Delivering services and/or products creatively
- Presenting products and services to cater to the predicted audience

In addition to using patterns to position sales and products in a competitive and novel fashion, the measurement of patterns over time is another useful way that pattern processing can be exploited.

Even if a pattern has been detected that does not have a strong correlation or if there is only a small population showing the characteristics of the pattern, if the pattern is growing stronger over time or if the population exhibiting the pattern is growing, the company can start to plan for the anticipated growth. Measuring the strength and weakness of a pattern over time or the growth or shrinkage of the population exhibiting the characteristics of the pattern over time is an excellent way to gauge changes in product lines, pricing, and so forth.

Yet another way that patterns can lead to commercial advantage is in the distinguishing of the populations that correlate to the pattern. In other words, if it can be determined that some populations do correlate to a pattern and other populations do not, then the business analyst can position advertising and promotions with a high degree of accuracy, thereby improving the rate of success and reducing the cost of sales. We will explore the process of exploitation in greater detail in Chapter 3.

1.7: THE APPROACH TO DATA EXPLORATION AND DATA MINING

The activities in the approach outlined in the previous section appear to occur in a linear fashion; that is, the activities appear to flow from one activity to another in a prescribed order. Although some projects may flow in this way, it is much more common for the activities to be executed in a more heuristic, nonlinear manner. First one activity is accomplished and then another activity is done. The first activity is repeated and another activity commences, and so forth. In other words, there is no implied order to the activities associated with data mining. Instead, upon the completion of an activity, any other activity may commence, and even activities that have been previously done may be redone. Such is the nature of heuristic processing.

DATA CORRELATION

Despite this seemingly random approach to data mining and discovery, the basis for all data mining activities is the concept of *data correlation*. When data can be correlated mathematically and from a business basis, assumptions can be made, and the basis for commercial exploitation can be formed.

The groundwork for correlation is a simple mathematical relationship between two or more variables. A wide variety of correlations of data are possible. Figure 1-9 shows some simple types of correlations.

The first correlation in Figure 1-9 is a perfect correlation of data. In this case, for every occurrence of A there is an occurrence of B, and vice versa. This is referred to as a perfect correlation with an *r* of 1.00.[1] Such an occurrence seldom happens, but when it does, the perfect correlation forms a very sound basis for exploitation.

FIGURE 1-9 Examples of Different Degrees of Correlation

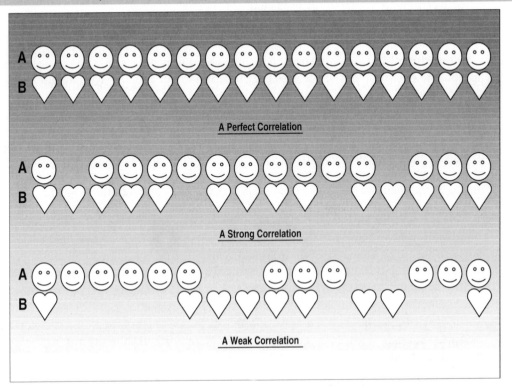

A Perfect Correlation

A Strong Correlation

A Weak Correlation

---

[1]Correlation is represented by *r*. The value of *r* can vary from 0.00, indicating no correlation, to 1.00, indicating a perfect correlation.

A more normal case is a strong correlation of data, which is represented by the second set of data shown in Figure 1-9. In the second set of data, in most cases where there is an A there is also a B. However, in a few cases A will exist when there is no B, and B will sometimes exist where there is no A. This correlation would probably have a value of r somewhere between 0.25 and 0.75. This correlation is fairly common and also forms a sound basis for further exploitation.

The third correlation shown in Figure 1-9 is an example of a weak correlation. In a weak correlation, in some cases when there exists an A there will also exist a B, or in some cases where there exists a B there will also exist an A. However, in many cases A and B will exist independently. Such a relationship would probably have an r somewhere between 0.00 and 0.25. As shown, the weak correlation between A and B does not form a particularly good case for commercial exploitation.

The Value of Weak Correlations

In some ways, however, weak correlations can be the most interesting of all. The allure of weak correlations is that they may point to important trends that are as yet undiscovered, and because they are undiscovered, they can lead to opportunities for exploitation that are as yet unknown. Therefore, two very important aspects of weak correlations are worth exploring:

- Is the correlation growing more significant over time?
- Is the correlation very strong for a subset of either A or B?

If the weak correlation is growing stronger over time, it is entirely possible that the weak correlation is an indication of a new trend that is just now developed enough to become visible. If this is the case, the trend may present massive opportunities for exploitation. Of course, how weak the correlation is and how fast the strength of the correlation is increasing are both important factors. If a correlation is increasing in strength at glacial speed, it will be very difficult to exploit the correlation. Further, if the correlation is so weak that it may be considered spurious, it may take a long time for it to become strong enough to be able to be exploited.

The second case where a weak correlation is of interest is where there is a weak correlation for the entire population but a quite strong correlation for a subset of the population. In other words, if there are other characteristics of A that can be used to select a subpopulation of A, and, if after having selected that subpopulation, the correlation between A and B becomes much stronger, then there will most likely be a significant opportunity for commercial exploitation by targeting the subpopulation of A that strongly correlates to B. We will explore this very issue when we discuss market basket analysis in Chapter 3.

Of course, types of correlations other than those based on simple existence criteria exist. The correlations that have been discussed so far are based on whether two variables exist in the presence of each other. Another very common type of correlation is not based on existence at all, but rather on values. As an example, suppose A and B always exist in each other's presence. When A has a value greater than 50, B has a value greater than 100, and when A has a value greater than 100, B has a value greater than 200, and so forth. In this case, the correlation is measured not in terms of existence of variables, but in terms of the values of the variables compared to each other.

The Spectrum of Correlation

Whether dual variables are correlated or multiple variables are correlated, the result will be a spectrum of strengths of correlation. Figure 1-10 depicts the spectrum of correlation that lies ahead for the data analyst.

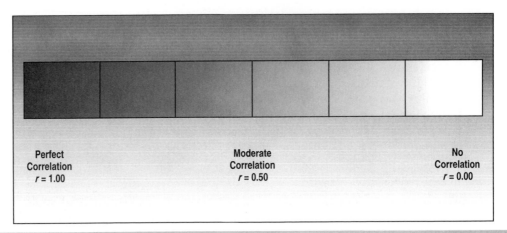

Perfect
Correlation
$r = 1.00$

Moderate
Correlation
$r = 0.50$

No
Correlation
$r = 0.00$

FIGURE 1-10 The Spectrum of Correlation

Corresponding to the spectrum of correlation is the spectrum of opportunity that awaits the data analyst who would exploit a correlation. As a general rule, the stronger the correlation, the greater the chance that the correlation is already well known. The greater the chance the correlation is well known, the greater the chance it is already being exploited. In other words, for well-known correlations, even though the correlation is strong, the opportunity for exploitation is minimal because the competition is probably already making use of the relationship. However, if a strong relationship develops between two variables that is not well known, then a major opportunity for exploitation emerges.

The next form of a relationship is a purely random one between two variables (A and B). This is often referred to as a spurious correlation. With a spurious correlation, there happens to be a relationship between A and B, but there is no valid reason for the relationship, and for another set of data the relationship may very well not exist. The existence of the relationship is merely a random artifact of the set of data upon which the analysis is being conducted. One famous example of this type of relationship was found by a group of statistics majors at MIT several years ago. They discovered that there was a highly significant ($r = 0.96$) relationship between the number of bicycles sold in Newark, New Jersey, and the number of packages of a particular brand of chewing gum sold in Chicago. For some unknown reason, this correlation was found to be present over a span of time exceeding a decade. Although clearly significant, no logical explanation can be offered for this relationship. In other words, just because two items are correlated does not mean that any relevant relationship exists between them. When there are a lot of data and many variables, it is virtually assured that there will be a fair number of spurious relationships discovered. Although mathematically valid, these relationships have no particular business meaning or relevance.

Methods to Determine Correlations
The simplest way to correlate data is to ask, for a given selection of data, how often variable B exists when variable A exists. This simple method is used quite often and forms the basis of discovering relationships. However, many refinements to the way that data can be correlated are available. Figure 1-11 illustrates several of these refinements.

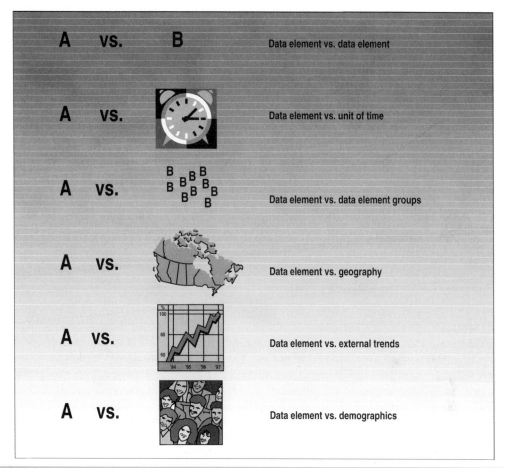

FIGURE 1-11 Various Approaches to Data Correlation

As can be seen in Figure 1-11, data can be correlated from one element to another, from one element to another over different time periods, from one element to a group of elements, from one element over a geographic area, from one element to external data, from one element to a demographically segmented population, and so forth. Furthermore, the one element can be correlated over multiple variables at the same time (e.g., time, geography, demographics, etc.).

As an example of correlating an element of data to another element of data, consider the analysis where the amount of a sale is correlated to whether the sale is paid for in cash or with a credit card. When a sale is below a certain amount, it is found that the payment is made with cash. When the sale is over a certain amount, the payment is made with a credit card. Moreover, when the sale is between certain parameters, the sale may be paid for with either a credit card or cash.

As an example of a variable being correlated with time, consider the analysis of airline flights throughout the year. The length of the flight and the cost of the flight can be correlated against the month of the year in which a passenger flies. Do people make more expensive trips in January? In February? As the holidays approach, do people make shorter and less expensive trips? What exactly is the correlation?

When correlating data against groups of other data, an analyst may want to know if the purchase of automobiles correlates to the sale of large ticket items in general, such as washers and dryers, television sets, and refrigerators. From this information, a particular pattern of buyer behavior can be predicted and used to develop a targeted advertising campaign.

The correlation of units of data to geography is a very common one in which data is matched against local patterns of activity and consumption. The comparison of the beer drinking habits of those living in the south versus those living in the southwest is an example of correlating units of data to geography.

One of the most useful types of correlations is that of correlating internal data to external data. The value of this kind of correlation is demonstrated by the comparison of internal sales figures to industry-wide sales figures.

Finally, as an example of demographic correlation, the savings rate for those with a college education can be correlated against the savings rate for those without a college education.

In other words, an infinite number of combinations of correlations can be calculated and explored. Some correlations are very revealing; however, others are just interesting and have no potential for exploitation.

Different Kinds of Trends

Trends are events that are found to repeat themselves in relation to some other event or over a predictable and measurable period of time. There are a multitude of trends—some useful, some not. In no small part, however, the usefulness of a trend is dependent on how permanent the trend is.

Generally speaking, the most interesting and useful trends are those that can be classified as long-term trends. *Long-term trends* are interesting in that, once detected, they can be used for market or behavioral prediction. Once a reasonably high degree of prediction can be achieved, it becomes easier to position the organization for market or competitive advantage. The downside of this, however, is that long-term trends tend to be obvious, and the competition will most likely have noticed the trend as well.

Another way of looking at trends is that a large trend is merely a part of a series of much smaller trends. Using this approach, each of the smaller trends can be exploited on its own, and the risk of overcommitting the organization to an inappropriate plan of action is reduced.

DATA WAREHOUSE AND DATA MINING/DATA EXPLORATION

Data mining and exploration can be performed on literally any body of data, and data mining does not absolutely require a data warehouse. There are, however, some compelling reasons why a data warehouse is the best foundation for data mining and data exploration.

One of the most compelling reasons for employing a data warehouse is that as the data analyst moves from testing one hypothesis to another, the need to hold the data constant is tantamount. The data analyst changes the hypothesis and reruns the analysis. As long as the data is held constant, the analyst knows that any changes in results from one iteration to another are due to the changes in the hypothesis. In other words, the data needs to be held constant if iterative development is to proceed on a sound basis.

Consider what happens when data is updated. In a typical operational data store, the data is updated regularly. If, at the same time, heuristic analysis is being conducted, the changes in the results the analyst sees will be questionable. The analyst never knows whether the changes in results are a function of the changing of the hypothesis, the changing of the underlying data, or some combination of both. The first reason why the data warehouse provides such a sound basis for data mining and data exploration is that the foundation of data is not constantly changing. But that reason—as important as it is—is not the only reason why the data warehouse provides such a good basis for data mining.

Perhaps the most compelling case that can be made for a data warehouse as a basis for data mining and data exploration is that the very essence of the data warehouse is integration. The proper building of a data warehouse requires an arduous amount of work because data is not merely "thrown into" a data warehouse. Instead, data is carefully and willfully integrated when it is moved into the warehouse.

When the data analyst wants to operate from a non-data-warehouse foundation, the first task the DSS analyst faces is scrubbing and integrating the data. This is a daunting task that can hold up progress for a lengthy amount of time. In contrast, when an analyst operates on a data warehouse, the data has already been scrubbed and integrated. The analyst can get right to work with no major delays.

Stability of data and integration are not the only reasons why the data warehouse forms a sound foundation for data mining and exploration. The rich amount of history is another reason why the data warehouse invites data mining. If the data analyst attempts to go outside of the data warehouse to do data mining, the analyst faces the task of locating the desired historical data. For a variety of reasons, historical data is difficult to gather:

- Historical data gets lost.
- Historical data is placed on a medium that does not age well, and the data becomes physically impossible to read.
- The metadata that describes the content of historical data is lost, and the structure of the historical data becomes impossible to read.
- The context of the historical data is lost.
- The programs that created and manipulated the historical data become misplaced, outdated, or lost.
- The version of DBMS that the historical data are stored under becomes out of date and is discarded.

The data analyst faces many challenges in trying to go backward in time and reclaim historical data. The data warehouse, on the other hand, has the historical data neatly and readily available.

Another reason why the data warehouse sets the stage for effective data mining and data exploration is that the data warehouse contains both summary and detail data. The analyst is able to immediately start performing effective macro analysis of data using the summary data found in the data warehouse. If the analyst must start from the foundation of operational or legacy data, very little summary data will be available to the analyst. Only detailed data resides (to any great extent) in the operational or legacy environment. Therefore, in the absence of a data warehouse, the data analyst can conduct only microanalysis of data. Starting with microanalysis of data in the data mining adventure is risky at best.

VOLUMES OF DATA—THE BIGGEST CHALLENGE

The single largest challenge the data analyst faces in conducting effective data mining and data exploration is that of coming to grips with the extreme volumes of data that accompany the data warehouse. The data warehouse has an enormous amount of data. As discussed earlier in this chapter, the cost of manipulating, storing, understanding, scanning, and loading the data is often quite large. Even the simplest activity becomes painful in the face of the large volumes of data that await the analyst. The data analyst must maneuver through many problems related to the volumes of data. The most insidious problem is that the volumes of data mask the important relationships and correlations that the analyst is most interested in.

The task of the data analyst is to find the needle in the haystack; that is, where there is both a mathematical basis and a business basis for a correlation. As we will see in the coming chapters, many tools are available to assist the analyst in finding the "needle," and many other tools can assist the analyst in determining whether the needle found was the right one. In the next and last section of this opening chapter, we will get an overview of one of the most powerful of these tools, *data visualization*.

1.8: FOUNDATIONS OF DATA VISUALIZATION

Five hundred people, all from the same section of London, England, died of cholera within a 10-day period in September 1854. Dr. John Snow, a local physician, had been studying this spread of cholera for some time. One of the earliest known examples of data visualization is Dr. Snow's use of maps to prove his long-held theory that cholera was a waterborne infection (Gilbert 1954).

In trying to determine the source of cholera, Dr. Snow located every cholera death in the Soho district of London by marking the location of the home of each victim with a dot on a map. Figure 1-12 contains a replica of Dr. Snow's original map.

As can be seen in the figure, deaths were marked by dots, and the area's 11 water pumps were designated by crosses. Examining the scatter over the surface of the map, Snow observed that cholera occurred almost entirely among those who lived near (and drank from) the Broad Street water pump. To test his hypothesis, he had the handle of the contaminated pump removed. Within a very short time, the neighborhood epidemic, which had taken more than 500 lives, was over. Of course, with some good luck and hard work, the link between the pump and the disease might have been revealed by computation and analysis without graphics. However, at least in this case, being able to visualize the data was far more efficient and effective than tables of figures and lengthy, complex calculations.

This is not to suggest that "number crunching" is not a useful method of data analysis. Rather, the point is that when the number crunchers have finished calculating, the analyst must find some way to make sense of the mountains of data produced. One of the most promising sense-making methods is data visualization, the process by which data are represented in dynamic images in order to reveal intrinsic patterns.

Born in the 1970s and 1980s from the twin technologies of computer graphics and high-performance computing, data visualization has attained maturity and is now widely employed in almost all fields of science and engineering. We will explore its application and use in detail in Chapter 3.

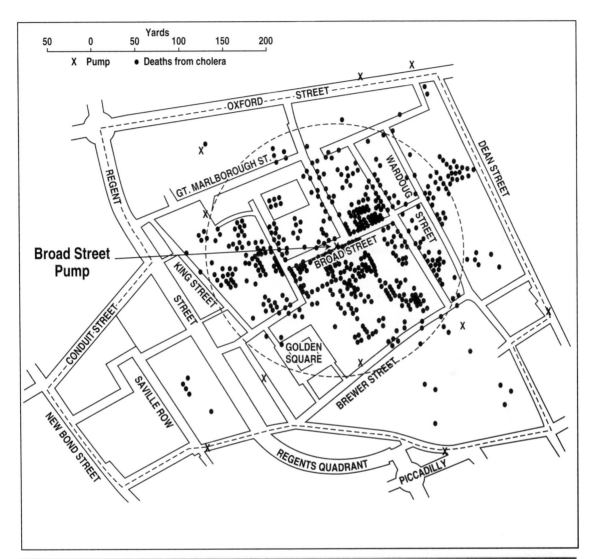

FIGURE 1-12 Replica of Dr. John Snow's Cholera Map

THE HISTORY BEHIND "SEEING THE DATA"

Data visualization and its animated counterpart, virtual reality, may have popped into the headlines only in the past few years, but their roots reach back more than four decades. It was in the late 1950s, just as the nation was shaking off stale traces of McCarthyism and dancing to the sounds of Elvis, that an idea arose that would change the way people interacted with computers and make data visualization possible.

At that time, computers were hulking Goliaths locked in air-conditioned rooms and used only by those conversant in esoteric, complicated programming languages. Few people considered them to be more than glorified adding machines. However, a young electrical engineer and former naval radar technician named Douglas Engelbart viewed them differently. Rather than limiting computers to number crunching, Engelbart envisioned them as tools for digital display. He knew from his days with radar that any digital information could be viewed on a screen. Why not, he then reasoned, connect the computer to a screen and use both to solve problems?

Opportunity and Timing

At first, Engelbart's ideas were dismissed, but by the early 1960s, other people were thinking the same way. Moreover, the time was right for his vision of computing. Communications technology was intersecting with computing and graphics technology. The first computers based on transistors rather than vacuum tubes became available. This synergy yielded more user-friendly computers, which laid the groundwork for personal computers, computer graphics, and later, the emergence of virtual reality.

During this same period, an infusion of self-styled computer wizards strove to reduce the barriers to human interactions with the computer by replacing keyboards with interactive devices that relied on images and hand gestures to manipulate data. In 1962, Ivan Sutherland developed a light pen with which images could be sketched on a computer. Sutherland's first computer-aided design program, called Sketchpad, opened the way for designers to use computers to create blueprints of automobiles, cities, and industrial products. By the end of the decade, the designs were operating in real time. By 1970, Sutherland also produced a primitive head-mounted display, and Engelbart unveiled his crude pointing device for moving text around on a computer screen—the first "mouse."

Get Real, Play Games

One of the most influential antecedents of virtual reality was the *flight simulator*. Following World War II and through the millennium, the military-industrial complex pumped millions of dollars into technology to simulate flying airplanes (and later driving tanks and steering ships). Figure 1-13 illustrates a screenshot from one of the most popular and realistic flight simulators available to the typical PC consumer enthusiast—Microsoft's *Flight Simulator*. The figure depicts the flight deck of a modern Boeing 747-400.

Then, as now, it was cheaper, and safer, to train pilots on the ground before subjecting them to the hazards of flight. The early flight simulators consisted of mock cockpits built on motion platforms that pitched and rolled. However, one limitation was that they lacked visual feedback. This changed when video displays were coupled with model cockpits. By the 1970s, computer-generated graphics had replaced videos and models. These flight simulations were operating in real time, though the graphics were primitive. In 1979, the military experimented with head-mounted displays. These innovations were driven by the greater dangers associated with training on and flying the jet fighters that were being built in the 1970s. By the early 1980s, better software, hardware, and motion-control platforms enabled pilots to navigate through highly detailed virtual worlds. Figure 1-14 shows a modern-day flight simulator used to train commercial airline pilots to fly large commercial jetliners. Of course, the military-industrial complex was not the only entity interested in computer graphics.

Get Virtual, Play Video Games

A natural consumer of computer graphics was the entertainment industry, which, like the military-industrial complex, was the source of many valuable spin-offs in virtual reality. By the 1970s, some of Hollywood's most dazzling special effects were computer generated, such as

FIGURE 1-13   Example of Flight Simulator Detail

the battle scenes in the big-budget, blockbuster science fiction movie *Star Wars,* which was released in 1976. Later came such movies as *Terminator* and *Jurassic Park.* In the early 1980s, the video game business began to boom, and its growth continues to this day as more powerful and sophisticated computing platforms are developed.

As pinball machines gave way to video games, the field of data visualization underwent its own metamorphosis from bar charts and line drawings to dynamic images.

Data visualization uses computer graphics to transform columns of data into images. This imagery enables analysts to assimilate the enormous amount of data required in some scientific investigations. Imagine trying to understand DNA sequences, molecular models, brain maps, fluid flows, or cosmic explosions from columns of numbers! Figure 1-15 contains an example of a data visualization model derived from a large, complex dataset.

One of the primary goals of data visualization is to capture the dynamic qualities of systems or processes in image form. In the 1980s, borrowing from as well as creating many of the special effects techniques of Hollywood, data visualization moved into animation. In 1990, the National Center for Supercomputing Applications (NCSA) created an award-winning animation of smog descending upon Los Angeles. The result of this compelling demonstration influenced air pollution legislation in the state. This animation was a clear testament of the value of this kind of imagery. Figure 1-16 contains a sequence of frames from the NCSA smog animation project.

FIGURE 1-14 Modern Flight Simulator for Boeing 747

Source: NASA.

However, animation had severe limitations. First, it was costly. After months of elaborate computer simulations, it still took 6 months to produce the NCSA smog animation from the resulting data; individual frames took from several minutes to an hour to render. Second, it did not allow for interactivity; that is, for changes in the data or conditions governing an experiment that produce immediate responses in the imagery. Once completed, the animation could not be altered.

Scientists wanted interactivity. So did those the military, industry, business, and entertainment. The demand for interactivity pushed computer visualization to the limits, towards virtual reality.

Back to Number Crunching, but with a Difference

The need for interactivity would have remained wishful thinking if not for the development of high-performance computers and microprocessors in the mid-1980s. These machines possessed the speed and memory for programmers and scientists to begin developing advanced data visualization software programs. By the end of the 1980s, low-cost, high-resolution graphic workstations were linked to high-speed computers, which made data visualization technology more accessible.

All the basic elements of data visualization had existed since 1980, but it took high-performance computers, with their powerful image rendering capabilities, to make it work.

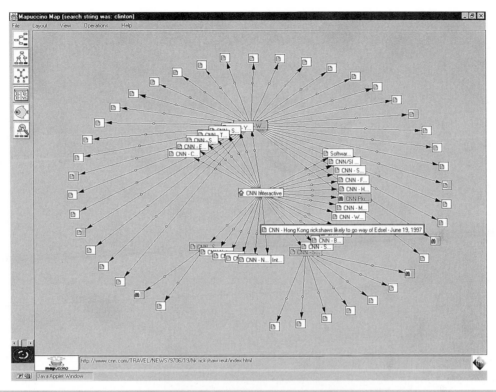

FIGURE 1-15 Data Visualization of a Large Web Access Data Set

Demand was rising for visualization environments to help scientists comprehend the vast amounts of data pouring out of their computers daily. As drivers for both computation and visualization, high-performance computers no longer served as mere number crunchers, but became exciting vehicles for exploration and discovery.

DATA VISUALIZATION AT THE FRONTIERS OF KNOWLEDGE

Today, data visualization is poised to change the way we interact with and analyze our data. Like the introduction of computers more than 50 years ago, its impacts are very much unknown, and the techniques are still in their infancy. About the only thing that does seem certain about data visualization is that it will grow and develop. As the technology matures, it will become better, cheaper, and more accessible. Clearly, the future of virtual reality is limited only by our imaginations. Throughout this text, you will begin to see more clearly both the immediate and potential value of data visualization. Being able to see the data brings an entirely new perspective to problem solving, exploration, and identification of new and exciting business opportunities.

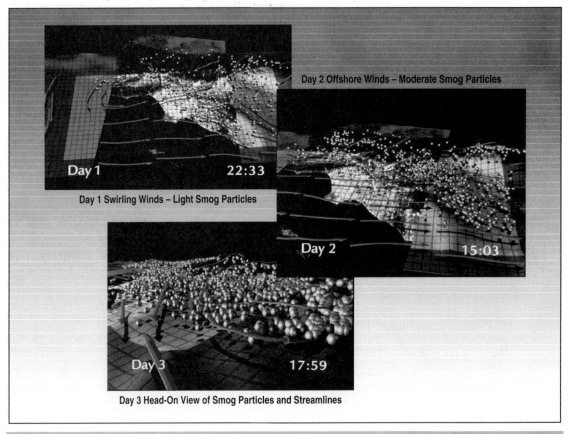

FIGURE 1-16 Data Visualization Frames from NCSA Los Angeles Smog Project

Source: National Center for Supercomputing Applications. www.ncsa.uiuc.edu/SCMS/DigLib/text/geosciences/Smog-Visualizing-Components-Siggraph90-McRae.html (Accessed August 29, 2002).

1.9: CHAPTER SUMMARY

The purpose of this chapter was to acquaint you with the basic concepts of data warehousing, mining, and visualization. In the following chapters, we will explore the application of each of these areas in greater detail with an emphasis on solving current business problems and exploiting new discoveries. By the end of the text, you should have a good understanding of how to use these new and powerful technologies. In addition, you will also develop an appreciation of the challenges of incorporating these new technologies into the modern organization.

Key Concepts

- A data warehouse is a copy of transaction data, specifically, structure for querying, analysis, and reporting.
- The data in a data warehouse is static, not dynamic.

- The data warehouse is set up to be the central repository of all organizational data deemed useful for reporting or exploration.
- A data mart is a smaller, more focused data warehouse.
- A data mart serves essentially the same function as the data warehouse, but for a subset of the business rather than for the business as a whole.
- Data warehouses can provide immediate information delivery, data integration from across the organization, a clear view of historical trends, and new tools for looking at data, as well as free users from IS department capacity constraints.
- The value from data warehouses comes from the reduced cost of system maintenance [assuming that the data warehouse is replacing another system(s)] and in the added revenue from the new business processes resulting from the additional information supplied by the warehouse.
- An organization that spends more on its data warehouse will not, necessarily, be happier with its data warehouse. It is dependent upon the design.
- Data warehouses will have users who have very set requirements for the system (farmers) and users who have various needs that they cannot define for the system (explorers).
- Data mining is the process of using raw data to infer important business relationships.
- Data must be extracted, analyzed, and generally scrubbed before effective data mining can take place.
- Based on the sheer volume of information in most data warehouses, the data miner must beware of the possibility of coming up with a correlation that is not, in fact, there or a "false positive."
- The basis for all data mining activities is the concept of data correlation.
- As a general rule, a correlation above 0.75 is considered very strong, a correlation between 0.25 and 0.75 is considered strong, and anything below 0.25 is considered weak.
- Spurious relationships are those that appear purely at random.
- Data mining can take place without a data warehouse, but a data warehouse offers data miners many advantages.
- Linking data from within and outside of the data warehouse can frequently lead to some of the biggest gains in terms of understanding and advantage.
- Data visualization involves examining data represented by dynamic images rather than pure numbers.

Questions for Review

1. What is data warehousing?
2. What does the concept of specific structure refer to?
3. What is a data mart?
4. What can a data warehouse do?
5. List five common data warehousing applications.
6. List some of the costs and benefits associated with implementing a data warehouse.
7. What are some of the factors that influence an organization's satisfaction with its data warehouse?
8. Where are the differences in the steps involved with generating a report from a data warehouse and with generating a report from a legacy system?
9. In data warehousing terms, what kind of user would be described as a "farmer"? What kind of user would be described as an "explorer"?

10. When cost justifying a data warehouse, which type of user should be used as the basis of the calculation?
11. What is data mining and why is it important?
12. What are the main categories of data mining?
13. What is metadata?
14. What does the term "granularity of the data" refer to?
15. What are some of the advantages and disadvantages associated with moving to a finer granularity in the data?
16. In data mining, what is a false positive? Why should we be concerned about these?
17. What are some of the considerations that a data miner must have when interpreting data? Why are these so critical?
18. As a general rule, what level of correlation is considered "strong"? Would you be comfortable making a decision based on data that was correlated at $r = 0.5$? Why?
19. Why would you be interested in a weak correlation?
20. What is a spurious relationship in data mining? How can it be identified? What are the dangers of not identifying it as spurious?
21. What is data visualization? Why is it important?

APPENDIX 1A

CALCULATING THE IMPACT OF A DATA WAREHOUSE ON THE ACCESS OF INFORMATION

1. How many sources (applications) do you have that will feed the need for reports and screens?

   1.a ＿＿ How many databases/files/datasets are there on average in the source systems (applications)?

   1.b ＿＿ DS (different sources) = 1.a ＿＿ 1.b ＿＿

2. What is the gathering cost per source (GC)?

   What is the cost of locating source information for reporting and screens?
   2.a ＿＿ (default = $1,000)
   What is the cost of writing code to gather source information?
   2.b ＿＿ (default = $10,000)
   What is the cost of converting/integrating source information?
   2.c ＿＿ (default = $10,000)
   What is the cost of merging data after conversion?
   2.d ＿＿ (default = $1,000)

$$GC = 2.a + 2.b + 2.c + 2.d$$

3. What is the cost of creating a report or a screen?

   3.a ＿＿ (CR) (default = $2,500)

4. How many screens/reports will be needed across the organization over the next 5 years?

   4.a ＿＿ RS

5. Calculate the infrastructure costs of a data warehouse. Determine the target size of the data warehouse in gigabytes. Now multiply the gigabytes by $7,500.

   5.a ＿＿ (DWC)

6. Calculate the cost of reporting from legacy/operational applications.

$$Report\ Costs = DS\_(GC + CR)\_RS$$

7. Now calculate the cost of reporting from a data warehouse.

$$DWReport\ Costs = (DS\_GC) + (CR\_RS) + DWC$$

Usually, the cost of reporting from legacy applications comes out so high that no reasonable organization would ever entertain spending that much money. Indeed, they do not spend that much money. Instead, the end users are frustrated in that they never get the information they need. This is why organizations without a data warehouse are said to be data rich and information poor.

CALCULATING WHETHER A DATA WAREHOUSE OR A DATA MART SHOULD BE BUILT FIRST (OR AT ALL)

1. How many sources (applications) do you have that will feed the data warehouse and/or data mart environment?

1.a ____ How many databases/files/datasets are there on average in the source systems (applications)?

1.b ____ *DS* (different sources) = 1.a ____ 1.b ____

2. How many data marts will be needed in the long run?

2.a ____ *(DM)* (default = 10)

3. How many interface programs will be needed?

$$IP = DM\_DS$$

4. What is the cost of creating an average interface program?

4.a ____ *(AIP)* (default = $20,000)

5. Calculate the infrastructure costs of a data warehouse. Determine the target size of the data warehouse in gigabytes.

5.a ____ *(DWC)* Now multiply the gigabytes by $7,500.

6. Calculate the cost of detailed redundant data that each data mart will have. Each data mart will have one-half of the detailed data found in the data warehouse.

6.a ____ = 5.a ÷ 2.

7. Estimate the number of gigabytes of redundant detailed data in an average data mart.   Multiply that number by $7,500.

$$DMRD = 5.a\_\$7,500$$

8. Calculate the cost of the data mart centric environment.

$$Cost\ of\ DM\ environment = (IP\_AIP) + (DM\_DMRD)$$

9. Now calculate the cost of the data warehouse centric environment.

$$Cost\ of\ DW\ environment = ((DS + DM)\_AIP) + DWC)$$

2
THE DATA WAREHOUSE

Learning Objectives

◆ Explain the goal of the data warehouse and its characteristics.

◆ Recognize the differences between an operational data store, a data mart, and a data warehouse.

◆ Describe each interconnected element of the data warehouse architecture.

◆ Understand the role of metadata in the data warehouse.

◆ Describe the components of the metadata.

◆ Identify the challenges to implementing a data warehouse.

◆ Examine the various data warehouse technologies and the future of data warehousing.

<DATA MINING MINICASE>

CAPITAL ONE

Mass customization transformed the credit card industry from a one-size-fits-all market into a microsegmented market offering thousands of product configurations tailored to individual consumers. Capital One, one of the top 10 U.S. credit card issuers, was founded on the premise that the credit card business is really an information business, and that mass customization is the key to growth and profitability.

Capital One uses information technology to implement a scientific testing approach to targeting profitable business. A strategy is formulated by mining behavioral data from the data warehouse. The target population is segmented and a test cell is established. The test cell is then exposed to the strategy and the results are recorded. An integrated economic evaluation is performed to judge the profit potential of the strategy. The results of the evaluation may lead to a larger-scale rollout, modification and retesting, or rejection of the strategy. No matter what the outcome, the data collected from the test become part of the data warehouse for use in evaluating future strategies.

DATA VOLUME

The amount of data needed to support Capital One's marketing efforts is enormous. The granularity of the segmentation being performed requires that all data be available at the individual account level. Also, the sophistication of the predictive models used requires low levels of transaction detail with a substantial set of measures. With approximately 9 million active accounts, 4,000 products, and 20,000 tests, some with up to 8 years of history, well over a terabyte of raw data are available.

Complex segmentation can potentially require many steps. Each step creates interim files, which need to be stored as input to subsequent steps. With dozens of analysts doing thousands of tests every year, the disk space needed to support analyst work areas accounts for more than 500 gigabytes of storage. Analysts' access to large amounts of table space allows them to create new tables potentially containing millions of rows. Mass updates of these tables are routine because of the complex nature of the segmentations being performed.

DATA STRUCTURE

Analysts at Capital One rarely ask the same question twice. The lack of a consistent access path to the data makes it almost impossible to utilize standard DSS architectures such as star schemas. Star schemas require users to restrict the framing of their questions around predetermined dimensions. With rich sources of data available to the analysts, the number of candidate dimensions would be physically impossible to implement given today's technology.

Most data are stored in slightly denormalized relational formats at a low level of granularity. Few prebuilt aggregations exist for the same reason: Stars are not effective. The analysts pay for the flexibility of the data structures by having to endure longer query turnaround times and more complex query syntax.

DATA WAREHOUSING PRODUCTS

Most data warehouse tools on the market today do not support the mass-customization environment. On the data acquisition side of data warehousing, most of the available tools cannot handle the complex integration of disparate, large-volume data sources. As tool offerings continue to address more sophisticated environments, this situation will improve. For now, companies such as Capital One are forced to build tools in-house.

DATA WAREHOUSING TALENT

Finding the right type of IT professional who can thrive in Capital One's unique culture is a constant challenge. The key characteristics of a successful data warehouse technician include a good balance of business and technical understanding, the ability to be a team player, and a great deal of flexibility. The demand for these types of professionals seems

(continued)

⟨ **DATA MINING MINICASE** ⟩

(continued)

endless and makes recruiting data warehousing talent a top priority.

Data warehousing is much more than an IT project for companies embracing the concept of mass customization. Armed with a data warehouse filled with quality information, Capital One has used mass-customization techniques and scientific testing methods to expand its customer base from one million to nearly nine million in 8 years.

Mass customization is the ultimate use of data warehousing, making it an integral part of the business process. Just like a muscle, a data warehouse increases in strength with active use. With each new test and new product, valuable information is added to the data warehouse, allowing the analysts to learn from the successes and failures of the past.

INTRODUCTION

During the 1980s, businesses and industries all over the globe participated in a "frenzy" of automation. Almost literally, if it moved, it was computerized. In this regard, the office became the new frontier for analysts and software engineers, much as the factory floor had been in the decade prior. This overwhelming concentration on the automation of business processes appeared to offer organizations the opportunity to improve from within and to realize the benefits associated with such improvement through increased profits and reduced costs.

Although many mission-critical business processes were improved during this period, the support of decision making throughout the organization remained focused on the operational and functional levels of the firm. Basic stock reports gushed out of the organization's information systems at alarming rates on a daily, weekly, and monthly basis. Often, the data used to construct these recurrent emanations were too old, too detailed, too aggregated, or not integrated. In some cases, the use of such reports led to negative consequences greater than if no information had been used at all. At the same time as this "rain" (or reign, in some cases) of data was occurring, the window of time to market and to respond to changes in global environments continued to narrow as well. By the end of the 1980s, it became clear to most organizations that the key to survival in the 1990s and beyond would be the ability to analyze, plan, and react to changing business conditions in a much more rapid fashion. This would require more and better information for management at all levels of the firm.

Despite this growing need for more information, every day organizations large and small created billions of bytes of data about all aspects of their business—millions of individual facts about their customers, products, operations, and people—without any formalized initiative beyond the transaction level to organize it. For the most part, these data were literally "locked up" in a thousand computer systems and were, metaphorically speaking, "imprisoned."

Only a small fraction of the data that are captured, processed, and stored in the enterprise ever actually make it to executives' and decision makers' attention. The concept of the data warehouse (DW) is part of the response by information technology to meet this identified need. It is a simple concept that, over time, could potentially evolve into a significant contributor to the success and stability of an organization in the global marketplace. The essence of the DW is a recognition that the characteristics and usage patterns of operational systems that automate business processes and those of a DSS are fundamentally different but, nonetheless, symbiotically linked (Kelly 1994). The DW provides a facility for integrating the data generated in a world of unintegrated information systems. A functional DW organizes and stores all of the available data needed for informational, analytical processing over a historical time perspective. The DW then reintegrates the data generated by a myriad of internal and external information systems to create a sense of unity about the data without surrendering any of its natural complexities.

2.1: STORES, WAREHOUSES, AND MARTS

The concept of the DW is brand new and, as such, is in a state of flux with regard to standardized terms and definitions. Some definitions focus on data, whereas others refer to people, software, tools, and business processes. The acknowledged father of data warehousing, W. H. Inmon, provided a clear and useful definition of the data warehouse concept in terms of measurable attributes, which will serve our purposes in this text:

> The data warehouse is a collection of integrated, subject-oriented databases designed to support the DSS (decision support) function, where each unit of data is nonvolatile and relevant to some moment in time. (Inmon 1992a, 5)

Inmon's definition of a DW makes two implicit assumptions: (1) the DW is physically separated from all other operational systems; and (2) DWs hold aggregated data and transactional (atomic) data for management separate from that used for online transaction processing.

The requirement of a separate environment for the DW is an essential element in the concept. In most cases, the systems employed in an operational environment are inadequate, in many respects, with regard to decision making and analysis. Primarily, the type, quantity, and quality of the data contained in such environments are not well suited to historical analysis. Warehouse data must be consistent, well integrated, well defined, and most important, time stamped. In addition, the need to merge a wide variety of internal and external environments with an equally wide variety of access methods suggests the need for separate data warehouse systems. Table 2-1 compares operational versus DW characteristics.

The blue-collar, distribution-channel metaphor of a "warehouse for data" extends easily to the primary components of a complete data warehouse environment. Although the focus of this chapter is on the warehouse itself, we must briefly examine three additional components of the DW environment: the data store, the data mart, and the metadata.

THE DATA STORE

The operational data store (ODS) is the most common component of the DW environment. Its primary day-to-day function is to store the data for a single, specific set of operational applications. Its function within the DW environment, however, is to feed the data warehouse a stream of desired raw data.

The data organization within an ODS is generally subject oriented, volatile, and current (or near current) and commonly focuses on customers, products, orders, policies, claims, and so forth. Normally, the ODS is fed by one or more legacy systems, and the DBMSs associated with such systems cleanse, transform, and integrate the data into homogeneous records of transactions or instances of occurrence. Although the data within an ODS lend themselves favorably

TABLE 2-1 Operational Data Store and Data Warehouse Characteristics

Characteristic	Operational Data Store	Data Warehouse
How it is built?	One application or subject area at a time.	Typically multiple subject areas at a time.
User requirements	Well defined prior to logical design.	Often vague and conflicting.
Area of support	Day-to-day business operations.	Decision support for managerial activities.
Type of access	Relatively small number of records retrieved via a single query.	Large data sets scanned to retrieve results from either single or multiple queries.
Frequency of access	Tuned for frequent access to small amounts of data.	Tuned for infrequent access to large amounts of data.
Volume of data	Similar to typical daily volume of operational transactions.	Much larger than typical daily transaction volume.
Retention period	Retained as necessary to meet daily operating requirements.	Retention period is indeterminate and must support historical reporting, comparison, and analysis.
Currency of data	Up-to-the-minute; real time.	Typically represents a static point in time.
Availability of data	High and immediate availability may be required.	Immediate availability is less critical.
Typical unit of analysis	Small, manageable, transaction-level units.	Large, unpredictable, variable units.
Design focus	High-performance, limited flexibility.	High flexibility, high performance.

Source: Adapted from Bischoff and Alexander (1997).

to analysis performed by one or more of its legacy systems, the data generally do not integrate easily with data from other nonrelated systems. Nonetheless, many data stores (both internal and external to the organization) may be drawn upon to feed the organizational DW for the purpose of analysis.

THE DATA MART

Although the concept of a central aggregation of disparate, yet relevant, data is appealing, the costs associated with such aggregation across an entire organization may be prohibitive. The need for certain types and sources of aggregated data may exist only within certain business units within the firm, and the specific needs of each unit may be tangential to those of the others. As an alternative, many firms adopt a lower-cost, scaled-down version of the DW called the data mart.

The data mart is often viewed as a way to gain entry into the realm of data warehouses and to make any mistakes on a smaller scale. In addition, vendors of data warehousing applications find it easier to deal directly with a small group of isolated users than with the IS department of an entire organization. Although the concept of the "mini-mart" is both appealing and useful, a single caveat regarding its proliferation must be acknowledged: Without careful planning from an enterprise-wide perspective, the data mart can become an isolated island of information that will be inaccessible to others in the firm. Assuming the data marts are constructed within the bigger picture of an enterprise-wide system, they offer a targeted and less costly method of gaining the advantages associated with data warehousing and can be scaled up to a full DW environment over time.

THE METADATA

One additional component of the DW environment is the metadata. Legacy systems generally do not keep a record of characteristics of the data, such as exactly what pieces of data exist, where they are located, where they came from, and how they can be accessed. The metadata are simply data about data—that is, information that is kept about the warehouse rather than information kept within the warehouse. We will cover metadata in detail in Section 2.3.

THE DW ENVIRONMENT

Figure 2-1 illustrates the flow of data within an organization and the position of the components of the DW environment with regard to other information systems. As shown in the figure, the organization's legacy systems and the relevant data stores of external systems provide the core sources of data for the data warehouse and data mart. During the transfer of data from the various data stores, a process of cleansing and transformation occurs to make the DW data more uniform. Simultaneously, the metadata are collected and associated with the DW data so

FIGURE 2-1   Organizational Data Flow and Data Storage Components

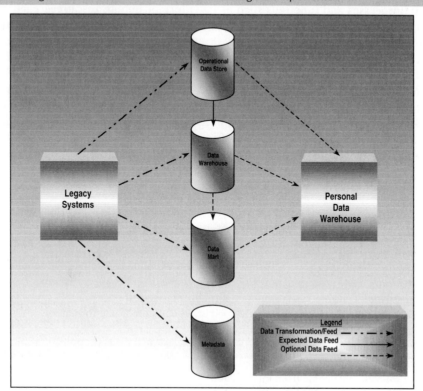

that potential users can determine the source and general characteristics of the DW data. Finally, the DW or data mart may be employed to create one or more personal data warehouses intended for isolated analysis. In the following sections, we will explore the details of the processes and architectures typically associated with a DW environment.

DW CHARACTERISTICS

Thus far, we have established the reasons why data warehousing is an important innovation in decision support, and we formally defined the DW to be:

- Subject oriented
- Data integrated
- Time variant
- Nonvolatile

Table 2-2 summarizes these essential characteristics of the DW and provides a brief description of each.

Subject Orientation

The first feature of the DW is its *orientation toward the major subjects of the organization,* which clearly contrasts with the more functional orientation of the various applications associated with the firm's legacy systems. Figure 2-2 illustrates this contrast in orientations.

As indicated by the figure, the operational world of the organization is typically designed around processes and functions such as inventory or human resources, each of which exhibit specific data needs, with most of the data elements local to that process or function. The DW, on the other hand, contains data primarily oriented to decision making and, as such, is organized more around the major subject areas relevant to the firm, such as customers or vendors.

This distinct subject orientation results in several specific differences between typical applications and the data warehouse. For example, design activities in the application world must be equally focused on both process and database design, whereas the DW world is primarily void of process design (at least in its classical form) and tends to focus exclusively on issues of data modeling and database design.

Another specific distinction can be found in the characteristics of the data contained within the DW. Operational data are normally stored in the form of an ongoing relationship between

---

TABLE 2-2 Characteristics of a Data Warehouse

- *Subject orientation.* Data are organized based on how the users refer to them.
- *Integrated.* All inconsistencies regarding naming convention and value representations are removed.
- *Nonvolatile.* Data are stored in read-only format and do not change over time.
- *Time variant.* Data are not current but normally time series.
- *Summarized.* Operational data are mapped into a decision-usable format.
- *Large volume.* Time series data sets are normally quite large.
- *Not normalized.* DW data can be, and often are, redundant.
- *Metadata.* Data about data are stored.
- *Data sources.* Data come from internal and external unintegrated operational systems.

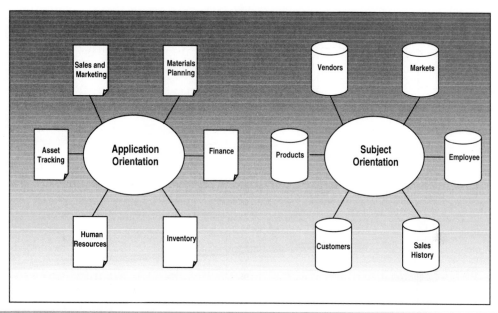

FIGURE 2-2 Application Versus Subject Orientation

two or more tables based on some established business rule such as "Each order must be related to one and only one customer." This business rule creates a relationship between the table containing instances of orders and the table containing instances of customers. One entry in the customer table may be related to many entries in the order table, whereas one entry in the order table will always be related to only one entry in the customer table. In contrast, data in the DW span a range of time and, as such, many business rules (and correspondingly, many data relationships) can be represented in the DW between two or more tables (Inmon 1992a).

Data Integration
According to Inmon (1992b), the essence of the DW environment is that the data contained within the boundaries of the warehouse are *integrated*. This integration manifests itself through consistency in naming convention and measurement attributes, accuracy, and common aggregation. Figure 2-3 illustrates the sharp contrast between the lack of integration found within the operational application environment and that of the DW environment.

Consistent Naming and Measurement Attributes
One of the freedoms associated with application design has always been the selection of a naming convention for variables, both as they are represented in the data dictionary and as they appear on the screen. The frequent exercise of this freedom made the inconsistency of applications throughout an organization legendary. For example, the typical data element of gender can (and has) been encoded in operational applications in a myriad of ways. In one application, the variable may be represented as M or F. In another application, the designer may choose to represent it numerically with 1 or 0, or 1 or 2, or possibly 0 or 1. In yet another, the representation may be as an X and a Y. As long as these representations are understood by their respective applications and users, then no serious problems will occur. However, when the databases

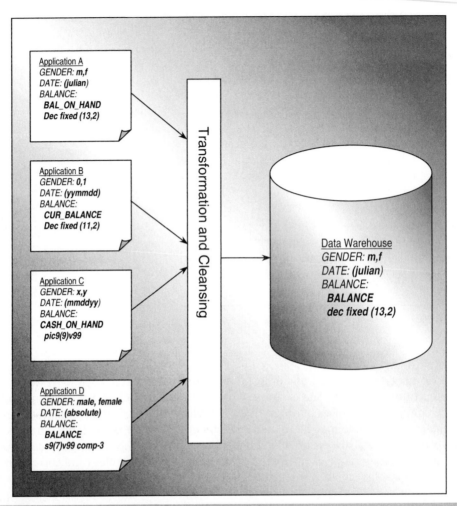

FIGURE 2-3 Integration and Transformation of ODS Data

associated with these dissimilar applications are loaded into the data warehouse, a decision as to what naming convention will be adopted must be made and a transformation process based on that naming convention must be effected. Therefore, it does not particularly matter how gender is represented in the DW as long as it is represented in a consistent and integrated manner. To ensure this consistency, each source of data needs an associated conversion process to "scrub" the data into a converted state.

Another result of the need for integrated data is the establishment of a common unit of measure for all synonymous data elements from dissimilar databases. This common measurement must not only serve to integrate the variety of measuring attributes being loaded into the DW, but it must also create a globally acceptable unit of measure for the final data. In one database, an employee's term of employment may be represented in weeks, whereas in another it may be represented in months or years or in decimal years. Just like the conversion of data element names to a common convention, units of measure must also be converted as the data are loaded into the warehouse. This conversion, although serving to standardize the unit of measure, must also create a standard that is universally acceptable to the decision makers and DSS technologies that will use the DW. In some cases, it is an easy decision as to how to represent a particular measurement. Temperature, for instance, will typically be a choice between the Fahrenheit, Celsius, or Kelvin scales. The decision will depend on the intended use of the data. In other cases, however, the decision may be constrained by a wide variety of intended uses for the data element in question. In these cases, it may become necessary to convert the data to some "nonstandard" unit of measure that will allow for the most flexible conversion schema to be employed. In the case of employee tenure, the conversion to a unit of days of employment during data loading of the DW may turn out to be the most flexible choice because this unit will allow easy conversion to any desired output. To extend this concept further, the needs analysis for this data element may suggest that it would be better to not store the length of employee service but, rather, to store the initial date of employment. In this way, a single mathematical process could be employed to convert the data to whatever unit of measure was deemed most desirable.

Whatever the issue, the data must be stored in the DW in an integrated, globally acceptable manner. It is important to the success of a DW that the DSS analyst focus on the use of the data contained in the warehouse rather than on issues of credibility or consistency.

Time Variant

In an operational application system, the expectation is that all data within the database are accurate as of the moment of access. When a customer service representative for a credit card company checks a customer's current balance, the representative's expectation (and the customer's) is that the value returned will be accurate as of that moment. It would not be particularly useful for the credit card representative to tell the customer that their balance was $459.00 as of 3 weeks ago. In the realm of data warehouses, however, data are simply assumed to be accurate as of some moment in time and not necessarily "right now." Typically, the data are assumed to be accurate at the moment they were loaded into the DW. In this regard, data within a data warehouse are said to be *time variant*.

The time variance of the warehouse data manifests itself in a variety of ways. Typically, the time horizon for the data in the warehouse is long—from 5 to 10 years. In contrast, the typical operational environment time horizon is much shorter—anywhere from current values to 60 to 90 days. The level of performance associated with high-volume transaction processing necessitates the shorter time horizons in operational applications. In DW environments, however, the desire is generally to analyze data over longer time periods in an effort to reveal trends and temporal relationships.

Another place where DW data display time variance is in the structure of the record key. Every primary key contained within the DW must contain, either implicitly or explicitly, an element of time (day, week, month, year, etc.). In an explicit representation, the time unit may be concatenated (appended) to the primary key (i.e., CUST-ORDER10992, where the second part of the key reflects month and year). In other cases, the time element will be implicitly stated, such as a file that is always loaded at the end of a month or quarter and is named for its associated time period. Regardless of the method employed, every piece of data contained within the warehouse must be associated with a particular point in time if any useful analysis is to be conducted with it.

Yet another aspect of time variance in DW data is that, once recorded, data within the warehouse cannot be updated or changed. In this regard, warehouse data can be thought of as a series of sequential photographs. Using this metaphor, an inaccurate snapshot may be replaced by an accurate one, but once the accuracy of the photos is ascertained, they cannot be altered.

Nonvolatility

In keeping with the restriction of not changing or updating the data contained in a DW, it makes sense that the typical activities of inserts, deletes, and changes performed regularly in an operational application environment are completely nonexistent in a DW environment. Only two data operations are ever performed in the data warehouse: data loading and data access.

This simplicity of data operations creates some extremely powerful differences between operational processing and processing in a DW environment. The design issues in a typical operational application must focus on data integrity and update anomalies. Complex processes must be coded to ensure that the data update processes allow for high integrity of the final product. Such issues are of no concern in a DW environment because data update is never performed. Liberties in the design of the DW databases can be taken to allow for optimal access to the data that could never be allowed in an operational environment. Recall from your study of database design the need to place data in a normalized form to ensure minimal redundancy. In this regard, the third normal form eliminates any derived data elements, such as those that can be calculated. In an operational application database, a designer would never store the total for a particular order. If this data element is desired, it can be easily calculated upon retrieval of the order. In the world of data warehouses, however, designers might actually find it useful to store many such calculations or summarizations not found in the operational data. For example, it might be useful to include weekly or monthly sales figures obtained by aggregating the daily sales figures found in the operational database.

Along with the simplicity of processing in a DW environment comes a relative simplicity in the necessary technology. In the operational realm, the technologies necessary to support issues of transaction and data recovery, rollback, and detection and remedy of deadlock are quite complex. In the realm of data warehouses, these processes are quite unnecessary.

ISSUES OF DATA REDUNDANCY

The lack of relevancy of issues such as data normalization in the DW environment that are so important to the reduction of data redundancy in the operational realm may suggest the prospect of massive data redundancy within the DW and between the operational and DW environments. Inmon (1992a) pointed out that, counter to that first impression, a minimum of redundancy actually occurs between the data in the operational application databases feeding the DW and the warehouse itself. Several points bear out the truth of this assertion.

First, consider that the data being loaded into the DW are filtered and "cleansed" as they pass from the operational database to the warehouse. Because of this cleansing, numerous data that exist in the operational environment never pass to the DW. Only the data necessary for processing by the DSS or executive information system (EIS) are ever actually loaded into the DW. Also, the DW contains a great deal of summarized data that are never reflected in the operational data store.

Consider also that the time horizons for warehouse and operational data elements are unique. Data in the operational environment are fresh, whereas warehouse data are generally much older. When viewed from a time-horizon perspective, the opportunity for overlap or redundancy between the operational and data warehouse environments is minimal.

Finally, recall that the data being loaded into the DW often undergo a radical transformation as they pass from the operational to the DW environment. Because of this transformation and alteration, most of the data that ultimately reside in the data warehouse are not the same data that once resided in the operational environment (at least not from a data-integration perspective).

Given these factors, Inmon (1992a) suggested that data redundancy between the two environments is a rare occurrence, with a typical redundancy factor of less than 1 percent.

2.2: THE DATA WAREHOUSE ARCHITECTURE

A data warehouse architecture (DWA) is a method by which the overall structure of data, communication, processing, and presentation for end-user computing within the enterprise can be represented. Figure 2-4 illustrates the various interconnected elements that make up the DWA.

OPERATIONAL AND EXTERNAL DATABASE LAYER

The operational and external database layer represents the source data for the DW. This layer comprises, primarily, operational transaction processing systems and external secondary databases. The goal of the data warehouse is to free the information locked up in the operational databases and to mix it with information from other, often external, sources. An additional

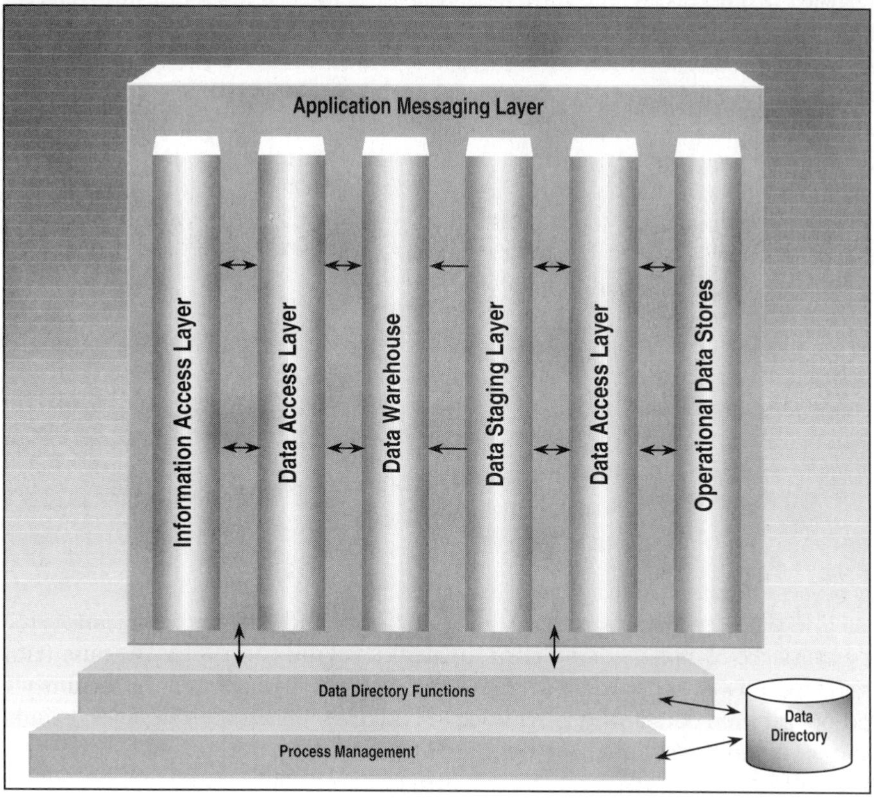

FIGURE 2-4 Components of the Data Warehouse Architecture

objective of the DW is to have a minimal impact on the performance and operation of the systems found in this layer. In other words, the addition of the necessary extraction software to this environment should go unnoticed in terms of performance of the operational applications whose databases are being accessed.

Large organizations frequently acquire additional data from outside databases. The ubiquitous nature of the Web and the Internet makes it easy and economical for firms to access and incorporate such data into their DW. Data related to demographic, econometric, competitive, and purchasing trends typically found in public- or subscriber-access databases via the Internet are treated in the same manner as the ODS data and, following extraction and conditioning for consistency, are loaded into the data warehouse.

INFORMATION ACCESS LAYER

The end user deals directly with the information access layer of the DWA. In particular, it represents the tools that the end user normally uses day to day to extract and analyze the data contained within the DW. This layer consists of the hardware and software involved in displaying and printing reports, spreadsheets, graphs, and charts for analysis and presentation. At the information access layer, the DSSs use the DW data to support the various categories and types of decision making throughout the organization.

DATA ACCESS LAYER

As shown in Figure 2-4, the data access layer serves as a sort of interface or intermediary between the operational and information access layers and the DW itself. This layer spans the various databases contained within the DW and facilitates common access by the DW users. The data access layer not only spans multiple databases and file systems on the same hardware, it also spans the wide variety of manufacturers and network protocols. A successful DW provides end users with universal data access so that, theoretically at least, end users should be able to access any or all of the enterprise's data necessary for them to do their job, regardless of location or information access tool. It is the role of the data access layer to make this access happen.

METADATA LAYER

In order to provide for universal data access, it is absolutely necessary to maintain some form of data directory or repository of metadata information. As discussed briefly in Section 2.1, metadata are data about the data stored within the DW. Examples of metadata include the directory of where the data are stored, the rules used for summarization and scrubbing, or possibly records of operational data sources.

PROCESS MANAGEMENT LAYER

The process management layer focuses on scheduling the various tasks that must be accomplished to build and maintain the data warehouse and data directory information. This layer can be thought of as the scheduler or the high-level job control for the many processes (procedures) that must occur to keep the DW up to date. Tasks such as periodic download from identified operational data stores, scheduled summarization of operational data, access and download of external data sources, and update of the metadata are typically performed at this layer of the DWA.

APPLICATION MESSAGING LAYER

The application messaging layer transports information around the enterprise computing network. This layer is also referred to as "middleware," but it can typically involve more that just networking protocols and request routing. Application messaging, for example, can be used to isolate applications, operational or informational, from the exact data format on either end, thus facilitating a seamless interface between the uniqueness of a particular data format and the specific format requirements of the analysis tool being used. This layer can also be used to collect transactions or messages and deliver them to a certain location at a certain time. In this sense, the application messaging layer can be thought of as the transport system underlying the DW.

PHYSICAL DW LAYER

The physical DW layer is where the actual data used for decision support throughout the organization are located. In some cases, one can think of the DW simply as a logical or virtual view of data, because, as we will see shortly, in some instances the data warehouse may not actually store the data accessed through it.

DATA STAGING LAYER

The final component of the DWA is the data staging layer. Data staging (sometimes referred to as copy or replication management) includes all of the processes necessary to select, edit, summarize, combine, and load data warehouse and information access data from operational and external databases.

Data staging often involves complex programming, but more and more vendors market data warehousing tools intended to reduce the complexities associated with this process. Data staging may also require data quality analysis programs and other such filters that identify patterns and data structures within existing operational data.

DATA WAREHOUSING TYPOLOGY

As mentioned previously, although the data warehouse may appear to be the source of data for various organizational analysis initiatives and decision-making activities, it may not physically be the location of the data being accessed. Numerous hybrid mechanisms exist to structure a DW, but three basic configurations can be identified: virtual (point-to-point), central, and distributed data warehouses.

Before we review each configuration, we must note that no single approach to configuring a DW schema is best in all situations. Each option fits a specific set of requirements, and a data warehousing strategy may ultimately include all three options.

The Virtual DW

A virtual, or point-to-point, data warehousing strategy allows the end users to access the operational data stores directly using tools enabled at the data access layer. This approach provides a great deal of flexibility as well as the minimum amount of redundant data that must be loaded and maintained; however, it can also put the largest unplanned query load and performance degradation on operational application systems.

Virtual warehousing is often an initial strategy in organizations with a broad but largely undefined need to get at operational data by a relatively large class of end users. In such situations, the likely frequency of requests is low. Virtual data warehouses often provide a relatively low-cost starting point for organizations to assess what types of data end users are really look-ing for.

The Central DW

Central data warehouses are what most people think of when first introduced to the concept of a data warehouse. The central data warehouse is a single physical database that contains all of the data for a specific functional area, department, division, or enterprise. This warehousing approach is often selected when users demonstrate a common need for informational data and large numbers of end users are already connected to a central computer or network. A central DW may contain data for any specific period of time and usually contains data from multiple operational applications.

The central DW is real. The data stored in the DW are physically located in and accessible from one place and must be loaded and maintained on a regular basis. This configuration is the most common of the three basic types and represents the de facto standard for DW implemen-tation due to the wide variety of construction and manipulation tools being offered.

The Distributed DW

A distributed DW is just what its name implies: a DW whose components are distributed across a number of different physical databases. As large organizations push decision making down to lower and lower levels of the organization, the data needed for decision making are also pushed down (or out) to the LAN or local computer serving the local decision maker. Many older DW implementations use the distributed approach because initially it was easier to create several small DW databases than to facilitate one all-encompassing one. The advent of modern DW implemen-tation and management applications, however, reduced the need for multiple or distributed DWs.

2.3: DATA ABOUT DATA: METADATA

The real problem with metadata is that the name suggests some high-level technological con-cept that requires far too much cognitive energy to discuss and understand. With the emergence of the DW as a primary decision-support resource, metadata are now considered as much a resource of the organization as the business data they describe.

The standard definition of metadata is "data about data." Although this definition exudes a comforting Zen-like quality that makes for a great slogan, it leaves a lot to be desired with regard to providing any useful description. For example, how can we add meaning to data by associating that data with more data? To answer this question we must first understand the pri-mary concept upon which metadata are built.

THE CONCEPT OF ABSTRACTION

To understand metadata, we focus on a relatively simple concept of general semantics called the chain of abstraction. For example, a sofa is a fairly concrete entity. Any particular sofa has a number of descriptive characteristics: It is made of wood, cloth, steel, and leather; it has two arms and a back; it is a particular shape or style; it has several cushions; and so on. We can abstract from that sofa, and others we encounter, to the word *sofa*. In other words, by using the word *sofa*, we can describe a wide variety of specific sofas; in fact, we can describe all sofas ever made. Moving from describing a particular sofa to representing all sofas by using a single word is but one step in the chain of abstraction. We can take additional steps. For instance, we could describe the word *sofa* and all the other words we know by the word *word*. The chain of abstraction for anything is essentially unlimited, provided the level of abstraction we use conveys some useful meaning.

Software is simply a link in the chain of abstraction. The word *sofa* that you are reading now, if stored in a computer, would be represented by a string of magnetic flux changes on the oxide surface of a hard disk or as minute pits in the surface of a compact disk. So would a source code statement such as:

LET CHECK_BALANCE = CHECK_BALANCE + CREDIT − DEBIT

The source code statement, in turn, is an abstraction of a banking transaction, which is an abstraction of a bank, which is an abstraction of an industry, which is an abstraction of an economy, which is . . . well, you get the point.

Metadata are simply abstractions from data. They are high-level data that provide us with concise descriptions of lower-level data. The world is full of metadata—consider these examples.

- Author, title, ISBN number, and publisher
- Headlines of stories in a paper
- Business definitions for all data elements in the DW
- Road maps
- Data flow diagrams in a CASE tool's repository

THE KEY TO THE DATA

Metadata are essential ingredients in the transformation of raw data into knowledge. For example, metadata in the form of a field definition tell us that a given stream of bits is a customer's order number, part of a bit-mapped graphic, or the name of a word-processing document we just created. Should the metadata get mixed up or out of alignment, none of the data will make sense. The order number will not match any of our orders; the document we created will not be retrievable; even the graphic will not look quite the way it should, though depending upon how jumbled the metadata become, our eyes may not detect the difference.

It may be helpful to think of metadata as "tongs" with which we can handle raw data (APT 1996). Without metadata, the data are meaningless. We do not even know where they are or what percentage to take. How could we query a database without data definitions? All we could hope to recover would be a string of ones and zeroes. In the early days of commercial computing, each application created and handled its own data files. Because the files' metadata were embedded in the application's data definitions, no application could make sense of another application's files. When databases were introduced, one of the greatest advantages they brought was that the metadata were stored in the database catalog, not in the individual programs. The one version of the truth was stored in the database.

THE METADATA IN ACTION

Assume for the moment that while exploring our organization's data warehouse we find three unique sets of data:

1. 615397 8350621 885214 0051023 6487921
2. A Garrison Group report dated 9/12/96 states that the Asian market for machine tools expanded by 33 percent in 1995
3. Leading sports marketing firms: IMG 45 percent, SportStarz 33 percent, Legends, Inc. 16 percent

How much can we learn from these data? In the first case, the answer is "absolutely nothing." The numbers may be sales figures for a department or region, the population of European cities, or maybe the number of blood cells in a set of samples. The numbers could even represent a sequence of machine code for a computer. This dataset is typical of tabular data found in a relational database. Meaning can, however, be assigned to the data in two specific ways: from the context or from the metadata. In the former case, these numbers are the result of a query on a given table, so we already know their meaning. In the latter, if we associate a metadata description with the data, it will tell us the name of the table and possibly a great deal more.

The second example appears to be more straightforward. It is free text and more self-descriptive. One small point, however: The date shown is ambiguous. Does "9/12/96" mean September 12, 1996 (U.S. convention), or December 9, 1996 (European/Asian convention)? In this case, the metadata clear up the confusion by indicating that all dates are displayed using "MM/DD/YY."

The third example contains some metadata: We know that the data represent leading sports marketing firms. What we do not know is what the percentages represent, what time period is referred to, how the data were collected, or even the source of the information. Without sufficient metadata, the data element in the example is useless.

These examples demonstrate the importance of metadata in the DW environment. Data analysts and executives look for useful facts and correlations that they can recognize when they find them—and often, not before. Routine applications are of no use to them: They need to get in among the data, and to do so successfully; they need to understand the data's structure and meaning. Passengers on a train do not need a map, although a timetable may be useful. A driver setting out by road across a foreign country to an unknown village, though, would be unwise to set out without a complete set of large-scale and small-scale maps (APT 1996). A DW without adequate metadata is like filing cabinets stuffed full of paper with no folders or labels. Try finding anything useful in that!

CONSISTENCY—AVOIDING MANY VERSIONS OF THE TRUTH

Unreliable or missing metadata lead to untenable situations in which one business unit reports that overall corporate profits are up 15 percent, while another business unit says they are down 10 percent. Each functional area uses its own numbers, collected in accordance with its own procedures and interpreted by its own applications. This "algorithmic differential" often results in organizational decision making that lapses into a morass of politics and personalities.

Unlike the individual ODSs established for the benefit of a specific business unit or department, the DW is set up for the benefit of business analysts and executives across all functional areas of the organization. If they need metadata—and they do—then it is the job of the DW support staff to make sure they get that information. In this regard, the DW support staff can be thought of as librarians. If you need help finding what you are looking for, they act as guides. If you do not require assistance, then you are free to browse at your convenience.

In a DW environment, both the data and the metadata are constantly updated. Organizational decision makers are always on the lookout for new and interesting patterns in the data, which can lead them to investigate and compare information from all corners of the enterprise and beyond. It can also lead to requests for new datasets, which must be replicated from operational application systems or imported from external sources. With each new addition to the DW, the warehouse's metadata map must extend to accommodate it.

AGREEING ON ONE VERSION OF THE TRUTH

Not only must DW administrators keep up with ever-changing data definitions and requests for new and disparate datasets, they must also agree on a single version of the truth. In the corporate world, the saying is that if the revenues for which credit was claimed by all the department managers were totaled, the amount would exceed the organization's actual revenue by several hundred percent. In aggregating all the data elements necessary for a useful DW, the metadata must be organized in such a way that accurate and useful comparisons across time and sources can be made. The greatest challenge developers and maintainers of a DW face is ensuring the integrity and accuracy of the data contained within the DW.

2.4: METADATA EXTRACTION

Inmon (1992b) suggested that, regardless of the specific nature of a given query to the DW, several general pieces of information, derived from the metadata, are important to all decision makers. Table 2-3 lists the generic information essential to using data from a DW.

   Data warehouse metadata are not all that different from operational database metadata, although DW metadata are versioned in order to permit historical analysis. The DW metadata must be tagged with some information that lets the user know the general conditions under which the DW data were collected. When collection methods or conditions change, then the metadata version must change as well. In this regard, we can think of metadata versioning as meta-metadata.

COMPONENTS OF THE METADATA

Collecting the right metadata at the right time is a foundational requirement for a successful DW implementation. Although specific metadata considered useful for one DW may not be useful to another, several categories of general metadata can be found in a typical DW environment.

Transformation Mapping

Transformation-mapping metadata records how data from operational data stores and external sources are transformed on the way into the warehouse. As the individual data elements from these sources are mapped to the existing DW structures, this mapping should be collected and maintained as metadata. With the advent of modern data warehouse development tools,

---

TABLE 2-3   General Metadata Issues Associated with Data Warehouse Use

- What tables, attributes, and keys does the data warehouse contain?
- Where did each set of data come from?
- What transformation logic was applied in loading the data?
- How have the metadata changed over time?
- What aliases exist and how are they related to each other?
- What are the cross-references between technical and business terms?
- How often do the data get reloaded?
- How many data elements are in the DW (to assist in avoiding the submission of unrealistic queries)?

the mapping process becomes virtually indistinguishable from the process of transformation. Table 2-4 lists several of the types of mappings that must be available as metadata.

Extraction and Relationship History

Whenever historical information is analyzed, meticulous update records must be kept. Often a decision maker begins the process of constructing a time-based report by reviewing the extraction history because any changes to the business rules must be ascertained in order to apply the right rules to the right data. If sales regions were reallocated in 1994, then the decision maker will know that results prior to that date may not be directly comparable with more recent results.

In addition to the extraction metadata, information regarding the various relationships contained within the DW must be maintained. DWs often implement data relationships differently from operational application databases. Metadata pertaining to related tables, constraints, and cardinality must be maintained, together with text descriptions and ownership records. This information and the history of changes to it can be valuable to decision makers when performing analyses with multiple aggregations of data.

Algorithms for Summarization

A typical data warehouse contains a wide variety of lightly and heavily summarized data, as well as fully detailed records. The summarization algorithms applied to the detail data are important to any decision maker analyzing or interpreting the meaning of the summaries. These metadata can also save time by making it easier to decide which level of summarization is most appropriate for a given analysis context.

Data Ownership

Operational data stores are often "owned" by particular business units or divisions within an organization. In a DW environment, however, all data are stored in a common format and are normally accessible to all, which makes it necessary to identify the originator of each set of data, so that inquiries and corrections can be made to the proper group. It is useful to distinguish between "ownership" of data in the operational environment and "stewardship" in the DW. The administrators of the DW are responsible for the collection, summarization, and dissemination of warehouse data, and in this regard are the caretakers or stewards of the data. The administrators of the source ODS, however, are responsible for the accuracy of the transaction-level data and are the actual owners of the data.

TABLE 2-4   Typical Mapping Metadata

- Identification of original source fields
- Simple attribute-to-attribute mapping
- Attribute conversions
- Physical characteristic conversions
- Encoding/reference table conversions
- Naming changes
- Key changes
- Values of defaults
- Logic to choose from among multiple sources
- Algorithmic changes

Patterns of Warehouse Access

It is often desirable to record patterns of access to the warehouse for the purpose of optimizing and tuning DW performance. Understanding what tables are being accessed, how often, and by whom can alert the DW administrators to ways of improving or simplifying the queries being performed by the end users. Less frequently used data can be migrated to cheaper storage media, and various methods can be employed to accelerate access to the data that are most in demand. Further, the identification and recording of queries can be a valuable resource to the organization because it can facilitate the reuse of queries. Instead of spending the time to figure out how to construct a new query, a decision maker can simply access a repository of past queries and choose the one that most closely resembles the immediate need.

Additional Common Metadata

In addition to the major categories of metadata already discussed, several other less common, yet equally important, categories of metadata can be identified. These miscellaneous metadata components are often context-specific or organization-dependent. When needed for analysis, however, they are as important as the more common categories.

Important members of this class of metadata are the logical business data models. In many instances, users need to understand the logical model that defines the entities, relationships, and rules that exist in a particular business environment where data were obtained. Building a data warehouse without including the source data models is both dangerous and prone to error. When the source data model is available, metadata describing the mapping between the data model and the physical design can be retrieved, thus resolving ambiguities or uncertainties.

Another category of metadata that can make the warehouse much more user friendly is alias metadata. By allowing a table to be queried by "Units produced by each region" rather than "REG_MFG_STATS," aliases make both the construction and subsequent interpretation of a query more understandable. Aliases are also useful when different business units use their own names to refer to the same underlying data. Careful tracking of aliases for data elements is an important part of the DW metadata.

Development-status metadata are yet another important source of information to the DW user. Often, parts of the same DW may be in various stages of development or completion. Status information can be used to convey information to the decision maker regarding, for example, the tables being accessed by a certain query. Such tables might be classified as in-design, in-test, or inactive.

Finally, volumetric metadata can be stored to inform users as to the exact volume of data they are dealing with so as to provide them with some idea about how much their queries will cost in terms of time and resources. Volumetrics often include such information as number of rows, table growth rate, usage characteristics, indexing, and byte specifications.

2.5: IMPLEMENTING THE DATA WAREHOUSE

The challenge of providing access to the aggregated data of an organization is not a new one. The 1970s saw the advent of the information center, an ill-fated concept that required a dedicated, high-powered computer and severely drained resources in terms of hardware, software, and personnel. The 1980s brought an emphasis on data reengineering using the extended relational model. This model, too, suffered from complexities and severe performance degradation issues. The twenty-first-century answer to this problem appears to be the data warehouse. If we are to avoid the problems of the past and realize the successes assumed to be associated with total access to data, IT management and organizational DW champions must not only understand what needs to be done, but also how to do it. Following a closer look in the next chapter at the DW from a data visualization perspective, in Chapter 6, we will focus in detail on the issues surrounding the implementation of a DW in the modern organization. For our purposes in this chapter, however, we simply need to begin thinking about the unique nature of the DW with regard to its implementation.

Denis Kozar (1997), vice president of Enterprise Information Architecture for Chase Manhattan Bank, assembled the "seven deadly sins" of DW implementation. Each of these errors can result in the failure of an otherwise valuable DW initiative. Table 2-5 lists the "seven deadly sins" of data warehousing.

SIN 1: "IF YOU BUILD IT, THEY WILL COME"

Kozar offered that the first of the seven sins is one of blind faith. This is the failure to recognize the importance of developing a clear set of business objectives for the DW prior to its construction. A successful DW plan considers the needs of the entire enterprise and develops a documented set of requirements to guide the design, construction, and rollout of the project. The DW cannot simply be built in the hope that someone will find a use for it.

SIN 2: OMISSION OF AN ARCHITECTURAL FRAMEWORK

One of the most important factors in a successful DW initiative is the development and maintenance of a comprehensive architectural framework. Such a framework serves as the blueprint for construction and use of the various DW components. Issues such as the expected number of end users, the volume and diversity of data, and the expected data-refresh cycle, among many others, must be considered (and reflected) in the DW architecture.

SIN 3: UNDERESTIMATING THE IMPORTANCE OF DOCUMENTING ASSUMPTIONS

The assumptions and potential data conflicts associated with the DW must be included in the architectural framework for the project. They must be ascertained and codified within the document as early in the project as possible to ensure their reflection in the final product. Several questions must be answered during the requirements phase of the project to reveal important underlying assumptions about the DW. How much data should be loaded into the warehouse? What is the expected level of data granularity? How often do we need to refresh the data? On

---

TABLE 2-5 The Seven Deadly Sins of Data Warehouse Implementation

1. "If you build it, they will come"
2. Omission of an architectural framework
3. Underestimating the importance of documenting assumptions
4. Failure to use the right tool for the job
5. Life cycle abuse
6. Ignorance concerning the resolution of data conflicts
7. Failure to learn from mistakes

what platform will the DW be developed and implemented? Accurate answers are essential to the success of a DW project.

SIN 4: FAILURE TO USE THE RIGHT TOOL FOR THE JOB

The design and construction of a DW is, in many ways, much different from the construction of an operational application system. A DW project requires a different set of tools than those typically used in an application development effort.

DW tools can be categorized into four discrete groupings: (1) analysis tools, (2) development tools, (3) implementation tools, and (4) delivery tools. Within each of these categories are specialized tools designed specifically to accommodate the unique design activities associated with DW development.

Analysis Tools

Analysis tools identify data requirements, the primary sources of data for the DW, and the construction of the data model for the warehouse. Modern CASE tools belong to this category. Another analysis tool is the code scanner. Code scanners scan source code for file or database definitions and data usage identifiers. This information is used to help build the initial data model for the warehouse by determining the data requirements contained within the source ODS.

Development Tools

Development tools are responsible for data cleansing, code generation, data integration, and loading of the data into the final warehouse repository. These tools are also the primary generators of metadata for the warehouse.

Implementation Tools

Implementation tools include the data acquisition tools used to gather, process, clean, replicate, and consolidate the data to be contained within the warehouse. In addition, information storage tools from this category may be used to load summarized data from external data sources.

Delivery Tools

Delivery tools assist in the data conversion, data derivation, and reporting for the final delivery platform. This category includes specific tools for querying and reporting and the generation of and access to data glossaries intended to help end users identify what data are actually contained within the warehouse.

SIN 5: LIFE CYCLE ABUSE

The fifth sin is the failure of the DW developers to realize the differences between the data warehouse life cycle (DWLC) and the traditional system development life cycle (SDLC) methodologies. Although similar, these two approaches differ in one critical aspect: The DWLC never ends. The life cycle of a data warehouse project is an ongoing set of activities that flow from initial investigation of DW requirements through data administration and back again. Typically, as each phase of the DW is completed, a new one is started due to new data requirements, additional user groups, and new sources of data. The DW developers must realize that the project must never end if the warehouse is to remain a viable source of decision-making support.

SIN 6: IGNORANCE CONCERNING THE RESOLUTION OF DATA CONFLICTS

The justification for a new data warehouse initiative is often predicated on the need for greater quality data for decision making within the organization. Although it offers a laudable objective for a DW project, it is simply the tip of the iceberg with regard to actually putting the warehouse into operation. People and organizations tend to be highly protective and territorial when it comes to their data and associated applications. As a result, a great deal of often tedious analysis must be conducted to determine the best data sources available within the organization. Once these systems are identified, the conflicts associated with disparate naming conventions, file formats and sizes, and value ranges must be resolved. This process may involve working with the data owners to establish an understanding with regard to future planned or unplanned changes to the source data. Failure to allow sufficient time and resources to resolve data conflicts can stall a warehouse initiative and result in an organizational stalemate that can threaten the success of the project.

SIN 7: FAILURE TO LEARN FROM MISTAKES

The ongoing nature of the DWLC suggests that one data warehouse project simply begets another. Because of this tendency, careful documentation of the mistakes made in the first round will directly affect the quality assurance activities of all future projects. By learning from the mistakes of the past, a strong data warehouse with lasting benefits can be built.

2.6: DATA WAREHOUSE TECHNOLOGIES

The real dream of anyone who suffered through the pre-development-tool days of data warehousing is that someday we will be able to place an order with Wile E. Coyote's favorite supplier, Acme. Seconds later, we will receive a big wooden crate with "Acme Data Warehouse" stenciled on the side with everything we need inside, including batteries.

That day may actually come, but current data warehouse products are still quite a ways from the "Acme" ideal. Today, organizations buy bits and pieces of complex hardware and software from a number of vendors. A typical sales pitch by a DW vendor might include, "A data warehouse is an architecture, not a product," or "It's a process, not a place," or even something such as, "It's 90 percent expertise, 10 percent technology." The translation for all this rhetoric is simple: Good luck making all this stuff work together!

To build a data warehouse that works, developers must be even more resourceful than a cartoon coyote when it comes to architecture, process, expertise, and dozens of other abstractions. However, resourcefulness, in itself, may still not be enough to guarantee a successful DW environment. The DW investment requires a thorough evaluation process that probes the promises and pitfalls of integrating data warehouse tools offered by the leading DW vendors.

No one currently offers an end-to-end data warehouse solution, but several companies such as SAS, IBM, Software AG, Information Builders, and Platinum are moving toward that goal, albeit slowly. For instance, the following is an example of the type of challenges facing one of the current key data warehouse vendors: IBM.

IBM's premier offering, Visual Warehouse, offers good integration if you run under OS/2; however, it is much less flexible under other leading operating system platforms such as

Windows NT and Novell. In addition, Visual Warehouse is, as yet, unable to manage databases beyond the LAN environment. Larger, more robust databases built around DB/2 Parallel Edition, DB2 MVS, and the new AS/400 parallel database (all IBM offerings) have yet to be accommodated by IBM's leading DW product. Although the company claims it is vigorously working on the problems, it is unwilling to offer any specific time horizons. In other words, even the vendors struggle to make it all work together in harmony.

The good news is that the marketplace is bursting with vendor offerings in the data warehouse arena and, given the plenitude of choices, an organization is likely to find the technology it needs to embark on a DW initiative. The bad news is that the constant state of flux and the high cost of operations make it difficult for the smaller players to stay afloat in this fiercely competitive marketplace, and, as such, the leader board changes daily. Table 2-6 contains a fairly comprehensive listing of the current data warehouse offerings (as of this writing).

2.7: CHAPTER SUMMARY

Due to the overwhelming concentration on process automation by business and industry, organizations, no matter how large or small, create enormous amounts of data every day. The biggest problem with this data explosion is the difficulty in integrating data generated in a world of unintegrated information systems. With data warehousing comes the ability to ask questions of the data that were previously unaskable and to discover new relationships contained within the data that were previously undiscoverable. The concept reintegrates the data generated by the wide variety of internal and external information systems. In the next chapter, we will build upon our understanding of data warehousing by focusing our attention on methods intended to "mine" the hidden resources contained within the data.

Key Concepts

- The data warehouse is "a collection of integrated, subject-oriented databases designed to support the DSS function (decision support), where each unit of data is nonvolatile and relevant to some moment in time" (Inmon 1992a, 5).
- The operational data store's function is to store the data for a single, specific set of operational applications.
- The data mart is often viewed as a way to gain entry to the realm of data warehouses and to make all the mistakes on a smaller scale.
- The following are characteristics of a data warehouse:

  Subject orientation

  Integrated

  Nonvolatile

  Time variant

  Summarized

  Large volume

  Not normalized

  Metadata

  Data sources

TABLE 2-6 Leading Data Warehouse Vendors and Products

DW Vendor	*Product Offering(s)*
Actuate Software	Report Server, Reporting System, Web Agent
Andyne Computing	GQL, PaBLO, Text Tool
Angoss Software	KnowledgeSEEKER
Aonix	Nomad
Applix	TM1 Server, TM1 Client, TM1 Perspective, TM1 Show Business
AppSource	Wired for OLAP
Arbor Software	Essbase, Essbase Web Gateway
Attar Software	XpertRule Profiler
Belmont Research	CrossGraphs
Brio Technology	BrioQuery Enterprise, brio.web.warehouse
Business Objects	BusinessObjects, BusinessMiner
Carleton	Passport
Cognos	Impromptu, PowerPlay, Scenario
Computer Associates	CA-LDM, CA-OpenIngres, Visual Express
Concentric Data Systems	Arpeggio
CorVu	Integrated Business Intelligence Suite (IBIS)
Data Distilleries B.V.	Data Surveyor
Data Junction	Data Junction, Cambio
Data Management Technologies	Time Machine, RQA-Remote Query Accelerator
DataMind	DataMind
Digital Equipment	Alpha Warehouse
Dimensional Insight	Cross Target
Enterprise Solutions	InfoCat
European Management Systems	Eureka
Evolutionary Technologies International	ETI-Extract
Harbor Software	Harbor Light
Hewlett-Packard	Intelligent Warehouse
Holistic Systems	HOLOS
Hyperion	OLAP, Spider-Man
IBM	Data Propagator, DB2 Database Server, Enterprise Copy Manager, Data Hub for OS/2, Data Hub for Unix, Flow-Mark, DataGuide, Application System, Visualizer family, Intelligent Decision Server, Query Management Facility, Intelligent Miner
Informatica	PowerMart
Information Advantage	DecisionSuite, WebOLAP
Information Builders	EDA/Copy Manager, Focus Fusion, Focus Six EIS Edition
Information Discovery	Data Mining Suite
Informix Software	OnLine Dynamic Server-Unix, OnLine Dynamic Server-Windows NT, New Era ViewPoint OnLine Extended Parallel Server, MetaCube, MetaCube Warehouse Manager

TABLE 2-6 Continued	
DW Vendor	*Product Offering(s)*
InfoSAGE	DECISIVE
Innovative Group	Innovative-Warehouse
Integral Solutions Limited	Clementine
Intersolv	DataDirect Explorer, SmartData
Intrepid Systems	DecisionMaster
IQ Software	IQ/SmartServer, IQ/Objects, Intelligent Query, IQ/Vision
Kenan Systems	Acumate ES
Liant Software	Relativity
Lingo Computer Design	Fiscal Executive Dashboard
Logic Works	Universal Directory
MathSoft	Axum
Mayflower Software	Sentinel, Information Catalog
Mercantile Software Systems	IRE Marketing Warehouse
Microsoft	Microsoft SQL Server
NCR	Teradata
NewGeneration Software	NGS Managed Query Environment
Oberon Software	Prospero
Oracle	Oracle8, Discoverer/2000, Oracle Express Server
Pilot Software	Decision Support Suite, Command Center
Pine Cone Systems	Data Content Tracker
Platinum Technology	InfoRefiner, Info Transport, Fast Load, Data Shopper, InfoReports, Object Administrator, Query Analyzer, Report Facility (PRF), InfoBeacon, Forest & Trees
Postalsoft	Postalsoft Library products
Powersoft	InfoMaker
Praxis International	OmniLoader
Precise Software Solutions	Inspect/SQL
Prism Solutions	Prism Warehouse Manager, Prism Change Manager, Prism Directory Manager
Progress Software	EnQuiry
QDB Solutions	QDB/Analyze
Red Brick Systems	Red Brick Warehouse, 5.0, Red Brick Data Mine Option, Red Brick Data Mine Builder, Red Brick Enterprise Control & Coordination
Reduct Systems	DataLogic/R
ReGenisys	extract:R
Sagent	Sagent Data mart
SAS Institute	SAS Data Warehouse, Warehouse Administrator, SAS System, SAS/MDDB
Seagate Software IMG	Crystal Reports, Crystal Info
SelectStar	StarTrieve
ShowCase	STRATEGY

(*continued*)

TABLE 2-6 Continued	
DW Vendor	***Product Offering(s)***
Siemens-Pyramid	Smart Warehouse
Silicon Graphics	MineSet
Smart Corporation	Smart DB Workbench
Software AG	Intelligon, Passport, SourcePoint, Esperant, ADABAS
Softworks	metaVISION
Spalding Software	DataImport
Speedware	Esperant, EasyReporter, Media
SPSS	SPSS
Sterling Software	Vision:Journey
Sybase	Sybase SQL Server 11, Sybase IQ, Sybase MPP
Syware	DataSync
Tandem	Tandem NonStop
Thinking Machines	Darwin
Torrent Systems	Orchestrate
Trillium Software	Trillium Software System
Visual Numerics	PV-Wave
Vmark Software	uniVerse, DataStage
Wincite Systems	WINCITE
WizSoft	WizWhy

- The data warehouse world is primarily void of process design (at least in its classical form) and tends to focus exclusively on issues of data modeling and database design.
- Only two data operations are ever performed in the data warehouse: data loading and data access.
- A data warehouse architecture is a method by which the overall structure of data, communication, processing, and presentation that exists for end-user computing can be represented.
- There are three data warehousing typologies.

  Virtual (point-to-point) data warehouse

  Central data warehouse

  Distributed data warehouse

- Metadata are simply abstractions from data. They are high-level data that provide us with a concise description of lower-level data (data about data).
- The "seven deadly sins" of data warehouse implementation are:

  Sin 1: "If you build it, they will come"

  Sin 2: Omission of an architectural framework

  Sin 3: Underestimating the importance of documenting assumptions

  Sin 4: Failure to use the right tool for the job

  Sin 5: Life cycle abuse

  Sin 6: Ignorance concerning the resolution of data conflicts

  Sin 7: Failure to learn from mistakes

Questions for Review

1. Define each of the following terms:
   - Data store
   - Data mart
   - Metadata
   - Subject orientation
   - Data integrated
   - Time variant
   - Nonvolatile
   - Chain of abstraction
   - Transformation mapping
2. What unique benefits does a data warehouse provide for management at all levels of the firm?
3. What is a data warehouse? How is it better than traditional information-gathering techniques?
4. Describe the data warehouse environment.
5. What are the characteristics of a data warehouse?
6. List and explain the different layers in the data warehouse architecture.
7. What are metadata? Why are metadata so important to a data warehouse?
8. What are the "seven deadly sins" of building a data warehouse?

For Further Discussion

1. The World Wide Web contains a vast amount of information about data warehousing and is, in fact, a data warehouse itself. Viewing the Web from the perspective of a data warehouse, describe and identify the various warehouse components and consider how an organization might harness the power of the Web as a useful data warehouse.
2. Proponents of data warehousing state that the concept is highly generalizable and can be used by any industry or knowledge domain. Think of several industries in which data warehousing could be useful in improving the management of information. Can you think of any industries where data warehousing would not be applicable?
3. Find an organization in your area that uses data warehousing. If possible, talk with the warehouse administrator about the trials and tribulations faced during the design and implementation of the warehouse. How did the administrator deal with the problems? What problems still exist today?
4. Metadata are everywhere. Find a database of information around your school, work, or home and identify as many pieces of metadata as you can.

References

APT Data Group. (November 1996). *Briefing Paper: What is Metadata?* Retrieved October 1997, from www.computerwire.com/bulletinsuk/212e_1a6.htm.

Bischoff, J., and T. Alexander. (1997). *Data Warehouse: Practical Advice from the Experts.* Upper Saddle River, NJ: Prentice Hall.

Inmon, W. H. (1992a). *Building the Data Warehouse.* New York: Wiley.

———. (1992b). "EIS and the Data Warehouse." *Database Programming and Design.*

Kelly, S. (1994). *Data Warehousing: The Route to Mass Customization.* New York: Wiley.

Kozar, D. (1997). The Seven Deadly Sins. In J. Bischoff and T. Alexander (Eds.), *Data Warehouse: Practical Advice from the Experts.* Upper Saddle River, NJ: Prentice Hall.

3

DATA MINING AND DATA VISUALIZATION

Learning Objectives

◆ Understand the concept of data mining (DM).

◆ Trace the evolution of decision support activities from verification to discovery.

◆ Understand the concept of online analytical processing (OLAP) and its rules.

◆ Learn the two approaches used to conduct multidimensional analysis of data—multidimensional OLAP (MOLAP) and relational OLAP (ROLAP)—and explore the different situations suited for MOLAP and ROLAP architectures.

◆ Recognize the four major categories of processing algorithms and rule approaches used to mine data: classification, association, sequence, and cluster.

◆ Assess current data mining technologies, including statistical analysis, neural networks, genetic algorithms, fuzzy logic, and decision trees.

◆ Learn the general process of knowledge discovery through examples.

◆ Examine market basket analysis procedures.

◆ Understand the current limitations and challenges to data mining.

◆ Survey the history of data visualization and how it can help with decision-making activities.

◆ Consider the typical applications of data visualization techniques.

◆ Review several current "siftware" technologies.

THE NATIONAL BASKETBALL ASSOCIATION GETS A "JUMP" ON DATA MINING

Anyone who follows professional basketball knows that the Dallas Mavericks are green, and not just because of the color of their uniforms. Like many National Basketball Association (NBA) franchises, the Mavericks are experiencing the growing pains associated with developing young players and building a winning professional basketball program. The Mavericks will probably not earn an NBA championship anytime soon. Assistant coach Bob Salmi knows this.

Salmi also knows that by the time Michael Jordan retires again, first from the Chicago Bulls and the next time from the Washington Wizards, at least 10 NBA teams will have assembled lineups of talent comparable to each other—including, he hopes, the Mavericks. Given this relatively level playing field, how can a coach create a competitive advantage for his team?

One way to create a competitive advantage is through information—specifically, the information gleaned through Advanced Scout, a data mining application for postgame analysis created by IBM for the NBA to showcase the use of the technology in professional sports.

Salmi uses Advanced Scout to mine for patterns in coaching data, such as winning player combinations. Advanced Scout is synchronized with digital video that is time-stamped by a uniform time clock that tabulates all the statistics—such as rebounding, matchups, and scoring—for all NBA games. Once a seemingly successful pattern is discovered, a coach can cue up the digital video to view additional factors that contributed to those combinations: what plays were run, how they were executed and defended, what other players were involved, and so on.

The data mining approach to postgame analysis is much less time-consuming than the old manual method of jotting down stats with pencil and paper and forever rewinding the videotape. That process greatly relied on guesswork and a coach's intuition, and often took all night. In contrast, Advanced Scout allows for analysis to be per-

formed in the few hours it takes to fly to the location of the next game.

Advanced Scout is based on a data mining technique written in C++ called attribute focusing, which looks for "interesting" patterns and statistical correlations. The key characteristic of the attribute focusing technique is that it is designed for use by lay people, or "domain experts," rather than professional data analysts. The attribute focusing technique's emphasis on the nontechnical user differentiates it from other methods, such as neural networks, decision trees, and regression analysis, that are typically used in data mining applications such as category management, market basket analysis, and sequence analysis. The complexity of most software tools for these applications makes them better suited for analysts.

Currently, the NBA is mining data on a per-season basis, but now that coaches have two seasons' worth of experience under their belt, they are ready to expand to historical statistical data, going back a number of years with Advanced Scout. Coaches can use the results not only for postgame analysis, but also in contract negotiations with players.

The benefits of Advanced Scout were clearly demonstrated during the 1997 NBA playoff series between the Orlando Magic and the Miami Heat. Like Bob Salmi, Orlando Magic assistant coach Tom Sterner has worked with Advanced Scout since its beginnings. The Heat eventually won the best-of-five series in a hotly contested fifth game. Without Advanced Scout's data mining, it would likely have ended in a three-game Heat blowout.

"We were beaten so badly in games 1 and 2 at Miami—99-64 in game 1 and 104-87 in game 2," Sterner recalls. "After game 2, we ran our analysis and watched the tape to determine what happened. Advanced Scout gave us some interesting pieces of data."

First, Advanced Scout revealed that the starting backcourt combination of Orlando Magic players Anfernee "Penny" Hardaway and Brian Shaw

(continued)

DATA MINING MINICASE

(continued)

was 217 in game 2. (Basketball coaches use a plus/minus system based on how many points are scored by or against a team while players are on the court as one indicator of the relative performance of a player or combinations of players.) It also revealed that in the same game, the combination of Shaw and point guard Darrell Armstrong—a backup player who usually saw little game time—was 16. Moreover, the combination of Armstrong and Hardaway was 114.

Based on Advanced Scout's analysis, Sterner concluded that the team should use Armstrong more in game 3 at Orlando. The results were stunning. "In game 3, with about 6 or 7 minutes left to go in the half, we were down 20 points again," he says. "We brought Darrell into the game, and by the end of the half we were tied, 42-42. By the end of the game, we had won, 88-75. Penny Hardaway had scored 42 points, and Armstrong scored 21. Most importantly, we avoided elimination."

Another example that illustrates how a pattern is discovered and interpreted comes from an analysis of the data from a game played between the New York Knicks and the Charlotte Hornets. The data revealed that when "Glenn Rice played the shooting guard position, he shot 5/6 (83 percent) on jump shots."

Through data mining, Advanced Scout identified a certain player (Rice), playing a certain position (shooting guard), shooting at a certain rate (83 percent), on a certain type of shot (jump shot). Advanced Scout not only found this pattern, but also pointed out that it was interesting because it differed considerably from the average shooting percentage of 54 percent for the Charlotte Hornets during that game.

Identifying the exact circumstances of an interesting pattern is something that a coach might not ordinarily detect. Advanced Scout was able to convey valuable information about a scenario that worked very well for the Hornets, but one that the Hornets used only a few times in the entire game. For the Hornets, it suggests a strategy that they should use more often. For the Knicks, it suggests that they might consider a different defensive strategy against Glenn Rice.

By using the NBA universal clock, Advanced Scout can automatically bring up the video clips that show each of the jump shots attempted by Glenn Rice at shooting guard, without requiring the coach to comb through hours of video footage. Those clips show Glenn Rice successfully using his strength and quickness against the player guarding him to free himself for a jump shot.

"The coach needs to determine how the information relates to his team—his insight is the art," says Sterner. He continues, "Why is Phil Jackson so successful? Michael Jordan and Scottie Pippen sure helped in Chicago and Shaquille O'Neill and Kobe Bryant contribute significantly to his successes in Los Angeles. But the human element in every team is still important to the success of the team."

Sterner says, "Talent goes a long way to winning. If you have more talent than your opponent, you'll win. When your talent equals theirs, then the competitive edge could be the technology you use to prepare for the game."

Advanced Scout also reinforces the business case for data mining. A more competitive game is money in the bank for professional sports teams. "Our fans' faith in the team was restored, and we played two more home games than anybody expected," Sterner says. "That's worth millions of dollars" in terms of the gate, TV advertising, even concession sales. "It's a snowball of positive effects."

INTRODUCTION
A PICTURE IS WORTH A THOUSAND WORDS

The title of this section is, admittedly, an old cliché. We use it when we need to point out that we can derive more information by looking at something than by reading or talking about it. Symbolically it may be true, but if it were literally true, I could deliver this book to you in approximately 350 pictures, if they were the right pictures.

It seems reasonable to assume that a cliché is not intended to be universally applicable, but rather applicable under a given set of circumstances. At times, we find it more useful to articulate with words concepts that are difficult to express with pictures alone. Other times, we might use words to make an inquiry to discover something new that is best represented by a picture. In still other situations, a picture is the only method by which certain information can be transmitted effectively (or even at all).

In this chapter, we will explore the new realm of data mining and data visualization. With the realization of the data warehouse comes the ability to ask questions of the data that were previously not possible and to discover new relationships contained within that previously undiscoverable data.

3.1: WHAT IS DATA MINING?

By its simplest definition, data mining (DM) is the set of activities used to find new, hidden, or unexpected patterns in data. Using information contained within the DW, DM can often provide answers to questions about an organization that a decision maker had previously not thought to ask:

- Which products should be promoted to a particular customer?
- What is the probability that a certain customer will respond to a planned promotion?
- Which securities will be most profitable to buy or sell during the next trading session?
- What is the likelihood that a certain customer will default or pay back on schedule?
- What is the appropriate medical diagnosis for this patient?

These types of questions can be answered surprisingly easily if the information hidden among the terabytes of data in your databases can be located and utilized.

An increasingly common synonym for DM techniques is knowledge data discovery (KDD). This more descriptive term applies to all activities and processes associated with discovering useful knowledge from aggregate data. Using a combination of techniques, including statistical analysis, neural and fuzzy logic, multidimensional analysis, data visualization, and intelligent agents, KDD can discover highly useful and informative patterns within the data that can be used to develop predictive models of behavior or consequences in a wide variety of knowledge domains.

For example, from using KDD techniques, we know that left-handed women tend to buy right-handed golf gloves. This pattern relates a customer's attributes to product sales. It is also known that AT&T's stock price predictably rises at least 2 percent after every 3-day slump in the Dow Jones Industrial Average. One can think of several uses for this single piece of information.

Another example of KDD at work is the relation of product consumption habits to each other: Men who buy diapers also buy beer; people who buy scuba gear take Australian vacations;

people who purchase skim milk also tend to buy whole wheat bread. Finally, the Minicase at the beginning of this chapter clearly demonstrates how data mining can be used to assist in play selection in the NBA. This small sampling indicates only a few of the pattern types that can be found using KDD techniques. The myriad of potential patterns, however, dictates the need for a wide variety of KDD approaches and technologies to assist in finding them.

One of the most recent applications of DM is in the explosive growth area of customer relationship management (CRM). DM and CRM software enable users to analyze large databases to solve business-decision problems. DM is, in some ways, an extension of statistics, with a few artificial intelligence and machine learning twists thrown in. Like statistics, data mining is not a business solution, it is a technology. CRM, on the other hand, involves turning information in a database into a business decision that drives interactions with customers. For example, consider a catalog retailer that needs to decide who should receive information about a new product. The information incorporated into the DM and CRM process is contained in a historical database of previous interactions with customers and the features associated with the customers, such as age, zip code, and individual responses. The DM software uses this historical information to build a model of customer behavior that could be used to predict which customers would be likely to respond to the new product. By using this information, a marketing manager can select only the customers who are most likely to respond. CRM software can then feed the results of the decision to the appropriate touchpoint systems (call centers, Web servers, e-mail systems, etc.) so that the right customers receive the right offers.

Even more recent is the application of data mining techniques to data collected from visitors to an e-commerce Web site. Companies venturing into e-commerce have a dream. By analyzing the tracks people make through their Web site, they can better optimize the design of their sites to maximize sales. Information about customers and their purchasing habits enables companies to initiate e-mail campaigns and other activities that result in sales. Good models of customers' preferences, needs, desires, and behaviors help companies simulate the personal relationship that businesses and their clientele had in the good old days.

The foundation of this dream is the log of customer accesses maintained by Web servers. A sequence of page hits might look something like this:

Page A => Page B => Page C => Page D => Page C => Page B => Page F => Page G

Or more explicitly:

Login => Register => Product Description => Purchase.

By analyzing customer paths through the data, vendors hope to personalize their interactions with customers and prospects. Companies will customize the homepage each customer sees, the responses to customer requests, and the recommendations of items to purchase. Vendors can also generate a list of related products. If you are a current customer of Amazon. com, you may already have noticed such personalization.

The business benefits of this customer intelligence are potentially enormous. For those sites providing such personalization, the number of people who come to a site and purchase will increase, and the average amount per purchase will rise, resulting in a dramatic increase in profitability—or at least that is what the dream says.

The reality is that achieving this goal of personalization and increased profits is difficult and expensive; however, it is possible. First, to be of any use at all, clickstream data, the data collected by monitoring the various "click" patterns of a typical user when navigating through the

Web, require enormous amounts of labor-intensive preprocessing. Even then, extracting meaning is still difficult. Second, many customers are reluctant to have vendors track what they do online. Their concern is so great that the government is actively considering privacy regulations to limit Web tracking. Nonetheless, DM is emerging as a major force in deep data analysis. Let's look at why DM is becoming so important.

VERIFICATION VERSUS DISCOVERY

In the past, decision support activities were based on the concept of verification. In this sense, a relational database could be queried to provide dynamic answers to well-formed questions. The key issue in verification is that it requires a great deal of a priori knowledge on the part of the decision maker in order to verify a suspected relationship through the query. One industry making extensive use of verification querying is the gaming, or casino, industry. The host of a casino can use a database of customer characteristics to develop a unique set of customer classifications. The host can then enter a new customer's observable or known characteristics into a query to assist in classifying the customer as a high roller, a souvenir buyer, a ticket purchaser, or any number of other categories related to casino services. Although this approach requires the casino host to manage a large volume of known relationships contained within the database, the ability to categorize a new customer has proven highly profitable.

As casinos embrace more sophisticated computer technologies, the concept of verification continues to evolve into one of discovery. By using siftware, software specifically designed to find new and previously unclassified patterns in data, the casino host can discover new patterns and classifications of customer spending habits that allow for the effective targeting of casino services and events to a specific group of customers.

It is easy to see the vast potential for decision support activities in virtually any domain using KDD. As with any technology, to use KDD effectively, we must first understand the foundations upon which it is based. Therefore, our exploration of the new world of DM must begin at the beginning: the conception of online analytical processing.

DM'S GROWTH IN POPULARITY

Several reasons can be cited in support of the growing popularity of DM. Probably the single greatest reason is the ever-increasing volume of data that require processing. The amount of data accumulated each day by businesses and organizations varies according to function and objective. A report from the GTE Research Center (2000) suggests that scientific and academic organizations store approximately 1 terabyte of new data each day, even though the academic community is not the leading supplier of new data worldwide.

Another reason for the growing popularity of DM is an increasing awareness of the inadequacy of the human brain to process data, particularly in situations involving multifactorial dependencies or correlations. Our biases formed by previous experience in data analysis often hold us hostage. As such, our objectivity in data analysis scenarios is often suspect.

Finally, a third reason for the growing popularity of DM is the increasing affordability of machine learning. An automated DM system can operate at a much lower cost than an army of highly trained (and paid) professional statisticians. Although DM has not entirely eliminated human participation in problem solving, it significantly simplifies the tasks and allows humans to better manage the process.

MAKING ACCURATE INDIVIDUAL PREDICTIONS WITH DM

Although quite valuable in the appropriate contexts, DM is developing into somewhat of an urban legend with regard to its abilities. Scanning data mining articles and texts reveals statements such as, "Data mining will allow us to predict who is likely to buy a particular product" or "We will be able to predict who is likely to cancel their service with us in the next 12 months." This scenario is exciting to consider, but it also tends to defy logic and human nature. Most people do not know what they are likely to do in the coming months or in the next year. It seems unlikely that a software application will be able to determine these actions with near-magical ability.

The real truth of the story is that, in a situation where DM is used to predict response to a direct marketing campaign, 95 percent of the people picked by the data mining application to be likely respondents will probably not respond. In other words, at the individual level of prediction, DM prediction will almost always be wrong! This result hardly qualifies it as a crystal ball.

It would seem, then, that DM is not especially valuable. However, quite the opposite is true. The reason that DM is so valuable in the direct marketing scenario, despite appearing to be so inaccurate, lies with an understanding of the correct level of analysis. At the individual prediction level, DM is not very good. However, despite the fact that only 5 percent of the people predicted to respond actually did so, this response rate is probably two to five times greater than if no data mining model were used. When dealing with direct marketing campaigns in which the normal expected response rate is 1 percent to 2 percent and the mailing list is 500,000 people, an increase of response rate to 5 percent just provided an additional 15,000 to 20,000 new customers. If each of those customers represents $10 in profits, the company just gained $150,000 to $200,000 at the bottom line. When we look at it from the group perspective, DM begins to look pretty good.

3.2: ONLINE ANALYTICAL PROCESSING

In 1993, E. F. Codd, the acknowledged founder of relational databases, introduced the term *online analytical processing* (OLAP). Codd suggested that the conventional relational database used for transaction processing had reached its maximum capability with regard to the dimensionality of the views of the data available to the user. He concluded that operational data and operational databases were simply not adequate for answering the types of questions typically posed by managers (a view held by members of the DSS and EIS communities for many years prior to Dr. Codd's revelation). From this conclusion, Codd developed a set of 12 rules for the development and use of multidimensional databases to assist decision makers within an organization in freely manipulating their enterprise data models across many simultaneous dimensions. Table 3-1 summarizes Codd's 12 rules for OLAP.

To date, it does not appear that any implementations exist where all the rules are strictly obeyed. In fact, some argue that it may not even be possible to implement all 12 rules simultaneously (Gray 1997). More recently, the term *OLAP* has come to represent the broad category of software technology that enables decision makers to conduct a multidimensional analysis of consolidated enterprise data. Along with the OLAP process, two new terms represent the specific approach used to conduct the analysis: (1) *multidimensional online analytical processing* (MOLAP) and (2) *relational online analytical processing* (ROLAP).

TABLE 3-1   Codd's 12 Rules for OLAP

1. Multidimensional view
2. Transparent to the user
3. Accessible
4. Consistent reporting
5. Client-server architecture
6. Generic dimensionality
7. Dynamic sparse matrix handling
8. Multiuser support
9. Cross-dimensional operations
10. Intuitive data manipulation
11. Flexible reporting
12. Unlimited levels of dimension and aggregation

MOLAP

Analyzing data across multiple dimensions is much easier to visualize than to describe. Figure 3-1 shows how sales data might be analyzed across the dimensions of time, product, and market region.

As the figure shows, data can be viewed as though they are stored in a three-dimensional array, or cube, with each side of the cube representing a single dimension. The intersecting cells of the three dimensions contain the actual data of interest, and each of the dimensions can contain one or more members. For example, the market region dimension might have north, south, east, west, and central as its members, and the product dimension would contain members representing each of the products being sold. The members of the time dimension could be months, quarters, years, or specific fiscal periods that represent particular sales cycles.

FIGURE 3-1   Multidimensional Analysis of Data

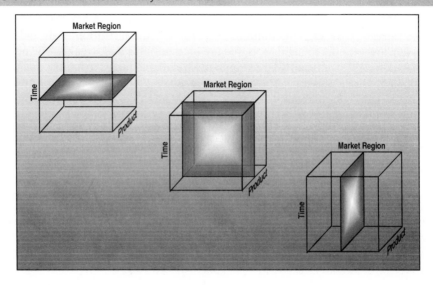

Although three dimensions of analysis may be useful in a limited setting, most multi-dimensional analysis is conducted using many more than three dimensions. In fact, MOLAP organizes and analyzes data as an *n*-dimensional cube.[1] The MOLAP cube can be thought of as a common spreadsheet with two extensions: support for multiple dimensions and support for multiple concurrent users.

In a hypercube, the data are stored as a multidimensional array where each cell in the array represents the intersection of all of the dimensions. Using this approach, any number of dimensions may be analyzed simultaneously, and any number of multidimensional views of the data can be created. In such a design, however, many cells in the hypercube may not have a value. For example, if the hypercube is analyzing a sales system across product, region, time, sales volume, and ratio of actual versus budgeted sales, it is conceivable that not all products will have been sold in all stores or regions during any given time period. In general, as the number of dimensions of the hypercube increases, so does the number of potentially empty cells. This phenomenon, called *sparcity,* can significantly increase the storage requirements of a MOLAP hypercube by requiring that storage space be allocated to all cells rather than only to those containing a value. New products are emerging, however, that incorporate special physical storage techniques such as data compression and complex indexing mechanisms that can reduce the negative impact of sparcity and thus ensure the fast access to hypercube cells.

One of the current limits to MOLAP is its scalability. Although it is good at handling summary data, MOLAP is not particularly well suited to handling large numbers of detailed data. Currently, MOLAP architectures are limited to data warehouses under approximately 50 gigabytes. To accommodate datasets larger than the current limitations and to address issues of scalability, the database world is, once again, embracing the relational model as an alternative approach to MOLAP.

ROLAP

In ROLAP, a large relational database server replaces the multidimensional database server. This "super" relational database contains both detailed and summarized data, thus allowing for "drill down" techniques to be applied to the datasets. In those cases in which a specific needed summarization is not contained within the database, the ROLAP client tool can build it dynamically. The ROLAP approach is a trade-off between flexibility or scalability and performance. On the plus side, ROLAP implementations offer robust administration tools and open SQL interfaces that allow vendors to build tools that are both portable and scalable. The negative side is that ROLAP requires a significantly large number of relational tables to handle the massive volume of data and dimensional relations. The extreme processor overhead needed for table joins and index processing results in significantly degraded performance over MOLAP implementations.[2]

One method being employed to reduce the processing overhead associated with ROLAP is the denormalization of the tables into a star schema. Figure 3-2 illustrates this approach to data organization.

---

[1]The term *cube* is used to describe the *n*-dimensional space occupied by the data. Once the number of dimensions increases beyond three, however, it is no longer a cube in the geometric sense. A data cube with more than three dimensions is, therefore, referred to as a hypercube.

[2]A *table join* is a basic database operation that links rows, or records, of two or more tables by one or more columns in each table. *Index processing* involves the creation, maintenance, and use of a lookup table that relates the value of a field in an indexed file to its record in that file. This allows for a lookup to be performed on a field value other than the primary key. Both of these operations require significant amounts of processing power, especially for large databases.

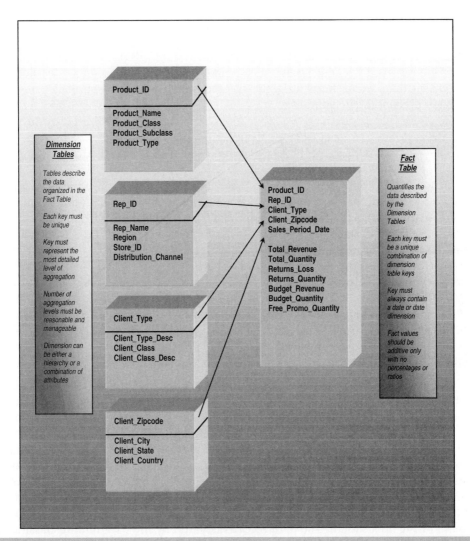

Dimension Tables

Tables describe the data organized in the Fact Table

Each key must be unique

Key must represent the most detailed level of aggregation

Number of aggregation levels must be reasonable and manageable

Dimension can be either a hierarchy or a combination of attributes

Product_ID

Product_Name
Product_Class
Product_Subclass
Product_Type

Rep_ID

Rep_Name
Region
Store_ID
Distribution_Channel

Client_Type

Client_Type_Desc
Client_Class
Client_Class_Desc

Client_Zipcode

Client_City
Client_State
Client_Country

Product_ID
Rep_ID
Client_Type
Client_Zipcode
Sales_Period_Date

Total_Revenue
Total_Quantity
Returns_Loss
Returns_Quantity
Budget_Revenue
Budget_Quantity
Free_Promo_Quantity

Fact Table

Quantifies the data described by the Dimension Tables

Each key must be a unique combination of dimension table keys

Key must always contain a date or date dimension

Fact values should be additive only with no percentages or ratios

FIGURE 3-2 Typical Star Schema Data Organization

Source: From *Managing the Data Warehouse,* by W. H. Inmon, J. D. Welch, and Katherine L. Glassey. Copyright © 1997 by Wiley Publishing, Inc. All rights reserved. Reproduced here by permission of Wiley Publications, Inc.

At the center of a star schema is a central fact table. This table contains numerical measurements that exist at the intersection of all dimensions. If any combination of dimensions does not yield a value, then no zero value is stored. The facts in the central fact table represent quantities of data that can be aggregated without losing their meaning and need to be described by more than two dimensions (Inmon, Welch, and Glassey 1997). The central fact table streamlines the processing associated with access to the facts contained within the fact table.

The dimension tables surround the central fact table. Dimension tables describe or categorize the data contained in the fact table. A concatenated (compound) key in the central fact table is made up of the keys from all of the dimension tables and results in a row in the fact table for every unique combination of the domains of all the keys of all of the dimension tables. This approach enables multidimensional analysis on datasets larger than the current 50-gigabyte limit imposed on MOLAP implementations. ROLAP architectures are especially appropriate when dynamic access to combinations of summarized and detailed data is more important than the performance gains offered by the MOLAP approach using only summarized or preconsolidated data.

3.3: TECHNIQUES USED TO MINE THE DATA

With the popularity of DM growing at a lightning-fast pace, the cadre of new and innovative techniques to mine the warehouse data is exploding as well. Many of the new techniques are refinements of previous methods, although some can truly be classified as major innovations. However, because of a lack of standardization across vendors, innovations in DM are often limited to a particular vendor platform and, thus, cannot be used across the board to advance the state of the art. Rather than concentrate on vendor-specific techniques and mining methods, we will focus on developing an understanding of the basic categories of mining techniques currently in use. Regardless of the specific technique, DM methods may be classified by the function they perform or by their class of application. Using this approach, four major categories of processing algorithms and rule approaches emerge: (1) classification, (2) association, (3) sequence, and (4) cluster.

CLASSIFICATION

The classification approach includes mining processes intended to discover rules that define whether an item or event belongs to a particular subset or class of data. This category of techniques is probably the most broadly applicable to different types of business problems. The technique involves two subprocesses: (1) building a model and (2) predicting classifications.

For example, suppose we want to look for previously undetermined buying patterns in a customer base. A classification model can be constructed that maps the various customer attributes (e.g., age, gender, income, etc.) with various product purchases (e.g., luxury automobiles, concert tickets, clothing, etc.). Given an appropriate set of predicting attributes, the model can be used against a list of customers to determine those most likely to make a particular purchase in the next month. The data records isolated by the data mining classification model could then be used to feed a selection query against a customer database to generate a targeted promotional contact or mailing list.

Other typical classification questions include: "Which households will likely respond to a forthcoming direct mail campaign?" "Which stocks in this portfolio will go up after the next major stock market correction?" and "Which insurance claims currently under process are most likely fraudulent?" By building and refining a predictive model of the business problem, DM classification methods can often provide useful and highly accurate answers to questions.

Generally speaking, classification methods develop a model composed of common IF-THEN rules. As the idea is to gain insight into probable members of a class, the standard approach to determining whether a specific rule is satisfied is relaxed to allow for three possible conditions and, thus, three possible subclasses:

1. **Exact rule.** This rule permits no exceptions; that is, each IF object is an exact element of the THEN class. This approach creates the highest probability class of members—100 percent probability.

2. **Strong rule.** With this rule, some exceptions are allowed but an acceptable range of exceptions is prescribed. This approach creates a subclass of strong probability members—90 to 100 percent probability.
3. **Probabilistic rule.** This rule relates the conditional probability P(THEN|IF) to the probability P(THEN). This approach creates a measured probability subclass of members—*x* percent probability.

ASSOCIATION

Techniques that employ association, or linkage analysis, search all details or transactions from operational systems for patterns with a high probability of repetition. This approach results in the development of an associative algorithm that correlates one set of events or items with another set of events or items. Patterns derived from the algorithm are generally expressed as, for example, "Eighty-three percent of all records that contain items A, B, and C also contain items D and E." The specific percentage supplied by the associative algorithm is referred to as the confidence factor of the rule. Associations can involve any number of items on either side of the rule.

A common example of the use of association methods is *market basket analysis.* Using a linkage approach, a retailer can mine the data generated by a point-of-sale system, such as the price scanner at the grocery store. By analyzing the products contained in a purchaser's basket and then using an associative algorithm to compare hundreds of thousands of baskets, specific product affinities can be derived. Example outcomes of an association method might be "Twenty-nine percent of the time that the brand X blender is sold, the customer also buys a set of kitchen tumblers" or "Sixty-eight percent of the time that a customer buys beverages, the customer also buys pretzels." This type of information can be used to determine the location and content of promotional or end-of-aisle displays (such as a 10-foot-high display of pretzels at the end of the aisle where the beverages are sold). Even though common associations such as yogurt and skim milk or wine and cheese are relatively intuitive, DM using a linkage approach can find less obvious, yet nonetheless useful, associations such as men who buy diapers also buy beer. We will explore market basket analysis in greater detail in the next section.

SEQUENCE

Techniques that use sequencing or time-series analysis relate events in time, such as the prediction of interest rate fluctuations or stock performance, based on a series of preceding events. Through this analysis, various hidden trends, often highly predictive of future events, can be discovered.

Common applications of sequence analysis methods can be found in the direct mail industry. Sequences are often analyzed as they relate to a specific customer or group of customers. Using this information, a catalog containing specific product types can be target mailed to a customer associated with a known sequence of purchases. For example, a known buying sequence might be that parents tend to buy promotional toys associated with a particular movie within 2 weeks after renting the movie. This sequence would suggest that a flyer campaign for promotional toys should be linked to customer lists created as a result of movie rentals. Another sequential pattern might be the determination of a set of purchases that frequently precedes the purchase of a microwave oven. By monitoring buying patterns of customers, particularly using credit card transactions, highly targeted mailing lists can be generated to focus promotions and marketing campaigns on those customers most likely to be persuaded to buy.

One additional technique within this class focuses on the determination of similar sequences. In a typical sequential analysis, the output is a pattern representing a sequence of events over time. In a similar-sequential analysis, however, the goal is to find groups of timed sequences. One of the most common examples of this approach is a large retailer using a similar-sequence approach to find unrelated departments with similar sales streams. This information can be used to determine more profitable promotions, customer flow, or store layouts. Similar-sequence techniques can successfully balance investment portfolios by identifying stocks or securities with similar price movements.

CLUSTER

In some cases, it is difficult or impossible to define the parameters of a class of data to be analyzed. When parameters are elusive, clustering methods can be used to create partitions so that all members of each set are similar according to some metric or set of metrics. A cluster is simply a set of objects grouped together by virtue of their similarity or proximity to each other. For instance, a clustering approach might be used to mine credit card purchase data to discover that meals charged on a business-issued gold card are typically purchased on weekdays and have a mean value of greater than $250, whereas meals purchased using a personal platinum card occur predominately on weekends, have a mean value of $175, and include a bottle of wine more than 65 percent of the time.

Clustering processes can be based on a particular event, such as the cancellation of a credit card by a customer. By analyzing the characteristics of members of this class, clustering might derive certain rules that could assist the credit card issuer in reducing the number of card cancellations in the future.

DM TECHNOLOGIES

By now you should begin to realize the potential power of DM with regard to providing new answers to old questions and to the development of new knowledge and understanding through discovery. Unlimited types of questions can be asked and answered. Numerous techniques are available to assist in mining the data, and there are numerous technologies for building the mining models. Most of these technologies are covered in greater detail in other chapters, but for purposes of continuity, they are briefly mentioned again here.

Statistical Analysis

Statistical analysis, despite requiring specialized capabilities to truly grasp its importance, is the most mature of all DM technologies and is the easiest to understand. If 69 percent of people who purchase product X using a credit card also purchase product Y, and product Y never sells independently, then it is relatively easy to build a model predicting product Y sales with an accuracy of 69 percent. Of greater interest, of course, is to be able to predict the sales of product X.

At this point, traditional statistical analysis methods and DM methods begin to diverge. Traditional statistical modeling techniques such as regression analysis are fine for building linear models that describe predictable data points; however, complex data patterns are often not linear in nature. In addition, traditional statistical methods can frequently be negatively affected or problematic if the data are not well described by a linear model or if the dataset contains a large number of outliers.[3] DM requires the use of statistical techniques—which are

---

[3]An *outlier* is a data point that is unusually distant from the mean of the dataset. In some cases, an outlier may represent simply an extremely low probability point. In other cases, it may be an indicator of a more complex relationship than is currently being modeled or assumed.

beyond the scope of this text—that are capable of accommodating the conditions of nonlinearity, multiple outliers, and nonnumerical data typically found in a DW environment.

Neural Networks, Genetic Algorithms, Fuzzy Logic, and Decision Trees

Discussed in detail in Chapter 4, neural networks attempt to mirror the way the human brain works in recognizing patterns by developing mathematical structures with the ability to learn. By studying combinations of variables and how different combinations affect datasets, it is possible to develop nonlinear predictive models that "learn." Machine learning techniques, such as genetic algorithms and fuzzy logic, can derive meaning from complicated and imprecise data and can extract patterns from and detect trends within the data that are far too complex to be noticed by either humans or more conventional automated analysis techniques. Because of this ability, neural computing and machine learning technologies demonstrate broad applicability to the world of DM and, thus, to a wide variety of complex business problems.

In contrast to the seemingly complex approaches just presented, decision trees offer a conceptually simple mathematical method of following the effect of each event, or decision, on successive events. For example, in a simple decision tree involving the performance of an activity indoors or outdoors, if "indoors" is selected from the initial choice set, then the next decision will more likely be "upstairs/downstairs" rather than "sun/shade." By continually breaking datasets into separate, smaller groups, a predictive model can be built. Decision trees used in DM applications assist in the classification of items or events contained within the DW.

In the appendix to this chapter, a complete outline of an actual decision tree analysis for Saudi Arabian Airlines is discussed. This analysis, using PolyAnalyst's Decision Trees exploration algorithm, determined which attributes influence the percentage of passengers flying in the first-class section. The analysis helped predict the optimal percentage of first-class seats for each flight, thus allowing Saudi Arabian Airlines to maximize revenue and increase customer satisfaction levels.

THE KDD PROCESS

Although no exact rules must be followed for mining a DW and each inquiry must be considered individually, some DM guidelines can be established. Table 3-2 contains the sequence of events in a generic DM "expedition."

One way to better understand the DM process is to actually see it in operation. Although we cannot do that completely within the pages of a book, we can look at examples of some queries that might be constructed during a typical DM session.

For example, a typical model-building SQL statement might take the following form:

CREATE MODEL promo_list
income character input, age integer input ... respond character output

Note the similarity of the CREATE MODEL statement to the standard SQL CREATE TABLE statement. DM software designers intentionally established this format because the newly created model is actually the same as a table or a view available for subsequent SQL processing. The CREATE MODEL statement creates a model that will relate various inputs, such as level of income (high, mid, or low) and age, to a desired output, such as a direct mail response rate (respond 5 yes or no). Bear in mind that this example is purposely simplistic and that the number or type of inputs that could be considered is not subject to any practical limit. A real application would typically include from several dozen to 100 or more such attributes.

TABLE 3-2   General Process of Knowledge Discovery

- *Select a topic for study:* Develop an understanding of the business problem.
- *Identify the target data set(s):* Determine what data are relevant for study.
- *Clean and preprocess the data:* Identify missing data fields, data noise, etc.
- *Build a data model:* Use the mining software to construct a mathematical model "explaining" the varying impacts of the inputs on the outputs.
- *Mine the data:* Search for patterns of interest. (Not all patterns identified by the model will be "interesting".)
- *Interpret and refine:* Review the results of the initial mining and use the results to refine the model, as necessary, to gain additional insight into identified patterns of interest.
- *Predict:* Use the refined model to predict the output for a set of inputs where the output is not yet known.
- *Share the model:* Once validated, make the model available to other warehouse users.

To provide the model with a dataset to process, it is simply a matter of inserting the data into the model using a standard SQL statement such as:

> INSERT INTO mail_list SELECT income, age, respond
>
> FROM client_list,
>
> WHERE mail 5 "Q2_Southeast"

This process automatically creates additional views of the model table that can be used for understanding the relationships and predicting future outcomes (mail_list_UNDERSTAND and mail_list_PREDICT tables). Once the model is built, it represents the best information available to the decision maker about the profile of people who respond to the organization's direct mail campaigns. To view the information generated by the model, an SQL statement is constructed to select from the table:

> SELECT * FROM mail_list_UNDERSTAND
>
> WHERE input_column_name 5 "income" and
>
> input_column_value 5 "high" and
>
> output_column_name 5 "respond"
>
> and output_column_value 5 "yes"
>
> ORDER BY importance, conjunctionid

To generate a mailing list for a new regional promotion in Miami, Florida, an SQL statement could be constructed to access the PREDICT table for only the records from which a positive response is predicted:

> SELECT name FROM client_list, mail_list_PREDICT
>
> WHERE city 5 "Miami" AND respond 5 "yes"

Notice that the model and its associated views, once created, are treated simply as tables in the database. They can be viewed and joined as appropriate to deliver the most benefit from the DM process. Also, the model tables are available to anyone with access to the DW and the ability to generate SQL, not just the person who created them. Other users may choose to use this model as a template with their own modifications. Although the actual process is much more involved than this example, the same basic steps are followed and the same types of SQL statements are constructed.

NEW DM APPLICATIONS

As DM matures, new and increasingly innovative applications for it emerge. Although a wide variety of DM scenarios can be described, two new categories of applications can be identified: text mining and Web mining (see Table 3-3).

Text mining is the process of searching large volumes of documents for certain keywords or key phrases. By searching literally thousands of documents, various relationships between the documents can be established. For example, let's say your company solicits customer feedback regarding the level of service they received during their last transaction. While much of the desired data could be collected using the typical checkbox or scale approach, you may also want to solicit comments related to issues that are not easily covered by the checkbox questions. Searching through these comments by hand would be both tedious and time-consuming. Furthermore, it would be difficult to derive any common patterns from the comments, particularly if they number

TABLE 3-3   Examples of Common Functions Found in a Text Mining Application

Functionality	Description
Distilling the meaning of a text	Formation and export of an accurate semantic network of the text or text base. A semantic network is a set of the most important concepts from the text and the relations between these concepts weighted by their relative importance. This network concisely represents the meaning of a text and serves as a basis for all further analysis.
Accurate summarization of texts	The quality of the summary is provided by a balanced combination of linguistic and neural network investigation methods. The size of the summary is controlled through the semantic weight threshold.
Subject-focused text exploration	User-specified dictionaries of excluded and included words allow the investigation to focus on a chosen subject.
Efficient navigation through a text base	The knowledge base can be navigated with hyperlinks from concepts in the semantic network to sentences in the documents that contain the considered combination of concepts. Individual sentences are in turn hyperlinked to those places in original texts where they have been encountered.
Explication of the text theme structure	A treelike topic structure representing the semantics of the investigated texts is automatically developed. The more important subjects are placed closer to the root of the tree.
Clustering of texts	Breaking links representing weak relations in the original semantic network enables clustering of the text base.
Semantic information retrieval	Natural language queries are analyzed for semantically important words, and all relevant sentences from the text-based documents are retrieved. In addition, a sub-tree of concepts related to the query is formed, which facilitates a simple search refinement.

in the thousands or tens of thousands. Using text mining, however, we can easily derive certain patterns in the comments that may help identify a common set of customer perceptions not captured by the other survey questions.

An extension of text mining is Web mining. Web mining is an exciting new field that integrates data and text mining within a Web site. It enhances the Web site with intelligent behavior, such as suggesting related links or recommending new products to the consumer. Web mining is especially exciting because it enables tasks that were previously difficult to implement, including personalized e-CRM, automated site navigation, and real-time e-business intelligence. Several advantages can be realized through Web mining:

- Unobtrusively learn the interests of Web site visitors based on their interaction with the Web site. User profiles are modified in real time as more information is learned.
- Automatically match the best available resource to the interests of the visitor. This capability allows the site owner to target banner ads, suggest related links, or provide dynamic, personalized content.
- Perform real-time response prediction: "Is this visitor going to make a purchase?"
- Perform real-time prospect valuation: "How much is this visitor going to spend?"
- Predict when a visitor is about to leave a site and provide incentives to stay.
- Identify and act on cross-sell and up-sell opportunities.
- Reveal clickstream patterns: "What paths do most users follow?" and "What paths do the most valuable users follow?"
- Increase overall user satisfaction with the Web site.
- Record all customer interactions through the Web site in the most efficient manner.
- Transform and store data on customers in a format suitable for further analysis.
- Use data for learning customer interests, preferences, and possible courses of action.
- Analyze the efficiency of Web site resources and architecture.
- Generate reports for executive managers.
- Recognize repetitive customers and access their profiles.
- Use all harvested knowledge to personalize communications with each customer.

Web mining applications typically run as a service in conjunction with a server operating system such as Windows 2000 or NT. They can be configured to monitor and gather data from a wide variety of locations and can analyze the data across one or multiple Web sites.

3.4: MARKET BASKET ANALYSIS: THE KING OF DM ALGORITHMS

As you will see from your exploration of the PolyAnalyst software provided to you with this text, 20-plus data mining and visualization algorithms are available, each of which is appropriate in certain analysis scenarios. Although the PolyAnalyst and TextAnalyst tutorials will familiarize you with the available algorithms, it is beyond the scope of this text to provide a detailed look at each one. For that reason, we focus on the most widely used and, in many ways, most successful data mining and visualization algorithm: *market basket analysis.*

Market basket analysis is one of the most common and useful types of data analysis for marketing.[4] It determines what products customers purchase together; it takes its name from

---

[4]The information in this section has been adapted from Ananyan (2001).

the idea of customers throwing all their purchases into a shopping cart (a "market basket") when they are grocery shopping. Knowing what products people purchase as a group can be helpful to a retailer or to any other company. A store could use this information to place products frequently sold together in the same area. Catalog or e-commerce merchants could use it to determine the layout of their Web site, e-catalog, and online order form. Direct marketers often use market basket analysis results to determine what new products to offer to their current customers.

In some cases, the fact that items sell together is obvious—go through the drive-up at any fast-food restaurant and you will probably hear, "Would you like fries with that?" However, sometimes the realization that certain items sell well together is far from obvious. Recall the well-known example from the previous section that diapers and beer sell well together. This relationship has been found to be particularly strong on Thursdays and Fridays. Though the result does make sense—couples stocking up on supplies for themselves and for their children before the weekend starts—it is not the sort of relationship one would normally think of when considering where to place products on the shelf or throughout the retail area. DM tools and market basket analysis eliminate the need for a person to focus on what products consumers would logically buy together. Instead, the customers' sales data speak for themselves. It is a prime example of the current trend toward data-driven marketing.

Once a firm knows that customers who buy one product are likely to buy another, it can market the products together or make the purchasers of one product the target prospects for another. If customers who purchase diapers are already likely to purchase beer, then a beer display just outside the diaper aisle will increase that likelihood. Likewise, if customers who buy a sweater from a certain mail-order catalog show a propensity toward buying a jacket from the same catalog, then sales of jackets can be increased by telephone representatives who describe and offer the jacket to customers who call in to order the sweater. By targeting customers who are already known to be likely buyers, the effectiveness of marketing—whether in the form of in-store displays, catalog layout design, direct offers to customers, or some other practical approach—is significantly increased. Thus, market basket analysis can improve the effectiveness of marketing and sales tactics using customer data already available to, and often already collected by, the company.

THE BENEFITS OF MARKET BASKET ANALYSIS

To a retailer, knowing which products are highly likely to sell together is the marketing equivalent to card counting in blackjack. It provides a distinct advantage in the highly competitive and often opportunistic world of consumer behavior. The most obvious effect is the increase in sales that a retail store can achieve by reorganizing its products so that things that sell together are also found together. This strategy facilitates impulse buying and helps ensure that customers who would buy a product do not forget to buy it simply because they did not see it. In addition, customers will begin to feel comfortable in their assumption that they will find whatever they need at a particular outlet, thus improving customer satisfaction. Every time they are reminded to buy an item because of intelligent placement of that item in the retail area, this customer assumption will be reinforced. Online or catalog merchants get the same benefit from conveniently organizing their catalogs or e-commerce Web sites so that items that sell together are found together. It is commonplace to see suggested products that are associated with the product being purchased displayed on the same screen. This savvy marketing probably can be attributed to market basket analysis.

Outside of the store environment, market basket analysis provides somewhat different benefits, though equally useful ones. For a direct marketer, it is far more preferable to market to existing customers, who are known to buy products and have a history with the company. The company's database already holds a significant amount of information about these people. After running a market basket analysis, a direct marketer can contact its prior customers with information about new products shown to sell well with the products they already bought; chances are, they will be interested. In addition, even when making sales to new customers, telephone representatives can offer buyers of a particular product discounts on any other products they know sell with it, in order to increase the size of the sale.

Finally, market basket analysis even has applications outside the realm of marketing. It can be useful for operations purposes to know which products sell together in order to stock inventory. Running out of one item can affect sales of associated items; perhaps the reorder point of a product should be based on the inventory levels of several products, rather than just one. In addition, market basket analysis can be used wherever several different conditions lead to a particular result. For example, by studying the occurrence of side effects in patients with multiple prescriptions, a hospital could find previously unknown drug interactions about which to warn patients.

Market basket analysis offers several advantages over other types of DM. First, it is undirected. It is not necessary to choose a product that you want to focus on in order to run a basket analysis. Instead, all products are considered, and the DM software reveals which products are most important to the analysis. In addition, the results of market basket analysis are clear, understandable association rules that lend themselves to immediate action, and the individual calculations involved are simple.

ASSOCIATION RULES FOR MARKET BASKET ANALYSIS

Association rules are a common, undirected DM technique that complements market basket analysis. All association rules are unidirectional and take the following form:

Left-hand-side rule IMPLIES Right-hand-side rule

Notice that association rules are unidirectional; they only go in one direction. In a restaurant market basket analysis, we might find that CAVIAR IMPLIES VODKA, but the reverse, VODKA IMPLIES CAVIAR, may not hold. In addition, both the left-hand side and the right-hand side of the rule may contain multiple items or combinations of items such as the following:

Yellow Peppers IMPLIES Red Peppers, Bananas, and Bakery

It should be obvious by now that any given market basket is chock full of potential rules, as any one item in the basket may imply all of the other items in that basket. As discussed earlier, however, DM is not valuable at the individual prediction level of analysis. To draw rules from a single basket would certainly not prove useful in marketing to the wider community. Only when these rules are formed from an analysis of thousands of market baskets can we begin to use them in a predictive sense.

To make effective use of a predictive rule derived from market basket analysis, three distinct measures of that rule must be considered: support (sometimes referred to as prevalence), confidence (also referred to as predictability), and lift.

Support
The *support measure* refers to the percentage of baskets in the analysis where the rule is true, that is, where both the left-hand side and the right-hand side of the association are found.

Confidence

The percentage of baskets from the analysis having the left-hand-side item that also contain the right-hand-side item is found via the *confidence measure*. This measure is different from support in that confidence is the probability that the right-hand-side item is present given that we know the left-hand-side item is in the basket.

Lift

The third measure of associative rule power, *lift,* is probably the closest to being useful on its own. It compares the likelihood of finding the right-hand-side item in any random basket. Lift measures how well the associative rule performs by comparing its performance to the "null" rule (that the left-hand-side item is present without the right-hand-side item). In this sense, lift can also be thought of as *improvement,* because it measures the improvement of the prediction over time. A typical example of an associative rule with its measures would look something like this:

Green Peppers IMPLIES Bananas

Lift = 1.37 Support = 3.77 Confidence = 85.96

An interpretation of this rule suggests that the vast majority of people in this market basket analysis bought bananas, including those who bought green peppers. Although not terribly interesting by itself, what happens when we combine it with two other associative rules generated by the market basket analysis algorithm?

Red Peppers IMPLIES Bananas

Lift = 1.43 Support = 8.58 Confidence = 89.47

Yellow Peppers IMPLIES Bananas

Lift = 1.17 Support = 22.12 Confidence = 73.09

In combination, we begin to see a pattern emerge: Because bananas are universally popular, green peppers sell in about the same quantities as either red or yellow peppers, they just are not as predictive. One reason may be that red and yellow peppers are produce items typically imported to the region under study, whereas green peppers are indigenous to the region. This factor would make red and yellow peppers generally more expensive and could imply a certain snob appeal to red and yellow peppers over the more common green ones. Given this set of rules, the store may want to try repositioning the red and yellow peppers away from the more common green peppers and closer to the other "exotic" imports such as fresh morels or other imported vegetables. Another experiment would be to triple the price of a few green peppers and display them with their higher-priced cousins. It is possible that the combination of all three colors would sell together at a higher price than if they were marketed individually.

Method

In order to perform a market basket analysis, it is necessary to first have a list of transactions and what was purchased in each one. Consider the following simple example of convenience store customers, each of whom bought only a few items.

Transaction 1: Frozen pizza, cola, milk
Transaction 2: Milk, potato chips
Transaction 3: Cola, frozen pizza
Transaction 4: Milk, pretzels
Transaction 5: Cola, pretzels

Each customer purchased a different basket of items, and at first glance, no obvious relationship exists between any of the items purchased and any other item. The first step of a basket analysis, however, is to cross-tabulate the data into a table, enabling the analyst to see how often products occurred together. These five convenience store purchases result in the following table.

	Frozen Pizza	Milk	Cola	Potato Chips	Pretzels
Frozen Pizza	2	1	2	0	0
Milk	1	3	1	1	1
Cola	2	1	3	0	1
Potato Chips	0	1	0	1	0
Pretzels	0	1	1	0	2

By looking at the diagonal data for each item, we can ascertain how often each item was purchased without purchasing any of the other items under study. Though this is significant for figuring some reliability statistics, it does not show how items sell together, and can be ignored for now. Look at the first row: Of the people who bought frozen pizza, one bought milk, two bought cola, and none bought potato chips or pretzels. This finding hints at the fact that frozen pizza and cola may sell well together and should be placed side-by-side in the convenience store. Nowhere else in the table do we find an item that sold together with another item as frequently, which suggests an actual cross-selling opportunity. Compare it to the second row: Of people who bought milk, one bought frozen pizza, one bought cola, one bought potato chips, and one bought pretzels. It appears that milk sells well with everything in the store, which limits good cross-selling opportunities. This finding makes sense for a convenience store, because people often come to a convenience store specifically to buy milk and will buy it regardless of what else they might want.

Results

A real example would usually contain more than five products and thousands of transactions. As a result, the distinction between products that sell well together and products that do not would be much sharper. Also, a market basket analysis of large amounts of data would be performed using DM software, rather than being entered into a table by hand as in our example. You will analyze some large datasets in your exercises with PolyAnalyst.

As shown, the results of a market basket analysis are particularly useful because they take the form of immediately actionable association rules. These rules allow a store to know right away that promotions involving frozen pizza and cola will pay off. Whether it places the cola display right next to the frozen pizza, advertises the two products together, or attaches cola discount coupons to the frozen pizza boxes, the convenience store will probably be able to increase sales of both items through directed marketing. Unlike most promotions, this promotion is almost sure to pay off—the convenience store has the data to back it up before even beginning the campaign.

This example demonstrates the best kind of market basket analysis result—one that is *actionable*. Unfortunately, two other kinds of association rules are sometimes generated by market basket analysis: the *trivial* and the *inexplicable*. A trivial rule is one that would be patently obvious to anyone with some familiarity of the industry at hand. For instance, the discovery that hot dog buns sell well with hot dogs would not surprise the owner of a grocery store, and would in fact not be at all useful for promotion purposes—people will buy hot dog buns with their hot dogs regardless of any marketing campaign encouraging them to do so. Another example of a trivial rule would be the discovery that people who purchase an extended warranty for a television generally purchase a television—the warranty would be pointless without the television. The DM software can only point out which items sell well together; it is up to the users to rely on their own business knowledge to determine which rules are valuable to the business.

Finally, market basket analysis occasionally produces inexplicable rules. These rules are not obvious, and they do not lend themselves to immediate marketing use. An example of this type of rule is one hardware store chain's discovery that toilet rings sell well only when a new hardware store is opened. No obvious reason can be found for this tendency—why do people only need toilet rings when a new store opens? In addition, even though the company could offer a sale on toilet rings during new store openings, it cannot tell whether this promotion will be successful, because it is still rather mysterious why they sell better at new openings in the first place. An inexplicable rule is not necessarily useless, but its business value is not obvious and it does not lend itself to immediate use for cross-selling.

Limitations to Market Basket Analysis

Though a useful and productive type of DM, market basket analysis does have a few limitations. The first involves the kind of data needed to do an effective basket analysis. A large number of real transactions is required to obtain meaningful data, but the accuracy of the data is compromised if all of the products do not occur with similar frequency. Thus, in our convenience store example, if milk is sold in almost every transaction, but glue only sells once or twice per month, putting both of them into the same basket analysis will probably generate results that look impressive without being statistically significant, and acting on these results is not likely to benefit profitability. With only one or two glue customers, the DM software can confidently state what sells well with glue, but the correlation may only be true for the one or two customers analyzed. However, this limitation can be overcome by classifying items into a taxonomy, as described in the next section.

Second, market basket analysis can sometimes present results that are actually due to the success of previous marketing campaigns. If the convenience store consistently places cola discount coupons on the frozen pizza, the fact that cola and frozen pizza sold well together probably does not surprise them. In this sense, it does not provide any new information; it just shows that previously existing marketing campaigns are already working. In fact, the previous campaign may even be overshadowing a real relationship. Perhaps people would normally prefer to buy beer with pizza but buy the cola because of the discount. In this case, the convenience store is missing out on a potentially better promotion.

PERFORMING MARKET BASKET ANALYSIS WITH VIRTUAL ITEMS

Suppose a marketer wants to consider more than just which items sell together in developing its promotions. It may be important to know which items sell better to families with children, to repeat customers, or to new customers. In such cases, the sales data can be augmented with the addition of virtual items. A virtual item is not a real item being sold, but is treated as one by the DM software. Thus, if a new customer calls a catalog retailer and orders a sweater and a jacket, this transaction can be entered into the database as:

Item 1: Sweater

Item 2: Jacket

Item 3: (new customer)

When the DM software is used to determine which items sell well together, it may discover that some items sell particularly well with the (new customer) virtual item. This connection could tell the catalog company which items are so interesting as to lure new customers, as opposed to only selling to longtime catalog buyers. By using virtual items, data about the customers themselves, which store the items sold at, or which sales representative sold the item can be considered in the analysis without changing the method by which it is performed. By adding the store number or sales representative number as a virtual item, patterns can be found that exist only in certain places or are brought out by certain salespeople. As far as the DM software is concerned, (new customer) or any virtual item is a real item like any other.

Virtual items are also useful for testing the effects of promotions. By adding virtual items to represent promotions or discounts, it is possible to see how these affect cross-selling. They can also be used to compare urban and suburban sales, seasonal or time-of-day differences, or gift-wrapped purchases versus those that people bought for themselves.

Measures of Association

Referring back to our table of transactions, we can calculate measures of association for each rule.

	Frozen Pizza	*Milk*	*Cola*	*Potato Chips*	*Pretzels*
Frozen Pizza	2	1	2	0	0
Milk	1	3	1	1	1
Cola	2	1	3	0	1
Potato Chips	0	1	0	1	0
Pretzels	0	1	1	0	2

The support measure for the rule "Cola IMPLIES Frozen Pizza" is 40 percent. Of five total records, two include both cola and frozen pizza. Note that support considers only the combination, and not the direction, as the support for the rule "Frozen Pizza IMPLIES Cola" is also 40 percent. Support can also be used to measure a single item. For example, the support for the item "Milk" is 60 percent, because it occurs in three of the five records. Measuring the support of a single item is where the central diagonal of the table can be useful.

Recall that the confidence of an association rule is the percentage of baskets from the analysis with the left-hand-side item that also contain the right-hand-side item. This percentage can be calculated by dividing the support for the combination by the support for the condition. For example, the rule "Milk IMPLIES Potato Chips" has a confidence of 33 percent. The support for the combination (Potato Chips + Milk) is 20 percent, as it occurs in one of the five transactions. However, the support for the condition (Milk) is 60 percent, as it occurs in three of the five transactions. This gives a confidence of 20 percent / 60 percent = 33 percent.

Note also that confidence is unidirectional—the confidence of the rule "Potato Chips IMPLIES Milk"" is 20 percent / 20 percent = 100 percent. However, this rule is based on only one transaction! Thus, like high support, high confidence alone does not indicate that a rule is necessarily a good one. This example also shows what happens when certain items with extremely low sales are thrown into a basket analysis with high sales. One customer's purchase of two items together can create an extremely high-confidence rule that may not mean much. This problem is overcome by using taxonomies, as described later in this section.

Performing a basket analysis that considers higher numbers of items in groups is done iteratively. First, pairs are found, then sets of three, then four, and so on. The number of calculations required to perform the analysis varies exponentially with the number of products to be considered simultaneously. The number of calculations for *n* items is proportional to the number of items to be considered at a time raised to the *n*th power. As a result, a pruning method has been developed to minimize calculation time by eliminating items as the number of items to be considered simultaneously increases. To perform a multidimensional market basket analysis, a minimum support threshold, say 2 percent, must be set. The DM software first eliminates all items that have less support than this minimum threshold, and then conducts an analysis comparing only pairs of items and generates a set of association rules.

At this point, the second round of pruning occurs. Any two items that, as a pair, have a support less than the minimum threshold are eliminated from consideration as conditions of an association rule. Then, these pairs of items are checked against all the items in the analysis (as results), and another set of association rules is generated.

This process continues, next eliminating all sets of three items that as a group fall below the minimum support threshold. In some environments, such as a convenience store, it is quite possible that customers buy so few items at a time that no rules involving more than two or three items will ever have the minimum support necessary to be considered significant. In contrast, in an environment such as a large grocery store, where customers buy more than 100 items at a time, rules of 10 to 12 items may be significant.

Performing basket analyses considering more than two items at a time results in the development of multidimensional tables that can be difficult to visualize. However, the use of DM software allows meaningful rules to be found in these data despite the difficulties in representing them.

USING THE RESULTS

Store Layout Changes

The results of market basket analysis can indicate how stores can change their layout to improve profitability. If the market basket analysis shows that lightbulbs and gardening tools sell well together in a hardware store, the obvious response is to put the lightbulbs next to the gardening aisle. However, a better response might be to put a shelf of the store brand of lightbulbs, a high-profit item for the store, next to the gardening aisle, leaving the rest of the lightbulbs where they are. By making it most convenient for the customer to buy high-profit items, the store owner can maximize profit. The market basket analysis shows that this tactic will probably work, because customers will already be looking to buy the item.

This same tactic is equally valid for "stores" that take some form other than the supermarket floor—anywhere that a customer browses for items is appropriate for reorganization based on market basket analysis. A catalog or Web page can also be reorganized to direct the attention of customers who are likely to buy a certain product toward high-profit items.

Product Bundling

For companies without a physical storefront, such as mail-order companies, Internet businesses, and catalog merchants, market basket analysis may be more useful for developing promotions than for reorganizing product placement. By offering promotions where buyers of one item get discounts on another they are likely to buy, sales of both items may be increased. In addition,

market basket analysis can help direct marketers reduce their number of mailings or calls. By only calling customers who previously showed a desire for a product, the cost of marketing can be reduced while increasing the response rate.

3.5: CURRENT LIMITATIONS AND CHALLENGES TO DM

It is important to remember that despite the potential power and value of DM to the business world, it is still a new and underdeveloped field. Most current developers of commercial DM products are relatively small and generally license or sell their products to larger, more established software vendors for incorporation into existing software products. Several of the challenges that significantly limit the advancement of DM products are identified in this section.

IDENTIFICATION OF MISSING INFORMATION

Until such time that DM becomes commonplace and legacy application databases are replaced by newer "warehouse friendly" databases, warehouse designers will continue to grapple with the conversion of data from an ODS into a homogenous form for the warehouse. This transformation, albeit quite thorough and technologically sophisticated, cannot yet detect whether the original dataset contains the necessary elements for effective mining. For example, the data contained in an ODS are normally not inclusive of domain knowledge. In other words, not all knowledge about a particular application domain is present in the data. We know from past discussion that the data within an ODS are normally limited to those needed by the operational application associated with that database. Even though application-relevant queries can be successfully made on the data, more generalized queries may not be possible. DM applications need to include mechanisms for "inventorying" the datasets so that attribute sufficiency can be determined prior to loading the data into the DW. For instance, if it is known that decision makers want to diagnose potential cases of malaria from a patient database, it is also known that all patient datasets loaded into the warehouse must include the patient's red blood cell count. Without these data, no diagnosis can be effectively made.

DATA NOISE AND MISSING VALUES

Virtually all operational databases are contaminated to some degree by errors. Data attributes that rely on subjective measurements or judgments can give rise to errors so significant that some examples may even be misclassified. Errors in either the values of the attributes or the classification of data are referred to as data noise. DM applications must address the problem of data noise in order to minimize its debilitating effect on the overall accuracy of rules generated from the data. Currently, DM systems are limited to the treatment of noise via statistical techniques that rely on known distributions of data noise. Future systems must incorporate more sophisticated mechanisms for treating missing or noisy data that include inference of missing values, Bayesian techniques for averaging over the missing values, and other methods of data inference.

LARGE DATABASES AND HIGH DIMENSIONALITY

Operational databases are inherently large and dynamic; their contents are ever changing as data are added, modified, or removed. Rules derived from a dataset at one moment in time may become less accurate as the data change. This need for timeliness of the data creates a parallel

need for increased dimensionality of the data for purposes of discovery. In other words, to ensure that discovered patterns are not "local" to a given time period, data patterns must be constantly updated by an expanding set of time-sensitive data values. This need in turn creates a problem space of significant breadth and depth that requires increasingly greater computing power to search. The spiraling nature of this problem must be addressed by future discovery applications that can portion the problem space into smaller, more manageable chunks without losing any of the intrinsic attributes of the data contained therein.

3.6: DATA VISUALIZATION: "SEEING" THE DATA

Data visualization is the process by which numerical data are converted into meaningful images. The raw data may come from any number of different sources, including satellite photos, undersea sonic measurements, surveys, or computer simulations, to name just a few. Typically, these sources create data that are difficult to interpret because of the overwhelming quantity and complexity of information and the embedded patterns. The human brain is capable of processing a significant amount of visual information, instantly recognizing millions of different physical objects. Data visualization techniques are intended to assist in analyzing complex datasets by mapping physical properties to the data, thus taking advantage of human visual systems. Reflectance and other lighting effects, color, direction and size of shadows, relative sizes of and distances between objects, speed, curvature, and transparency are just a small sample of the characteristics that help visualize data.

For example, Table 3-4 contains an example of some real-life weather balloon data. As you can see, our ability to extract any useful information from looking at the numbers is virtually nonexistent.

Using a data visualization technique that allows for the creation of a three-dimensional model of the sensor data reveals the shape in Figure 3-3. The various shadings contained within the figure indicate relative degrees of thunderstorm activity, with the darkest portions of the figure indicating the most violent storm activity.[5] The ability to create multidimensional structures and models from raw data is one of the most important innovations in decision support technologies. In this section, we continue our discussion (begun in Section 3.2) of multidimensional analysis and examine the visualization of data across n dimensions.

A BIT OF HISTORY

The early concepts of data visualization originated in the statistical and scientific disciplines. Most of the early work involved a series of two-dimensional analyses of multidimensional or multivariate datasets. Such analyses involved the use of static images and graphs that could then be sequenced to effect a quasi-layering of the data across dimensions.

Much of the advancement in data visualization can be credited to the National Center for Supercomputing Applications (NCSA) at the University of Illinois at Champaign-Urbana. One of the first practical applications of multidimensional data analysis was the Los Angeles smog project conducted by NCSA. By creating a computer animation of smog data superimposed

---

[5]Normally, data visualization images are rendered in color so that colors, rather than shades of gray, can be used as data value indicators. As we are limited to a gray scale medium for this text, we will determine data values using relative shades of gray.

TABLE 3-4   Sample Weather Sensor Data

Offset	X	Y	Z	Vector
0.000000	−17.833000	6.661000	0.011000	−0.118000
0.000000	−17.773001	6.683000	0.015000	−0.122000
0.000000	−17.673000	6.718000	0.009000	−0.143000
0.000000	−17.563999	6.757000	0.008000	−0.163000
0.000000	−17.461000	6.802000	0.011000	−0.165000
0.000000	−17.375000	6.865000	0.012000	−0.149000
0.000000	−17.297001	6.940000	0.009000	−0.127000
0.000000	−17.239000	7.016000	0.010000	−0.114000
0.000000	−17.200001	7.091000	0.018000	−0.116000
0.000000	−17.170000	7.167000	0.030000	−0.133000
0.000000	−17.169001	7.256000	0.050000	−0.148000
0.000000	−17.187000	7.345000	0.064000	−0.152000
0.000000	−17.226000	7.429000	0.074000	−0.153000
0.000000	−17.290001	7.509000	0.088000	−0.152000
0.000000	−17.375999	7.583000	0.106000	−0.146000
0.000000	−17.488001	7.645000	0.112000	−0.145000
0.000000	−17.620001	7.692000	0.118000	−0.156000
0.000000	−17.768000	7.724000	0.126000	−0.158000
0.000000	−17.931000	7.737000	0.133000	−0.143000
0.000000	−18.106001	7.736000	0.128000	−0.134000
0.000000	−18.284000	7.719000	0.121000	−0.132000
0.000000	−18.450001	7.688000	0.121000	−0.129000

FIGURE 3-3   Data Visualization of Weather Sensor Data Depicting Storm Cell Activity

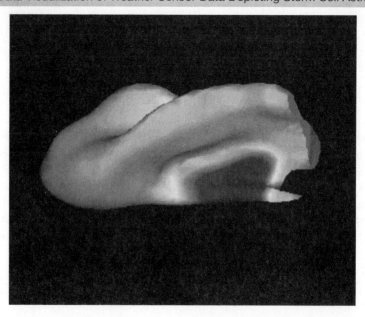

over a three-dimensional map of the Los Angeles basin, NCSA was able to pinpoint locations of major contributors to pollution and to accurately predict smog levels and movement over a wide area of the basin.

Some of the newest developments in data visualization have come from the work conducted at Xerox PARC in the area of virtual reality. Three-dimensional visualization programs allow the user to "fly through" large datasets, view the data from infinite angles, and examine and rearrange virtual object representations of the data interactively. Military and industrial simulations are two examples of the practical application of these innovative data analysis methods. Computers can be used to display realistic visuals of tank combat in urban areas or large tankers docking in busy harbors, thus allowing for learning through experience and avoiding the messy cleanup associated with mistakes made during the early phases of training.

HUMAN VISUAL PERCEPTION AND DATA VISUALIZATION

If you were to go outside right now, your sense of vision would immediately detect a variety of objects—automobiles, buildings, people, trees, dogs—all organized in a neatly coherent and meaningful framework. Your brain would be processing all of these objects by assembling edges, movements, and distances into multidimensional wholes from which you would seamlessly retrieve identities and labels. This apparently effortless processing is both continuous and subconscious.

Data visualization is so powerful not only because the human visual cortex dominates our perception, but because the process of converting objects into information occurs so quickly. Using data visualization, massive amounts of information can be presented, thus accelerating the identification of hidden patterns contained within the data. Stop for a moment and contrast how easily you processed the image presented in Figure 3-3 with how difficult it was to process the rows and columns in Table 3-4, and you will immediately realize the value of data visualization as an analytical tool.

Applying the old adage of a picture being worth a thousand words, we may better come to appreciate the value of data visualization by simply looking at several examples of complex datasets from a variety of knowledge domains represented in visual form.

The graphic in Figure 3-4 represents a model of a dynamic dataset related to the connectivity, relative throughput, and usage of a global private computer network. The lightest shaded lines connecting the nodes indicate the lowest values of throughput, and the darkest shades indicate the highest values. The relative vertical size of each of the ground-based and satellite-based nodes represents the current number of active processes or users accessing that node. Although this figure is a static representation of network activity, these data could be easily converted into a dynamic animation of the network, which would allow analysts to see patterns of usage over time and indications of peak or overload conditions at a given node.

Figure 3-5 is a static screenshot of an interactive visualization of the multiple variables affecting the monitoring of a natural gas pipeline. The underlying map and pipeline network diagram shows each of the compressor stations, with the total flow through each station represented by the height of each station. Although not easily detectable in gray scale, the large station in the foreground indicates an alert condition (shown in bright red in a color rendering), in this case highlighting a station with a particularly high flow volume. Drill down permits the operator to explore the situation—pointing to a station elicits a pop-up text report of all the underlying data, or pop-up charts and graphs, or detailed graphics, such as the state of each turbine within the station, shown as small, light-colored bars on top of the station.

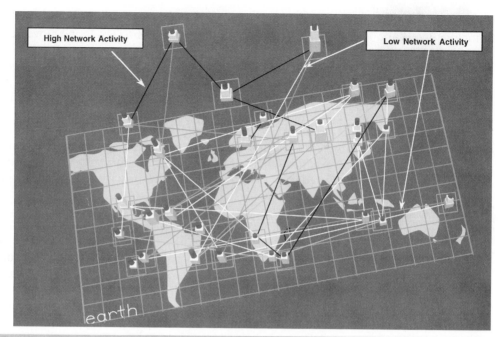

FIGURE 3-4 Data Visualization of Global Private Computer Network Activity

FIGURE 3-5 Natural Gas Pipeline Analysis

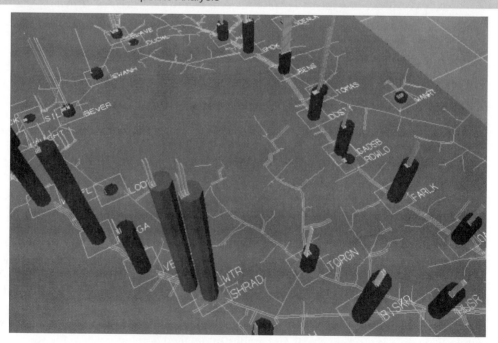

The visualization in Figure 3-6 shows the benefit that three-dimensional representation can have on the most mundane printed reports. Instead of seeing just a yield curve and the overnight impact on the portfolio, the manager is enticed by an interactive yield curve of "what-if" interactions, without having to wait for reports detailing various scenarios.

If you have ever received a telephone survey call around dinnertime or during the most exciting part of a televised sporting event or movie, then you know how annoying it can be. Your opinions are important, and the process of polling is often quite expensive. Frequently, the subject of the poll, although interesting to the pollster, is not something you are particularly interested in, and the pollster must randomly call thousands of homes until enough interested parties express their opinions. Using data visualization, however, a polling application could be developed that would allow people to participate in surveys on only those issues that they feel strongly about. Consider the following scenario: A new poll question is advertised on TV or radio with a 1-800 phone number. Interested voters call the 1-800 number and press 1, 2, or 3 based on whether their vote is yes, no, or other. A database correlates the votes and can even verify through caller identification that no originating phone number votes twice. The data visualization application converts the collected opinion data into a three-dimensional map of the calling area and depicts the frequency of answers as differently shaded vertical bars (such as those shown in Figure 3-7). The user clicks on the area of interest to see the results in that area and can successively click down to poll results by districts.

FIGURE 3-6   Risk Analysis Report

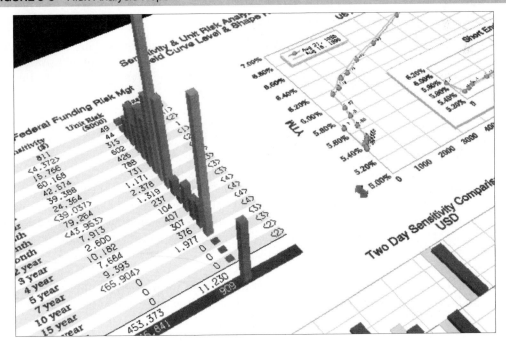

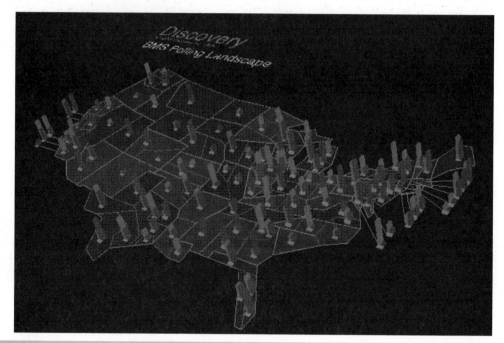

FIGURE 3-7 Interactive Telephone Polling Discovery

GEOGRAPHIC INFORMATION SYSTEMS

A geographic information system (GIS) is a special-purpose digital database in which a common spatial coordinate system is the primary means of reference. Comprehensive GISs require a means of (1) data input from maps, aerial photos, satellites, surveys, and other sources; (2) data storage, retrieval, and query; (3) data transformation, analysis, and modeling, including spatial statistics; and (4) data reporting, such as maps, reports, and plans.

The many definitions offered for GISs emphasize their various aspects. Some definitions miss the true power of the GIS—that is, its ability to integrate information and to help in making decisions—but all include the essential features of spatial reference and data analysis.

For the purposes of this text, we define a GIS as follows: A GIS is a system of hardware, software, and procedures designed to support the capture, management, manipulation, analysis, modeling, and display of spatially referenced data for solving complex planning and management problems. In other words, a GIS is both a database system with specific capabilities for spatially referenced data and a set of operations for working with those data.

Spatial Data

Spatial data are elements that can be stored in map form. These elements correspond to a uniquely defined location on the Earth's surface. Spatial data contain three basic components: points, lines, and polygons.

- *Points* are single locations in two- or three-dimensional space (e.g., the dot representing a city on a map of the United States).

- *Lines* can be isolated, within a tree structure, or elements of a network structure (e.g., river or road systems).
- *Polygons* can be isolated, adjacent, or nested (e.g., state boundaries or contour lines on a map).

Attribute Data

A GIS must also be able to handle attribute data. Simply put, attribute data are the description of the spatial data seen on a map. For example, a map of Pittsburgh, Pennsylvania, will have corresponding "attribute" data that describe it, such as elevation numbers, land use designations, and boundary information. This information is usually kept in tabular form and managed as a normal database. If something on the map changes (e.g., city zoning areas), the attribute data can be modified, and the map will reflect the changes.

The GIS is often referred to as the "spreadsheet of the 1990s." Today, the GIS is changing the way people organize and use information, much in the same way the computer spreadsheet changed data organization and retrieval in the 1980s. The GIS facilitates wise use of limited resources by clarifying characteristics and patterns over space.

Examples of decision-making scenarios in which a GIS may be appropriate include the following:

- Does it make sense to put a megamall in a particular location?
- Where should legislative district boundaries be located?
- Do we expand the existing airport or build a new one in a different location?
- Will the current school facilities be sufficient for the number of students expected 10 years from now?
- Which pockets of endangered environment should be protected?
- What is the impact of waste facilities on local health patterns?
- Where might restocking of native species be environmentally wise?
- Are we adequately prepared to service the local and surrounding population in the event of various possible disasters?

APPLICATIONS OF DATA VISUALIZATION TECHNIQUES

We live in an age of fierce competition and ever-increasing needs for more information. Data visualization is one response to meeting these needs, and it appears that its value can be applied across a wide variety of application domains. Currently, industries ranging from banking, where data visualization is used in credit scoring and risk analysis, to government, where data visualization is used in fraud analysis and drug enforcement, are making effective use of available data visualization techniques and applications. Table 3-5 contains a brief listing of typical data visualization business applications.

3.7: SIFTWARE TECHNOLOGIES

Although the market is in a constant state of flux with the entry and exit of data visualization product vendors on a daily basis, a number of vendors are establishing a stronghold in the marketplace as they develop significant brand loyalty among their customers. This next section briefly outlines the characteristics of several of the more prominent players in the data visualization field.

TABLE 3-5 Typical Applications of Data Visualization Techniques

Retail Banking
- Customer/product cross-selling analysis
- Electronic banking management
- Credit risk
- Product pricing strategy

Government
- Budget analysis
- Resource management
- Economic analysis
- Fraud detection and drug trafficking analysis

Insurance
- Asset/liability management
- Actuarial modeling
- Workflow management and analysis

Health Care and Medicine
- Claims analysis
- Patient behavior analysis
- Therapy analysis

Telecommunications
- Call-center management
- Network operations management
- Service policy analysis
- Market analysis
- Loading pattern analysis

Transportation
- Yield analysis
- Asset utilization
- Fleet management

Capital Markets
- Risk assessment
- Derivatives trading
- Institutional sales systems
- Retail marketing

Asset Management
- Portfolio performance analysis
- Asset allocation
- Portfolio optimization

RED BRICK

Red Brick offers a number of case studies that demonstrate how its DM technology can be used in the real world. Here we will examine two of these cases studies.

H.E.B. is a grocery store chain based in San Antonio, Texas, that as of 2000 had sales of approximately $4.5 billion across 225 stores and 50,000 employees. H.E.B. was able to design and implement a category management application in under 9 months because it kept the application requirements simple and used database support from Red Brick and server support from Hewlett-Packard.

Prior to the implementation of the category management application, the marketing information department would take ad hoc requests for information from users, write a program to extract the information, and return the information to the user a week or so later—not timely enough for most business decisions, and in some cases not what the user really wanted in the first place.

The organization implemented category management in 1990. With category management, a category manager is characterized as the "CEO" of the category, with profit and loss responsibilities, final decision over which products to buy and which to delete, and where the products are to be located on the shelves. The category manager also decides which stores get which products. Although H.E.B. stores are only within the state of Texas, it is a diverse market: At some stores near Mexico, 98 percent of the customers are Hispanic, whereas in suburban Dallas stores, only 2 percent of the customers are Hispanic. The change to category management centralized all merchandising and marketing decisions, removing these decisions from individual stores.

As category managers built up their negotiating, technical, and partnering skills over 3 years, the need for more timely decision support information grew. An enterprise-wide survey of users to determine requirements for the new category management application took until September 1993. The final system was delivered in March 1994, and the application has been up and running without problems ever since. The company maintains 2 years of data by week, by item (257,000 universal product codes, or UPCs), and by store, which amounts to approximately 400 million detail records. Summary files are maintained by time and total company only, which can be an advantage.

To meet one of the system goals, all queries would be answered in 4 seconds, but some trend reports dealing with large groups of items over long time periods take 30 to 40 seconds. The users are not always technically oriented, so the design of the application is intentionally simple. The system is ad hoc to the extent that the user can specify time, place, and product.

H.E.B. believes that by using the new system, category managers are able to make better fact-based decisions to determine which products to put in which stores, how much product to send to a store, and the proper product mix. Historically, the company promoted buyers from the stores based on their considerable product knowledge. Category managers now come from other operational areas such as finance and human resources. The new system supports people with diverse backgrounds because it gives those with limited product knowledge the equivalent of years of experience.

Another example of Red Brick technology in the marketplace can be found at Hewlett-Packard (HP), a premier global provider of hardware systems. HP is known for manufacturing high-quality products, but to maintain its reputation, it delivers service and support during and after product delivery.

The Worldwide Customer Support Organization (WCSO) within Hewlett-Packard is responsible for providing support services to its hardware and software customers. For several years, the WCSO used a DW of financial, account, product, and service contract information to support decision making. WCSO Information Management is responsible for developing and supporting this DW.

Until 1994, WCSO Information Management supported business information queries with a DW architecture based on two HP3000/Allbase systems and an IBM DB2 system. It was a first attempt at collecting, integrating, and storing data related to customer support for decision-making purposes. As WCSO users increasingly relied on the DW, they began to demand better performance, additional data coverage, and more timely data availability.

The DW architecture failed to keep pace with the increased requirements from WCSO users. Users wanted to get information quickly. Both load and query performance were directly affected as more data were added. WCSO decided to investigate other DW alternatives that would significantly improve load/query performance, be more cost effective, and support large amounts of data without sacrificing performance.

HP chose to use Red Brick software on an HP9000, and the project began with the consolidation of the existing three databases into a single DW named Discovery. This downsizing provided significant cost savings and increased resource efficiencies in managing and supporting the warehouse environment. Today, Discovery supports approximately 250 marketing, finance, and administration users in the Americas, Europe, and Asia-Pacific regions. Users pull query results into their desktop report writers, load information into worksheets, or use the data to feed EISs. User satisfaction rose dramatically due to Discovery's vastly improved performance and remodeled business views.

ORACLE

For large-scale data mining, Oracle on the SP2 offers its users robust functionality and excellent performance. Data spread across multiple SP2 processor nodes are treated as a single image, affording exceptionally fast access to large databases. Oracle Parallel Query allows multiple users to submit complex queries at the same time. Individual complex queries can be broken down and processed across several processing nodes simultaneously. Execution time can be reduced from overnight to hours or minutes, enabling organizations to make better business decisions faster.

Oracle offers products that help customers create, administer, and use their DW. Oracle's large suite of connectivity products provides transparent access to many popular mainframe databases and enables customers to move data from legacy mainframe applications into the DW on the SP2.

Some examples of Oracle technology at work include the following:

- John Alden Insurance, based in Miami, Florida, uses Oracle Parallel Query on the SP2 to mine health care information, which permits orders-of-magnitude improvements in response time for typical business queries.
- ShopKo Stores, a $2-billion, Wisconsin-based mass merchandise chain that operates 128 stores throughout the Midwest and Northeast, chose the SP2 to meet its current and projected needs for both DM and mission-critical merchandising applications.
- Pacific Bell and Qwest, two telecommunications providers, use the Oracle Warehouse, which was introduced in 1995, to improve their ability to track customers and identify new service needs. Pacific Bell's DW provides a common set of summarized and compressed information to base decision support systems. The first system analyzes product profitability, and similar decision support systems are in development for marketing, capital investment, procurement, and two additional financial systems.
- Qwest implemented a DW to analyze intra-area code calling data from its three operating companies. Running Oracle7 Release 7.2 on a nine-CPU symmetric multiprocessing system from Pyramid, Qwest's initial centralized architecture supported use by 20 executives and marketing specialists. The next phase delivered DW access to more than 400 service representatives, which will ultimately be expanded up to 4,500 service representatives.

INFORMIX

As a major player in the DM field, Informix can claim a number of success stories. For example, Associated Grocers, one of the leading cooperative grocery wholesalers in the northwest United States, with revenues of $1.2 billion, replaced its traditional mainframe environment with a three-tiered client/server architecture based on Informix database technology. The new system's advanced applications cut order-fulfillment times in half, reduced inventory carrying costs, and enabled the company to offer its 350 independent grocers greater selection at a lower cost.

In 1991, Associated Grocers embarked on a phased transition from its mainframe-based information system to an open system. The company initially used IBM RS/6000 hardware, and subsequently included Hewlett-Packard and NCR. In evaluating relational database management systems, Associated Grocers developed a checklist of requirements that included education and training, scalability, technical support, solid customer references, and future product direction.

After selecting Informix as its company-wide database standard, Associated Grocers then assembled the rest of its system architecture using a three-tier model. On the first layer, the "client" presentation layer, graphical user interfaces use Microsoft Windows and Visual Basic. The second layer, based on Hewlett-Packard hardware, runs Micro Focus COBOL applications on top of the OEC Developer Package from Open Environment Corporation, which helps Associated Grocers develop DCE-compliant applications. The third layer, the data layer, is the INFORMIX-OnLine database.

Associated Grocers' pilot Informix-based application provides real-time inventory information for its deli warehouse. In the past, merchandise was received manually, and pertinent product information was later keyed into Associated Grocers' financial system. In contrast, the new system recognizes merchandise right at the receiving dock. Handheld radio frequency devices allow merchandise to be immediately scanned into the Informix database. Product is assigned to a warehouse location and its expiration date is noted. When orders are filled, products with the earliest expiration dates are shipped first.

As an extension to the deli warehouse system, the new postbilling system provides separate physical and financial inventories. Previously, merchandise could not be released for sale until the financial systems had been updated, which typically occurred overnight. The new Informix-based system allows for immediate sale and distribution of recently received merchandise.

A third Informix-based application enables Associated Grocers to sell unique items economically; that is, slow-moving merchandise that is ordered monthly versus daily. Rather than incurring the high cost to warehouse these items, Associated Grocers created a direct link to outside specialty warehouses to supply the needed items on demand. Independent stores simply order the merchandise from Associated Grocers. The order goes into Associated Grocers' billing system, which transmits it to the specialty warehouse, which immediately ships the merchandise to Associated Grocers. The specialty items are loaded onto Associated Grocers' delivery trucks and delivered along with the rest of an independent store's order.

SYBASE

As testimony to the interest and activity in data warehousing, recent surveys (Meta Group information) show that more than 70 percent of *Fortune* 1000 companies have data warehousing projects budgeted or underway at an average cost of $3 million and a typical development time of 6 to 18 months.

Today, conventional warehousing applications extract basic business data from operational systems, edit or transform them in some fashion to ensure their accuracy and clarity, and move them by means of transformation products, custom programming, or "sneaker net" to the newly deployed analytical database system. This extract-edit-load-query, extract-edit-load-query system might be acceptable if business life were simple and relatively static. However, new data and data structures are added, changes are made to existing data, and even whole new databases are added on a regular basis.

The Sybase Warehouse WORKS Alliance Program provides a complete, open, and integrated solution for organizations building and deploying DW solutions. The program addresses the entire range of technology requirements for DW development, including data transformation, data distribution, and interactive data access. The alliance partners are committed to adopting the Warehouse WORKS architecture and APIs, as well as to working closely with Sybase in marketing and sales programs.

Sybase Warehouse WORKS was designed around four key functions in data warehousing:

1. Assembling data from multiple sources
2. Transforming data for a consistent and understandable view of the business
3. Distributing data to where they are needed by business users
4. Providing high-speed access to the data for those business users

SILICON GRAPHICS

New DM solutions are extending the advances in data analysis realized through breakthroughs in data warehousing. Sophisticated tools for three-dimensional visualization, coupled with DM software developed by Silicon Graphics, make it possible to bring out patterns and trends in the data that may not have been realized using traditional SQL techniques. These "nuggets" of information can then be brought to the attention of the end user, yielding bottom-line results.

Using fly-through techniques, the user can navigate through models on consumer purchasing and channel velocity to follow trends and observe patterns. In response to what the user sees, the user can interact directly with the data, using visual computing to factor critical "what-if" scenarios into the models. By making it possible to go through many such iterations without overburdening IS staff with the need for analytical assistance, the user can eliminate days—even months—from the review process.

IBM

IBM provides a number of decision support tools that offer users a powerful, easy-to-use interface to the DW. IBM Information Warehouse Solutions, in keeping with their commitment to provide open systems implementations, offers the choice of decision support tools that best meet the needs of the end users.

IBM announced a Customer Partnership Program to work with selected customers to gain experience and validate the applicability of DM technology. This program offers customers the advantage of IBM's powerful new DM technology to analyze their data. For example, Visa and IBM announced an agreement in 1995 that changed the way in which Visa and its member banks exchange information worldwide. The structure facilitates the timely delivery of information and critical decision support tools directly from Visa to member financial institutions' desktops worldwide.

IBM Visualizer provides a powerful and comprehensive set of ready-to-use building blocks and development tools that can support a wide range of end-user requirements for query, report writing, data analysis, chart/graph making, business planning, and multimedia databases. As a workstation-based product, Visualizer is object-oriented, which makes it easy to plug in additional functions. Visualizer can also access databases such as Oracle and Sybase, as well as the DB2 family.

A number of other decision support products are available from IBM based on the user's platform, operating environment, and database. For example, the IBM Application System (AS) provides a client/server architecture and the widest range of decision support functions available for the MVS and VM environments. AS is the decision support server of choice in these environments because of its capability to access many different data sources. IBM Query Management Facility (QMF) provides query, reporting, and graphics functions in the MVS, VM, and CICS environments. The Data Interpretation System (DIS) is an object-oriented set of tools that enables end users to access, analyze, and present information with little technical assistance. It is a LAN-based client/server architecture with access to IBM and non-IBM relational databases as well as host applications in the MVS and VM environment. These and other products available from IBM provide the functions and capabilities needed for a variety of implementation alternatives.

3.8: CHAPTER SUMMARY

"Seeing" the data is becoming a major component in decision support and the formation of organizational strategies. The coming "Age of Information" will bring with it increased demands for organizing and using the multitude of information and knowledge resident within a typical organization, and the discovery of hidden structures and patterns within that information will be a key activity. Through DM technology, we will fundamentally transform our understanding of the concept of information from its present form of "something we need to know" into its future form of "something we could otherwise never have known."

Key Concepts

- Data mining (DM) is the set of activities used to find new, hidden, or unexpected patterns in data. A synonym for DM techniques is knowledge data discovery (KDD).

- Online analytical processing (OLAP) software enables decision makers to conduct multidimensional analysis of consolidated enterprise data. Two approaches can be used to conduct the analysis.

  Multidimensional OLAP (MOLAP). MOLAP organizes and analyzes data as a hypercube, an n-dimensional cube, which allows a number of dimensions to be analyzed simultaneously and any number of multidimensional views of data to be created. Although MOLAP is good at handling summarized data, it is not particularly adept at handling large amounts of detailed data.

  Relational OLAP (ROLAP). In ROLAP, the multidimensional database server is replaced with a large relational database server. ROLAP architectures are especially well suited to those situations in which dynamic access to combinations of summarized and detailed data is more important than the performance gains offered by the MOLAP approach using only summarized or preconsolidated data.

- The four categories of processing algorithms and rule approaches are classification, association, sequence, and cluster.

  Classification. By building and refining a predictive model of the business problem, DM classification methods can often provide useful and highly accurate answers.

Association. By searching all details or transactions from operational systems, an associated algorithm that includes the rules that will correlate one set of events or items with another can be developed.

Sequence. Sequencing and time-series analysis are used to relate events in time and can discover hidden trends for predicting future events.

Cluster. By creating clusters of data according to some metric or set of metrics and analyzing the characteristics of members in the class, clustering might derive certain rules.

- DM technologies include statistical analysis, neural networks, genetic algorithms, fuzzy logic, and decision trees.

Statistical analysis. DM requires the use of statistical techniques capable of accommodating the conditions of nonlinearity, multiple outliers, and nonnumerical data typically found in a DW environment.

Neural networks, genetic algorithms, and fuzzy logic. By using machine learning techniques to derive meaning from complicated and imprecise data, patterns and trends within the data can be detected and extracted.

Decision trees. By continually breaking datasets into two separate smaller groups, a predictive model can be built. This technique is often used in DM applications to assist in the classification of items or events contained within the DW.

- The general process of knowledge discovery has seven steps.
  1. Select a topic for study.
  2. Identify a target dataset.
  3. Clean and preprocess the data.
  4. Build a data model.
  5. Interpret and refine.
  6. Predict.
  7. Share the model.

- DM has a number of limitations and challenges.

Identification of missing information. Even with thorough and sophisticated technologies, we cannot yet detect whether an original dataset contains the necessary elements for effective mining. Therefore, DM applications need to include mechanisms for "inventorying" the dataset so that a determination of sufficiency in attributes can be made prior to loading the data into the DW.

Data noise and missing values. Currently, DM systems are limited to the treatment of noise via statistical techniques that rely on known distributions of data noise. Future systems must incorporate more sophisticated mechanisms for treating missing or noisy data.

Large databases and high dimensionality. Dimensionality ensures that discovered patterns are not "local" due to the constant update of the data by an expanding set of time-sensitive data values.

- Data visualization is the process by which numerical data are converted into meaningful images. The ability to create multidimensional structures and models from raw data can assist in analyzing complex datasets by mapping physical properties to the data, thus taking advantage of human visual systems. The identification of hidden patterns contained within the data can be accelerated.

Questions for Review

1. Define data mining.
2. Describe the evolution of decision support activities from verification to discovery.
3. What is OLAP?

4. Explain MOLAP.
5. Describe how ROLAP works.
6. Compare the two approaches of conducting OLAP analysis. How do the two approaches differ?
7. Explain how data are classified.
8. How does the association technique apply to data mining?
9. List and briefly describe several data mining technologies.
10. List the KDD process and briefly describe the steps of the process.
11. Describe the three measures of association used in market basket analysis.
12. What are the current limitations and challenges to data mining?
13. What is data visualization?
14. What is text mining? How does it differ from typical data mining?
15. What are some Web mining applications?

For Further Discussion

1. After gaining an understanding of the evolution of decision support activities from verification to discovery, find an example of this evolution and what makes it possible.
2. Analyze a commercial DM product that uses OLAP. Describe the approaches and techniques it applies and how it works.
3. Analyze a commercial DM product that does not use OLAP. Identify the benefits of this product and discuss its limitations.
4. How can data visualization help in decision making?
5. Compare the siftware technologies discussed in Section 3.7. How are they similar? How do they differ?

PolyAnalyst Exercises

1. POLYANALYST: SUMMARY STATISTICS AND LINK ANALYSIS

In this exercise, we will compare the characteristics of cars manufactured at different locations using the Autompg.csv dataset provided in the PolyAnalyst Examples folder.

CASE DESCRIPTION

The dataset consists of 398 records characterizing various car types. The following attributes are provided for each car type: the miles-per-gallon value (mpg) measured for each car model in a test performed in 1982, the number of the engine cylinders (cyl), the cylinder displacement in cubic inches (displ), the engine power (power), the car weight in pounds (weight), the number of seconds required to accelerate to the speed of 100 miles per hour (accel), the car's production year (year), the country of production (origin), and the name of the model (model).

TASKS

a. Load Autompg.csv into PolyAnalyst and select the number of cylinders (cyl) to be a categorical attribute.

b. Use Rule Assistant to create a new attribute representing the car age at the time of the experiment from the year of production of the car and create a new dataset "Explored" where the age attribute is included instead of the production year (year). Create a histogram illustrating the distribution of the age of cars included in the experiment; use Chart Wizard to reformat the histogram to appear in the depicted form; save the picture in BMP format; and insert this graph in your report. What conclusions can you make about the age of cars considered in the experiment?

c. What is the statistical mean and standard deviation of power, mpg, and accel?

d. Split the Explored dataset into three datasets containing only cars manufactured at each particular location (origin). Determine the distribution of the number of cylinders (cyl) in cars manufactured at different locations (origin) to the overall distributions. What conclusions can you make? Support your conclusions with the relevant graphs. Hint: Use the PolyAnalyst Summary Statistics engine.

e. Depict the relationship between where a car was produced (origin) and the number of cylinders (cyl) in the car with the help of PolyAnalyst's Link Chart. What are the most prominent positive and negative correlations that you see? What conclusions can you make? Is it easier to arrive at your conclusions using the Link Chart or Summary Statistics engine? What are the benefits and drawbacks of each method?

f. Compare cars manufactured at different locations (origin) on all their characteristics at once. What conclusions can you make? Support your conclusions by including the graphs saved from PolyAnalyst to your report. *Hint:* Use the PolyAnalyst Snake Chart.

2. POLYANALYST: LINEAR REGRESSION

In this exercise, we will discover simple relations in medical data. Consider the 2med.csv dataset provided in the PolyAnalyst Examples folder.

CASE DESCRIPTION

The data for this problem are taken from the heart surgery archive of a large hospital. Each record corresponds to one patient. The record fields, or attributes, are as follows: file number ID (FILE), sex, age, diagnosis, weight, body surface area (bsa), and height. The purpose of this exercise is to determine if the weight of a patient can be reliably predicted based on other attributes.

TASKS

a. Start PolyAnalyst and load the 2med.csv dataset. Exclude attributes FILE and bsa. Launch the Linear Regression exploration engine with the weight attribute as a target. Interpret the results and record the accuracy of the prediction.

b. Note that it might be somewhat more reasonable to expect that weight be linearly proportional to body volume rather than the height of a patient. Create a new attribute "cube_of_height" representing weight to the third power and include this new attribute instead of height in the same analysis. Interpret the results and compare the accuracy of the obtained model to that obtained in the previous step.

c. Plot a chart displaying the dependence of weight against patient height. Add the obtained linear regression rules to the same chart. Use the sliders on the right-hand side of the chart to test the dependence of the models on other attributes.

d. What other PolyAnalyst exploration engines can be used to develop a model predicting the value of height based on other independent attributes?

3. POLYANALYST: DECISION TREE

In this exercise, we will determine the profile of those consumers who are not likely to purchase the Land Rover Discovery. Consider the Lrover.csv dataset provided in the PolyAnalyst Examples folder. *Note:* The data in this example are real, but both the data and the company name are disguised for reasons of privacy.

CASE DESCRIPTION

To better understand the lifestyles of potential purchasers of the Discovery SUV produced by Land Rover, the Land Rover marketing research manager commissioned a study of consumers' attitudes, interests, and opinions. A 30-question questionnaire was designed that covered a variety of dimensions, including consumers' attitudes toward risk, foreign versus domestic products, product styling, spending habits, self-image, and family. The questionnaire included a final question measuring the consumer's attitude toward purchasing the Land Rover Discovery.

The respondents used a nine-point Likert scale where a value of "1" meant that they definitely disagreed with a statement and a "9" meant that they definitely agreed. A total of 400 respondents were obtained from the mailing lists of *Car and Driver, Business Week,* and *Inc.* magazines. The respondents were then interviewed at their homes by an independent surveying company.

TASKS

a. Read through the corresponding PolyAnalyst Tutorial to learn what questions were asked and how the marketing research manager was able to build a profile of a typical buyer of the Land Rover Discovery.

b. Consider "nonbuyers" as respondents who expressed little interest in the possibility of purchasing a Land Rover Discovery (marked their attitude as a 1 or 2). With the help of the Decision Tree algorithm, determine a profile of a typical nonbuyer and interpret your results.

c. Compare the profiles of typical buyers and nonbuyers. What recommendations can you make to the management of Land Rover regarding market positioning of the Discovery?

4. POLYANALYST: MARKET BASKET ANALYSIS

In this exercise, we will discover purchase patterns in transactional data. Consider the Grocery.csv dataset provided in the PolyAnalyst Examples folder.

CASE DESCRIPTION

Transactions are the lifeblood of any corporation. It is common knowledge that companies record transactional data in order to fulfill orders, manage the supply chain, facilitate accounting, process product returns, and support their daily operations in many other ways. Daily records of customers, products, dates, and amounts provide an unbiased corporate history.

The technology that helps solve the task of discovering purchase patterns in transactional data is called market basket analysis. This technology can be used to find which products sell together well and what drives these sales. The key sales drivers are identified in the form of association rules. Association rules can capture relations that are one-to-one (the purchase of cereal often implies that milk will be purchased in the same transaction) or many-to-one (the purchase of a computer and printer will most probably imply that the customer is going to purchase the corresponding connecting cable). Association rules are usually unidirectional. For example, a rule that steak will be purchased when barbeque sauce is purchased does not necessarily imply that the opposite rule holds true.

The data in Grocery.csv are provided in transactional format. In this format, each transaction (or basket) is marked by an ID in one data column, and the other data column contains all products purchased in the transaction. Therefore, each shopping basket may contain several products. In the Grocery.csv file, the attribute Customer contains a unique identifier for each shopping basket and the attribute Product lists all products associated with every basket.

TASKS

a. Launch PolyAnalyst and load the Grocery.csv file. What are the 15 most commonly purchased and 15 least commonly purchased products from the grocery store?
b. Use the PolyAnalyst Transactional Basket analysis algorithm to learn which products are most commonly purchased together and the corresponding association rules. List those groups of products discovered by the system that we would intuitively predict would often be purchased together. *Hint:* Use the following settings for the Transactional Basket exploration engine:

   Min. Support: 1 percent
   Min. Confidence: 30 percent
   Min. Improvement: 2 percent

c. Provide the definitions of Support, Confidence, and Improvement, which are the measures of the quality of the results obtained by Transactional Basket analysis. Interpret the key product associations discovered in the Transactional Basket analysis performed in the previous step and interpret the discovered rules according to these definitions. Provide a written interpretation of the relationship found between Hot Dogs, Hot Dog Buns, and Sweet Relish in terms of Support, Confidence, and Improvement.
d. Based on your results, what recommendations would you make to the manager of the grocery store to use the discovered cross-sell opportunities to increase sales?

5. POLYANALYST: TEXT ANALYSIS

In this exercise, we will determine occupational trauma hazards through text analysis. Consider the UnitedMutual.csv dataset provided in the PolyAnalyst Examples folder. *Note:* The data in this example are real, but both the data and the company name are disguised for reasons of privacy.

CASE DESCRIPTION

The Research Center of United Mutual, a health insurance company with more than 1,000 offices throughout the world, needed to determine the causes of accidents and injuries and identify appropriate methods for preventing these accidents. The goal of the project was to drive down the incidence of occupational injuries and reduce the disabilities arising from those that do occur. The main source of accidents and claims data is the call center data, which contains natural language textual notes entered into the database by call center operators when they interview claimants.

The important fields and their definitions are as follows:

Cause. Reported cause of injury (natural language text data reported by the insured and entered into the database by a call center operator)
Diagnosis. Doctor's report of patient's injury (also unstructured text data)
Localization. Trauma localization (category selected from a predetermined drop-down list)

TASKS

a. Count all of the records that describe cases involving trucks (a vehicle used for hauling). What senses of the word *truck* have you selected? *Hint:* Use the PolyAnalyst Text Analysis exploration engine and allow the system to include word generalizations.
b. How many cases out of those selected in the first step do not contain the word *truck* itself, but contain related words (e.g., *tractor* or *van*)? How many cases were treated erroneously as being related to trucks?
c. Compare the distribution of trauma localization for cases involving trucks with all cases. What are the main differences between the most-represented trauma localizations?
d. List trauma localizations that occur unusually frequently in cases involving trucks (even if the absolute number of these cases is not high). List trauma localizations that occur rarely in cases involving trucks. Which PolyAnalyst instrument did you use to arrive at your results?

6. TEXTANALYST: SUMMARIZATION

In this exercise, we will document summarization and semantic search for information. Consider the Web_Intelligence.txt file provided in the Data_TA folder on the Megaputer software CD.

CASE DESCRIPTION

Industry analysts who process large amounts of documents are often overloaded with work and seek automated tools to reduce that burden. When an analyst is monitoring a particular subject or when a venture capitalist wants to assess the value of a proposal and must search the Internet, both end up with a huge collection of documents. Some of those documents contain the key answers that they are searching for, but the majority of the collected documents are usually irrelevant to their research. Analysts must skim through the entire collection of documents to decide which documents are worth further investigation. The technology for automated document summarization can dramatically increase the effectiveness of this work and save analysts vast amounts of time.

"Web Intelligence" is an eight-page white paper discussing the benefits and techniques of Web data mining. The objective of this exercise is to carry out semantic analysis, automated summarization, and a natural language search for information with the help of the text mining tool TextAnalyst, which is offered by Megaputer Intelligence. TextAnalyst operates via a unique neural network technology combined with some linguistic analysis tools, enabling the system to analyze large volumes of unstructured text quickly and efficiently.

TASKS

a. Launch TextAnalyst and load the *Web_Intelligence.txt* file. Browse through the automatically created Semantic Network (a list of most important terms and relations between these terms in the text). Use TextAnalyst to locate all of the sentences in the text that deal simultaneously with the terms *Web site* and *prospects*. Include the found sentences in your report on the problem. What is the meaning of the numbers to the left of each term included in the Semantic Network? What does it mean when two numbers appear to the left of a term?

b. Use TextAnalyst to run an automated summarization. Does the summary generated by the system provide you with a sufficient initial understanding of the subject of the text? Compare the size and quality of the summaries generated by TextAnalyst with a minimum semantic importance threshold set to 90 and 99. Include both summaries in your report, listing the semantic weight of each sentence in the summaries.

c. Run a natural language query against the considered text. A good sample query would be: "How does data mining help in learning visitor interests?" Include the response generated by the system in your report. How many fragments found by the system are relevant to your query?

d. What is the basic idea of the search mechanism implemented in TextAnalyst? Why do you think terms that were not included in your query were still presented in the list of terms in the Query control window? Are they related to your initial query?

7. TEXTANALYST: KEY CONCEPT EXTRACTION

In this exercise, we will extract knowledge from customer surveys. Consider the ITT_survey.txt file provided in the Data_TA folder on the Megaputer software CD. *Note:* The data in this example are real, but both the data and the company name are disguised for reasons of privacy.

CASE DESCRIPTION

One of the basic tasks of a text mining system is to automatically identify key concepts and the links between them in documents. The created semantic network of concepts and relations serves as the foundation for many further analysis techniques. The network is also displayed graphically to provide a convenient navigation mechanism for the considered text. The background knowledge about the considered application domain can be utilized through customized user dictionaries.

ITT is an Internet service provider. ITT created an online survey soliciting customer comments about the quality of its service. ITT's goal was to monitor the overall satisfaction of its customers with its Internet access service and to identify any problems. Knowledge of these issues could help the company address the identified problems and thus improve customer satisfaction.

TASKS

a. Launch TextAnalyst and load the ITT_survey.txt file. The initial results do not take into account the presence of synonyms in the text, but these preliminary results are quite useful because they reveal the main topics customers are concerned about. These topics include e-mail, ads, the navigation bar, page, service, the search engine, and so on. List in your report other topics that are most important to customers. Which of these concepts might be of primary concern to ITT managers? Why?

b. Extract customer comments dedicated to ads. How many sentences were retrieved? Include the results in your report. Do customers perceive ads as a benefit or a drawback of the provided service? What is the ratio of positive to negative comments related to ads?

c. As useful as they are, these results can be significantly improved by making the following observation: Some terms can be used interchangeably within the considered domain. For example, in the present context, the terms *mail* and *e-mail* refer to the same subject, e-mail. This conclusion is made based on a visual evaluation of the results furnished by TextAnalyst. Launch the Dictionary Editor module of TextAnalyst and add the following terms and their synonyms, as used by the survey respondents, to the dictionary:

> advertise (synonyms: *ad, advertising,* and *advertisement,* and even *add*)
> toolbar (synonyms: *bar* and *menu*)
> rid (synonym: *remove*)

> *Hint:* When adding words with their synonyms to the dictionary, mark the main added words as *exception words,* as defined in the TextAnalyst User Manual. Add "dont" to the dictionary as *not analyzed word.* Save the resulting dictionary under a different name and then link TextAnalyst to this new dictionary so that the new synonym list is used in the further analysis. Close and reopen TextAnalyst in order for all the changes to take effect.

d. Reload the ITT_survey.txt file. Observe that with the new dictionary, TextAnalyst obtains more accurate and informative results. Summarize the most significant differences between the newly obtained results and the results generated in the first step of the analysis.

> What issues did you find to be the main problems for customers when they use the ITT Internet access service? Obtain and copy to your report all text fragments corresponding to the three main problems as perceived by customers. *Hint:* Because the concept page is too unspecific and can be related to many different situations, ignore this concept in your analysis.

e. Export the resulting semantic network to CSV format. Open these CSV results in Microsoft Excel, sort the results in order to obtain the list of the most important concepts in descending order, and then plot an Excel graph illustrating the frequency of occurrence of the top 30 concepts representing customer comments and suggestions.

8. RECOMMENDATION MODULE

In this exercise, we will analyze data in order to offer product recommendations to assist call center operators. Install the Online Recommendation system from Megaputer Intelligence on your machine and launch the Online Recommendation Demo through the regular Windows Start menu. *Note:* The data in this example are real, but both the data and the company name are disguised for reasons of privacy.

CASE DESCRIPTION

Scores of transactions are recorded and stored by thousands of companies daily. The advent of e-commerce, which requires the recording of millions of transactions each day, accelerated the growth of volumes of stored data. The analysis of transactional data can help improve the quality of business decisions and increase the value of every customer interaction.

The purpose of a recommendation system is to provide the most probable additional purchases in response to any transaction performed by the customer. Customers might enjoy receiving an accurate and unobtrusive recommendation for other products of interest to them. These recommendations can help customers better navigate through the store and reduce their shopping time.

MITA Group performs analytical research for various high-tech industries ranging from broadband and cellular communications to biotech companies. The company analysts create industry-specific reports. The average price of a report ranges from $7,000 to $10,000, and the volume of business-to-business sale transactions with these reports is rather low. The point of sale for a report is a call center, where operators handle requests for particular reports from customers. The utilization of the Recommendation module from Megaputer Intelligence helped call center operators identify the best cross-sell opportunities on the fly in each particular case. This recommendation of the most relevant additional reports of interest to the individual customers simultaneously generated additional revenue to the company and increased customer satisfaction.

TASKS

a. Launch the Online Recommendation (OR) demo and view the Transactions table in the opening Microsoft Access database demo. This database is the main source of data for the application. The two most important fields are Company_Name, which represents a customer who purchased products, and Product_Name, which represents the purchased report. In our application, the data are so sparse (few products are purchased by a single customer) that we can view all purchases performed by a single customer as a single transaction in order to identify the best cross-sell opportunities. What are the four main industries that MITA Group covers? Which industries have the largest number of reports dedicated to them? How many individual purchase records are included in the demo data? *Note:* In many cases, a vendor would want to recommend not only products with a high probability of being purchased, but to recommend those products that have the highest profit margin. This issue is addressed in the OR module by incorporating the Margins table, where the business user can specify different margins for products and influence the recommendations made in each case.

b. Click the Create button on the Online Recommendations form in the Access demo. The OR module will process historical transactional data contained in the database and distill and store in a recommendation table all frequent purchase patterns for each product. With the creation of the recommendation table, you can select a product from a drop-down list of all products in the lower part of the form. For example, select 4F Cellular (the real report name: 3D Cellular) and click Add, which implies that the customer purchased this report. What other products does the system recommend that might be of interest to the customer? What recommendations have sufficiently high probability (the number in the square brackets) to be recommended to customers? How many products from the biotech sector are included in the recommendations returned by the system? Why?

c. Set the Number of Recommendations to "4" to include only the most important recommendations. Select one of the products recommended by the system, for example, "Core Ultra-fast Nets: Market Options for Ultra-fast Switching, Routing, and Crossconnect in DASA

Nets" as the next purchase by the same customer. How did the list of recommendations returned by the OR module change?

d. Assume that you assist the next customer. Click New Customer on the form to "forget" the last transactions. Select the report "Diagnostic Imaging Equipment and Systems Global Market" as a purchase by a new customer. What additional reports are recommended by the system? How many reports dedicated to broadband communications are recommended? Why? Which products can indeed be recommended, taking into account our certainty in the outcome? Does it help the business if we try to recommend more?

e. Determine manually from the Access Transactions table why the OR module recommended the products you see in the list. Provide simple mathematical reasoning for your conclusion.

Note: It is relatively easy to trace the reason for the system decision in this case because the data are so sparse and so few transactions are considered. In more realistic situations involving millions of products and transactions, as well as more than one product in the basket, this analysis might become a formidable task.

f. What other businesses, in addition to call centers, could successfully use an expert system with the results obtained by the OR module? What would be a typical corresponding system implementation?

References

Codd, E. F., S. B. Codd, and T. S. Clynch. (July 1993). "Beyond Decision Support." *Computerworld 26.*

Gray, P. (1997). The New DSS: Data Warehouses, OLAP, MDD, and KDD. In J. M. Carey (Ed.) *Proceedings of the Americas Conference on Information Systems.* (pp. 917–19). Phoenix, AZ: Association for Information Systems.

Inmon, W. H., J. D. Welch, and K. L. Glassey. (1997). *Managing the Data Warehouse.* New York: Wiley.

APPENDIX 3A
SAUDI ARABIAN AIRLINES

OBJECTIVE AND EXPLORATION

The objective of the performed analysis was to determine which attributes influenced the percentage of passengers flying in the first-class section. These influential attributes could then be manipulated to influence the number of first-class passengers present on each flight, thus increasing revenue. The analysis also helps to predict the optimal percentage of first-class seats for each flight, thus allowing Saudi Arabian Airlines to maximize revenue and increase customer satisfaction.

The data provided for the analysis contained various characteristics of flights originating from or arriving to major cities in Saudi Arabia: Riyadh (RUH), Jeddah (JED), Medina (MED), and Mecca (DMM).

To simplify the analysis, we began by creating a dataset that consisted of flights departing from a single location, designated by JED_DEP, which listed all flights departing from Jeddah. Breaking the departure field down to one location allowed us to concentrate on the flight analysis of just this location: The analyses for other locations can be performed similarly. We then created a variable that indicated the season when the fight took place called D_Season. This variable indicates whether any relationship is evident between the number of first-class passengers and a certain season. Third, we created two ratios to allow comparison of the prices of first-class tickets to economy-class tickets (FtoY) and business-class tickets to economy-class tickets (JtoY) on each individual flight. Fourth, we created an attribute named FC_percent that indicates the percentage of first-class passengers on a given flight.

Customer-provided attributes used in the analysis include the following:

- REVPAX is a given attribute that indicates the total number of passengers on the flight.
- L_MAILKILO is the total weight of the mail on the flight in kilograms. Additional analysis is required to determine how this variable is applicable to the model.
- FREIGHT is the total amount of freight weight in kilograms on the flight.
- L_COMAT is the total amount of commercial mail weight in kilograms on the flight.
- FC_PREV is the total number of first-class passengers on the flight.
- BC_PREV is the total number of business-class passengers on the flight.
- EC_PREV is the total number of economy-class passengers on the flight.

Derived/Added attributes used in the analysis include the following:

- F gives the price of the first-class ticket for the given flight.
- J gives the price of the business-class ticket for the given flight.
- Y gives the price of the economy-class ticket for the given flight. (*Note:* F, J, and Y are actionable attributes that management can manipulate to change consumers' response to purchasing first-class tickets.)
- JED_origin indicates that the departure is from JED, which is used to break the dataset down to a single airport.
- Weekday indicates whether the flight took place on a weekday. (We assumed the number of passengers who fly on weekends would differ from the number of passengers who fly on weekdays.)
- Flight_class indicates whether a flight is primary or secondary.
- FC_percent indicates the percentage of the first-class passengers on each flight.
- FC_perc_class indicates whether the number of first-class passengers is high, low, or zero.
- FtoJ indicates the ratio of the first-class ticket price to the business-class ticket price.
- FtoY indicates the ratio of the first-class ticket price to the economy-class ticket price.
- D_Season indicates one of the four seasons in which the flight took place. (We felt this attribute would help in determining when the airline industry increases were due to passengers who do not travel on a regular basis; for example, people who only travel during summer vacations.)
- Flight_class is a derived variable that indicates the value as "Yes" if the FLIGHTNO variable is less than 1,000 and "NO" if FLIGHTNO is greater than or equal to 1,000. (This attribute was created in order to separate primary flights serving popular routes, which were given three-digit flight numbers, and supplementary flights serving less-popular routes and having four-digit flight numbers. The Flight_class attribute was created after observing the difference in the number of passengers carried by flights with three- and four-digit flight numbers.)

We divided the percentage of first-class passengers carried by individual flights into three categories: 0, to indicate that the category contained no first-class passengers; low, to indicate that less than 6 percent of the passengers are first class; and high, to indicate that 6 percent or more are first-class passengers. We used the percentage value of the number of first-class passengers rather than the absolute number of first-class passengers on each flight because the latter would give a solution based mainly on the plane's size. The percentage of first-class passengers on each plane was split by 6 percent to give us three almost evenly populated categories, with 6 percent as the mean number of first-class passengers on all the flights. The resulting new attribute, named FC_perc_class, provided the target variable in our exploration. Creating this categorical attribute allowed the use of the Decision Trees exploration engine in order to predict whether a considered flight will have a large or small percentage of first-class passengers.

With the data initially explored and all derived attributes applied to the dataset JED_DEP, we then created a testing dataset called JED_DEP_Check10P by randomly sampling 10 percent of the records from the JED_DEP dataset. These data were not used when training the model but were used to test the created model for significance. A complement to this dataset produced a dataset that contained 90 per-cent of records of flights originating from JED. This dataset was called Training; it contains 16,350 records of the JED_DEP dataset.

First, to identify a small set of variables that influence the percentage of first-class seats on an air-plane most significantly, we ran the Find Dependencies (FD) exploration engine with the FC_perc attribute selected as a target and only some independent variables included. The first round of the FD exploration suggested that two attributes, L_COMAT and Flight_class, are the most important predictors for FC_perc, which indicates that the amount of commercial mail and whether the flight is a primary flight can determine what percentage of first-class passengers it will carry. The second round of FD, with L_COMAT and Flight_class excluded from the exploration, suggested that three other most important attributes are prices F, J, and Y, which is not surprising. Although this result is interesting, we would like to find out how various attributes influence the percentage of first-class passengers.

To create a model to predict the target variable FC_perc_class, we used PolyAnalyst's Decision Trees exploration engine. This engine clearly indicates the most influential attributes (using a graphical decision tree) in determining the target variable: FC_perc_class. The Decision Trees exploration model named DT_FC_perc_class was the first algorithm run, and it returned a decision tree using the attribute DEST as the initial split composed of approximately 44 different nodes with a high classification probability of 59.35 percent. (Individual classes were predicted with errors of 27 percent, 60 percent, and 36 percent, respectively). By testing this model on the JED_DEP_Check10P dataset, we can see that the created model delivers only slightly worse results on the data that were not used in training. This conclusion increases our confidence in the significance of the model. This model can be used to determine the num-ber of first-class seats that should be reserved to a given destination. For example, flights destined for AMS, BWN, BRU, MAA, CMB, CPH, DAC, DUS, ISB, LAX, MCT, and THR should reserve a low num-ber of first-class seats because a low number of the flights to these locations contains passengers in the first-class section. At the same time, flights to AUH, AMM, CAI, DXB, and KRT have a large percentage of first-class seats on them. To further investigate other actionable attributes that influence the target, we created a second Decision Trees model.

We ran Decision Trees again, but this time we excluded the DEST variable. The Decision Trees exploration model named DT_No_Destination returned the following classification statistics:

Classification probability: 64.44 percent
Classification efficiency: 46.42 percent
Classification error for class 0: 29.29 percent
Classification error for class 1: 53.80 percent
Classification error for class 2: 23.88 percent

These statistics show that the second Decision Trees model provides a higher classification probabil-ity than the first Decision Trees model. Thus, if the second model proves to be significant through testing it on unseen data, it would be the better model in predicting the objective. The classification error for class 1 (low percentage of first-class passengers) is relatively high, but it is not of great concern because we are more interested in whether the percentage of first-class passengers is high or none.

The Decision Trees exploration engine made the initial split on variable F, which is the first-class price for a ticket. F, as the initial splitting attribute, indicates that it is the most important variable in deter-mining the objective. The following decision tree was produced by the algorithm; for easier visibility, the tree is split into two different pictures by the initial split on variable F.

In the figure, the nodes' color indicates the predicted classes: Blue is class "High"; red is class "0"; and green is the class "Low." The shade of each node relates to the share of records that correspond to it; bright nodes have a higher number of corresponding records and light nodes contain fewer records. The Decision Trees algorithm found the attributes Flight_class, REVPAX, FtoJ, FtoY, D_Season, and L_MAILKILO to be important attributes in predicting the target attribute. One can follow individual branches of this tree to see how these attributes predict either a large or small portion of passengers flying first class or none at all.

BUSINESS DISCUSSION

Note that this business analysis covers just one branch of the Decision Trees model. In determining the attributes that predict the percentage of first-class passengers, the decision tree indicates that the price of the first-class ticket is the most influential as the initial split. (*Note:* Nodes closer to the root have a stronger influence on the model.) If the first-class ticket price is less than 2,380, then 52 percent of these flights will contain passengers of the High first-class section. If the first-class ticket price is more than or equal to 2,380, then only 14 percent of these flights will contain passengers of the High first-class section.

For the higher first-class ticket prices, the next most-influential parameter is whether the flight is a primary flight or secondary flight. We assumed that three-digit flight numbers refer to primary flights, whereas four-digit flight numbers indicate secondary flights. For the secondary flights, the majority of the passengers purchase either business or economy tickets. For the primary flights, a much higher percentage of the passengers are first class. This statistic would indicate the need to reserve a much larger section for first-class passengers on primary flights and smaller sections for secondary flights. However, we could be wrong in our assumption here as secondary flights may not offer first-class seats.

For the higher first-class ticket prices and primary flights, the next most-influencing parameter in determining our objective is the total number of passengers a given flight carries. It is assumed that lower-revenue-producing flights use smaller planes. These planes can either accommodate first-class passengers or they cannot, because the flights either contain a high number of first-class passengers *or* they contain a high number of business and economy passengers. For higher-revenue-producing flights, the probability is higher that the flights will contain a large number of first-class passengers. We assumed the higher-revenue-producing planes to be larger planes that are able to accommodate first-class arrangements.

For the higher first-class ticket prices, primary flights, and higher-passenger-booked planes, the next most-influencing attribute in reaching our object is the ratio of first-class ticket price to business-class ticket price. This ratio indicates that when the value is greater than or equal to 1.28, there is a higher chance that more passengers will be flying in the first-class section. This result appears to be paradoxical, but the Decision Trees exploration engine found it to be soundly based on the data. This finding may indicate that higher-ratio flights offer better first-class service, which consumers may desire. Thus, providing a higher, more-expensive first-class service could increase the number of first-class passengers on board a flight, and thus increase the ratio.

For the higher first-class ticket prices, primary flights, higher-passenger-booked planes, and lower first-class to business-class price ratio, the next most-influencing parameter is the ratio of first-class ticket price to economy-class ticket price. A high ratio means a higher number of first-class passengers on these flights. We assumed this parameter to be due to better first-class service, which usually attracts customers.

For the higher first-class ticket prices, primary flights, higher-revenue-producing planes, lower first-class to business-class price ratio, and a high first-class to economy-ticket price ratio, the next most-influencing variable is the very high-passenger-booked planes. These nodes indicate that planes with a large number of passengers are more likely to have more people in the economy sections than planes that hold fewer than 129 passengers. The assumption here is that planes that can handle many passengers allow for more room by not having as many first-class seats that tend to take up more space, thus not allowing for as many first-class tickets. To increase the number of first-class passengers, you could increase the space allowed for the first-class area in the plane.

MODEL TESTING

After analyzing the results of the Decision Trees algorithm, the algorithm was tested on data that were not used for training in order to manually test the model for significance. PolyAnalyst contains a unique feature that allows models to be tested for their ability to successfully predict outcomes of future situations. The results returned statistical values that indicate that the Decision Trees algorithm was successful on the unseen data. The following classification statistics can be compared to the classification statistics of the Decision Trees algorithm in showing the significance of the model.

Classification probability: 64.54 percent
Classification efficiency: 45.38 percent

Left panel:

```
⊟ Root
  ⊟ F<2.38e+003
    ⊟ Flight_class=yes
      ⊟ REVPAX<16.5
          REVPAX<10.5
          REVPAX>=10.5
      ⊟ REVPAX>=16.5
        ⊟ FtoJ<1.28
          ⊟ FtoY<1.46
              F<1.45e+003
              F>=1.45e+003
          ⊟ FtoY>=1.46
            ⊟ REVPAX<129
                REVPAX<30.5
                REVPAX>=30.5
              REVPAX>129
        ⊟ FtoJ>=1.28
          ⊟ FtoJ<1.28
              REVPAX<96.5
              REVPAX>=96.5
          ⊟ FtoJ>=1.28
            ⊟ L_MAILKILO<138
                REVPAX<70.5
              ⊟ REVPAX [2]=70.5
                  F<1.39e+003
                ⊟ F>=1.39e+003
                  ⊟ L_MAILKILO<56.5
                      REVPAX<240
                      REVPAX>=240
                    L_MAILKILO>=56.5
            ⊟ L_MAILKILO>=138
                F<1.39e+003
              ⊟ F>=1.39e+003
                  F<1.69e+003
                  F>=1.69e+003
    ⊟ Flight_class=No
        REVPAX<250
      ⊟ REVPAX>=250
          REVPAX<395
          REVPAX>=395
  ⊟ F>=2.38e+003
    ⊟ FtoY<1.5
```

Right panel:

```
          REVPAX>=395
  ⊟ F>=2.38e+003
    ⊟ FtoY<1.5
      ⊟ REVPAX<61.5
          REVPAX<16.5
        ⊟ REVPAX>=16.5
            FtoY<1.41
          ⊟ FtoY>=1.41
              FtoY<1.5
              FtoY>=1.5
      ⊟ REVPAX>=61.5
        ⊟ REVPAX<386
          ⊟ FtoY<1.41
              F<3.14e+003
              F>=3.14e+003
          ⊟ FtoY>=1.41
              Flight_class=No
            ⊟ Flight_class=Yes
              ⊟ D_Season=2
                  REVPAX<110
                  REVPAX>=110
              ⊟ D_Season=4
                  FtoY<1.5
                  FtoY>=1.5
                D_Season=1
                D_Season=3
          REVPAX>=386
    ⊟ FtoY>=1.5
      ⊟ Flight_class=Yes
        ⊟ REVPAX<49.5
            REVPAX<16.5
          ⊟ REVPAX>=16.5
              FtoJ<1.3
              FtoJ>=1.3
        ⊟ REVPAX>=49.5
          ⊟ FtoY<1.5
              FtoY<1.5
            ⊟ FtoY>=1.5
                REVPAX<103
                REVPAX>=103
          FtoY>=1.5
        Flight_class=No
```

Classification error for class 0: 33.22 percent
Classification error for class 1: 52.05 percent
Classification error for class 2: 22.29 percent

CONCLUSIONS

The performed analysis suggests the following conclusions:

1. The attribute ratios FtoJ and FtoY can be manipulated by changing the ticket prices to influence the number of first-class passengers on each individual flight. Increasing the benefits of the first-class section results in higher percentage occupancy of the first-class seats.
2. The primary flights could use planes that accommodate more first-class passenger seats, secondary flights could decrease the area of the first-class section to allow for more economy and business seats. Using the first Decision Trees model, you could increase or decrease the number of reserved first-class tickets to increase profit based on the destination of the flight from JED.
3. Flights destined for AMS, BWN, BRU, MAA, CMB, CPH, DAC, DUS, ISB, LAX, MCT, and THR should reserve a low number of first-class seats because a low number of the flights to these locations carry passengers in the first-class section.
4. At the same time, flights to AUH, AMM, CAI, DXB, and KRT have a large percentage of first-class seats. The company should proactively manipulate the attribute ratios FtoJ and FtoY in order to increase the occupancy rates of the first-class seats on flights to these destinations.

Source: Richie Kasprzycki, Analyst at Megaputer Intelligence.

4
MACHINES THAT CAN LEARN

Learning Objectives

◆ Understand the types of problems that can be solved by machine learning systems.

◆ Understand the basics of how fuzzy logic processing employs set membership and how linguistic ambiguity can be modeled.

◆ Understand the strengths and limitations of fuzzy logic systems.

◆ Understand the basic concepts and components of artificial neural networks (ANNs) and their structures.

◆ Understand the strengths and limitations of neural computing.

◆ Understand the basic components and functioning of genetic algorithms (GAs).

◆ Know which intelligent systems are best suited to different kinds of problems.

CHASE MANHATTAN BANK CREDIT SCORING SYSTEM

In 1985, Chase Manhattan Bank began a search for new quantitative techniques to assist senior loan officers in forecasting the creditworthiness of corporate loan candidates. Chase established a 36-member internal consulting organization called Chase Financial Technologies to oversee the development of pattern-analysis network models for evaluating corporate loan risk.

The resulting models, called the Creditview system, perform 3-year forecasts that indicate the likelihood of a company being assigned a Chase risk classification of good, criticized, or charged-off. In addition to the overall forecast, Creditview provides a detailed listing of the items that significantly contributed to the forecast, an expert system (ES)-generated interpretation of those items, and several comparison reports.

Creditview models run on a Chase Financial Technologies host computer. A user system resides at each user's PC and communicates with the host through telephone lines. In addition, conventional financial statement analysis may be performed using Chase's Financial Reporting System, an independent financial spreadsheet and analysis package. The Financial Reporting System also resides on the user's PC for access to a company's standard financial statements.

The "secret" to the success of Chase's analysis systems lies with an embedded pattern-analysis technology for constructing a hybrid neural network based on sufficient high-quality historical data. Each hybrid net represents a separate "model" produced by the pattern-analysis module. The PLCM (Public Loan Company Model), the first model implemented at Chase, derives information from Chase's extensive loan history of large, publicly traded companies and their past financial data. (Chase's client base contains both publicly and privately owned corporations.) The historical data analyzed by the pattern-analysis module to produce forecasting models consist of a large col-

lection of data units. Each data unit contains as much as 6 years of consecutive financial data for a particular company, corresponding industry norms, and the company's status 3 years after the last year of data. (The last of the 6 years is called the "year of the data unit.") The data unit's status is the company's rating—G stands for good, C stands for criticized, and X stands for charged-off. The system uses these data to construct a large set of candidate variables that may or may not indicate a company's future financial condition. These variables become the basis for forming patterns.

A pattern is fundamentally a statement about the value of a particular financial variable or set of variables. A simple pattern may have the following form: C1, V1, C2, where V1 is a financial ratio or variable and C1 and C2 are constants. For example, 1.75, quick ratio, 2.00 could be a simple pattern. Typically, patterns are more complex; several elements of this kind are combined by using *and, or,* and *not.* The following example could be a small complex pattern:

$$C1, \ V1, \ C2$$
$$V2, \ C3$$
$$C4, \ V3, \ C5 \text{ and } C6, \ V4, \ C7$$
$$C8, \ V5, \ C9$$

where all the Cs are constants and Vs financial variables or ratios. Candidate variables are arranged into thousands of complex patterns and analyzed by the system to produce an optimal set of variables and patterns that form a pattern network called the Forecaster. The criteria for selection of patterns are as follows:

• **Score.** The score (as observed in the historical data) measures the ability of the pattern to differentiate between the categories good, criticized, and charged-off—in other words, the ability of the pattern to classify correctly.

<DATA MINING MINICASE>

(continued)

- **Complexity.** A measure of how complicated the pattern is (in terms of number of variables), the simple patterns within it, and the amount of historical data it satisfies.
- **Spuriousness.** A measure of the likelihood that the pattern's score (how well it predicts) is due solely to chance.

These statistics are used to evaluate the predictive power of the patterns and to ensure that whatever predictive power is uncovered is not by chance. To each pattern and status a probability (called the "precision") exists that a data unit corresponding to the pattern will have that status. The system uses a proprietary network-balancing technique that selects the patterns for the network to maximize precision and minimize bias.

The benefits of this system to Chase are obvious. Chase can now identify the strengths and vulnerabilities in the financial structure of an obligor and forecast the impact of these factors on the firm's financial health 3 years into the future. The savings associated with being able to "predict the future" are a key element in the longevity of Chase Manhattan Bank.

INTRODUCTION

The advent of the digital computer brought with it a general misconception that the majority of information processing at any given moment in our world is being carried out by an automated device. The ubiquitous nature of the computer allows us to forget about the most complex and powerful information processing device on Earth: the human mind. If we look at cybernetics and other disciplines that form the basis of information science, we see that the true nature of information processing is rooted in the actions of living creatures as they struggle to survive and adapt to their environments. Viewed in this light, the information being processed by today's computers accounts for only a small part of the total. Therefore, we can begin to seriously consider the development of information processing devices that mimic the structures and operating principles found in humans and other living creatures.

One of the new multidisciplinary fields of research—neural computing and the development of artificial neural networks—evolved in response to the attractiveness of digital information processors that can simulate the human brain's potential for solving ill-structured business problems. Neural computing involves processing information by means of changing the states of networks formed by interconnecting extremely large numbers of simple processing elements that interact with one another by exchanging signals. This interconnection approach to information processing directly simulates the way the human brain processes information and learns. This chapter will introduce one of the core concepts of DM: *machine learning.* We will focus our attention on specific methods such as neural computing and genetic algorithms and will discuss numerous applications and domains in which such systems play an integral part.

As a preface to our focus on machine learning, however, we need to develop a better understanding of the way the human brain actually works. The world of human thought and reasoning is characterized by vagueness, linguistic ambiguity, and fuzzy descriptions.

4.1: FUZZY LOGIC AND LINGUISTIC AMBIGUITY

Fuzzy logic is a relatively recent alternative to the traditional notions of set membership and logic, with their origins in ancient Greek philosophy and applications at the leading edge of AI research (Brule 1985). Fuzzy logic is a method of reasoning that allows for the partial or "fuzzy" description of a rule. Combining this approach to reasoning with the realm of digital processors results in a class of computer applications that can "learn" from their mistakes and can "understand" the vagaries commonly found in human thought.

LINGUISTIC AMBIGUITY

Our language is replete with vague and imprecise concepts. Sometimes a rule is clear-cut, and sometimes it is difficult (if not impossible) to describe things in terms of well-defined distinctions. Take, for example, the phrase "Dan is very tall" or the phrase "It is extremely hot today." Statements such as these are commonplace in our daily interactions and are representative of a reasoning process of measurable complexity. Yet the translation of these statements into ones of "greater precision" often causes them to lose some of their semantic richness and meaning. For example, the statement "The current temperature is 97.65 degrees Fahrenheit" does not explicitly state that it is hot, and the statement "The current temperature is 1.1 standard deviations above the mean temperature for this geographic region at this time of the year" is also fraught with many linguistic difficulties. Would it still be hot today if the current temperature were 1.099 standard deviations above the mean? Do I need to know precisely where I am in the world to determine whether it is hot today?

The point is that our language evolves to allow for the conveyance of meaning through semantic approximation rather than precise content. We are quite comfortable with adjectives of categorization that describe intelligent people, midsize automobiles, tall buildings, and powerful computer systems, among many others. This method of categorization enables our expression of general terms and allows us to interpret these generalizations based on the context in which they are made. Although quite useful to humans, these context-based meanings do not lend themselves to the common rule-based or case-based codification schemes necessary for an expert system knowledge base. Fuzzy logic, however, is quite adept at supporting reasoning about these kinds of situations because it focuses on gradation rather than precise distinction.

The kinds of categorizations we often use to describe something do not have precise boundaries. Rather, the categories often encompass a range of values. For example, the term *highly skilled* encompasses a range of values that is context-specific. If the context is a group of elementary school students playing baseball, and one of the young students tends to hit the ball farther than anyone else, she may be referred to as "highly skilled." If, on the other hand, this same student were to be placed in a major league baseball game, the term highly skilled (as it directly relates to her) would no longer be applicable. The "truth" of these categorizations can be thought of as varying much like a light does with a dimmer switch. A switch completely off indicates 0 percent agreement concerning the categorization. A switch completely on means 100 percent agreement; but the switch allows an infinite number of gradations in between.

If we think of the world in terms of the degree to which something is a member of a category or set, we can see how fuzzy logic could be used to express many problem contexts. A verbal protocol obtained from the operator of a production line might come in the form of "When the line gets near capacity, I begin to slow the feed." Converting this statement into a set of precise rules could prove problematic, if not impossible. With fuzzy logic, however, rules such as these are completely acceptable and quite easy to accommodate.

THE BASICS OF FUZZY LOGIC

Fuzzy logic is based on an approach to logic that dates back to the days of Plato. Its primary distinction from the early conceptualizations of the world by Aristotle and others is that it defines truth to be a value that is contained within the range of values [0.0, 1.0], with 0.0 representing absolute Falseness and 1.0 representing absolute Truth. It is important to note that fuzzy logic does not mean vague answers but, rather, precise answers that vary mathematically within a given range of values. Fuzzy logic can deal with any degree of precision from the input data and can react just as precisely in returning the results.

Rather than carry around a lot of mathematical baggage, however, let's develop our understanding of fuzzy logic using a commonplace example. Consider the phrase "Dan is very tall." From this phrase we can infer that a subset of all people classified as tall exists, and Dan is contained within that subset. Further, we can infer that Dan is considered an extreme value within the subset of tall people because his membership within the subset is further qualified by the adjective *very*. By formally defining the fuzzy subset TALL_PEOPLE, we can answer the question "To what degree is person *x* tall?" We must assign a degree of membership in the fuzzy subset TALL_PEOPLE to every member of the set ALL_PEOPLE. The easiest way of defining the set is by creating a membership function based on a person's height. Figure 4-1 illustrates this membership function and shows the shape of a graph of the derived function.

Using the derived membership function for the fuzzy subset TALL_PEOPLE, we can compute values that represent the degree of tallness for any member of the set ALL_PEOPLE. Table 4-1 contains some tallness values for a sample of people drawn from the set. A "precise"

FIGURE 4-1 Membership Function for Inclusion in Subset TALL_PEOPLE

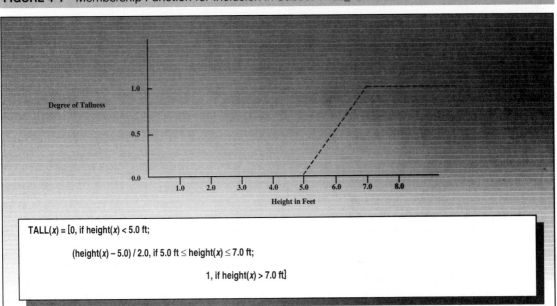

TALL(x) = [0, if height(x) < 5.0 ft;

(height(x) – 5.0) / 2.0, if 5.0 ft ≤ height(x) ≤ 7.0 ft;

1, if height(x) > 7.0 ft]

TABLE 4-1	Sample Values Obtained from Tallness Function	
Person	*Height*	*Degree of Tallness*
Tom Thumb	2′10″	0.000
Mugsy Bogues	5′3″	0.125
Albert Einstein	5′5″	0.208
Thomas Edison	5′10″	0.417
Michael Jordan	6′6″	0.750
Kareem Abdul-Jabbar	7′2″	1.000

mathematical value for degree of tallness is assigned to each person sampled. Using this approach, a rule for determining tallness could be constructed in the form of a "tallness algorithm" that could be contained within a knowledge base for an ES. By developing a network of these algorithms, a complex set of categorizations can be analyzed and a high level of reasoning can be brought to bear on a given problem context. This process is the essence of fuzzy logic reasoning in the development of expert systems and the focus of this chapter: machine learning.

It is important to note, however, that membership functions are rarely as simple as the one used in our example. Often, they involve degrees of membership in multiple subsets based on multiple criteria. For instance, a membership function for the subset TALL_PEOPLE may depend not only on physical height but on chronological age as well ("He's tall for his age"). In fact, it is not uncommon for a particular membership function to contain elements from a wide variety of criteria and populations. The complexity of such functions is significant and requires a deep level of understanding of sophisticated mathematical concepts to be fully appreciated. This level of understanding is best left to the computer scientists who will build these systems for use by the managerial community. Important here, in the realm of management, is the notion that fuzziness can be codified and that the linguistic ambiguities so commonplace in human interaction can be modeled and systematized in an intelligent computer system.

FUZZINESS VERSUS PROBABILITY

Before we move away from the concept of fuzzy logic, one last point needs clarification. A confusion sometimes arises between the concept of fuzziness and that of probability. Both operate over the same continuous numeric range and at first glance have similarities in the interpretation of their values: 0.0 representing False (or nonmembership) and 1.0 representing True (or membership). However, some fundamental differences between fuzziness and probability are significant.

To fully understand these differences, consider, again, our statement "Dan is very tall." Let's assume that by using our membership algorithm, we assign a degree of tallness value to the statement of 0.80. From this, we can render the statement symbolically as follows:

$$m\text{TALL\_PEOPLE}(\text{Dan}) = 0.80$$

where m is the membership function operating on the fuzzy subset of TALL_PEOPLE.

From a probabilistic approach, we might interpret the degree of tallness value to mean "There is an 80 percent chance that Dan is tall." Conversely, the fuzzy logic approach would yield a statement corresponding to "Dan's degree of membership within the set of tall people is 0.80." The semantic difference between these two statements is critical. The first statement supposes that Dan is or is not tall; it is just that we have only an 80 percent chance of knowing which set he is in. In contrast, the fuzzy statement supposes that Dan is "more or less" tall. In other words, probability deals with the likelihood that something has a particular property, whereas fuzzy logic deals with the degree to which a particular property is present in something. In the former, we are guessing about the presence of a property; in the latter, we are assuming the presence of a property and comparing its strength relative to all other members of the set. With probability, we can only determine membership in a set, but with fuzzy logic, we can determine where on the continuum of membership a particular set member resides.

ADVANTAGES AND LIMITATIONS OF FUZZY LOGIC

A truly beneficial aspect of rules is that they allow you to state relationships generally and compactly as associations (Dhar and Stein 1997). On the other hand, they do not require you to be as precise as mathematical models, which is good, because we know that the complexity of a system increases when variables begin to interact in a nonlinear fashion. The acknowledged modern-day "father of fuzzy logic," Lotfi Zadeh, suggested that "as complexity rises, precise statements lose meaning and meaningful statements lose precision." Fuzzy rules offer an attractive trade-off between the need for accuracy, compactness, and scalability as reasoning systems and processes within a particular knowledge domain become more complex. Fuzzy rules generalize the concept of categorization because, by definition, the same object can belong to any set to a certain degree and can belong to multiple sets as necessary. In this sense, fuzzy logic eliminates the problems associated with borderline cases, such as where the value 1.1 causes a rule to fire but the value 1.099 does not. The net result is that fuzzy logic tends to provide greater accuracy than traditional rule-based systems when continuous variables are involved. In this section, we explore the key benefits derived from the use of fuzzy logic and identify several limitations to its use that must be both acknowledged and understood.

Advantages of Fuzzy Systems

Fuzzy logic systems are used in a wide variety of applications and can be found in many facets of business and society. Their use in microprocessor-based appliances and products is pervasive, proving their value beyond doubt. Regardless of the application or context, fuzzy logic offers several generalizable advantages and benefits over traditional rule-based logic.

Modeling of Contradiction   Fuzzy logic allows for the modeling and inclusion of contradiction within a knowledge base. Fuzzy rules can be completely contradictory and yet exist in complete harmony. Compared to traditional logic where opposing instructions would result in an inability on the part of the computer to resolve the contradiction, fuzzy logic imparts a certain degree of tolerance to such ambiguities, thus allowing compromise. For example, by allowing for membership in multiple sets, a 6-foot-tall person might be simultaneously assigned a degree of membership in the set TALL_PEOPLE of 0.80, a degree of membership of 0.45 in the MEDIUM_PEOPLE set, and a value of 0.01 in the SHORT_PEOPLE set. Using fuzzy logic, the designer exercises complete control over the accuracy of a given conclusion or reasoning process by simply increasing or decreasing the number of rules required and the degrees of sensitivity to membership allowed.

Increased System Autonomy   The rules contained within the knowledge base of a fuzzy system can function completely independently of one another. In a traditional rule-based system, if a single rule is faulty, it can result in outcomes ranging from erroneous conclusions to complete inability of the system to resolve. In a fuzzy system, however, one rule could be faulty and the others will "compensate" for the error. Fuzzy systems actually change the common trade-off relationship between system robustness and system sensitivity. Unlike conventional rule-based systems, properly constructed fuzzy systems actually increase in sensitivity as the robustness of the system is increased. Fuzzy rules will continue to "work" even in circumstances where the whole system is completely changed.

Limitations to Fuzzy Systems

Despite its advantages, fuzzy reasoning presents certain limitations to both the knowledge engineer (KE) and the end user. Its application cannot be construed to be universally better than traditional reasoning methods and, as with all forms of problem-solving strategies, it must be carefully assessed in terms of its appropriateness to a given problem context.

Obstacles to System Verification   Fuzzy reasoning can become an obstacle to the verification of a system's stability or reliability. Under situations of high complexity, it may become impossible to know whether the correct rules are firing. Further, the redefinition of membership associated with fine-tuning a fuzzy system has no set guidelines or prescriptions that are easily followed. As a result, designers may find it difficult to determine whether their actions improve the system or result in a move away from a better solution. One response to this limitation is the use of simulation in the verification of a fuzzy system. Results of multiple simulations can be used to analyze small refinements in set memberships and their relative sensitivities to outcomes derived from the system.

Fuzzy Systems Lack Memory   Basic fuzzy reasoning mechanisms cannot learn from their mistakes and possess no memory. As such, fuzzy logic is not yet capable of optimizing the efficiency of a system. Presently, no precise mathematical method allows for the verification of the correctness of a fuzzy system. Furthermore, the high degree of complexity of a given situation that can be modeled using fuzzy reasoning can result in a literal simultaneous firing of rules. This phenomenon is referred to as *fuzzy set saturation,* which means that the fuzzy set gets so full of inferences that consequent fuzzy sets are overloaded. The end result is that the entire system loses the information provided by the fuzzy rules and the entire fuzzy region begins to "balance itself" around its mean value. Systems that can learn from their mistakes and can "learn to forget" information that is no longer applicable to the problem context are being developed to solve these problems of constant retention and saturation. Such systems are the focus of our next topic in this chapter: neural networks.

4.2: ARTIFICIAL NEURAL NETWORKS

Artificial neural networks (ANNs) were first proposed in the early 1940s at the University of Chicago as an attempt to simulate the human brain's cognitive learning processes. Their ability to model complex, yet poorly understood, problems for which sufficient data can be collected make ANNs particularly applicable in numerous domains such as business and finance. Their capacity to learn can result in solutions that are superior to those achieved using traditional statistical or mathematical methods.

ANNs[1] are simple, computer-based programs whose primary function is to construct models of a problem space based upon trial and error. Conceptually, the process is easily described: A piece of data is presented to a neural net. The ANN "guesses" an output and then compares its prediction with the actual, or correct, value presented as a form of feedback. If the guess is

---

[1]The terms *artificial neural network, neural network, network,* and *net* will be used interchangeably throughout this chapter.

correct, then the network performs no further action. If, however, the prediction is incorrect, then the network analyzes itself in an effort to figure out which internal parameters to adjust to improve the quality of the prediction. Once these adjustments are made, the net is presented with another piece of data and the process is repeated. Over time, the ANN begins to converge on a fairly accurate model of the process.

FUNDAMENTALS OF NEURAL COMPUTING

To better understand how the ANN "learns" from experience, we must begin with an understanding of the biological principles that underlie both human neural processes and artificial neural computing.

The Human Brain

The basic processing element in the human nervous system is the neuron. Our nervous system is made up of a network of interconnected nerve cells that receive information from various sensors—our eyes, ears, skin, and nose—that are positioned at various places along the network. Figure 4-2 provides a simple representation of a single human neuron and its component parts.

As shown in the figure, the human neuron is composed of a nucleus and connectors called dendrites that are responsible for providing input signals to the neuron and axons, which, in turn, carry away the output of the neuron to other parts of the network. The transmission of signals from one neuron to another occurs at the neural synapse via a complex chemical process in which specific substances, called neurotransmitters, are released from one side of the synaptic junction. The effect is to raise or lower the electrical potential inside the body of the neuron. If the electrical potential within a specific neuron reaches a certain threshold, a pulse is sent down the axon, and the neuron is said to have "fired." These bursts of electricity that occur when a neuron fires transmit information along the network to other neurons. Conceptually speaking, the larger the burst of electricity at the synapse, the more important the information contained within.

Information received at a neuron can have one of two effects: It can either excite the cell or it can inhibit it. If the neuron is excited, it will immediately fire and pass its information along the network to the other neurons. If the neuron is inhibited, however, it will not fire, in effect suppressing the flow of that information along the network. Through this process, each neuron processes the incoming raw input and then determines whether it is important enough to pass along.

The synaptic connections that exist among the neurons can be strengthened or weakened as a result of the passing of time or the gaining of experience. Strengthening of the connection

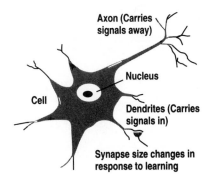

Axon (Carries signals away)

Nucleus

Cell

Dendrites (Carries signals in)

Synapse size changes in response to learning

FIGURE 4-2 Typical Human Neuron Cell

results in learning, whereas the lack of use of a connection over time results in forgetting. This dynamic process results in the establishment of new responses to new stimuli, modifications to existing stimuli, and the complete removal of unused responses.

Putting a Brain in a Box

Following a biological metaphor, the ANN involves an interconnected system of nodes called neurodes that are associated with one or more weighted connections that are equivalent to human neural synapses inside the memory of a digital computer. The ANN is constructed of multiple layers with the connections running between the layers. Figure 4-3 shows a simple ANN.

As shown in the figure, the ANN is composed of three basic layers. The layer that receives the data is referred to as the input layer, and the layer that relays the final results of the net is called the output layer. The internal layer, also referred to as the hidden layer, is where the processing and transformation of the input signal takes place and where the type of output signal is determined. The hierarchical network dynamics among the neurodes are determined by a mathematical combination of the weight of each input to the neurode and the threshold parameters associated with that neurode. Each pass of the net causes adjustments to these weights in response to the feedback received by the net regarding the accuracy of its last output. Over time, these weight adjustments increase the accuracy in the transformation of the input data. Learning, in a neural network, results from this adjustment of weights.

Inside the Neurode

Figure 4-4 illustrates the component parts of a typical neurode. The basic structure consists of a set of weighted input connections, a bias input, a state function, a nonlinear transfer function, and an output connection. We will explore each of these primary components and their functions in greater detail.

FIGURE 4-3 A Typical Artificial Neural Network Configuration

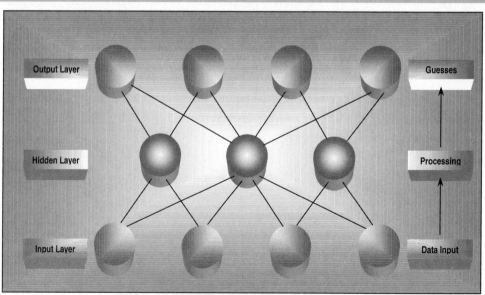

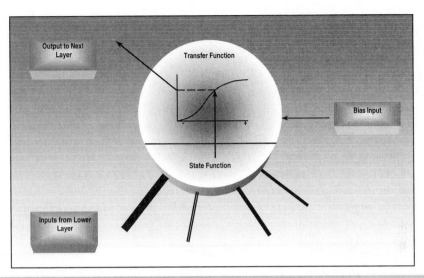

FIGURE 4-4 Typical Neurode Component Structure

Weighted Inputs   As shown in the figure, each of the inputs to a neurode is a connection from a lower layer of the network. The neurode can, and usually does, have multiple inputs, each with its own associated weight or importance. In the figure, we depict the relative weights of each of the inputs by varying the thickness or style of the line representing that input. The thickness of the line is proportional to its weight or importance. A hollow line indicates a negative weight. The weight of an input determines the importance of its contribution to the output of the neurode. Because all of the weights are added together inside the neurode, the more important inputs will be those with larger weights, and the lesser contributors will be those with the smaller weights.

The Bias Input   The bias input is not normally connected to the network and is assumed to have an input value of 1.0 for the state function. Its purpose is to allow for the individual adjustment of the firing threshold of the neurode to facilitate the final adjustment of the ANN following the learning process. Under normal circumstances, the bias input is not used and its value to the state function remains a constant throughout the network. If, however, the need for adjustment of a specific neurode becomes necessary, the bias input for that neurode can be set within a range of 21.0 to 1.0 to allow for the appropriate "bias" in the transfer function.

The State Function   The state function, although conceivably a mathematical algorithm of any form or complexity, is typically a simple summation function. Its purpose is to consolidate the weights of the various inputs to the neurode into a single value that can be passed to the transfer function for processing. The value obtained by the state function determines the degree of impact the combined inputs will have on the transfer function and, thus, on the final output of the neurode. Figure 4-5 illustrates this process.

The Transfer Function   As implied by its name, the primary purpose of the transfer function is to serve as the vehicle by which the summed information is passed on as output. It performs this function, however, in a rather unique manner. Refer to Figure 4-5 and note that the value of the output (and ultimately the threshold at which the neurode will fire) is not linear with respect to

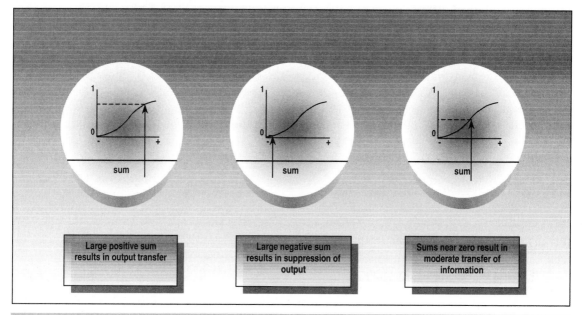

FIGURE 4-5   Relationship Between State Function Value and Transfer Function Value

the summed inputs. The transfer function acts metaphorically like a dimmer switch for turning the neurode on and off.

Note that in the figure we depict the transfer function in the shape of the typical logistic function. The logistic function is characterized by its "lazy S-shaped" form. Transfer functions can be either continuous (as shown in the figure) or discrete (such as a series of "on" or "off" ranges of values) and can take any appropriate mathematical form. Although the logistic function is the most commonly used, another popular transfer function is the radial basis function, which takes on a more bell-shaped form. The important issue, here, is that the transfer function must contribute a sense of nonlinearity between the summed inputs and the resultant output.

TRAINING THE ANN

The process of training a neural net to associate certain input patterns with correct output responses involves the use of repetitive examples and feedback, much like the training of a human being. The operation begins by setting all of the connection weights in the net to small random values, which allows the net to begin with no specific "memory" or imprint. Next, the net is presented with a single data example drawn from a training set with known outputs. The net processes this example and then provides a "guess" at the answer based on the example provided.

As you can probably imagine, the first guess provided by the net is usually incorrect because the weights for each of the input connections are not yet set correctly. However, just as humans can learn from their mistakes, so can ANNs. Once the example data are processed, the ANN compares the results of its calculations with the feedback received regarding the desired, correct output and records that comparison in a training record. If the calculation performed by the net compares favorably with the feedback, then no action is necessary. If, however, the guess is deemed incorrect when compared to the feedback, the net begins an iterative process of making small adjustments to the input weights of certain neurodes in an attempt to bring its own output more in line with the feedback. Figure 4-6 depicts this iterative adjustment process.

The actual process by which the net determines an appropriate adjustment to each input weight is a complex mathematical procedure. Essentially, however, it can be thought of as a form of sensitivity analysis in which the size of the error is determined and an adjustment is made to see the effect (and in what direction) of the change on the size of the error. This process continues for each hidden layer in the network until all neurodes have been subjected to the sensitivity analysis and the net is ready for another trial.

SENDING THE NET TO SCHOOL: ANN LEARNING PARADIGMS

The actual procedure used by a neural network to find the appropriate weight settings is referred to as its learning paradigm. Again, similar to the ways in which humans can acquire knowledge and learn, learning paradigms for ANNs can be loosely classified into those that are largely unsupervised and those that are supervised.

Unsupervised Learning Paradigms

The wide variety of specific unsupervised learning paradigms developed in response to particular problem context needs all possess the same basic characteristics and approaches. Therefore, we will limit our discussion to the general characteristics of all unsupervised learning methods.

The unsupervised nature of an unsupervised learning paradigm simply means that the ANN receives the input data and examples but no feedback in the form of desired results. To affect its learning process, an unsupervised net begins by developing clusters of the training records it generates based upon similarities it detects in the data examples. The net continues to process data examples, creates a training record, and then reclusters the records until a set of definable patterns begins to emerge. With each successive pass, the net finds a pattern more

FIGURE 4-6 Typical Training Sequence for Neural Networks

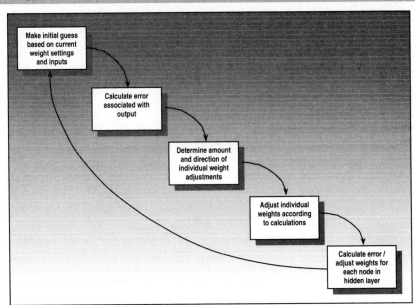

closely matched with the input data than any of the others. Over time, the net refines this pattern recognition until the difference between the input and the output patterns for the training set reach a close approximation of each other.

One way to envision the unsupervised learning process is to imagine a scenario in which you present a group of strangers with a stack of randomly ordered photographs of different situations and ask each of them to classify the photos in some way. Without any specific instructions regarding the method of classification, each stranger will probably choose an approach that is unique, based upon some common characteristic contained within each picture. One stranger might set up a classification based upon the type of scene (indoor, outdoor, day, night, landscape, portrait, etc.). Another may classify the pictures according to the situation depicted (people interacting, pictures of machines, pictures of natural settings, etc.). Yet another may choose to classify the pictures according to their specific photographic characteristics (black-and-white, color, glossy, matte, etc.). Although each grouping would be logical from a given perspective, the relationships among the photos would be different from one grouping to the next. By comparing the relationships within each group, as well as the relationships across groups, we might begin to discover new relationships that were not discernable in any of the previous clusters.

The unsupervised learning paradigm for an ANN works in much the same manner as the situation just described. The net is unsupervised with respect to what it is supposed to discover or conclude. As such, it finds relationships among the input data examples and uses those relationships to create accurate output. Using this approach, a neural net can begin to "specialize" its learning with respect to a specific dimension of the data.

Supervised Learning Paradigms

In contrast to the unsupervised approach, the most common supervised learning paradigm is called back propagation. With back propagation, the net receives an input example, generates a guess, and compares that guess to feedback containing the desired results. In this sense, the ANN is being "supervised" by the feedback, which shows the net where it made mistakes and how the answer should look. The name of this technique is based on the fact that the algorithm used to adjust the neurode weights propagates some measure of the calculated error between the guess and the feedback back through the various layers of the network in the direction of the input layer.

The most common form of the back propagation algorithm uses a sum-of-squared-errors approach to generate an aggregate measure of the difference error. Following this calculation, a progressive adjusting of the weights along the network is conducted to bring the network "closer" to the correct response. This adjustment process is based on a combination of the calculated error measure and an adjustment increment established by the net trainer. This adjustment increment, or learning rate, is a specification of how much adjustment should occur in each training session. If too large a learning rate is specified, then the net may constantly "overshoot" its optimized weights and never reach the desired level of accuracy. If, conversely, the learning rate is specified in too small an increment, the net may take a long time to reach the desired level of accuracy, if at all.

As with most of the inner workings of an ANN, the mathematics are complex and require a high level of understanding to successfully construct a working ANN. For those with a flair for the calculus, an appendix to this chapter describes the mathematical foundations of the back propagation algorithm. For others, understanding exactly how the algorithm works is not as important as understanding how, and under what conditions, the technology should be applied.

Therefore, we turn our attention to some of the advantages and disadvantages that must be acknowledged in the application of neural computing technologies.

BENEFITS AND LIMITATIONS ASSOCIATED WITH NEURAL COMPUTING

One of the most obvious benefits of neural computing is the ability to obtain inferential insights not readily available through the use of other knowledge-based techniques and technologies. In addition to this capability, however, ANNs provide several other advantages over more traditional problem-solving systems. Table 4-2 lists several of those benefits.

A key advantage to ANNs is the elimination of the need for direct input from domain experts. In some cases, soliciting knowledge from a domain expert may be too costly in terms of economic resources or the time involved. In other cases, an expert simply may not exist. Our forays into diverse knowledge domains framed within the physical, biological, and social sciences can often venture beyond the bounds of domain experts. In these cases, ANNs provide a valuable vehicle for the discovery of new relationships and knowledge that is beyond the capabilities of other problem-solving and support technologies.

Another unique advantage of ANNs is their inherent ability to deal with noisy or incomplete datasets. Most often, the availability of clean, high-quality datasets is limited, if not nonexistent, and the problem solver is faced with analyzing data that are poorly distributed and inconsistent. The structural nature of ANNs makes them better suited to deal with such data than more traditional statistical or AI methods. As each of the neurodes looks at only a small portion of the problem and the neurodes and layers are positioned to look at each of these small elements from different angles, ANNs can often reconstruct missing or corrupt data by inferring what the data "should" look like and then using that inference as an input to its current guess. Such inferences can be modified as necessary, along with the weights for each input, as the network seeks to reduce the error associated with previous training sessions.

Along these same lines, the ability of an ANN to look at the small parts of a large and complex problem also makes it uniquely capable of scaling up as necessary to accommodate problems of increased complexity. Intuitively, more complicated problems can be solved by adding more hidden layers to the network, thus increasing the ability of the network to use the output of neurodes in lower layers and allowing for a greater number of neurodes to interact. In this way, many complicated, highly nonlinear relationships and processes can be modeled effectively.

We must be prepared, however, to acknowledge that these advantages and benefits associated with neural computing do not come without a price. Table 4-3 lists several of the

---

TABLE 4-2   Benefits Derived from Neural Computing

- Avoids explicit programming and detailed IF-THEN rule base.
- Reduces need for expensive or limited availability experts.
- ANNs are inherently adaptable and do not require update when inputs change.
- Eliminates need for redefined knowledge base.
- ANNs are dynamic and continue to improve with use.
- Able to process erroneous, inconsistent, or even incomplete data.
- Allows for generalization from specific information context.
- Facilitates the creation of abstractions from diverse datasets.
- Allows for the inclusion of "common sense" into the problem-solving domain.

TABLE 4-3 Limitations to Neural Computing Techniques

- ANNs cannot "explain" their inferences.
- The "black box" nature of ANNs makes accountability and reliability issues difficult.
- The repetitive training process is often extremely time consuming.
- Highly skilled machine learning analysts and designers are still a scarce resource.
- Neural computing technologies generally push the limits of existing hardware.
- ANNs require that a certain amount of faith be imparted to the final output.

limitations and drawbacks associated with application of neural computing techniques to a problem context.

ANNs are often successfully applied in finding solutions to complex problems involving pattern recognition and nonlinear relationships because of their unique ability to find subtle relationships within datasets. Unfortunately, however, once such subtleties are revealed, the ANN has no mechanism for explaining or justifying them. The fact that an ANN can effectively differentiate items based on inherent, yet latent, characteristics within the dataset does not mean that such differentiation is based on the desired set of discriminating characteristics. In fact, it is possible for the ANN to develop an understanding and ability to discriminate between patterns contained within the noise in the data rather than in the data themselves.

One famous example of this potential comes from the military. A neural net was developed to distinguish between pictures containing specific military armaments and those without such elements. In the early training sessions, the net was presented with two sets of photographs: one containing combat tanks and one without any tanks in the pictures. Each of these pictures was converted to machine-readable format and presented to the net for training. Within a relatively short number of passes, the net displayed an excitingly high degree of discrimination between the pictures containing combat tanks and those without. To ensure the success of the training, a new set of photographs was digitized and presented to the net for analysis. The excitement from the training session soon turned to disappointment when the net failed to correctly discriminate the desired elements. An inspection of the training set quickly revealed the problem: The photographs containing tanks were all taken on sunny days, whereas the photos without the tanks were taken on generally overcast days. The net had learned to discriminate between sunny and overcast days rather than to identify images of combat tanks.

The evolution of neural computing and machine learning techniques is rapidly accelerating, with new approaches emerging each day that are intended as improvements over the current methods. One such improvement over "conventional" neural computing techniques is the subject of our next discussion.

4.3: GENETIC ALGORITHMS AND GENETICALLY EVOLVED NETWORKS

You may recall from one of your systems analysis courses the concept of bounded rationality. Offered by Simon (1960), the concept suggests that human beings, although desiring the optimal solution, tend to "satisfice" and accept a solution of lesser quality than optimum. Even though Simon's explanation suggests that optimization is a laudable, yet unattainable, cognitive goal, we nonetheless continue our quest for the best possible solution to our daily problems. We "know" an optimal, very best solution to our problem exists, if we could only find it.

THE CONCEPT OF OPTIMIZATION

The goal of any problem solver is to arrive at a solution that effectively solves the problem within the constraints (perceived or real) imposed on the problem context. This goal suggests that for a given problem context and set of constraints, there exists an optimal solution based on some predetermined measure of goodness. Although Simon's position on optimizing versus satisficing holds true from a human cognition perspective, in other situations, optimization is not only desirable, but attainable as well. The field of management science successfully developed mathematical techniques intended to derive optimal solutions under a given set of often complex constraints. Such techniques make the best of an imperfect situation by taking the fullest advantage of the limited resources available to the problem. The advent of the computer, combined with these mathematical optimization models, further extends our ability to find the best solution available. Our problem is that as we become more proficient and capable of solving increasingly complex problems, we also develop an appetite for achieving optimal solutions to even more complex problems and constrained contexts. This cycle of complexity stimulates the need for innovative methods of deriving such optimal solutions.

Consider the classic traveling salesperson problem. Recall that one of the problems was to determine the number of unique routes without visiting any city along the route more than once. We can easily determine that the need to visit 10 cities yields a total of 181,440 unique routes.[2] Assuming we have a relatively powerful computer that can evaluate 1 million (10^6) unique routes per second, we could perform an exhaustive search of the problem space in approximately 0.18 seconds—not much time considering the potential return in the form of efficient performance and cost savings. If, however, our zeal for this newfound optimization power suggests that we might want to increase the size of the problem, our limitations for an exhaustive search will soon be revealed. By increasing the number of cities to 25, we also increase the number of unique routes to 3.10×10^{23} possibilities. No problem, though. Our computer will figure out the optimal route based on the constraints we have placed on the solution. Unfortunately, however, our computer, operating at a speed of 1 million evaluations per second, will require just a bit longer to process the 25-city problem. At that rate, it will take the computer somewhere around 10 billion years to perform an exhaustive search and determine the optimal solution.[3] It would appear that conventional approaches to optimization do have their limits.

Recall further from the traveling salesperson problem that a heuristic approach to the solution results in a pretty good outcome with a minimum of effort. Such techniques find their way into the realm of machine learning, and one such method, the genetic algorithm, is gaining widespread acceptance and application.

INTRODUCTION TO GENETIC ALGORITHMS

Similar to the conceptual foundations of ANNs, genetic algorithms (GAs) are based in biological theory. In contrast to the neuroscience roots of ANNs, however, GAs find their roots in Darwin's evolutionary theories of natural selection and adaptation.

---

[2]Using the formula 0.5(number of cities–1)!
[3]Assuming 365.25 days per year: 3.10×10^{23} unique routes would require approximately 8.62×10^{13} hours to solve. This approximates to 9,830,411,719 years.

The theory of natural selection offers some compelling arguments that individuals with certain characteristics are better able to survive and pass on those characteristics to their off-spring. A genetic algorithm is an elegantly simple, yet extremely powerful, type of optimization technique based on the ideas of genetics and natural selection. Originally developed by John Holland at MIT during the 1940s, a GA employs a set of adaptive processes that mimic the concept of "survival of the fittest" by regenerating recombinants of the algorithm in response to a calculated difference between the network's guess and the desired solution state. The power of a GA results from the mating of population members and their production of offspring that have a significant chance of retaining the desirable characteristics of their parents, perhaps even combining the best characteristics of both parents. In this manner, the overall fitness of the population can potentially increase from generation to generation as we discover better solutions to our problem. The primary advantage of a GA over conventional, unsupervised neural networks is its ability to overcome the combinatorial limitations associated with the development of complex ANNs with intricate combinations of performance criteria.

The Concept of Natural Selection

To better understand the fundamentals of GAs, we must first understand the theoretical foundation upon which they are built. The primary problem faced by all organisms found in nature is that of survival. Those that come up with successful solutions survive, and those that fail to solve the problem become extinct. The Darwinian approach to the evolution of species suggests that surviving organisms are able to adapt themselves to the conditions within the environment that best support them and insulate themselves from harmful environmental factors. This adaptation to the environment serves as the basis for the development and use of genetic algorithms.

Basic Components of GAs

In keeping with its root biological metaphor, the GA's smallest unit is called a gene. The gene represents the smallest unit of information in the problem domain and can be thought of as the basic building block for a possible solution. If the problem context were, for example, the creation of a well-balanced investment portfolio, a gene might represent the number of shares of a particular security to purchase. If the problem context focused on the traveling salesperson problem, the gene might represent one of the cities that must be visited on a route. Continuing with the metaphor, a series of genes that represents the components of one possible solution to the problem is referred to as a chromosome. Figure 4-7 illustrates examples of chromosome strings that might be found in a typical GA.

The chromosome is represented in computer memory as a bit string of binary digits that can be "decoded" by the GA to determine how good a particular chromosome's gene pool solution is for the given problem. The decoding process simply informs the GA what the various genes within the chromosome represent. For the traveling salesperson problem, for example, the decoder would know how to convert the genes into cities along the route. This representation of the solution as a bit string is probably the only significant limitation with regard to the application of a GA to a problem context. For the GA to be effective in reaching a solution to the problem, the solution must be able to be represented as a digital bit string. Figure 4-8 outlines the basic processes associated with the operation of a GA.

Initialization The first step in the creation of a GA is the development of an initial population of chromosomes that are possible solutions to the problem under investigation. This population of

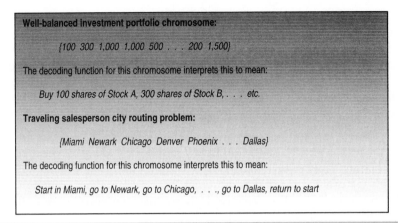

Well-balanced investment portfolio chromosome:

$\{100 \ 300 \ 1,000 \ 1,000 \ 500 \ . \ . \ . \ 200 \ 1,500\}$

The decoding function for this chromosome interprets this to mean:

Buy 100 shares of Stock A, 300 shares of Stock B, . . . etc.

Traveling salesperson city routing problem:

$\{Miami \ Newark \ Chicago \ Denver \ Phoenix \ . \ . \ . \ Dallas\}$

The decoding function for this chromosome interprets this to mean:

Start in Miami, go to Newark, go to Chicago, . . ., go to Dallas, return to start

FIGURE 4-7   Examples of Genetic Algorithm Chromosome Strings

initial genetic structures should be constructed in such a way that it represents solutions randomly distributed throughout the solution space.

Evaluation   In the evaluation stage, each chromosome is decoded by the decoder function and evaluated using a fitness function to determine which genetic structures are good and which are not so good. The fitness function is analogous to an objective function commonly found in optimization techniques such as linear programming. The function represents some constraint or requirement to minimize or maximize the use of some resource. In the traveling salesperson example, typical fitness functions might include requirements to minimize time en route, minimize fuel or travel expense, and maximize individual city contact time.

FIGURE 4-8   Basic Process Flow of Genetic Algorithm Problem Solving

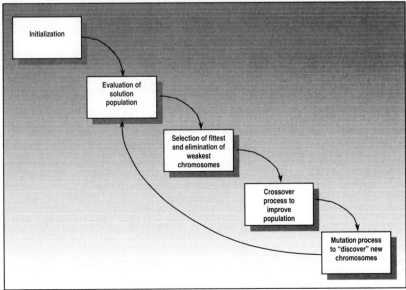

Figure 4-9 illustrates the decoding process using a binary chromosome that represents the cities along a route, their distances from a home base, and the desired contact time in each. In terms of the problem domain, the decoder function and the fitness function are the only two GA components that are specific to the problem context. As such, the GA can be altered with respect to how it ranks solutions simply by changing the nature of the fitness functions. Additionally, the same GA can be used to solve a wide variety of problems simply by changing the decoder function and the fitness functions to those relevant to the new problem domain.

Selection   Once the initial pool of chromosomes is evaluated by the fitness function, the GA experiments with new solutions by iteratively refining the initial solutions so that those with the best fit are more likely to be ranked higher as solutions. In essence, the GA begins to "experiment" with the existing set of chromosomes by combining and refining the genes contained within each chromosome. The objective is to produce new chromosomes that form a new generation of possible solutions to evaluate.

In the first step, selection, the GA chooses the fittest species to remain and reproduce within the population of solution chromosomes. Poorer, less fit solutions are eliminated. The most common method for this evolution is called fitness proportional selection. In its simplest form, this method determines the relative fitness of each chromosome to all the other chromosomes in the current generation. If chromosome A is determined to be twice as fit as chromosome B, then chromosome A is given twice the chance of survival as chromosome B. The fittest

FIGURE 4-9   Example of Chromosome Encoding and Decoding

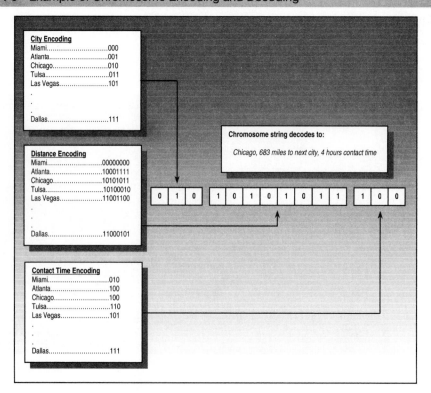

evolve, and the weaker species "die off." The selection process weeds out the poorer solutions and passes the remaining chromosomes on to the crossover process.

Crossover   Continuing the refinement process, the crossover phase involves the exchange of gene information between two selected chromosomes. Figure 4-10 illustrates this activity in which a portion of one chromosome crosses over into another chromosome, and vice versa.

The crossover operation allows the GA to create new chromosomes that share positive characteristics while simultaneously reducing the prevalence of negative characteristics in an otherwise reasonably fit solution. This process is analogous to the concept of "strengthening the breed" in the field of biogenetics.

One important limitation in the crossover phase, however, is that it can only rearrange gene information that already exists within the population of chromosomes. For example, in our traveling salesperson problem, if we fail to include a city or a specific characteristic in the original population, then that value will never become a part of any solution set and, thus, will never be swapped into a better solution chromosome. Just as in nature, however, GAs demonstrate a mechanism for spontaneous evolution of new genetic code.

Mutation   The final step in the refinement process is mutation. The mutation phase randomly changes the value of a gene from its current setting to a completely different one. Figure 4-11 shows the mutation of a chromosome.

Most mutations formed by this process are, as is often the case in nature, less fit rather than more so. Occasionally, however, a highly superior and beneficial mutation will occur. Mutation provides the GA with the opportunity to create chromosomes and information genes that can explore previously uncharted areas of the solution space, thus increasing the chances for the discovery of an optimal solution. In conformance with natural laws, however, mutation is normally set to a low frequency of occurrence and is primarily used to ensure that the probability of searching any point within the solution is never zero.

BENEFITS AND LIMITATIONS ASSOCIATED WITH GAs

Despite the power of GAs, some precautions must be taken when setting up or coding a GA problem. Several parameters significantly affect the speed with which an optimal solution is discovered.

FIGURE 4-10   Chromosome Crossover Process

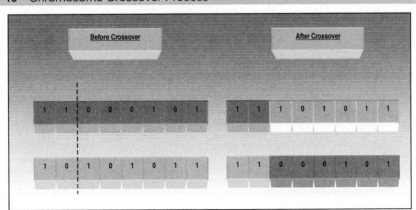

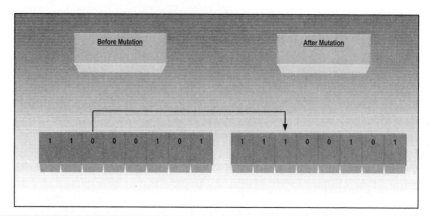

FIGURE 4-11 Chromosome Mutation Process

One of the most important parameters is population size. The ideal number of initial solution chromosomes is based on a trade-off between the time to carry out the processes and the degree of diversity in the solution population. Wayner (1991) provided evidence that, for most problems, a population size of 10 appears to be optimal. Fewer than 10 chromosomes causes excessive failures to reach a solution; greater than 10 increases the process time with no measurable advantage.

One of the advantages noted in using GAs to solve complex problems also can be attributed to population size. GAs tend to zero in on a solution much faster than a neural network and generally are highly predictable in their process time. As the GA is always following the same steps, the total process time is based upon the number of chromosomes in the initial solution population and the number of generations that is chosen to run. A reasonably accurate prediction of time to solution can be derived by multiplying the time necessary to evaluate a single chromosome by the number of chromosomes, and then multiplying that result by the number of generations.

Other parameters that may directly affect the efficiency of the GA include the processes of crossover and mutation. Mutation should be used judiciously to ensure that duplication of solution space members can never occur. Crossover must be set such that an appropriate number of new recombinants can be evaluated without wasting the resources allocated to the GA. If no crossover is conducted, then no new structures will ever become available for evaluation. If all chromosomes in the population are subjected to crossbreeding, then good genes will begin to disappear along with the bad ones. Heuristically speaking, it is recommended that 90 percent of the chromosome population be subjected to crossover with mutation occurring less than 5 percent of the total evaluation time.

The greatest advantage that GAs offer for solving complex problems lies in their ability to "stretch" themselves across a vast solution space in search of the optimal solution. Further, because all initial populations are composed of possible solutions, GAs generally come up with a proposed optimal solution based on the initial population. In other words, with the application of a GA to an optimization problem, you are usually guaranteed to find at least some reasonable solution. In many cases, the proposed solution will be superior to any that were used to seed the initial chromosome population.

Recall from our discussion of Simon and the concept of satisficing that humans are willing to settle for a suboptimal solution as long as it is a good one and meets their criteria for successful outcome. The processes of nature and the evolutionary processes of living organisms also tend to conform more to Simon's theories than to those of optimization. It is unimaginable that any population of human species will ever yield a single member that possesses the vision of a Thomas Edison, the charisma and empathy of a Princess Diana, the intellect of a Carl Sagan, and the athletic prowess of a Michael Jordan. We accept the fact that the evolution of our species will be suboptimal, and we must also accept the fact that the solutions we derive will also be suboptimal. The important issue is that the evolution of species appears to be constantly improving and is, for the most part, responsible for improvements in quality of life within the species. Likewise, the generation of a suboptimal solution that shows improvement over prior solutions is also beneficial to the advancement of our understanding of complex problems and to our abilities to deal with them. In this regard, GAs play an important part in the decision challenges facing tomorrow's manager.

Another significant benefit associated with the application of GAs is that they can be used to solve problems that we have no clue how to solve. If we can describe the components of a reasonably good solution and provide a fitness function that is usable by the GA, we can derive one or more solutions that would otherwise be unattainable. This ability to "invent" solutions makes GAs more attractive than conventional expert system applications, where a great deal of explicit knowledge about the domain must exist. In other words, GAs do not need to know how to solve a problem but simply need to recognize a good solution when one presents itself.

One final advantage associated with GAs is that their power does not result from a complex algorithmic perspective, but rather from a relatively simple and widely understood set of concepts. This basis increases the potential for widespread acceptance of a GA approach across an organization composed of individuals without a deep technical background. Almost everyone took at least one class in biology, and the concept of survival of the fittest is familiar in almost every knowledge domain. The familiarity with the underlying concepts of genetic algorithms makes their acceptance and credibility relatively easy to establish over other machine learning and AI-based techniques.

4.4: APPLICATIONS OF MACHINES THAT LEARN

MACHINE LEARNING APPLICATION DOMAINS

Table 4-4 contains a brief listing of the types of problem contexts in which machine learning systems such as neural networks and genetic algorithms have been successfully applied. Although it is not intended to be comprehensive, the list's diversity illustrates the wide variety of problems and domains in which AI-based systems can be useful.

A number of developmental projects involving ANN technology have been reported by the media. For example, Nippon Steel Corporation built a blast furnace operation control support system that makes use of ANNs. The neural network employed in this system comes equipped with functions that enable it to learn the relationship between sensor data and the eight kinds of temperature distribution patterns known from experience to pertain to the overall operation of blast furnaces and to instantaneously recognize and output that pattern that most closely approximates sensor data input into the system. The neural network learns quickly and achieves a better than 90 percent pattern recognition ratio following learning. Because this system performed extremely well during operational testing, Nippon Steel plans to introduce it

TABLE 4-4   Typical Applications of Machine Learning Systems

- Predict staffing requirements at different times of the year and for different conditions.
  Brooklyn Union Gas Corp. predicts in advance the number of crew members that will be needed for service calls based on the time of year, predicted temperature, and day of the week.
- Predict which job a job applicant is best suited for.
- Predict which customers will pay their bills.
- Spot odd trading patterns.
  This is how Ivan Boesky, the rogue trader, was caught.
- Predict the properties of chemical mixtures.
- Diagnose diseases.
  A neural net has been developed that outdid an expert system in diagnosing smell disorders.
- Predict the stock market, futures markets, and the like.
- Flag faulty parts on an assembly line.
- Regulate industrial processes using inputs from sensors at different points in the process.
- Classify medical ailments (such as hearing losses), living things, and cells (as cancerous/noncancerous).
- Predict pollution based on the composition of trash coming into an incinerator.
- Predict sales and/or costs.
- Predict a company's corporate bond rating.
- Appraise real estate.
- Predict the outcome of sports events (such as horse racing).
- Predict solar flare activity.
- Predict the length of survival for medical patients with certain ailments.
- Recognize welds that are most likely to fail under stress in nuclear containments.
- Test beer.
  Anheuser-Busch identifies the organic contents of its competitors' beer vapors with 96 percent accuracy.
- Predict which prison inmates could benefit from less expensive alternative programs.

into other aspects of its operations in addition to blast furnace control, including the diagnosis of malfunctions and other control processes.

A second example is the experimental work started by Daiwa Securities Company and NEC Corporation, which applies neural network technology to the learning and recognition of stock price chart patterns for use in stock price forecasting. NEC previously developed neural network simulation software for use on its EWS 4800 series of workstations, and, by limiting stock price chart pattern learning to a few dozen major stocks, improved the accuracy of this software's forecasting capabilities. Based on these results, the Daiwa Computer Services Company (DCS), an information-processing subsidiary of the Daiwa Securities Group, transferred the NEC system to its supercomputer and taught it to recognize the stock price chart patterns for 1,134 companies listed on the Tokyo Stock Exchange. Since then, DCS has put this system to good use for stock price forecasting.

Yet another recent example is the project at Mitsubishi Electric, which combines neural network technology with optical technology to achieve the world's first basic optical neuro-computer system capable of recognizing the 26 letters of the alphabet. The system comprises a set of light-emitting diodes (LED) that output letter patterns as optical signals, optical fibers, liquid crystal displays (LCD) that display letter patterns, and light-receiving devices that read these letters. This system is capable of 100-percent letter recognition, even when slightly mis-shapen handwritten letters are input.

A fourth example is a development project for a facilities diagnosis system that employs a neural network system at Nippon Oil Company in cooperation with CSK Research Institute. This project is attracting considerable attention because, for the first time, research is examining the application of neural network systems to facilities diagnosis. Initially, the project will be aimed at developing a diagnosis system based on vibration analysis for pump facilities. Nippon Oil operates 1,500 pumps at its Negishi Oil Refinery in Yokohama, Kanagawa Prefecture alone, and must retain large numbers of experienced personnel to maintain these pumps. The company decided to apply neural network technology to pump facilities diagnosis operations in order to reduce the amount of labor required.

Bond rating is another successful ANN application domain. Bond rating refers to the process by which a particular bond is assigned a label that categorizes the ability of the bond's issuer to repay the coupon and par value of that bond. For example, the Standard and Poor's organization might assign a rating varying from AAA (very high probability of payment) to BBB (possibility of default in times of economic adversity) for investment-grade bonds. The problem is that no hard-and-fast rule governs the determination of these ratings. Rating agencies must consider a vast spectrum of factors before assigning a rating to an issuer. Some of these factors, such as sales, assets, liabilities, and the like, might be well defined. Others, such as willingness to repay, are quite nebulous. Thus, a precise problem definition is not possible.

Still other areas where machine learning systems are regularly applied are credit scoring and target marketing. Credit scoring is used to screen an applicant for credit cards based on known facts about the person applying. These facts usually include such things as salary, number of checking accounts, and previous credit history. Large banks and other lenders lose millions each year from bad debts. Even a small increase in the ability to predict accurately which accounts will go unpaid can result in hundreds of thousands of dollars saved each year for large lenders. To address this problem, major banks and finance companies actively pursue new technologies and systems that can aid in credit prediction.

Machine learning applications also take up a long-standing problem in advertising. For years, advertising agencies and other companies tried to identify and sell to target, or specific, markets. For example, a company selling life insurance might send out an advertisement enclosed in a monthly credit card bill. The company would prefer to send out a small percentage of these advertisements to consumers and keep information on what type of person responds. Once the company obtains data on who responded, it can then build a predictive model to analyze potentially good customers. Thus, a life insurance company may be able to save money by only sending out advertisements to a select 1 million credit card holders who are more likely to buy life insurance, rather than to all credit card holders. Successful target marketing can significantly reduce marketing expenses.

The statistical-based hybrid neural network at Chase Manhattan Bank, discussed in the Minicase at the beginning of this chapter, is one of the largest and most successful AI applications in the United States. It addresses a critical success factor in the bank's strategic plan: reducing losses on loans made to public and private corporations. Most of Chase's transactions with corporations involve an assessment of a corporation's creditworthiness. Chase loans $300 million annually and can benefit greatly from tools that improve loan assessment. This assessment allows Chase to mitigate risk and seek out new business opportunities. Financial restructuring deals are promising business opportunities for the bank.

Various international conferences and academic and professional journals and magazines report many recent studies and success stories. An example of a typical multipurpose neural application, NeuroForecaster, is described at the end of this chapter.

THE FUTURE OF MACHINE LEARNING SYSTEMS

A key question that normally arises when reflecting on the advancements in neural computing and other machine learning realms focuses on how close we are to building a truly intelligent machine. For isolated capacities, some ANNs already exceed humans. However, the development of large-scale networks that mirror complex human endeavors, such as creating a musical work or carrying on a wide-ranging conversation, is not in our foreseeable future.

The greatest obstacle to building such systems is the acquisition of sufficient training data. The speed of signal transmission in the human brain is estimated to be approximately 100 meters per second; the speed of a typical copper wire transmission system is at least 1 million times faster. Although it is theoretically possible for a computer to think and learn at a speed 1 million times faster than humans, for it to actually occur, the system will need to acquire data at the same speed. This bottleneck is a function of the cognitive limitations imposed on humans to create such training sets and to feed them to the net. In the meantime, we must satisfy ourselves with the development of machines that can learn how to support us in many of our more complex activities such as medical diagnosis, flying an aircraft, sending explorers to other planets, and other endeavors intended to improve our quality of life.

4.5: CHAPTER SUMMARY

We are, rightfully so, fascinated with the processes of the human brain and with the prospects of capturing those processes in a computer-based system. In our quest, however, the lack of clarity and specificity with which the human brain quite comfortably functions on a daily basis looms as a major obstacle to the development of a truly humanlike machine. Nonetheless, the advent of fuzzy systems, GAs, and neural computing systems takes us another step closer to the goal.

Key Concepts

- Neural computing and the development of artificial neural networks (ANNs) evolved in response to the attractiveness of digital information processors that can simulate the human brain's potential for solving ill-structured business problems.

- Fuzzy logic is a method of reasoning that allows for the partial or "fuzzy" description of a rule. Combining this approach to reasoning with the realm of digital processors results in a class of computers that can "learn" from their mistakes and can "understand" the vagaries commonly found in human thought.

- Fuzzy logic does not mean vague answers, but, rather, precise answers that vary mathematically within a given range of values. By developing a network of mathematical algorithms, a complex set of categorizations can be analyzed and a high level of reasoning can be brought to bear on a given problem context.

- Probability deals with the likelihood that something has a particular property, whereas fuzzy logic deals with the degree to which a particular property is present in something. With probability, we can only determine membership in a set, but with fuzzy logic, we can determine where on the continuum of membership a particular set member resides.

- Fuzzy systems offer a number of advantages.

  Modeling of contradiction. Fuzzy logic allows for the modeling and inclusion of contradiction within a knowledge base. Using fuzzy logic, the designer exercises complete control over the accuracy of a given conclusion or reasoning process by simply increasing or decreasing the number of rules required and the degrees of sensitivity to membership allowed.

  Increased system autonomy. The rules contained within the knowledge base of a fuzzy system can function completely independently of one another. Fuzzy rules will continue to "work" even in circumstances where the whole system is completely changed.

- Fuzzy systems have a number of limitations.

  Obstacles to system verification. Fuzzy reasoning can become an obstacle to the verification of a system's stability or reliability. Designers may find it difficult to determine whether their actions improve the system or result in a move away from a better solution.

  Lack of memory. Basic fuzzy reasoning mechanisms cannot learn from their mistakes and possess no memory. As such, fuzzy logic is not yet capable of optimizing the efficiency of a system.

- The fuzzy set may become so full of inferences that consequent fuzzy sets are overloaded, which results in the entire system losing the information provided by the fuzzy rules in an attempt to "balance itself" around its mean value.

- ANNs are simple computer-based programs whose primary function is to construct models of a problem space based upon trial and error.

- An ANN has three basic layers.

  Input layer. The layer that receives the data.

  Output layer. The layer that relays the final results.

  Internal layer (hidden layer). The layer where the processing and transformation of the input signal takes place and where the type of output signal is determined.

- The hierarchical network dynamics among the neurodes is determined by a mathematical combination of the weight of each input to the neurode and the threshold parameters associated with that neurode. Learning, in a neural network, results from the adjustment of weights.

- The basic structure consists of a set of weighted input connections, a bias input, a state function, a nonlinear transfer function, and an output connection.

  Weighted inputs. The neurode can, and usually does, have multiple inputs, each with its own associated weight or importance. The weight of an input determines the importance of its contribution to the output of the neurode.

  Bias input. The purpose of the bias input is to allow for the individual adjustment of the firing threshold of the neurode to facilitate the final adjustment of the ANN following the learning process.

  State function. The purpose of the state function is to consolidate the weights of the various inputs to the neurode into a single value that can be passed to the transfer function for processing.

  Transfer function. The primary purpose of the transfer function is to serve as the vehicle by which the summed information is passed on as output. The transfer function must contribute a sense of nonlinearity between the summed inputs and the resultant output.

- The process of training a neural net to associate certain input patterns with correct output responses involves the use of repetitive examples and feedback. This iterative adjustment process continues for each hidden layer in the network until all neurodes have been subjected to the sensitivity analysis and the net is ready for another trial.

- The actual procedure used by a neural network to find the appropriate weight settings is referred to as its learning paradigm. The learning paradigms for ANNs can be loosely classified into two categories: unsupervised learning and supervised learning.

Unsupervised learning paradigms. The unsupervised nature of an unsupervised learning paradigm means that the ANN receives the input data and examples but no feedback in the form of desired results. Using the clustering approach, a neural net can begin to "specialize" its learning with respect to a specific dimension of the data.

Supervised learning paradigms. The most common supervised learning paradigm is called back propagation. In this approach, the net receives an input example, generates a guess, and compares that guess to feedback containing the desired results. The ANN is being "supervised" by the feedback that shows the net where it made mistakes and how the answer should look.

- Neural computing offers a number of benefits:

  The ability to obtain inferential insights not readily available through the use of other knowledge-based techniques and technologies

  The elimination of the need for direct input from domain experts

  The inherent ability to deal with noisy or incomplete datasets

  The capability of scaling up as necessary to accommodate problems of increased complexity

- A genetic algorithm (GA) is an elegantly simple, yet extremely powerful, type of optimization technique based on the ideas of genetics and natural selection. The GA is a set of adaptive processes that mimic the concept of "survival of the fittest" by regenerating recombinants of the algorithm in response to a calculated difference between the network's guess and the desired solution state.

- GAs are composed of genes and chromosomes.

  Gene. The GA's smallest unit is called a gene, which represents the smallest unit of information in the problem domain. It can be thought of as the basic building block for a possible solution.

  Chromosome. A series of genes that represent the components of one possible solution to the problem is referred to as a chromosome. The chromosome is represented in computer memory as a bit string of binary digits that can be "decoded" by the GA to determine how good a particular chromosome's gene pool solution is for the given problem.

- The basic processes of the operation of a GA are initialization, evaluation, selection, crossover, and selection.

  Initialization. The first step in the creation of a GA is the development of an initial population of chromosomes as possible solutions to the problem under investigation.

  Evaluation. In this stage, each chromosome is decoded by the decoder function and evaluated using a fitness function to determine which genetic structures are good and which are not so good.

  Selection. The selection process weeds out the poor solutions and passes the remaining chromosomes on to the crossover process. In this process, the GA chooses the fittest species to remain and reproduce within the population of solution chromosomes. The objective of this process is to produce new chromosomes that form a new generation of possible solutions to evaluate.

  Crossover. The crossover phase involves the exchange of gene information between two selected chromosomes. The purpose of this operation is to allow the GA to create new chromosomes that share positive characteristics while simultaneously reducing the prevalence of negative characteristics in an otherwise reasonably fit solution.

  Mutation. In order to provide the GA with the opportunity to create chromosomes and information genes that can explore previously uncharted areas of the solution space, thus increasing the chances for the discovery of an optimal solution, the mutation phase randomly changes the value of a gene from its current setting to a completely different one.

- GAs offer a number of benefits.

  GAs tend to zero in on a solution much faster than a neural network and generally are highly predictable in their process time.

The advantage of GAs in solving complex problems lies in their ability to "stretch" themselves across a vast solution space in search of the optimal solution.

The applications of genetic algorithms can be used to solve problems that we have no clue how to solve.

The power of GAs does not result from a complex algorithmic perspective, but rather from a relatively simple and widely understood set of concepts.

Questions for Review

1. How does fuzzy logic deal with the concept of categorization? How does this method differ from our typical process of categorization?
2. Describe how membership functions often rely on inclusion in multiple sets.
3. Explain the similarities and the differences between fuzziness and probability.
4. List and briefly describe the advantages and limitations of fuzzy systems.
5. What is fuzzy set saturation?
6. Describe the basic structure of an ANN. What is the purpose of each layer?
7. What is the purpose of a transfer function?
8. How does feedback in ANNs work?
9. Briefly describe and compare supervised and unsupervised ANNs.
10. What is the primary advantage of GAs over ANNs?
11. Describe genes and chromosomes as applied to GAs.
12. Describe each step of GA processing: initialization, evaluation, selection, crossover, and mutation.
13. Summarize the benefits of GAs.

For Further Discussion

1. Discuss the utility of fuzzy logic's ability to model inclusion in multiple sets that intuitively are mutually exclusive or contradictory. In what situations might this prove useful?
2. Use an example to explain the typical neurode component structure described in this chapter.
3. ANNs deal well with noisy or incomplete data. Describe some situations in which ANNs would perform better than other techniques for eliciting patterns from the data.
4. How can mutation enhance a GA's ability to arrive at a satisfactory solution? Is mutation necessary?
5. Describe the effect of the number of chromosomes on the performance of a GA.

Back Propagation Algorithm (adapted from Dhar and Stein, 1997)

The primary objective of a back propagation algorithm is the minimization of error between the output of a neural network and the true solution contained within the training data record. Assuming a logistic transfer function, we can update the weight, ω_{ij}, from a given node, η_i, to the current node, η_j, as follows:

$$\omega_{ij,(t+1)} = \omega_{ij,t} + (\lambda)(\varepsilon\omega_{ij})(n_j)$$

where λ is the learning parameter, the subscript t refers to the number of times the net has been updated, and $\varepsilon\omega_{ij}$, is the sensitivity of node n_j to the change in the weight ω_{ij}.

Recall that the total input to a given neurode is described as:

$$s_j = \sum n_i \omega_{ij}$$

where s_j represents the sum of all inputs to the neurode, n_i is the output from the ith neurode in the previous layer, and ω_{ij} is the weight of the input connection between the ith neurode in the previous layer and the current neurode.

The result of this summation is passed to a nonlinear transfer function to yield the total output, n_j, of neurode j. Typical of the transfer function forms used is the *logistic function* shown as:

$$n_j = \frac{1}{1 + e^{-s_j}}$$

With these equations in place, we can determine the overall error for a single pass of the ANN using the following steps:

- Calculate the (RMS) error, E, for the output layer as:

$$E = \frac{1}{2} \sum_{output} (n_j - d_j)^2$$

where d_j is the desired output for output neurode j.
- Calculate the error term for each output neurode and determine the sensitivity of the error terms to changes in neurode output:

$$\varepsilon o_j = \frac{\partial E}{\partial n_j}$$

$$\varepsilon o_j = (n_j - d_j)$$

- Determine the relationship of change between input and output:

$$\varepsilon s_j = \frac{\partial E}{\partial s_j}$$

$$\varepsilon s_j = \frac{\partial E}{\partial s_j} \frac{dn_j}{ds_j}$$

$$\varepsilon s_j = \varepsilon o_j n_j (1 - n_j)$$

- Next, we calculate how much to adjust each weight, w_{ij}, from a given neurode on the layer below the current layer, n_i, to the current neurode, n_j:

$$\varepsilon \omega_{ij} = \frac{\partial E}{\partial \omega_{ij}}$$

$$\varepsilon \omega_{ij} = \frac{\partial E}{\partial s_j} \frac{ds_j}{d\omega_{ij}}$$

$$\varepsilon \omega_{ij} = \varepsilon s_j n_i$$

- We continue this operation on the neurodes in the hidden layers by summing all the contributions of inputs to the errors of the hidden neurodes in the lower layers. The variable εh replaces the variable εo from the previous equations to differentiate the error of the output layers from that of the hidden layers:

$$\varepsilon h_i = \frac{\partial E}{\partial n_i}$$

$$\varepsilon h_i = \sum_j \frac{\partial E}{\partial s_i} \frac{\partial s_j}{\partial n_i}$$

$$\varepsilon h_i = \sum_j \varepsilon s_j \omega_{ij}$$

Using this approach, we can back propagate the error recursively through the entire ANN with all the weights being adjusted to minimize the overall error of the net.

NeuroForecaster and GENETICA

NeuroForecaster is an advanced Windows-based, user-friendly business forecasting tool. It is packed with the latest technologies, including neural network, genetic algorithm, fuzzy computing, and nonlinear dynamics. It excels at the following tasks:

- Time-series forecasting (e.g., stock and currency market forecasts, GDP forecasts)
- Classification (e.g., stock selection, bond rating, credit assignment, property valuation)
- Indicator analysis (e.g., moving averages, price action alerts)
- Identification of useful input indicators (e.g., which of the variety of available indicator variables is most appropriate for a particular forecast trend)

With NeuroForecaster, you can create neural networks of any size—the only limit is the memory constraint of your computer. It is also an excellent tool for analyzing the effectiveness of neural network architecture (numbers of hidden nodes, hidden layers, transfer functions) for problem solving. It accepts numerical input attributes, patterns, codes, technical indicators, and fundamental indicators, and allows them to be combined to build univariate or multivariate models. Like other numerical tools, it cannot handle descriptive information such as news, rumors, or fiscal policies unless such information is accompanied by numerical information, reflected in other indicators, or can be quantified.

NeuroForecaster is a general-purpose forecasting tool with adaptive learning capability. You can turn it into an automatic trading system if you train it with a good trading strategy to generate the buy/sell signals.

GENETICA Net Builder, another neural computing application, is supported by NeuroForecaster 3.0 and above. It searches for the best combination of input data and the most predictable forecaster horizon (i.e., how many steps ahead to forecast) and automatically creates and optimizes forecaster structures and control parameters by evolution and genetic search.

GENETICA is seamlessly integrated with the training process of NeuroForecaster—it determines when to pause the training, purge the poor-performing networks, and evolve new offspring to inherit the knowledge acquired by outperforming parents.

GENETICA has a number of unique features:

- Reads various file formats, including MetaStock, CSI, Computrac, FutureSource, ASCII, and VisuaData, and displays data in its built-in spreadsheet
- GENETICA Net Builder searches for the best input data combination and forecast horizon and builds the best forecaster networks
- Rescaled range analysis and Hurst exponent to unveil hidden market cycles and check for predictability
- Correlation analysis to compute correlation factors to analyze the significance of input indicators
- Weight and accumulated error index (AEI) histograms to monitor the learning process

References

Brule, J. F. (1985). *Fuzzy Systems—A Tutorial*. Retrieved January 1998, from www.austinlinks.com/Fuzzy/tutorial.html.

Dhar, V., and R. Stein. (1997). *Intelligent Decision Support Methods*. Upper Saddle River, NJ: Prentice Hall.

NIBS Pte, Ltd. (1996). *NeuroForecaster Genetica Software Package*. Retrieved November 1997, from www.singapore.com/products/nfga.

Simon, H. A. (1960). *The New Science of Management Decision*. New York: Harper & Row.

Wayner, P. (January 1991). "Genetic Algorithms." *Byte*, pp. 361–64.

INTRODUCTION

The CEOs of today's organizations are not so far removed from their predecessors of decades before. Now, as then, information is the mainstay of the executive suite; the majority of an organization's resources allocated to the executive branch are deployed in an effort to gather and maintain that information. The character of the information needed by the CEOs has not changed that much either. Top executives generally need much broader information than that required by middle or line management. What has changed, however, is the speed with which this vital information is being generated and the speed with which the CEO needs access to it. The typical decision support system (DSS) designed to focus on providing support for a particular problem or decision context, which works so effectively at the line and middle management levels of the firm, cannot provide the diversity of information access and decision support needed by top management. To address the unique information needs of the CEO, a unique and powerful interface to both the organization's production data and DW emerged. This chapter will focus on the information needs of the top executive and the architecture of the executive information system (EIS) used to address those needs.

5.1: WHAT EXACTLY IS AN EIS?

In basic terms, an EIS is a special interface and decision support system uniquely designed to facilitate the analysis of information critical to the overall operation of an organization and to provide tools that can support the strategic decision-making processes conducted by top executives. More specifically, an EIS can help a CEO get an accurate and almost immediate picture not only of the operations and performance of the organization, but of the activities of its competitors, customers, and suppliers as well. An EIS performs these functions by constantly monitoring both internal and external events and trends and then making this information available to the top executive in a manner that best suits the needs of the moment. An EIS can provide a wide range of summarization or detail at the convenience of the executive. For example, a CEO can use the EIS to quickly view sales activity categorized by product, region, subregion, month, local market, or any number of other methods of organization. Simultaneously, the CEO can also monitor the sales activity of the firm's competitors in much the same way. This high degree of summarization provides a quick, comparative snapshot of what is going on in the company and/or the market. Should this snapshot reveal some discrepancy, unusual variance, or anomaly, the executive can drill down into the organization's DW to display a greater level of detail and to explore trends in prior periods. This process of decomposition can continue until the individual transaction level is reached, if necessary, to provide the CEO with the information that explains the variance and helps decide a course of action. The design of an EIS combines access to a wide variety of information sources with a mechanism for relating and summarizing those sources. It also provides the user with the tools necessary to examine and analyze the gathered information so that a swift, yet well-informed, decision can be made.

Regardless of the context in which the EIS is deployed, all have certain characteristics in common. Table 5-1 contains a summary of common characteristics associated with all EIS technologies.

Building upon the common EIS characteristics and the various definitions offered in the literature on EISs, we adopt the following definition in this text: *An EIS is a computer-based*

TABLE 5-1 Common Executive Information System Characteristics

- Used directly by top-level executives
- Tailored to individual executive users
- Designed to be easy to operate and require little or no training to use
- Focused on supporting upper-level management decisions
- Can present information in graphical, tabular, and/or textual formats
- Provides access to information from a broad range of internal and external sources
- Provides tools to select, extract, filter, and track critical information
- Provides a wide range of reports including status reporting, exception reporting, trend analysis, drill down investigation, and ad hoc queries

system intended to facilitate and support the information and decision-making needs of senior executives by providing easy access to both internal and external information relevant to meeting the stated goals of the organization. Throughout the literature on this subject, the terms *executive information system* and *electronic support system* (ESS) are used interchangeably, though often ESS connotes a system of much broader capabilities than an EIS. With the advent of distributed groupware technologies and improvements in existing decision-making and information-gathering technologies, this distinction is rapidly becoming blurred. For our purposes, we use the term *EIS* to refer to all executive support systems regardless of content or specific target.

At this stage of our discussion, it is not particularly important to position various EIS structures within a taxonomy or categorization scheme (although we will ultimately do just that). What is important, however, is to realize that EISs differ considerably in both scope and purpose and, therefore, must be designed and implemented for a particular executive environment and must be based on a particular executive's information needs. As both of these design requirements are extremely fluid, the EIS must be considered an evolutionary tool in an organization that requires a significant commitment to its ongoing support and development.

A TYPICAL EIS SESSION

To better understand the unique nature of an EIS, let's walk through the activities in a typical EIS session. The session might begin with a report of the organization's financial and business situation. This report would contain several graphics of sales revenues by region or categorical costs of goods sold, but it would also have a section displaying the value of key performance indicators ranging from typical financial ratios, such as assets to liabilities, to more targeted indicators, such as the average waiting time for customers accessing telephone support services. The body of the report may use arrows or color to highlight those measures that are going up, staying steady, or declining. Other colors or graphics may be used to indicate those measures that have transcended some predetermined operating range or threshold. At a quick glance, the executive can form an overall assessment of the organization's state.

After reviewing the summary information, the executive may notice a color-coded trend indicator that appears troublesome. Let's say the current ratio appears to be declining unusually fast. The executive will use the drill down capabilities of the EIS to explore the underlying data used to compile the current ratio. In this case, the drill down feature would bring up screens listing asset and liability categories separately. If this level of disaggregation does not give the executive the answer, additional drilling down may be warranted. Drilling down further on assets may reveal itemized dollar figures for cash, inventories, receivables, and other specific assets. This process can occur until the level of detail is sufficient to reveal the root of the change in the ratio.

The drill down capability of an EIS is one of its most important characteristics. This process of decomposition can be selected and controlled by the executive and can be different for every situation. The executive merely selects the level of detail deemed necessary for the situation at hand, using a keystroke or mouse click on the interface to bring forth the story behind the information displayed. By going down one layer from a summary of company-wide sales to regional sales, for instance, an executive might learn that a slump in a product category can be attributed to a specific area of the country. Continuing to drill down in the specific region may reveal a lack of promotion. Drilling down in the other regions where sales are good may indicate that sales expectations were actually exceeded wherever distributors advertised the product properly.

Drilling down through the data allows the executive to seek solutions to problems by employing a "top-down" analysis. The EIS summary highlights potential problem areas, and the drill down feature allows for further structured investigation. This process leads to better decisions, more successful solutions, and better management performance.

WHAT AN EIS IS NOT

One additional issue of importance is the acknowledgment of what an EIS is not. The organizational EIS is not a panacea or substitute for other forms of information technologies and computer-based systems. Transaction processing systems (TPS), the core management information systems (MIS), and the individual DSS support systems are all still vital elements in bringing relevant information to the various levels of a modern organization. The EIS actually feeds off the various information systems within an organization for its internal information needs and then attaches itself to external information sources as necessary to fill in the bigger picture.

Along these same lines, an EIS does not (and above all, should not) turn the executive suite into a haven for computer techies and geeks. The well-designed EIS should offer an interface that is intuitive, flexible, and easily managed by the nontechnical user. In this regard, the EIS should be positioned and viewed by senior management as more of a trusted confidant or assistant who can be easily called upon and relied upon when and where necessary.

5.2: SOME EIS HISTORY

The term *executive information system* was coined at the Massachusetts Institute of Technology (MIT) in the late 1970s. The first EISs were developed by a few organizations in private industry that were willing to take rather large risks in return for the significant competitive advantage perceived to be associated with the use of an EIS. The "coming out" party for the EIS is historically associated with the publishing of a *Harvard Business Review* article by Rockart and Treacy (1982) entitled "The CEO Goes On-Line." This article vividly describes the emergence of the computer in the executive suite—often assumed to be the last bastion of successful resistance to the computing technology monster. Although many were skeptical of the widespread acceptance of this new organizational tool, the skeptics were soon silenced. By the mid-1980s, several vendors such as Pilot Software (Command Center) and Comshare (Commander EIS) were making huge inroads into large corporations by providing relatively easy application environments for EIS development that included easy screen design, flexible interface design, preprogrammed access to electronic news sources, mechanisms to facilitate widespread data importation, and a wide variety of easy-to-use analytical tools. One of the major driving forces behind the adoption of both large-scale data warehouses and enterprise resource planning (ERP) systems in the next decade will be the ability to easily feed real-time data to an organizational EIS. It is becoming almost axiomatic that where you find enterprise resource planning (ERP), you will also find a mission critical EIS.

As excitement and support for EIS technology grew throughout the 1980s and early 1990s, new vendors and emerging products increased the scope of available information sources and analytical techniques that allowed the EIS to be used at other levels of the organization. Modern EISs contain a wide variety of data, including mission-critical business processes, research and development efforts, customer-related information, financial activity, and, of course, external data to support the necessary environmental scanning activities. The current generation of EISs addresses a much broader audience, and the available applications transcend the boundaries of typical corporate hierarchies. The adoption of an EIS is not without risk, but the number of success stories associated with EIS development and use suggests that the risks are well worth the benefits.

To fully understand and appreciate the value and power of an EIS, we must first understand and appreciate the unique information needs of its users. Section 5.3 focuses on the issues surrounding the information needs of the CEO.

5.3: WHY ARE TOP EXECUTIVES SO DIFFERENT?

What makes top executives different from other decision support users? To help answer this question, we must begin by defining who top executives are and what constitutes their realm of activities. No generalizable definition captures the full meaning of the term *executive*, and its application varies from organization to organization. As with other such constructs that lack a focused definition, executives tend to be defined by their common characteristics. Table 5-2 lists several commonalities associated with the executive branch of management.

EXECUTIVE INFORMATION NEEDS

To fully appreciate the information needs of any decision support system user, we begin with the nature of the work and the various tasks associated with the process. In the design of an EIS, the unique nature of the target user makes this understanding essential for success.

TABLE 5-2 Common Characteristics of Executives

- They manage entire organizations or autonomous subunits.
- They are enterprise-oriented in their thinking.
- They possess the broadest span of control in the organization.
- They are future-oriented and focus on strategic horizons rather than day-to-day activities.
- They are responsible for establishing policies.
- They represent the organization and its interactions with the external environment.
- Their actions can have considerable financial, human, and business consequences.
- They must concern themselves with a wide range of internal and external issues.

Source: Adapted from Watson, Houdeshel, and Rainer (1997).

From your first management class, you learned that all managers perform five basic functions: planning, organizing, staffing, directing, and controlling. You may also recall that even though all managers may perform tasks within each of these functions, they do not spend equal time in all areas. One method of differentiating the various managerial roles within the hierarchy of an organization is to categorize them by frequency of function. The nature of work at the top executive level suggests that executives spend more time focusing on planning and controlling than managers at other levels of the firm. Specific tasks at the executive level include management and operational control, strategic planning, negotiation, and disturbance management. Studies by Rockart (1979) and Jones and McLeod (1986) focused on the identification of the specific tasks performed by top executives and the frequency of their occurrence. In these studies, executives were asked to keep careful track of every activity they performed during the course of their work over an extended period. In addition, they were asked to indicate the sources of information they used during the conduct of each activity and the relative importance of that activity. The results suggested that executive activities can be divided into five basic categories. Figure 5-1 shows these activities and their relative frequency of occurrence.

Disturbance Management

The word *disturbance* may belie the real nature of tasks contained in this area. When something unexpected occurs, particularly something that could materially and negatively affect the financial health of the organization, the immediate attention of executives and the deployment of resources are usually warranted. In times of disturbance, all other executive activities are usually subordinated to those directly related to the crisis. Furthermore, disturbance management activities may require around-the-clock attention during the early stages of the crisis and may continue for weeks or months before the disturbance is fully managed and under control. As you can see by the figure, the majority of executive time is spent in some form of disturbance management activity.

The events following the May 11, 1996, crash of ValuJet Flight 592 are a vivid example of disturbance management activities. ValuJet President Lewis Jordan was immediately thrust to the forefront of media attention and was charged with the responsibility of representing ValuJet in press conferences, internal and external investigations, and public relations activities,

FIGURE 5-1 Frequency of Executive Activities

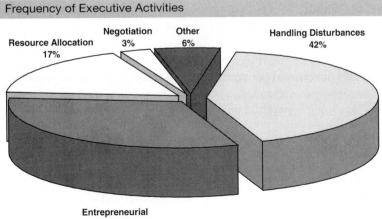

as well as the preparation for the inevitable mire of legal proceedings to come. FAA scrutiny caused so many disruptions in ValuJet's schedule that Jordan faced the decision to cut the number of ValuJet's flights in half so its planes could be inspected in a more orderly fashion. What Jordan called "unprecedented regulatory and media scrutiny" was immediately focused on the airline. Jordan said ValuJet was subjected to 4 years' worth of inspections in 4 weeks.

Jordan then decided to add a "safety czar" and began upping quarterly bonuses to employees despite a less-than-stellar first quarter. "It's clear we're going to forgo a significant amount of revenue," Jordan said. "And we're going to forgo the opportunity to carry a number of people, but we have said we're putting safety first." In the end, Jordan predicted "we will weather this just fine." In fact, these actions were serious efforts to reclaim public confidence and build employee morale.

Even more recently, the events following the tragic loss of life on September 11, 2001, also emphasize the importance of disturbance management activities. New York City Mayor Rudolph Giuliani, New York Governor George Pataki, and President of the United States George W. Bush all faced a nation in turmoil. Their actions became immediately and simultaneously focused on rescue efforts, expectation management, economic stability, national security, and military action. All consummate executives, these men, and many others, faced their greatest challenge with resolve, clarity, and skill. The ability to conduct successful disturbance management activities was never more valuable to a nation and the world than on September 11, 2001, and the days and weeks that followed.

Entrepreneurial Activities

Entrepreneurial activities fall under the general heading of strategic planning tasks. Executives spend a significant portion of their time focusing on the selection, design, and implementation of projects to improve performance and initiate controlled change within the organization. In most cases, the entrepreneurial activities of an executive are triggered by real or perceived changes in the external environment. Executives must focus their attention on understanding the dynamic forces in their markets and the global environment and must use the information gathered to predict changes that can be viewed as opportunities to the firm. Because of the risk associated with making such predictions and the subsequent commitment of present and future resources to projects intended to take advantage of environmental changes, executives must spend a large percentage of their time in this area.

Allocation of Resources

In one form or another, and regardless of where in the organizational hierarchy the actual deployment occurs, top executives completely control resource allocation. Typically, managers at various levels are given authority to manage and deploy resources from a predetermined allocation based on a control mechanism such as a budget or operational plan. The authority to deploy those resources, and the various behind-the-scenes activities to obtain them, is normally held by top executives. Organizational resources include more than just dollars, however. They also include people, equipment, plant and warehouse space, and all other entities associated with reaching the strategic goals of the firm. In general, the demand for resources is greater than their availability, and, as such, top executives must decide where and to whom the limited cache of organizational resources will be allocated.

Negotiation

Executives represent the organization in both internal and external disputes. Typically, this role involves responsibility for the resolution of disputes and conflicts and, thus, involves a significant amount of negotiation among the parties. Internal disputes can occur when functional areas within the organization disagree on an issue of procedure or span of authority. In such cases, top executives must facilitate the resolution of the dispute through negotiation among the principal members of the firm who are directly affected by the conflict. External disputes occur when the perspectives of one or more constituencies outside the organization are in conflict with the actions of the firm. Such situations include hostile acquisitions, strikes and labor disputes, shareholder relation issues, and government investigations. Despite the relatively small amount of time spent by executives on these activities (only 3 percent as shown in Figure 5-1), the need for rapid information and decision support may be as critical here as it is during times of disturbance or crisis. Further, situations can occur that require an almost simultaneous conduct of the primary areas of executive actions.

In late 1997, United Parcel Service (UPS) truck drivers went on strike after a vote by the members of the Teamsters Union. The 15-day standoff cost UPS more than $500 million and was characterized by periods of literally around-the-clock negotiations by both sides. During this time, the need for rapid and accurate information was vital to the successful resolution of the dispute. In addition, the UPS executives had to divide their time between activities of negotiation and activities related to disturbance management. Every minute they spent in attempting to resolve the strike was also a minute spent in managing the crippled operations of the organization. Because of the nature of the dispute, the consequences of the various outcome scenarios had to be analyzed with regard to their impact on the availability of present and anticipated resources, the overall strategic plan, and, thus, the future of the company.

TYPES AND SOURCES OF EXECUTIVE INFORMATION

Executive Information Types

We know from past discussion that decisions come in many forms, and the information necessary to make a particular decision carries with it certain attributes relevant to the problem context. In addition to the variance in attributes associated with certain types of information, the relative importance of those attributes varies with regard to management level. Table 5-3 lists the various common attributes of information and compares their relative importance to lower- and higher-level managers.

Given the relevance of the various information attributes, it seems reasonable to expect that the kinds of information sought by executives and their sources may also be uniquely

TABLE 5-3 Differences in Information Attributes Between Management Levels		
Information Attribute	*Lower-Level Management*	*Top Executive Management*
Accuracy	High	Low
Timeliness	High	Low
Scope	Narrow	Broad
Time horizon	Past and present	Future
Relevance	High	Low
Level of detail	High	Low
Summarization	Low	High
Orientation	Internal	Internal and external
Source	Written	Verbal and graphical
Quantifiability	High	Low

Source: Adapted from Watson, Houdeshel, and Rainer (1997).

identifiable. Rockart (1979) made several observations concerning the various types of information needed by top executives:

1. Cost accounting systems that relate revenues and expenses to specific functions and operational areas are more useful to top executives for tracking critical success factors than the more traditional financial accounting systems.
2. Externally obtained information about markets, customers, suppliers, and competitors is extremely valuable in determining strategy.
3. Top executives require information that is typically spread across several computer systems and is located throughout the organization.
4. Top executives rely on both objective and subjective assessments of issues internal and external to the organization.
5. High-level executives use information focused on current results and short-run performance levels.
6. Top executives require information that is often both short-term and extremely volatile.

Executive Information Determination and Sources

Given the unique characteristics of executive information needs, mechanisms for determining and satisfying those needs in a given situation are required. Rockart (1979) identified five basic methods for such determination. Table 5-4 lists these methods in order of increasing formality and level of detail.

By-Product   The by-product method expends the least amount of effort of any of the identified approaches to determining the information needs of top executives. The primary level of support comes from traditional TPSs and other MISs that summarize and aggregate the various informational by-products of the current operations of the organization. Using this method, exception highlighting is limited to those areas with predefined ranges of values or easily summarized historical data. The delivery mechanism for this method is primarily through a collection of online or hard copy reports and summaries.

Null   Using the null approach, no formal effort is made to supply the executive with desired information. The reasoning is that the information needs of executives are so dynamic and fluid that the predefined reports generated by typical information systems are not especially useful. In contrast to the by-product method, the null approach involves the constant, but informal, collection of mostly subjective information from trusted sources via "word of mouth." This method was made famous by Peters and Waterman (1982) in their classic book *In Search of Excellence*, in which they discussed the philosophy of Hewlett-Packard executives using the term *management by walking around*. The null method relies on the spontaneous exchanges and discoveries that take place during informal tours of an organization. Although this method recognizes the value of subjective information, it ignores the value of more objective information such as that obtained through computer-based information systems.

TABLE 5-4   Methods for Determining Executive Information Needs

- By-product method
- Null method
- Key indicator method
- Total study method
- Critical success factors method

Key Indicator   This method for determining executive information needs is based on three basic notions:

1. The health of an organization can be determined by comparison to a set of key financial indicators.
2. Organizations can be managed based on exception reporting where only those areas operating outside of a preestablished set of norms are of interest.
3. Technology is available to allow for flexible display of key indicator information in graphical form.

The first notion requires the identification of relevant financial indicators such as internal financial ratios, production levels, revenues and expenses, and market share. Once these indicators are identified, information about each of them is collected on a continual basis and used to make adjustments or decisions critical to the ongoing success of the organization.

The second notion suggests that a range of operational values and norms can be accurately established in such a way that the concept of "no news is good news" becomes operational. Top executives monitor only that information that reflects an out-of-nominal condition and gather additional information as a basis for making decisions intended to correct the condition.

The third notion requires that the information be made available in graphical rather than tabular form. Using this approach, the executive can more easily "see" the exceptional condition and respond to it more rapidly than would be expected through analysis of tabular data.

Total Study   The total study approach gathers information from a sample of top executives in the organization concerning the totality of their information needs. Following these interviews, system developers make a comparison between the stated needs of the executives and the present information capabilities of the organization's computer systems. Where voids can be identified, the developers create new subsystems to supply the missing information. This method — while more comprehensive than its predecessors — is nonetheless both expensive and somewhat problematic with regard to its ability to meet the needs of any single executive well. As such, this method, although intuitively attractive, has not manifested itself as a practical approach to EIS design.

Critical Success Factors   The fifth and most comprehensive of the approaches identified by Rockart seeks to overcome the various weaknesses associated with the other methods. Regardless of the nature of the organization, certain areas of activity, called critical success factors (CSFs), exist in which satisfactory results will ensure the health and competitiveness of that organization. According to Rockart, CSFs are those things that simply must be done right if the organization is to be successful. Similar to the key indicators approach, this method requires information on the identified CSFs to be constantly gathered and supplied to top executives. This information is used as the basis for making decisions that affect the organization.

The primary method for establishing the CSFs of an organization is through structured interviewing of the top executives of the firm. Following this step, CSFs are further refined through a series of facilitated collaborative sessions in which executives discuss the goals and objectives of the firm, the CSFs related to those goals, and just how they might be measured.

Of the five approaches identified and discussed, any or all of the last three methods could easily serve as the basis for the design of a computer-based EIS. In the next section, we look at the various components of a typical EIS and explore several available application environments used in their design and implementation.

5.4: EIS COMPONENTS

Many organizations are still evolving from their "big iron" days of the mainframe to the more flexible and functional client/server environment. In many cases, this evolution enables easier development and implementation of computer-based decision support technologies (as well as many other organizational information systems). Several companies already completed this transition in their environments with deployment of their first EIS.

The client/server architecture allows rapid additions and modifications to business applications and facilitates the widespread access and dissemination of databases located throughout the globe. Several of the early EIS products were originally developed for use in a high-powered computing environment, but all of the currently marketed products target the client/server platform, designed to be deployed in a variety of settings (local, mobile, Internet access, etc.). Several of the specific benefits of the client/server architecture are as follows:

1. Multiple views of geographically dispersed data residing on corporate computer platforms ranging from mainframes to personal computers (PCs) regardless of data format
2. Reduction of investment costs in new computer hardware and physical plant
3. Establishment of a flexible platform that can change and adapt to the dynamic needs of the organization
4. Facilitates management use of both real-time and archival data, which results in faster, more informed decisions and provides a competitive advantage based on the reduced decision time
5. Facilitates the use of information as a competitive weapon through the easy creation of "strategic" applications that can reveal the "hidden treasures" within an organization's data

Figure 5-2 illustrates a typical EIS implementation within an organization's client/server environment.

HARDWARE COMPONENTS

The EIS does not require any unique computing hardware or peripherals other than those typically found in a modern client/server environment. The important considerations regarding sufficient RAM memory, hard drive space, removable storage, high-speed graphics, data access, large display terminals, and multimedia capabilities relevant to any client-side setup are equally relevant in an EIS environment. A key issue, however, is to be sure that the components of the EIS optimize and conform to the organizational computing resources as well as adapt to the legacy, or existing system, data. The executive user, in many cases, will require the most support in terms of both training in the early stages and modifications to the system in the later ones. The system must be configured so that the organization's resources and capabilities with regard to providing such support are well matched. Otherwise, a disgruntled executive will result, and the benefits surrounding the EIS will never be realized.

SOFTWARE COMPONENTS

In contrast to the rather "generic" nature of the hardware components of an EIS, the software components are normally highly specialized and designed to meet the specific needs of specific users. The trend toward open, modular development environments, however, makes the con-

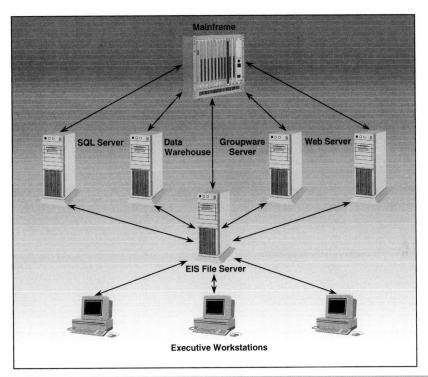

FIGURE 5-2 Typical Client/Server Architecture for EIS Implementation

cept of an "off-the-shelf" EIS a reality. Many vendors offer general-purpose EIS application environments that contain the features and capabilities most often required in a typical EIS. These general-purpose environments permit the addition and integration of a wide variety of add-on packages from third-party vendors through which the EIS designer can easily customize the application to meet the specific needs of the executive user group. More recently, EIS applications built around groupware packages provide collaborative features in addition to the standard EIS functions. Two such examples are GroupSystems from Ventana Corporation and Lotus Notes from Lotus Development. GroupSystems can facilitate the complete design and ongoing maintenance associated with an EIS, and Notes can be used as either a partial integration to an existing EIS system or as a total EIS software development platform.

The essential individuality in an EIS, then, comes from the software components rather than from the hardware. Regardless of the specific needs of the executive, all EIS systems tend to possess many commonly requested features and functions. Table 5-5 lists the various common features and functions of a modern client/server-based EIS.

CURRENT EIS TECHNOLOGIES

The EIS marketplace contains various offerings that provide EIS designers with application environments ranging from off-the-shelf solutions to highly customizable and proprietary systems. The components previously discussed render the various EIS offerings relatively similar.

TABLE 5-5 Common Features and Functions of Modern EIS Applications

- Status access, drill down, exception reporting, trend analysis, and ad hoc queries/reports
- Multiple user interfaces
- Multiple search engines and algorithms
- Graphical user interface (GUI) navigation (pull-down menus, pop-up lists, etc.)
- Multiple output channels (screen, hard copy, transparency, etc.)
- Seamless integration with commercial office suites
- Integrated DSS
- Widespread access to external databases and information repositories
- Data management capabilities
- Multidimensional data mining and visualization
- Electronic messaging
- Calendaring and scheduling
- Open architecture
- Online, context-sensitive help mechanisms
- Screen design templates and wizards
- Application design shells
- Multilevel access control security
- Backup and recovery functions
- Usage monitoring

To assist in categorizing the current offerings, Dobrzeniecki (1994) proposed a three-tiered functional categorization:

- **Category 1.** EIS products that include a full set of applications developed by the same vendor
- **Category 2.** EIS products that are implemented on top of DSS products previously developed by the same vendor
- **Category 3.** Applications that serve to bind together any number of products currently owned by the client organization into a cohesive, integrated EIS

To be considered an EIS, the software application product(s) should address the needs of the executive in the following areas:

- Office support

  Provide e-mail services and access to intracompany and external industry news services
  Support common office automation functions, including word processing, calendaring and scheduling, address book, and to-do lists

- Analytical support

  Provide unstructured system query support
  Provide DSS assistance and capabilities
  Provide graphic output of trends, key indicators, summary documents, and exception reporting
  Provide key word searching, drill down capability, and text-based explanations or help systems

- Customization

    Allow flexible modification of report formats, graphic style and type, and menu content

- Graphics

    Provide a full range of graphic generation and display options

- Planning

    Provide project management and scheduling functions

- Interface

    Provide a user-friendly environment, be easy to learn, and use data navigation modes

- Implementation

    Provide cost-effective integration with organizational computing resources
    Provide training and long-range technical support
    Allow for remote access
    Provide data security features

The EIS commercial marketplace is constantly changing with new vendors and applications emerging on an almost daily basis. A section at the end of this chapter contains a fairly comprehensive listing of the major EIS products currently available and provides a short description of each along with sample screenshots of several of the more popular offerings.

5.5: MAKING THE EIS WORK

In one sense, building an EIS is much like building any other type of modern information system. A structured development approach needs to be followed, requirements gathered, prototypes developed, logical models revised, cost analyses performed, and the final system implemented. In another sense, the unique character of an EIS indicates that we still have much to learn about successfully building one. For some developers, their next EIS project will also be their first. They will be thrust into the realm of executives: a world where success has often been realized without a computer, time and patience may be both precious and limited, the problems are often unstructured, and computer literacy and acumen may vary considerably. Furthermore, the physical considerations associated with building an EIS, such as determining the hardware, finding and accessing the necessary data, and integrating the system into the existing computing infrastructure, also contribute to the uniqueness of the challenge. Top these issues off with political issues such as middle management's fear that "Big Brother will be watching," and it becomes easy to see why building a successful EIS may be one of the most formidable development efforts analysts and developers will ever face. This section focuses on many of the issues surrounding these challenges.

AN EIS DEVELOPMENT FRAMEWORK

Numerous researchers and practitioners have focused their efforts on studying and refining our understanding of the processes associated with building and implementing a successful EIS. Watson, Rainer, and Koh (1991) provide a touchstone to this ongoing investigation with their EIS development framework. A development framework provides the terminology, concepts, and guidelines necessary for building a system; it is somewhat analogous to a generic instruction manual or road map. Their framework is divided into three major components: (1) the structural perspective, where the key elements that are critical to EIS development and their relationships are delineated; (2) the development process, where the dynamics and interactions of the necessary activities are identified; and (3) the user-system dialog, the interface that directs the system's actions, presents the output, and provides the user with the tools to use the system effectively. A detailed discussion of this framework is beyond the scope of this text; however, we will briefly discuss the three components and their importance to a successful EIS. Figure 5-3 illustrates the elements contained in the structural perspective and their relationships to the EIS.

Structural Perspective

In this component, the focus is on people and data as they relate to the EIS. Key players such as the sponsors or advocates of the system, the user group, the developers and designers, personnel from the various functional areas within the organization, and any vendors and consultants associated with the system are identified and positioned. In addition, the various sources of internal and external data are identified and positioned. Finally, an acknowledgment of the various forces and pressures either driving or affecting the successful development of the system is included. The *structural perspective* provides a model for understanding the relationships among the various elements and their potential interaction during the various phases of development of the EIS.

EIS Development Process

The *development process* builds upon the elements and their relationships contained within the structural model and adds a time dimension to the framework. In this component, the various activities and sequences of events are delineated and actual project management issues relating

FIGURE 5-3 Structural Perspective of EIS Development Framework

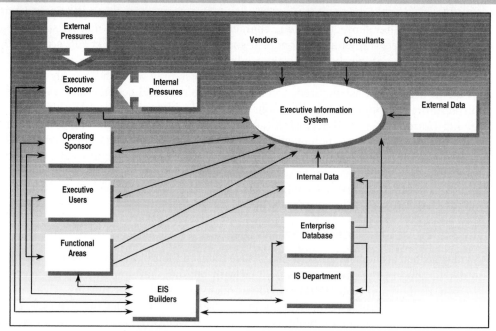

Source: Watson, Rainer, and Koh (1991).

to time, critical path, and milestones are established. Figure 5-4 illustrates the various phases of the EIS development process.

User-System Dialog

In this component of the framework, we can see the most commonalities between the design and development of an EIS and other related tools such as decision support systems. The *dialog system* contains an action language for processing the various commands and elements of manipulation. With this language, the user is directed in how to use the system. The action language element can be thought of as the incoming communication channel from the executive to the EIS.

In contrast, the dialog component also contains a presentation language that serves as the EIS counterpart to the action language. The presentation language component guides the outflow of information and the form in which this information is presented. Characteristics typical of this component include textual, graphical, and tabular formats, voice annotation, and audio and video capabilities.

The third element in this component is the *knowledge base*. The knowledge base is the sum of what the executive knows about using the system and all of the support mechanisms designed to assist in its use. Experience shows that executives simply do not read documentation (unlike you or me, of course). Therefore, the knowledge base must provide the executive with a consistent and context-dependent help system if the EIS is to be used effectively.

The *development framework* establishes boundaries and guidelines for development of an EIS. In addition to the component elements of the framework, however, Watson, Singh, and Holmes (1995) offer two additional considerations when designing and developing an EIS. First, the EIS must be easy to use. The authors suggested that "because of the nature of the

FIGURE 5-4 Development Process

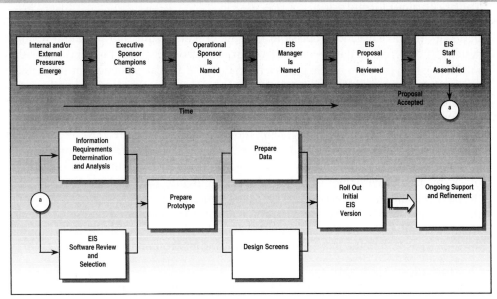

Source: Used with permission from EIS Development Process. From *Building Executive Information Systems & Other Decision Support Applications* by Watson, Houdeshel, and Rainer. Copyright © 1997 by John Wiley & Sons.

executive user, the system has to go beyond user friendly and be 'user intuitive' or even 'user seductive.'" Second, the EIS must have an acceptably fast response time. Some designers attempt to establish a quantifiable benchmark minimum for response time of 5 seconds or less. Watson, Singh, and Holmes suggest, however, that executive tolerance for response time will vary depending upon the nature of the inquiry; ad hoc queries will elicit greater tolerance for response than simple scanning of prefabricated analyses. The authors cite an unnamed EIS developer who defined acceptable EIS response time when moving from screen to screen as "the time it takes the executive to turn a page of *The Wall Street Journal.*"

SOME EIS LIMITATIONS AND PITFALLS TO AVOID

The development and implementation of an EIS brings significant benefits to an organization, and its potential for improving both competitive advantage and performance is a driving factor in its increasing popularity. Its benefits are not without some caveats, however. Here, we summarize several of the limitations and caveats associated with EIS development.

Cost

Watson, Rainer, and Koh (1991) conducted a survey of organizations using EISs and found the mean development cost to be $365,000. A breakdown of this figure revealed an allocation for software of $128,000, hardware costs of $129,000, personnel costs of $90,000, and the remainder allocated to training. In this same survey, they found the mean annual operating costs for an EIS (including ongoing upgrade and enhancement) to be in excess of $200,000. The majority of this annual operating cost was allocated to personnel and additional training. In other words, the benefits derived from an EIS are costly, and the cost of maintenance of the system after development can easily exceed the original development costs over the life of the system. The decision to adopt an EIS into an organization must be made with the understanding that the ongoing commitment of significant organizational resources is critical if the expected benefits are ever to be realized.

Technological Limitations

The essence of an EIS resides in its ability to bring all of the dispersed data and information necessary to make executive decisions into the executive suite and contain it in an easy-to-use system. The myriad of data sources necessary to accomplish this task and the wide variety of media in which they can reside poses a formidable technical challenge for the EIS designer. To accomplish this seemingly magical feat, developers may need to learn new file structures, data formats, and programming languages, as well as enlist the services and support of a variety of data providers and other MIS personnel.

To add to the technical issues facing the EIS designer, the seamless integration of the EIS into the existing computing and data warehousing infrastructure of the organization poses a challenge. As discussed previously, many organizations are still immersed in the transition from older "big iron" environments to the client/server architecture. The presence of this dynamic in the environment must be accounted for in the initial design stages of an EIS. The momentum of this change can often dictate the platform and software selected to design and deploy the EIS. Nonetheless, the EIS must be able to access the data in residence in the legacy system and during data transition to the more modern computing environments.

Organizational Limitations

Aside from the technological issues facing the EIS designer, we must also consider those of an organizational nature. These issues can often be more complex and, thus, more difficult to address than the technical limitations. Millet and Mawhinney (1992) suggested three main categories of potential negative impacts of an EIS on organizations: (1) biased agendas and time orientations, (2) loss of managerial synchronization, and (3) organizational destabilization.

Agendas and Time Biases   Despite the EIS designer's goal of providing the executive with a total information and decision-making package, the system is usually only a part (albeit often a large one) of the totality of information that an executive should ideally consider in making the critical strategic decisions of an organization. The EIS provides information associated with the measurable aspects of the organization and the environment. The less quantifiable aspects of the problem context most often must be obtained from sources other than the EIS. As such, the EIS represents only part of the executive's total agenda. It may become easy to be overly reliant on the EIS, thus focusing the executive's attention on that which can be measured rather than that which is both relevant and necessary. This form of information channeling can cause an executive's agenda to be biased toward a superficial analysis of the environment.

Another potential pitfall associated with EIS use is rooted in the nature of the EIS itself. Because of its ability to produce relevant information with greater frequency and with greater accuracy and depth than an executive is accustomed to, an EIS may lure the executive into concentrating on the more short-run, lower-level decisions within the organization, thus losing focus on big-picture decisions. An EIS sometimes promotes a more micromanagement approach to conducting business, disrupting the activities of middle and lower-level managers. Simply knowing that the top executives can monitor their every move via the drill down capabilities of the EIS can force a shifting of time orientation. The lower-level managers will begin to turn their attention to decisions with shorter time horizons in an effort to create improvement in the more closely monitored aspects of their work, thus losing their focus on more long-term performance issues.

Managerial Synchronization   This issue is an extension of the time and agenda issues just discussed. The various managerial processes of an organization must not only be carefully delineated and effectively allocated, but also must be coordinated or synchronized toward reaching the goals of the firm. One method of accomplishing synchronization is through a periodic reporting mechanism. Such an approach serves to orchestrate the shared review of key indicators and CSFs across managerial levels. Even though most EISs can, and do, produce a variety of periodic reports, they can also be used extensively to produce on-demand, *ad hoc* reports. Although virtually all of the reports generated from the DW will be *ad hoc*, heavy reliance on such reports can sometimes disrupt the stable and well-established reporting cycles designed to synchronize management activities within an organization. The important point here is that while *ad hoc* reporting is a valuable tool in the executive's EIS arsenal, it must not be used as a replacement for the more stable periodic reporting systems.

Destabilization   Through the use of airplane metaphors, the issue of destabilization can be better understood. The physics associated with flying an airplane are in constant flux across the three dimensions of altitude, forward motion, and direction. A pilot must respond to changes in each of these dimensions with the intention of reaching a goal, such as increasing altitude or changing direction, while simultaneously performing actions that return the aircraft to stable flight following the attainment of the goal. If the pilot overreacts to a particular short-term flux in one or more of the flight dimensions, the aircraft may destabilize and require additional, more focused actions to take place. The concept of stability is better thought of as an average of conditions over time. The key to stability is not simply to affect an average, but to affect an average based on small variances in change.

TABLE 5-6 Factors Contributing to EIS Failures

- Management failures (lack of support, loss of interest, unwillingness to train)
- Political problems (middle management resistance, lack of resource commitment)
- Developer failures (slow development, inadequate needs analysis, doubtful data integrity)
- Technology failures (inadequate speed or capacity, insufficient functionality)
- Costs (development, training, political)
- Time (development, training, maintenance)

In the organizational setting, the executive must be positioned to decide rather than to simply react. The fast responses to spur-of-the-moment inquiries made by an executive to an EIS can provide the ability to react swiftly to changes in the organization's operations. It is important, however, that such fast responses do not encourage the executive to react too swiftly by making adjustments to the organization that are too frequent or too strong. Such overreactions by executives can destabilize an otherwise stable organization in much the same manner as an over-reactive pilot can destabilize an otherwise smooth-flying aircraft.

FAILURE IS NOT AN ACCEPTABLE ALTERNATIVE

As with any development effort, the possibility of partial or total failure for a particular EIS is always present. An EIS failure occurs when the development effort fails to produce a working system or when the installed system fails to be usable or deliver the desired benefits. Crockett (1992) clearly demonstrated that an EIS development effort that fails to satisfy its targeted users can be a severe setback not only for the organization, but also for the individuals involved. Competitive edge and opportunity can be lost, many people will be disappointed, careers will undoubtedly be adversely affected, and most important, the organization will likely become reluctant to engage in any future EIS development efforts. As *Apollo 13* Flight Director Gene Kranz put it, "Failure is not an option." Table 5-6 lists many of the factors identified by Crockett that can contribute to the failure of an EIS.

Prevention of EIS failure is not readily prescriptive in nature. The need for broad-based executive support for the project is essential, however. Training and regular communication among all the participants are also key elements to success. Finally, being aware of the various factors that can contribute to EIS failure and paying constant attention to minimizing those factors are both important steps toward the successful implementation of an EIS within today's organization.

5.6: THE FUTURE OF EXECUTIVE DECISION MAKING AND THE EIS

The future of EIS technology and, thus, executive decision making, is one where several conditions will merge to transform the technology. Some of these conditions are fairly easy to predict because they exist today, whereas others have yet to emerge. Nonetheless, we will spend some time looking forward to see what the EIS of the future might be.

CONDITIONS OF TRANSFORMATION

Increased Comfort with Computing Technology

One current condition that will continue is executives' increasing comfort with technology. In the early years of EIS development, a significant roadblock to the acceptance of the technology was executives' lack of experience with hands-on use of computers. An increased focus on training combined with the growing realization that information systems such as EISs are valuable to the organization significantly reduces this roadblock. In addition, the executive suite is becoming younger. Emerging leaders grew up in the age of technology and developed an early understanding of and comfort level with computer-based systems throughout the organization. As the resistance to computers dissipates, new and more powerful EIS systems will emerge.

Broadening of Executive Responsibilities

The organization will continue to flatten and "right size." These conditions will create a leaner, more flexible and responsive structure, but will also increase the worker-to-executive ratio. Most of the reduction in workforce will come from staff and middle management levels, and the future executive will have direct contact with and responsibility for a much broader span of personnel. We can assume that EIS technology will play a major role in facilitating the management of this flatter organizational structure.

The boundaries of the organization will also continue to expand. Global markets will intensify the competition for market share, natural resources, and labor. With these factors will come continued increases in regulation driven by social and environmental concerns. The scope of responsibility of the executive will clearly include these increasing complexities, and the need for accurate, more diverse, and immediate information will continue to grow.

THE EIS OF TOMORROW

The trend toward the integration of applications and technologies into seamless enterprise-wide systems bodes well for the future of EISs. Technological and conceptual advances in telecommunications, information systems, and decision support systems will all contribute to new EIS features and potentially new and more powerful EIS applications. Watson, Houdeshel, and Rainer (1997) suggest that the EIS of the future may become an executive intelligence system.

The Intelligent EIS

The amount of data provided to the executive is literally overwhelming. Even with an EIS, the potential for information overload is constant. AI can perform some of the data screening for the executive, reducing the amount of time spent searching for relevant data.

Advances in voice input capabilities promote the use of AI. Executives accustomed to delivering verbal instructions would find that voice input reduces both the data entry time and the potential for errors. Properly deployed, voice input and output would clearly add greater flexibility to the EIS and allow for further understanding and comprehension of information. Voice command software is available today, but it is still in a relatively primitive form. The current state of speech recognition system technology, therefore, limits the use of voice input as an interface. Nonetheless, voice annotation technology has already demonstrated its value in increasing comprehension while reducing the need for page after page of reports. As the challenges related to voice recognition technology begin to dissolve, the advent of the intelligent voice-controlled EIS will occur.

Managing the large storage requirements for voice handling presents a major hurdle in voice technology. Physically storing a system that can recognize all the language instruction, accents, and other natural speech phenomena takes huge amounts of magnetic or optical storage space and has proven difficult. In addition, the technology necessary to overcome issues associated with speaker-dependent recognition is still in its infancy. Current systems require the user to "train" the system by participating in a rather protracted preparation exercise. The user is prompted to speak a series of words, phrases, syllables, and numbers repeatedly while the application creates a voice fingerprint for the user. Although this method dramatically increases recognition rates (currently as high as 99.7 percent with the Kurzweil Voice Plus system), it is nonetheless tedious and extremely time-consuming, two conditions that are antithetical to the nature of executives. Several speaker-independent recognition technologies are currently under development, however, and when refined, will become an immediate enhancement to current EIS systems.

Another branch of AI is expert systems (ESs). An ES can be used within an EIS to assist the user with appropriate model selection to analyze a problem. Based on rules provided to the ES, the ES can instruct the user on which model would best fit the problem context. An ES is similar to an EIS in that they both contain components that manipulate data. They differ in the way knowledge is maintained, however. An EIS uses predefined models and associated algorithms, whereas an ES operation is based primarily on heuristics.

The Multimedia EIS

An EIS requires a database component for retrieving, analyzing, manipulating, and updating files. A multimedia database management system (MMDBMS) can increase the future EIS user's resources to manipulate text, voice, and images effectively within an integrated database structure. MMDBMSs provide the traditional benefits of a database management system, as well as voice concatenation, transformation of information, rotation of images, scaling of objects, and merging of various data types. The problem with these systems, especially for the executive user, is the complex interface. As the functionality of these systems continues to increase, more applications for their use will be developed. By combining more applications with an easy-to-use system, an opportunity for a competitive advantage develops.

The Informed EIS

We know that most of the decisions made by executives require some element of external data. Strategic decisions require significant access to data about the market, the environment, the economy, regulatory and technological changes, and the competition. Although access to external data via an EIS is not new, the degree to which the EIS will be able to manipulate and assemble those data will be.

Literally thousands of private sector and government-maintained databases currently exist, and the present volume is expected to double by the turn of the century. The information in these databases is available, but the scanning, filtering, and extraction tools that allow for efficient and effective use of those data are still being refined. The challenge for the next generation of EIS designers will be to integrate data access tools into the applications that will allow the EIS to systematically find and organize the necessary information for the executive from the world's data stores and to deliver it to the EIS desktop in a manner that allows it to be readily understood and applied.

The Connected EIS

The Internet and the World Wide Web facilitate the electronic interconnection of companies to their customers and suppliers. The addition of Web-centric groupware technologies such as Lotus Notes moves organizations even closer toward mass interconnectivity. One massive current development is the dawning of electronic commerce (e-commerce). Firms use the Internet to advertise and communicate new product developments to both current and future customers. Emerging virtual markets are making Internet-based commerce and finance a reality.

With the widespread availability of high-bandwidth communications media, a logical extension of this interconnectivity frenzy would include the executive suite. The EIS of tomorrow may allow for controlled access by a variety of stakeholder groups, such as key suppliers, customers, stockholders, and partners, to that part of the EIS that is important to the conduct and maintenance of a particular relationship. This sharing of resources and information will strengthen the relationship between the parties by simultaneously facilitating the coordination of the relationship and building a common knowledge base. This concept is simply an electronic extension of today's account manager concept. The EIS of tomorrow will not eliminate the need for human relationship management, but it will serve as a valuable resource for improving the relationship building and maintenance processes.

5.7: CHAPTER SUMMARY

Despite the increasing awareness of the value of information to the successful implementation of organizational strategy, the concept of the EIS is still in its infancy. As new decision support and information gathering technologies emerge, new and more robust EIS designs will develop. Regardless of its power, however, the purpose of tomorrow's EIS will be the same as today: to provide senior managers with the information they need about their operating environment, internal operations, industry knowledge, and events, markets, customers, and suppliers. The future EISs will be bigger and more powerful and will surely differ in the scope of data sources available to them, but their purpose will be unwavering. The EIS will be a common tool found in every executive suite in the Information Age.

Key Concepts

- To address the unique variety of information needs of the CEO, a particular class of decision support technologies has emerged: executive information systems (EISs).

- An EIS is a computer-based system intended to facilitate and support the information and decision-making needs of senior executives by providing easy access to both internal and external information relevant to meeting the stated goals of the organization.

- An EIS must be designed and implemented for a particular executive environment. An EIS must be designed and implemented based upon a particular executive's information needs. Because both of these requirements are extremely fluid, the EIS must be considered an evolutionary tool in an organization, requiring a significant commitment to its ongoing support and development.

- The drill down capability of an EIS is a process of data decomposition that is selected and controlled by the executive and will be different for every situation. This feature of an EIS allows the executive to seek solutions to problems by employing a "top-down" analysis and a structured investigation.

- By gaining an understanding of the unique nature of work at the top executive level, we can fully appreciate the information needs of top executives. Executive activities can be divided into several basic categories:

  Disturbance management. This activity requires the immediate attention of executives as well as the deployment of resources to an unexpected occurrence, particularly one that could materially and negatively affect the financial health of the organization.

Entrepreneurial activities. These activities are strategic planning tasks usually triggered by real or perceived changes in the external environment. Executives must focus their attention on understanding the dynamic forces in the markets and the global environment and must use the information gathered to predict changes that can be viewed as opportunities to the firm.

Allocation of resources. The authority to deploy resources and the various activities to obtain them are normally performed by top executives. Moreover, top executives must decide to whom and where to allocate the organizational resources because, in general, the demand for resources is greater than their availability.

Negotiation. Executives represent the organization in both internal and external disputes. This role involves responsibility for the resolution of disputes and conflicts and a significant amount of negotiation among the parties.

- Given the relevance of the various information attributes to management levels, we can identify the various types of information needed by top executives.

- Executive information determination and sources include the following:

By-product. The primary support comes from TPSs and other MISs that summarize and aggregate the various information by-products of the current operation in the organization.

Null. The null approach involves the constant, but informal, collection of mostly subjective information from trusted sources via "word of mouth." This method relies on the spontaneous exchanges and discoveries that take place during informal tours of an organization.

Key indicator. Top executives monitor only that information that reflects an out-of-nominal condition and gather additional information as a basis for making decisions intended to correct the condition.

Total study. The total study approach gathers information from a sample of top executives in the organization concerning the totality of their information needs.

Critical success factors (CSFs). Information on the identified CSFs is constantly gathered and supplied to top executives. This information is used as the basis for making decisions that affect the organization.

- Client/server architecture allows for rapid additions and modifications to be incorporated into business applications and facilitates the widespread access and dissemination of disparate databases located throughout the globe.

- EISs are composed of hardware and software.

Hardware components. The hardware components of the EIS should be optimized with and conform to the organizational computing resources as well as adapted to the legacy data. Also, the system must be configured with the organization's resources and capabilities so that support is provided to both train executives and facilitate the systems' modifications.

Software components. The individuality of an EIS comes from the software components rather than from the hardware. The software components of an EIS are normally highly specialized and designed to meet the specific needs of specific users.

The EIS development framework provides the terminology, concepts, and guidelines necessary for building an EIS. It can be divided into three major components:

Structural perspective. The structural perspective provides a model for understanding the relationships among the various elements and their potential interaction during the various phases of development of the EIS.

EIS development process. The development process builds upon the elements and their relationships contained within the structural model and adds a time dimension to the framework.

User-system dialog. The user-system dialog includes the action language, presentation language, and knowledge base. The action language is the various commands and elements that direct users how to use the system. It is the incoming communication channel from the executive to the EIS. The presentation language serves as the EIS counterpart to the action language. This component guides the outflow of information and the form in which this information is presented. The knowledge base is the sum of what the executive knows about using the system and all of the support mechanisms designed to assist in its use.

- Two considerations of designing and developing an EIS are that the EIS must be easy to use and have an acceptably fast response time.

- EIS has a number of limitations.

  Cost. The benefits derived from an EIS are costly, and the cost of maintenance of the system after development can easily exceed the original development costs over the life of the system.

  Technological limitations. The myriad of data sources necessary to accomplish the functionalities of an EIS and the wide variety of media in which they can reside pose formidable technical challenges for the EIS designer.

  Organizational limitations. An EIS may be limited by biased agendas and time orientations, a loss of managerial synchronization, and organizational destabilization.

    Biased agendas and time orientations. This form of information channeling can cause an executive's agenda to be biased toward a superficial analysis of the environment. Also, an EIS can serve to promote a more micromanagement approach to conducting business, which can disrupt the activities of middle and lower-level managers.

    Loss of managerial synchronization. A heavy reliance on ad hoc reports can sometimes disrupt the stable and well-established reporting cycles within an organization that have been designed to synchronize management activities.

    Organizational destabilization. The fast response to spur-of-the-moment inquiries may cause the executive to react too swiftly by making adjustments to the organization that are too frequent or too strong. Such overreactions by executives can destabilize an otherwise stable organization.

- Failure is not an option. An EIS development effort that fails to satisfy its targeted users can be a severe setback not only for the organization, but also for the individuals involved.

- The following factors can prevent EIS failure:

  Broad-based executive support for the project is needed.

  Training and regular communication among all the participants is a key element to success.

  Be aware of the various factors that can contribute to EIS failure and pay constant attention to minimizing those factors.

- Conditions of transformation in executive decision making include increased comfort with computing technology and a broadening of executive responsibilities.

- The EIS of tomorrow will be intelligent, multimedia friendly, informed, and connected.

  The intelligent EIS. AI can perform some of the data screening for the executive, reducing the time spent searching for relevant data.

  The multimedia EIS. An MMDBMS can increase the EIS user resources in order to manipulate text, voice, and images effectively within an integrated database structure.

  The informed EIS. The challenge for the next generation of EIS designers will be to integrate data access tools into the applications that will allow the EIS to systematically find and organize the necessary information for the executive from the world's data stores and to deliver it to the EIS desktop in a manner that allows it to be readily understood and applied.

  The connected EIS. With the widespread availability of high-bandwidth communications media, a logical extension of this interconnectivity frenzy would include the executive suite. The EIS of tomorrow will serve as a valuable resource for improving relationship building and maintenance.

Questions for Review

1. Define executive information system (EIS).
2. List two EIS design requirements.
3. Describe the drill down feature of an EIS.
4. Is the organizational EIS a substitute for other forms of information technology and computer-based systems? Why or why not?
5. List and briefly describe executive activities.
6. List and briefly describe the five basic methods for executive information determination.
7. What is the primary method for establishing the CSFs of an organization?
8. What are the benefits of client/server architecture?
9. Depict the key consideration of the computing hardware environment for developing and deploying an organizational EIS.
10. List and briefly describe the categories of current EIS technologies.
11. Describe the components of an EIS development framework.
12. Identify the three basic components of the user-system dialog.
13. List and briefly describe several EIS limitations.
14. Explain the three main categories of potential negative impacts of an EIS on organizations.
15. How can the failure of an EIS implementation project be prevented?
16. Describe the conditions of transformation in executive decision making.
17. Briefly describe the EIS of tomorrow.

For Further Discussion

1. Analyze an EIS application in the market. Describe its drill down capability and how this function helps executives.
2. Review the categories of executive activities and the information needs for the activities in each category. Relate these factors to a fast-food company. What about a service organization?
3. Find and study a case of disturbance management in an organization. How can an EIS support the executives in this case?
4. Assume you and your team are the top executives of an insurance company. Identify the information you need through key indicator and CSF approaches.
5. Review the areas of support that should be provided by an EIS application. Analyze an EIS application product in the market. Describe its functionalities based on these areas of support.
6. Assume you and your team are assigned to develop an EIS for your organization. Design the EIS using the development framework. Identify the factors that may cause the failure of this project. How can you and your team prevent the failure?
7. Use a common development platform such as Excel or Access to develop a prototypical EIS for your department at work or at school. Use color to highlight exceptions where appropriate and include models for forecasting and prediction. Prepare a report that outlines the steps you took in the development of the system and the problems you encountered during its design.
8. It appears that the EIS is no longer being used exclusively in the executive suite of large organizations. The system is rapidly spreading throughout the organization to all levels of management. Discuss why this phenomenon is occurring and make suggestions about how this diffusion may be facilitated by senior management.

9. Analyze the types of information you use in your daily tasks. Using the various categories of information discussed in this chapter, outline the types of information you regularly use. Do you see any patterns of information in your daily activities? Could you benefit from a "personal EIS"?

10. Consider the development of an EIS for the CEO of a major commercial airline. Choose a specific airline and do some basic research on its senior management and its organizational structure.

- Who would be the target users? List the actual names of the people involved in the EIS.
- Who would be the most appropriate project sponsor? Why?
- What sources and types of information would be made available to the target users via the EIS? What would be in summary form? What levels of detail would be provided? What formats for presentation would you choose?
- Would the EIS need to be real-time or archival?
- What limits or controls would you place on various target user subgroups?
- What sources of external data would you include in the EIS?

References

Crockett, F. (Summer 1992). "Revitalizing Executive Information Systems." *Sloan Management Review*, *38*, pp. 17–29.

Dobrzeniecki, A. (1994). *Executive Information Systems*. IIT Research Institute White Paper Series.

Jones, J. W., and R. McLeod. (1986). "The Structure of Executive Information Systems: An Exploratory Analysis." *Decision Sciences*, *17*, 2: pp. 220–49.

Millet, I., and C. H. Mawhinney. (1992). "Executive Information Systems—A Critical Perspective." *Information and Management*, *23*, 1: pp. 83–93.

Peters, T., and R. H. Waterman. (1982). *In Search of Excellence*. New York: Harper & Row.

Rockart, J. F. (March–April 1979). "Chief Executives Define Their Own Data Needs." *Harvard Business Review*.

Rockart, J. F., and M. E. Treacy. (1982). "The CEO Goes On-Line." *Harvard Business Review*, *60*, 1: pp. 82–87.

Watson, H. J., G. Houdeshel, and R. K. Rainer, Jr. (1997). *Building Executive Information Systems and Other Decision Support Applications*. New York: Wiley.

Watson, H. J., R. K. Rainer, and C. Koh. (1991). "Executive Information Systems: A Framework for Development and a Survey of Current Practices." *MIS Quarterly*, *15*, 1: pp. 13–31.

Watson, H. J., S. Singh, and D. Holmes. (1995). "Development Practices for Executive Information Systems: Findings of a Field Study." *Decision Support Systems*, *14*, 2: pp. 171–85.

6

DESIGNING AND BUILDING
THE DATA WAREHOUSE

Learning Objectives

◆ Understand the enterprise model approach to building a DW.

◆ Explore the issues related to defining the project scope.

◆ Examine the concepts associated with the economic justification of the project.

◆ Review the various analysis tools used to gather system requirements.

◆ Explain the design of a project plan for construction of a DW.

◆ Understand the process of economic feasibility analysis and the importance of intangibles.

◆ Review the various DW architectures and development methodologies.

◆ Determine the project success factors associated with DW implementation.

SALES BLOSSOM AT EFLOWERS.COM
WITH WEB MINING

eFlowers.com came to be when Bill McClure, chairman and CEO of Flowers Direct LP and Universal American Flowers LP, decided to sell flowers over the Internet. The company obtained nationwide publicity in April 2000 by acquiring its domain name in exchange for agreeing, in addition to a cash payment, to send a dozen long-stem roses to the previous owner's wife every month for the rest of her life.

When McClure founded eFlowers.com, he had already built two substantial businesses selling flowers wholesale to supermarkets and directly to consumers over the telephone. Together with eFlowers.com, these businesses occupy a 35,000-square-foot, fully refrigerated facility and employ more than 100 full-time employees.

eFlowers.com leverages its experience and a strong business infrastructure to surpass other Web florists by offering the freshest product and the most creative designs. Today, it takes the company no more than 3 days to deliver cut product direct from its farms in South America—2 days faster than the industry standard. According to eFlowers, flowers are more than just a decorative accessory. Flowers have the power to deliver the sender's thoughts and feelings, just as those emotions were meant to be expressed.

THE BUSINESS CHALLENGE

eFlowers.com experienced problems with a low-end traffic analysis solution for their Web site. Potential traffic builders, advertisers, and investors used the number of unique visitors as their primary metric, yet the low-end tool was only able to measure the number of visitor sessions. The problem grew large when eFlowers' partners began expressing their concerns over the accuracy of the numbers and the overall validity of the application used to collect the metrics.

Inability to track referrals from various search engines hampered the company's efforts to improve its search engine positioning. As most search engines charge per clickthrough, it also meant that eFlowers.com had no way to validate the actual numbers for which they were paying. Finally, the traffic analysis tool provided no assistance in addressing another critical issue: extremely short sales periods during holidays. The company's marketing team needed immediate feedback on the performance of sales promotions in order to make adjustments that could have a major financial impact.

THE SOLUTION

Virtually all of the partners who expressed concern over the tool were users of WebTrends, a popular Web mining application. Their recommendations weighed heavily in eFlowers.com's decision to adopt WebTrends as its Web mining solution. eFlowers.com found the WebTrends solution to be a blessing because it required virtually no support infrastructure, which eliminated the need to purchase and set up hardware, install software, and maintain everything. All they had to do was paste a bit of JavaScript code on each of the pages they wanted to analyze. The cost was reasonable, the process simple, and on the few occasions they ran into snags, they received excellent technical support from WebTrends.

THE RESULTS

Implementing a robust Web mining solution immediately improved their credibility with traffic builders and potential advertisers. They can provide information in a format that everyone is used to seeing, and the WebTrends name meant instant credibility.

The fact that Web mining is able to provide unique user statistics is especially important, and the service saved eFlowers.com time by eliminating disagreements. For example, if a search engine tells them that they received 252 referrals but the Web mining system says it was only 158, the WebTrends' statistic ends the argument. Just as important is the additional information the service provides. Having continual, accurate information on referrals from each search engine helps eFlowers.com increase

(continued)

DATA MINING MINICASE

(continued)

traffic by allowing them to focus marketing efforts on sites where they have a low number of referrals. The Web mining solution goes beyond reporting the source of the traffic by providing a count of key words used to reach the eFlowers.com site. Then, if they see they are getting very little traffic from a search engine for a keyword that is generating a lot of traffic from other sites, the marketing staff can change the metatags or headlines to try to improve the results.

The ability of the Web mining application to track transactions helped the company significantly increase revenues during key flower holidays. The specials they run during holiday periods generate a significant part of eFlowers.com's revenues. The problem they encountered in the past was that it often took a day or two before they were able to generate meaningful figures from their back-end systems on which promotions were taking off

and which ones were falling flat. By the time eFlowers.com received the information, many sales were already lost. Now, the marketing and sales staff can query the Web mining application and get a real-time determination of exactly how their products are moving. Based on that information, they can make decisions such as moving a popular promotion to the homepage, dropping a promotion that is not working, ordering new inventory of a popular item, or reducing the price of something that is not selling. By closely tracking what is happening in the early hours of the holiday, eFlowers.com can make decisions that affect sales over these hot selling periods. For Thanksgiving 2000, the Web mining solution helped eFlowers.com determine which centerpieces were the best sellers. The products were moved to the homepage, and they beat their projected sales targets for the period.

6.1: THE ENTERPRISE MODEL APPROACH TO DW DESIGN

In Chapter 2, we explored the concept of a data warehouse (DW) and looked briefly at some of the challenges associated with implementing one within a modern organization. In this chapter, we extend our focus to specific issues regarding the construction and implementation of an organizational DW.

Regardless of the level of sophistication of an organization's strategic deployment of technologies, the DW poses a significant challenge to the technology infrastructure. If the DW project is to be successful and generate information for the widest possible audience, the first step in planning a DW must be to define the information requirements of the enterprise in a holistic sense. This definition normally requires a description of the business at the enterprise level in terms of its various information characteristics. These activities constitute the creation of an *enterprise model* (EM).

EM DEFINED

The EM of a firm consists of a number of separate models that, when properly integrated, provide a coherent picture of the enterprise. The various submodels may describe the enterprise in terms of strategy, organization, data, processes, or culture. The goal is to ascertain the level of alignment between the business and its cadre of systems.

Although all of the components of a fully specified EM will be of interest to the DW designers, two specific elements of the model are particularly important: *the corporate process model* and *the corporate data model.*

The corporate process model represents a highly structured description of the elementary processes within the enterprise that identify the interrelationships among the different processes. The corporate data model describes the entities generated by or required by the elementary processes carried out by the enterprise. We will explore the content and construction of each of these models in greater detail later in this section. For the moment, it is only important for us to realize the benefits of developing an EM prior to launching a DW venture of any size.

The long-term benefit of the construction of an EM is found primarily through the increased integration of the business processes throughout the firm. Simply constructing the model does not, however, create this benefit. The increased integration is a direct result of the redesign of the processes themselves and of the information systems that support them. Most organizations cannot, however, afford the luxury of having a fully integrated set of business processes. They need, or simply want, an integrated view of their data immediately. The construction of an EM can deliver a short-term benefit to the organization by serving to integrate the data, if not their associated processes. The organization can use its EM to determine which data to offload to the data warehouse from its currently disintegrated data model. The DW can then serve to integrate the offloaded data according to the desired enterprise data model before moving on to the longer-term (and more costly) goal of total integration of the business processes.

TOP-DOWN DW DESIGN

The decision to construct an accurate EM prior to commencement of a DW is heavily dependent on which approach to DW construction the organization chooses to adopt. A top-down approach to DW design is firmly based on the EM itself. It implies a strategic rather than an operational perspective of the data.

Many organizations are reluctant to accept the daunting task of constructing an EM before beginning the more urgent DW initiative. The perception is that too much organizational change will be generated by organizational, competitive, and economic uncertainties for the model to ever be truly accurate at any given point in time. Another common reason for resistance is that the construction of a holistic model of the enterprise will likely identify deficiencies throughout the organization that could be potentially damaging to individuals and groups and disrupt an otherwise stable power structure. Finally, IS personnel, continually under the gun to deliver high-quality systems, may not feel that the resources necessary to construct the enterprise model can be effectively diverted to an activity that does not result in the delivery of a new system.

Regardless of the reason for resistance, building an EM means putting the *important* before the *urgent*. It is precisely because of the constant fluctuation and change in the business environment and the relatively poor productivity in the IS function that the EM needs to be built first. The model serves as a jointly created charter of an agreed course for the future and the proper alignment of the organization's information systems with its business goals and objectives.

BOTTOM-UP DW DESIGN

In contrast, a bottom-up approach to DW design focuses more on making use of data available in the current operational systems. The decision of which approach to take can ultimately affect the nature and functionality of the final DW. Wherever possible, the top-down approach brings more benefit to the project, albeit with much more effort.

To be clear, however, an organization can build a successful DW without first going through the process of constructing an accurate and strategic EM. If this direction is chosen by the organization, two significant factors must be given careful consideration. First, no EM, regardless of how well it is constructed, will solve the immediate problem of integrating data on existing operational systems. In other words, the construction of an EM is not a substitute or alternative to building a DW. Second, if the chosen route is to bypass the EM, the DW will most likely end up a solution to some of the organization's information needs, but certainly not all of them. If this "80 percent right" approach is acceptable to the organization, then the enterprise model step can be skipped altogether.

THE CONCEPT OF ENTERPRISE INTEGRATION

Enterprise modeling and its associated software and hardware standards are at the heart of the concept of integration. To be effective, integration must occur on three distinct levels: (1) *horizontal,* (2) *vertical,* and (3) *enterprise.*

Horizontal Integration

Horizontal integration can be thought of as the most basic form of integration because it seeks to ensure that each application under development or in operation is fully integrated within its own boundaries and to eliminate any inconsistencies in the final software product. This level of integration is often achieved without any reference to an EM and is limited to providing quality within each isolated software application.

Vertical Integration

Vertical integration is much less prevalent in organizations. Vertical integration is the means by which the application designer ensures that the software application is in harmony with its stated business requirements. To make a comparison across applications, some form of high-level EM (at least from a strategic perspective) must exist. Vertical integration is a move toward enterprise integration because the determination is based on the mission, goals, objectives, and critical success factors of the business.

Enterprise Integration

At the enterprise level of integration, consistent definitions of all data and processes across the enterprise will occur. To arrive at this level of integration, the organization engages in a literal refinement of all naming conventions used to identify, describe, and define objects within the enterprise. Once this task is completed, the data and processes throughout the organization and all interactions between them will be standardized. This level can only be achieved via the construction of an EM that has been validated by all business users of the information systems within the organization and where strict compliance to all standards set by the model are observed by all software developers within the firm.

Although it is beyond the scope of this text to discuss the detailed steps in constructing an EM, Table 6-1 contains a brief listing of the various activities and techniques of enterprise modeling.

6.2: THE DW PROJECT PLAN

As we have seen thus far, no easy prescription or recipe precedes the formal initiation of a DW project. Each organization is unique and, thus, few of these activities can be repeated across organizations. Regardless of the situation, however, the first item on the agenda must be an

TABLE 6-1 Activities Associated with Construction of an Enterprise Model

Activity	*Description*
Entity identification	Entities, the main building blocks of the DW, are identified by nouns that occur within the organization. Typical examples include: **CUSTOMER, ORDER, EMPLOYEE, INVOICE, PRODUCT.**
Entity relationship diagramming	Every identified entity within the organization is described along with a depiction of the relationships, ordinalities, cardinalities, and optionalities associated with each relationship. The identified relationships ultimately are aggregated into the business rules under which the organization operates. A typical example of such a relationship would be: **Each CUSTOMER may place one or more ORDERS.**
Elementary process identification	This activity identifies and describes all high-level processes within the organization. Each logical unit of work identified should occur as a result of a response to some event. Those units that do not conform to this requirement should be assessed with the intent of eliminating or redesigning them. A typical example of the description for each high-level process should include **NAME, PROCESS DESCRIPTION, TRIGGER EVENT, LOCATION, FREQUENCY OF OCCURRENCE.**
Entity life cycle analysis	This activity associates the data model and the process model for each business area as well as validates the completeness and consistency of both. A typical example of the outcome of this activity would be: **Each ORDER may be related to a number of elementary processes that can change the state of the entity from PLACED to CONFIRMED to CANCELLED to REORDERED.**
Event analysis	This activity describes the events clustered around inter-dependent processes such that the analyst can subdivide the enterprise into lower-level functions.
Association diagramming	This technique captures for analysis the association that exists between two objects resident in the enterprise model. Analysis results are usually presented in matrix form.
Critical success factor analysis	This activity identifies the high-level conditions critical for the enterprise to function effectively in the marketplace. A typical example of a CSF would be: **The organization will possess a thorough understanding of its customers' behaviors.**
SWOT analysis	SWOT analysis identifies the strengths, weaknesses, threats, and opportunities associated with a specific course of action.
Information needs analysis	This activity guides the key information needs of the decision makers at the strategic and operational levels. A typical example of this activity might provide the following knowledge: **The key information need of a certain operational decision maker is to know how many units of the product were sold within a given week.**
Current systems evaluation	This analysis provides the basis for determining the distance between the current information systems architecture and the constructed conceptual model of the enterprise. This analysis demonstrates the ability (or lack thereof) of the existing information systems architecture to meet the demands of the business, which provides a key input to the justification of a DW project.

assessment of the organization with regard to its readiness to undergo DW development and implementation.

DW PROJECT DEFINITION AND READINESS ASSESSMENT

An organization's readiness for a DW can be assessed using five key factors. It is not necessary for the organization to achieve high scores in each of the factors to proceed, but rather for the key players to have a clear understanding of the project and an awareness of any potential vulnerabilities. If you find that you are unable to confidently give your organization a passing grade on the combined factors, however, it may be time to pull the plug on the project and revisit the issue later. Weaknesses in any given readiness factor will not correct themselves over time alone. When identified, a weakness in readiness should be addressed before proceeding with the DW development effort. Each of the five factors of readiness is discussed briefly.

Strong Management Sponsorship
Strong management sponsorship for the DW project may be the single most critical factor to its success. Strong project sponsors generally possess a clear vision of the DW's impact on the organization. They also hold a strong conviction with regard to their vision, enough to allow themselves to be held accountable for it.

One strong sponsor is good; multiple sponsors from different areas of the business are even better. Effective sponsors are realistic and will be able to accept and address the short-term problems normally associated with a typical DW endeavor.

Compelling Business Motivation
By itself, a DW will do nothing. Its value lies in its role as an enabler of specific business processes and strategic initiatives. In this sense, your organization can be considered ready on this dimension when a clear and easily articulated motivation for having the DW is present. A DW that can demonstrate an alignment with the stated strategic mission of the organization can be considered to display compelling motivation for its existence.

Level and Quality of the IS/Business Partnership
In an ideal world, one would never hear the phrase "IS and the business." IS is simply a facet of the business, just like marketing or finance. The degree to which you can determine the conscious elimination of the phrase is one way to measure the strength of the IS portion of a business and its potential to make a positive contribution to the DW initiative. The firm cannot build a successful DW without significant effort from IS, and the IS group cannot build a successful DW without the rest of the business functions as its partners. The good news is that a DW may be the perfect project to bring all of the functions of the business together to form a more cohesive culture.

Analytic Culture of the Organization
My good friend, Alan Dennis, is often fond of turning a common phrase with regard to decision making: "You can lead a group to information, but you can't make them think."[1] This phrase offers an appropriate way of thinking about the current analytic culture of the organization with regard to DW readiness. If the organization does not place a high value on information and analysis, then its readiness for a DW becomes questionable. The most successful DWs can

---

[1] Dr. Alan R. Dennis is the John T. Chambers Chair of Internet Systems in the Kelley School of Business at Indiana University.

be found in organizations that reward fact-based decision making. If the culture in your organization is better described as heuristic rather than holistic, you may want to reconsider your readiness for data warehousing.

Feasibility of the DW

This factor is concerned specifically with the feasibility of converting the existing organizational data into a common form for storage in the DW. If the current data model indicates that the typical organizational data are questionable with regard to accuracy, redundancy, colocation, or even physical existence, then a DW should not be in your immediate future. Further, if common business rules and definitions in the form of data relationships do not currently exist, the time line for launching the DW initiative will be severely extended.

Kimball and his colleagues (1998) developed a DW litmus test, which makes it relatively easy to see how an organization stands up to the challenge. Table 6-2 contains each of the readiness factors along with a description of what both high and low readiness looks like. Look over the chart and see how your organization or one that you know is contemplating a DW project scores. Use a weighting of 60 percent for the sponsorship category, 15 percent each for the business motivation and feasibility categories, and 5 percent each for the two remaining categories of readiness.

ADDRESSING DW READINESS SHORTFALL

As already discussed, stellar grades on all categories will not automatically ensure a successful DW initiative, and less than stellar grades on one or two categories does not mean the project should not go forward. If the litmus test for readiness identifies a weakness in one or two areas, then several techniques can be used to address the shortfall and get the organization ready for the big project.

In this section, we identify several techniques commonly used to address a readiness shortfall in one or more areas. Although the techniques are presented as isolated activities, they are more commonly used in conjunction with one another to address any readiness shortfall.

High-Level Business Requirements Analysis

The basic tools and techniques associated with business requirements analysis are described in any good systems analysis and design text.[2] Therefore, we will defer any discussion of the details of interviewing, survey preparation, joint application development (JAD), and direct observation. If a readiness shortfall is discovered during the litmus test, it may be time to conduct a thorough business requirements analysis to determine exactly what the business needs and where the disconnect is between its actual needs and its perceived needs. Generally speaking, a high-level business analysis effort should answer several key questions essential to the success of the DW initiative:

- What are the key strategic business initiatives as perceived by management?
- What are the key performance indicators or success metrics to be used for each of the key business initiatives?

---

[2]The reader is referred to Marakas, G. M. 2001. *Systems Analysis and Design: An Active Approach.* Upper Saddle River, NJ: Prentice Hall.

TABLE 6-2 Litmus Test for Data Warehouse Readiness Determination		
DW Readiness Factor	*Low-Level Readiness*	*High-Level Readiness*
Strong management sponsor	Not widely respected. Hard to gain access to. "Let me get back to you." "Good luck with the project." "Can we get this done in a month?" "What's a data warehouse?"	Widely respected and high clout. Easily accessible. Decisive with regard to problem resolution. Active, vocal, and visible sponsor of the project. Demonstrates realistic expectations with regard to project completion. Demonstrates understanding of DW concepts.
Compelling business	"So what's the point of this again?" "Can we afford to do this?" Nebulous, blurry vision of the project. Multiple views of the solution. Project viewed as tactical rather than strategic. Project viewed as a cost savings mechanism. Inability to satisfactorily quantify payback.	Project viewed as necessary for survival. "We can't afford to not do this." Clear articulation of the project vision. Clear and consistent view of the solution. Project viewed as strategic rather than tactical. Project viewed as a revenue generation opportunity. Clearly articulated and demonstrated payback.
Level and quality of IS/business partnership	Business engages outside consultants with IS knowledge. Business creates internal DW team without IS participation. "We can trust our current systems to be accurate." "It will take years to get IS involved."	Business and IS work as a team from the beginning. IS is actively engaged in all business activities. Business has strong confidence in current systems. IS is quick to respond to ad hoc project requests.
Analytic culture of the organization	Decisions are still made from the "gut." User community generally does not ask for more data. Current reports are not aggressively employed. Finance believes they own the bottom-line performance figures.	Fact-based decision making is prevalent. Business users are constantly asking for data. Current reports are widely used for other related analysis projects. Information is shared openly throughout the organization.
Data warehouse feasibility	DW project would require a large-scale purchase of all new technology. All experienced personnel are committed to other "highly strategic" projects. Data reliability is in question throughout the organization.	Organizational information systems architecture is robust and stable. Experienced human resources are available for the project. Data quality is perceived to be high throughout the organization.

Source: Adapted from Kimball, Reeves, Ross, and Thornthwaite. *The Data Warehouse Lifecycle Toolkit.* New York: John Wiley & Sons Publishing, 1998.

- What are the core business processes that management regularly monitors and wishes to affect positively through one or more key business initiatives?
- What is the potential impact on each of the existing performance metrics with improved access to higher-quality business process information?

The answers to these questions will identify the area(s) of the business that need attention to correct the overall DW readiness shortfall.

Business Requirements Prioritization

Business requirements prioritization is adapted from the formal step of project prioritization advocated by James Martin in his Rapid Application Development (RAD) methodology. Following the identification of key strategic initiatives, you will probably find that the organization believes that several initiatives are important rather than settling on just one. Until some method of prioritization can be agreed upon, any attempts to build organizational consensus for a DW project will be difficult, if not impossible, to achieve.

Although various techniques can be used to determine an unbiased ranking of projects on the basis of priority, the important issue is for the characteristics that drive a prioritization project to be carefully selected and agreed upon. Often a less complex approach will be more widely accepted than a highly complex mathematical method, such as analytical hierarchy process (AHP), and will be more easily understood by the various constituencies involved.[3]

One approach to the prioritization project is to rank the set of initiatives across two dimensions: perceived impact on the core business and feasibility of near-term completion. With the first dimension, each person assigns a rating on a scale from 1 to 10 with regard to the potential dollar payback to the organization, its strategic significance, availability of alternative solutions, political strength, and so on. Each characteristic should be calculated in terms of dollars, with an appropriate level of justification for each estimate provided.

This ranking of the projects and initiatives, based on potential impact on the business, can then also be prioritized in terms of feasibility of near-term completion. Feasibility can be determined in terms of data availability, ease of development, availability of necessary resources, and human factor requirements related to overall experience with similar projects. Using a simple 2×2 matrix approach, the various projects under consideration can be plotted into one of four quadrants. Figure 6-1 illustrates a typical plot of eight identified projects.

As you can see from the figure, Project 6 appears to represent the only project of the group that demonstrates both high business impact and high near-term feasibility. Based on this analysis, Project 6 would get an immediate nod. What would the next project likely be?

Proof of Concept

The proof of concept technique stems from the widely used software development approach of prototyping. In this case, however, proof of concept allows for a relatively low-cost approach to demonstrating the perceived benefits and feasibility of a given project. It can take the form of a small pilot study or isolated rollout of a technology to demonstrate its ability to succeed in a relatively low-risk environment. Once the small-scale proof of concept is established, the necessary buy-in for its large-scale counterpart is much easier to obtain.

---

[3]AHP is a mathematical ranking technique that can create an unbiased set of metrics to determine the exact order of priority for a set of characteristics or events. Although quite effective, it can also be quite complex and often yields results similar to that of other less complex approaches.

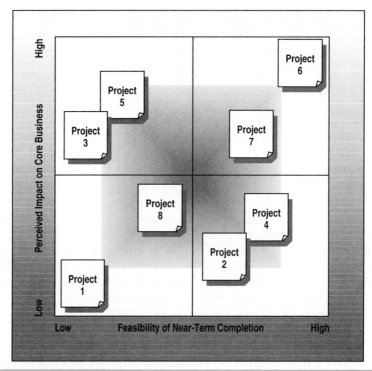

FIGURE 6-1 Example Project Prioritization Matrix

DEFINING THE DW PROJECT SCOPE

After the overall organizational readiness is determined to be within acceptable boundaries, the DW project can begin. The first item on the agenda is the formal definition of the project scope. It establishes an agreed boundary for the project and defines not only what the project is, but equally important, what the project is not.

Interestingly, one of the first challenges associated with project scope definition is the determination of exactly what it is we are scoping. Are we defining a project scope for the near-term requirements determination and DW design activities? Are we scoping a project that will result in the delivery of the first generation of the warehouse? Are we providing a project scope for a 3-year phased rollout? It is somewhat axiomatic that the farther one tries to see into the future, the more blurry their vision becomes. It is, therefore, important to determine the scope in terms of how far into the future one can see with 20-20 vision.

One of the unwritten rules concerning initial project scope definition is that the project manager wants to make as few promises as possible while simultaneously painting a broad enough picture to effectively identify the benefits and costs associated with the effort. To this end, several guidelines can be used for developing the preliminary scope for a DW project. Table 6-3 lists and briefly describes these guidelines.

The primary deliverable from this activity is the formally documented statement of project scope. Although it is clearly destined to change over time, this document provides the road map for each of the future development stages and reminds everyone what the objective of the project is. The more one gets involved in the details of an endeavor, the greater the likelihood that

TABLE 6-3   Guidelines for Developing Initial DW Project Scope

Project Scope Guideline	*Description*
Joint effort between IS and other business functions.	While the specific business requirement upon which the project scope is being developed may not be driven by IS, all relevant business functions, including IS, must materially participate in the development of the project scope for the DW.
Initial scope is meaningful and manageable.	*Meaningful* refers to the value to or impact on the organization derived from successfully addressing a well-defined business requirement.
	Manageable translates into *doable*. The value of starting small and growing cannot be overstated at this stage. By starting with smaller, quicker-to-market projects, the organizational knowledge as it relates to DW issues can be greatly enhanced without the fear of large-scale failures.
Initial focus is on a single business requirement from a single-source process.	Scope should be defined in terms of a single business process that requires a bounded set of data sources. Projects attempting to extract and integrate information from multiple business processes suffer from an exponential growth in the data staging effort necessary. Satisfy one constituency at a time.
Number of initial users is limited.	In general, an initial rollout limited to the needs of 20 to 25 users is considered manageable. Once the core user base can be established and stabilized, a plan to roll out to a larger community of users can be executed.
Success criteria are developed in conjunction with project scope.	The scope should be driven by the expectations of the business community with regard to the DW. To this end, success criteria should be established simultaneously with the definition of project scope to ensure the expectations are properly managed.

they will begin to forget the objective of their activities. The statement of project scope makes for a useful reminder in such times of temporary memory loss.

One last point to address before leaving project scope definition is the discussion of *scope creep*. This phenomenon is often found with projects that are complex and highly organizational in nature. Scope creep occurs when the initial scope of the project continues, sometimes imperceptibly, to expand as affected parties begin to think of features they would like to see incorporated into the project. Over time, scope creep can result in inflated budgets, missed deadlines, and projects that never seem to end. It is important to recognize the distinct difference between project scope refinement and scope creep. The former is a natural result of the gathering of more detailed information and requirements. The project still fits in the same-sized box, it just fits more snugly. The latter always results in the project needing a continually larger box in which to reside.

DEFINING THE BUSINESS JUSTIFICATION FOR A DW PROJECT

Once project scope is successfully established and agreed to by all related parties, the process of making the business case for the project can begin. This exercise formally articulates the various arguments that justify the allocation of resources necessary to design, construct, and deliver the DW. As with the definition of project scope, all related parties, including IS, must be involved in the construction of the business case for the DW.

The business case is really no mystery or magical exercise, although some people fear it as such. The justification for the project simply identifies and quantifies the appropriate anticipated benefits and costs, both tangible and intangible, to a level of accuracy that is both reasonable and from which common financial performance measures can be derived. Two distinct areas of concentration can be identified: investment (cost) and benefits (value). Each of these areas can be explored independently of the other and, when appropriately combined, can provide a clear justification (or lack thereof) for the proposed DW initiative. Remember, if the project cannot be adequately justified before it begins, no such justification will be forthcoming after money and time are already invested in it. At that point, it simply becomes sunk cost and wasted resources. Better to face that issue before the money is gone rather than after.

ISSUES IN MAKING THE BUSINESS CASE

One way to view the justification stage of the project is to think of the proposed DW as a business case for a major capital investment by the organization. If we adopt this approach, we can identify three perspectives from which the argument to pursue the investment may be made: (1) *facts,* (2) *faith,* or (3) *fear.*[4] Figure 6-2 provides several examples for each of these perspectives.

In the late 1980s, economic researchers discovered the *productivity paradox.* Despite an immense investment in information technologies—more than $1 trillion since the beginning of the PC revolution in about 1980—productivity growth in the United States has been either stagnant or weak. Growing productivity, more than anything else, contributes to expanding opportunity and a better material life. The effects of computerization, such as the speeding up of production and consumption and the ubiquity of computers, are clear, but wages and productivity stalled during the years of heavy investment in information technologies.

MIT researchers Erik Brynjolfsson and Lorin Hitt (1998) completed a comprehensive study of productivity in 380 large firms that together generate yearly sales in excess of $1.8 billion. They found that computing technologies were far from unproductive: They were significantly more productive than any other type of investment these companies made. The gross return on investment averaged about 60 percent annually for computers, including supercomputers, mainframes, minis, and micros. In addition, IS staffers were more than twice as productive as other workers.

Although many reasons explain why the productivity paradox appears to exist or, more recently, why it is a myth, one fact remains indisputable: If an investment cannot be justified in fact before it is made, then it will never be justifiable in fact after it is made. One theory behind the inability of researchers and economists to find a justifiable basis for investment in information systems is because many of them were never justifiable in the first place.

This point brings us back to facts, faith, and fear. Many IT investments in the past were made based on faith: "Look, we need to do this if we are to grow as an organization and remain technically competitive with the marketplace. You really have to trust me on this one." Others were made based on fear: "If we don't implement this new system, our competitors will eat us alive!" The important point here is that the feasibility assessment of an information system, at this point in the development process, must be made purely on fact and must be devoid of faith-based statements or threats of extinction. If the facts support the implementation of the proposed solution, then it is justifiable on all dimensions and should be implemented. If not, then

---

[4] I am indebted to my good friend and colleague, Dr. Bradley C. Wheeler, for allowing me to use his excellent conceptualization of making the business case.

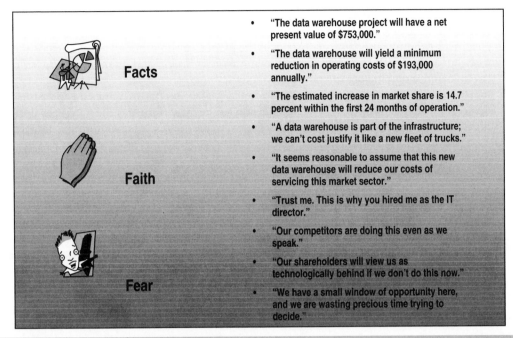

Facts
- "The data warehouse project will have a net present value of $753,000."
- "The data warehouse will yield a minimum reduction in operating costs of $193,000 annually."
- "The estimated increase in market share is 14.7 percent within the first 24 months of operation."

Faith
- "A data warehouse is part of the infrastructure; we can't cost justify it like a new fleet of trucks."
- "It seems reasonable to assume that this new data warehouse will reduce our costs of servicing this market sector."
- "Trust me. This is why you hired me as the IT director."

Fear
- "Our competitors are doing this even as we speak."
- "Our shareholders will view us as technologically behind if we don't do this now."
- "We have a small window of opportunity here, and we are wasting precious time trying to decide."

FIGURE 6-2   Three Bases of Project Justification

the present is precisely the time to realize the potential for failure and deal with it prior to the unwarranted investment of millions of dollars of organizational resources.

ECONOMIC FEASIBILITY ANALYSIS

This issue of business justification is not unique to DW proposals. Regardless of the nature of the project, we must assess the *economic feasibility* of the proposed system. This dimension identifies the financial and net economic impacts to the organization of the proposed system. Is it worth doing? Do the benefits outweigh the costs?

This activity can be thought of as a cost-benefit analysis, but it is actually much more complex. A great number of the expected benefits from a new DW system may appear to be intangible (i.e., improved customer service, improved customer satisfaction, increased employee morale). We will soon see that this complexity can be managed and, using common financial analysis techniques, the true economic value of a system can be determined.

Although economic feasibility assessment may be arguably the most important of all dimensions of justification, it must be performed last if it is to be comprehensive in its analysis. The true economic impact of a system must account for all components, including required changes to the technology and the organization, additional specialized human resources or training, and compliance with or management of any material legal or political constraints. Further, the final decision to invest in the proposed system will be made primarily on the outcome of the economic analysis rather than any specific information requirements or favorable feasibility dimension. Thus, to ensure that all other dimensions of feasibility can be reconciled in favor of the system, we perform the economic assessment last. If it passes this analysis, then it is ready for the next step.

Identifying the Costs and Benefits

It is often said that the good parts of an investment are a lot easier to identify than the bad parts. This generalization is equally true in the identification of the benefits and costs associated with a proposed DW initiative. We will begin by identifying and quantifying the benefits, both tangible and intangible, of the new DW.

By definition, a *benefit* is something that, either directly or indirectly, increases profit or decreases cost. Benefits are the desirable side of the equation, and the goal is to design a DW that has more benefit than cost. The task then is to identify all the benefits and, as accurately as possible, quantify them in terms of dollars and cents. Benefits can be classified as either tangible or intangible.

A *tangible benefit* is one that can be identified with certainty and easily expressed in dollars. Table 6-4 identifies some common tangible benefits associated with a typical information system.

Intangible benefits, although believed to be directly associated with the operation of the new information system, cannot be identified with certainty or easily expressed in dollars. The intangible benefits, even though they are difficult to quantify, contribute to the overall economic analysis of the system and can improve the benefit side of the economic feasibility

TABLE 6-4 Typical Tangible Benefits Associated with a New Data Warehouse

Benefit Category	Common Examples
Cost reduction	Reduction in labor or head count
	Reduction or elimination of overtime
	Consolidation of jobs or employee roles
	Reduction in supply usage
	Less paperwork
	Smaller inventory needs or carrying costs
	Efficiencies in distribution
	Less need for travel
	Efficient use of utilities
	Lower costs of hardware and/or software
	Less maintenance
	Increase in product/process quality
	Improved production throughput or costs
	Reduction in overall cost of funds
	Improved subcontractor or external vendor control
	Reduction in or improved effectiveness of training
Revenue increase	Introduction of new products
	Decreased time to market
	Improved product quality
	Increased efficiency in sales processes
	Product enhancements
	Improved advertising support and target marketing
	Effective bidding tools
	Development of, or access to, new markets

assessment. Table 6-5 summarizes several common intangible benefits associated with a new information system.

Just as with the benefit side of the analysis, the cost side contains both tangibles and intangibles. Tangible costs can be identified with certainty and easily expressed in dollars. The intangible costs are not easily identified with certainty and cannot be readily expressed in terms of dollars. One additional classification of costs distinguishes between those associated with DW development and those dealing with DW operation. Development costs are typically incurred once during the development project, whereas operating costs generally follow the implementation of the system and are considered to be ongoing. Table 6-6 contains examples of both tangible and intangible costs typically associated with a new DW.

Tangibles and Intangibles

The most difficult problem in performing a thorough economic feasibility assessment lies with the intangibles. They are, admittedly, difficult to identify and even more difficult to quantify. For this reason, the tendency is to ignore them in the preparation of the assessment. Yielding to this tendency, however, can be a most serious mistake in a business justification exercise.

Think of it this way: The intangible benefits are like icing on a cake. They are not the primary reason for pursuing the new DW, and their presence or absence in the analysis will probably not make or break the decision to pursue the project. If you are wrong about the intangible benefits, so what?

Unfortunately, however, the same cannot be said for the intangible costs. The fact that they can be identified at all suggests that they have the potential to negatively impact the economic assessment. They represent one or more potential "black holes" where money can go in but can never be recovered. Failing to quantify the intangible costs as accurately as possible can be disastrous. If you are wrong about the intangible costs, then what? To ensure an accurate analysis, all costs and benefits, both tangible and intangible, must be identified and quantified as

---

TABLE 6-5   Typical Intangible Benefits Associated with a New Data Warehouse

- Improved employee morale
- Improved corporate or public image
- Increase in perceived quality of products or services
- Perceived decrease in time to market by customers
- Improved decision making
- More timely information
- Increased organizational flexibility
- Improved resource allocation and control
- Increased strategic or competitive advantage
- Improved public and community relations
- Improvements in addressing environmental concerns
- Reduced employee turnover
- Increased quality of work for employees
- Proactive attention to ethical issues
- Proactive addressing of legal issues
- Increased workplace and/or community safety

TABLE 6-6	Typical Costs Associated with a New Information System
Cost Category	*Common Examples*
Tangible development	Development personnel
	Analysis and design consulting fees
	Predevelopment training
	Materials and supplies
	Vendor installation and consulting
	Hiring costs for new operating personnel
	Hardware and software acquisition or development
	Physical plant acquisition and/or conversion
	Documentation preparation and distribution
	Data conversion costs
Tangible operating	Maintenance and upgrades (hardware and software)
	Annual or renewable software licenses
	Repairs (hardware and software)
	Operational personnel
	End user training
	Connectivity and communication charges
	Materials and supplies
	Equipment lease payments
	Depreciation of system assets
Intangible	Potential disruption to existing productivity and environment
	Loss of customer goodwill
	Reduction in employee morale
	Diversion of attention to daily responsibilities

accurately as possible. The question then becomes, "How do we make that which is intangible tangible?" The answer in its simplest form is, we guess.

The validity of an economic assessment that is based on completely unquantified components becomes somewhat difficult to accept. If we are to obtain an accurate assessment of the economic feasibility of the new system, we must take the position that there is no such thing as an intangible cost or benefit. They are all costs and benefits, some of which can be accurately quantified and some that require a reasonable estimation process. To that end, the intangibles must be calculated using a logical set of underlying assumptions that lead to an estimate. The estimate, although probably not 100 percent accurate, is nonetheless much closer to reality than simply ignoring the cost or benefit altogether. In reality, all of the numbers in an economic justification are estimates—some are just more accurate than others. Let's look at an example.

Suppose the issue is to determine the potential cost of a temporary reduction in employee morale during the first 6 months of implementation for the new DW. This intangible cost, identified through past experience, suggests that a certain number of employees will be distressed by the intrusion of the new technology into their environment and their productivity will be temporarily reduced as a result of this distress. A series of surveys and focused interviews reveals that approximately 10 percent of our workforce will experience this loss of productivity based on their concerns expressed during the information gathering process. Further, we know from reviewing other similar DW projects and by consulting industry professionals that the probability of this reduction in morale occurring is about 60 percent. Our problem is that we do not know the dollar value of a 60 percent chance of a 10 percent reduction in employee morale. What we need is a logical surrogate measure for employee morale. In other words, we need something we can quantify to logically represent something we cannot.

Suppose we make the assumption that the overall morale of our workforce is directly related to the profits of our company. In other words, if our employees are unhappy, then we will not sell our products or services and will, therefore, not make any money. We could argue that morale is directly related to company revenues but, for purposes of illustration, profit becomes a more conservative approach to the problem. Given this assumption, we still do not know what a 10 percent reduction in employee morale is worth, but we now know what a 100 percent reduction in morale would cost: 100 percent of our annual profits! Consider the following:

100 percent reduction in employee morale = Nominal annual profits

Nominal annual profits = \$2,000,000

100 percent reduction in employee morale = \$2,000,000

10 percent reduction in employee morale = (0.1)(\$2,000,000) = \$200,000

60 percent probability of a 10 percent reduction in employee morale
= (0.6)(\$200,000) = \$120,000

By performing this analysis, on either intangible costs or benefits, using assumptions that can be agreed upon as logical, we quantify the intangible. Although this approach still may not yield an accurate assessment of the cost or benefit, it nonetheless provides a working boundary for the problem. Other assumptions can be considered and tested until one is found that all agree will provide enough reliability to be useful. An estimate is just that: an estimate. The important issue is that a reasonably derived estimate is infinitely more useful in assessing the economic feasibility of a project than no estimate at all.

ECONOMIC FEASIBILITY MEASURES

Numerous financial methods and approaches to the assessment of economic feasibility—often referred to as tests of *cost-effectiveness*—can be employed. For our purposes, we will examine the use of three common approaches: (1) net present value (NPV), (2) internal rate of return (IRR), and (3) breakeven analysis.[5]

All of the assessment approaches mentioned share a common concept called the *time value of money*. In essence, this concept suggests that a dollar today is worth more than a dollar in the future. The reasoning behind this concept is that if you have a dollar today, you can invest that dollar in some interest-bearing manner and have more than a dollar in the future. In assessing the economic feasibility of a project, we must consider the time value of money because we must incur cash outflows today, in the form of dollars spent to design, develop, acquire, and implement the proposed system, so that we can enjoy cash inflows in the future through the benefits expected from the new system. To ensure that we are comparing "apples to apples," we convert all future dollars in the present value of today's dollars. In this way, we can accurately assess the value of the system over its useful life in today's dollars.

---

[5]A detailed coverage of each of these methods is beyond the scope of this text. The explanations provided here are intended to demonstrate the basic use of the assessment approach in a manner that will allow for its application. For more detailed explanations of these methods, the reader is referred to any good financial analysis textbook.

NPV

Probably the most common technique for assessing the economic feasibility of an investment is the NPV approach. This method calculates the present value of a series of cash outflows and expected future cash inflows. The logic behind this technique is that if the net of all current and future outflows and all current and future benefits using a reasonable cost of capital or rate of return (called the discount rate) is positive, then the investment is a good one. If it is negative, then the investment will not yield the necessary returns, and it should be abandoned in favor of one that will. This technique also can be used to compare two or more competing investment alternatives. The one with the largest NPV will be the one that should be chosen based on the value of its return to the organization. Figure 6-3 contains a spreadsheet model used to conduct an NPV analysis of a project.

Note that each of the expected cash outflows and inflows for the project is calculated and then *discounted* back to today's dollars by applying a factor based on an acceptable rate of return for the organization. This factor can be thought of as the opportunity cost associated with investing those dollars in other projects, including stocks, bonds, or other less risky investments. In many cases, the NPV analysis is conducted using a discount rate deemed to be risk-free to determine the relative level of risk in the project. Probably the most common risk-free rate is based on the return on a U.S. Treasury bill and the assumption that the United States will not go bankrupt or out of business.

It is also important to note that the actual value calculated in an NPV analysis is not an important number. What is important is whether the final calculation is positive or negative. If it is positive, then the investment will yield a return greater than the required return. If it is negative, then the project, at least in its present form, is not economically feasible. The present value of a dollar for any period in the future can be easily calculated using the following formula:

$$PV_n = 1 / (1 + i)^n$$

where

$$PV_n = \text{present value of \$1 } n \text{ years from now}$$
$$i = \text{the accepted discount rate or rate of return}$$

Thus, the present value of a dollar 3 years from now assuming a discount rate of 10 percent is:

$$NPV = PV_1 + PV_2 + PV_3 + \ldots PV_n$$
$$PV_3 = 1 / (1 + 0.10)^3 = 0.751$$

This calculation suggests that $1 received 3 years from now is the same as receiving 75.1 cents today if a 10 percent rate of return is required. As shown in the calculations and in Figure 6-3, the NPV of an investment is simply the sum of the present value calculations for each period.

Although simple enough to calculate, most financial textbooks contain detailed tables of discount factors for a dollar at various interest rates and for various periods. Table 6-7 contains a partial listing of discount factors using common interest rates and discount periods. A more complete listing can be obtained from any good financial analysis reference book.

Internal Rate of Return (IRR)

Another equally popular method of assessing the economic feasibility of a project, closely related to the NPV approach, is to calculate its IRR. The IRR is mathematically more complicated than calculating an NPV, but it is actually the rate of return of the project when the NPV

FIGURE 6-3 Spreadsheet Model of Net Present Value Analysis

	Year 0	Year 1	Year 2	Year 3	Year 4	Year 5	Totals
Net economic benefit		$ 920,168.30	$ 926,977.32	$ 934,286.92	$ 941,703.65	$ 949,228.60	
Discount rate (8.25%)	1.0000	0.9238	0.8534	0.7883	0.7283	0.6728	
PV of benefits		$ 850,040.00	$ 791,067.06	$ 736,540.37	$ 685,808.14	$ 638,603.49	
NPV of all benefits		$ 850,040.000	$ 1,641,107.06	$ 2,377,647.42	$ 3,063,455.56	$ 3,702,059.05	$ 3,702,059.05
One-time costs	(831,579.65)	(322,659.82)					
PV of equipment depreciation		$ (56,086.46)	$ (51,811.97)	$ (47,863.25)	$ (44,215.47)	$ (40,845.70)	
Recurring costs		$ (325,576.80)	$ (341,855.64)	$ (358,948.42)	$ (376,895.84)	$ 395,740.64	
Discount rate (8.25%)	1.0000	0.9238	0.8534	0.7883	0.7283	0.6728	
PV of recurring costs		$ (300,763.79)	$ (291,733.93)	$ (282,975.17)	$ (274,479.38)	$ (266,238.66)	
NPV of all costs	$(831,579.65)	$(1,511,089.71)	$(1,854,635.61)	$(2,185,474.03)	$(2,504,168.89)	$(2,811,253.25)	$(2,811,253.25)
Overall NPV							$ 890,805.80
Overall ROI							32%
IRR							38%
Breakeven analysis							
Yearly NPV cash flow	$(831,579.65)	$ 549,276.21	$ 499,333.13	$ 453,565.19	$ 411,328.75	$ 372,364.83	
Overall NPV cash flow	$(831,579.65)	$ (661,049.71)	$ (213,528.55)	$ 192,173.39	$ 559,286.67	$ 890,805.80	
Project breakeven occurs at 2.576 years							

TABLE 6-7 Partial Table of Values for the Present Value of a Dollar

Period	8%	10%	12%	14%
1	0.926	0.909	0.893	0.877
2	0.857	0.826	0.797	0.769
3	0.794	0.751	0.712	0.675
4	0.735	0.683	0.636	0.592
5	0.681	0.621	00567	0.519
6	0.630	0.564	0.507	0.456
7	0.583	0.513	0.452	0.400
8	0.540	0.467	0.404	0.351

is zero. The result of an IRR calculation is the true net return on the investment expressed as an interest rate. The IRR of an investment is mathematically defined as the largest number d that satisfies the equation:

$$x = \sum_{t=1}^{T} \frac{R_t}{(1 + d)^t}$$

where

T = the expected life of the project in years

X = the total cost of the project

R_t = the expected net return in year t

Given the obvious complexity of the preceding calculation, it is much better to use a computer when determining an IRR.[6] Most spreadsheet programs include a simple function for calculating IRR. As shown in Figure 6-3, the calculated IRR of our project is 38 percent.

Breakeven Analysis

The objective of a breakeven analysis is to determine at what point over the expected life of the project (if ever) the benefits derived from the project equal the costs associated with implementing it. The first step in determining the breakeven point is to calculate the NPV of the yearly cash flows for the project. Next, a running total of the overall NPV cash flow during each period of the project must be determined. The year in which the overall NPV cash flow for the project is positive is called the *payback period*. To determine the actual breakeven point for the project, the following formula can be used:

$$\frac{\text{Payback Period NPV Cash Flow} - \text{Overall NPV Cash Flow}}{\text{Payback Period NPV Cash Flow}}$$

Referring to Figure 6-3, we can see that the project will reach a breakeven point in approximately the seventh month of year 2.

---

[6]A related calculation sometimes employed in investment analysis is *return on investment* (ROI). Although useful as an analysis tool, its applicability in assessing the economic feasibility of a proposed project is limited because it takes into account only the net results at the endpoints of the investment (i.e., the beginning and the end of the project). Because it accounts for the net cash flows during each period, IRR is preferred over ROI.

Another equally effective method to determine the breakeven point of a project is to simply plot the expected costs against the expected benefits on a graph. The point at which the two lines intersect is the breakeven point. Figure 6-4 illustrates the graphical approach to the assessment.

DEVELOPING THE DW PROJECT PLAN

The next step in the process is the development of a formal *project plan,* which involves looking at staffing needs, time estimates, constraints, and other project management activities. Put on your project manager hat, and let's get started.

Project Staffing Issues

Any DW project, regardless of size or scope, requires a number of different roles and skills to be successful. Rarely will these roles align themselves in a one-to-one fashion with individuals. Instead, it will more likely be the case that certain individuals will serve in several roles throughout the DW project. When determining initial staffing requirements for the project, you should actively seek synergies across roles and match those synergies to individuals who possess the necessary skill set to successfully perform the duties required.

Table 6-8 lists the various roles associated with a typical DW project along with a brief description of each. Table 6-9 illustrates a typical staffing plan for the user requirements definition phase of a typical DW project.

The Formal DW Project Plan

If we identify two key characteristics of a well-designed DW project plan, they would be high integration and high detail. The former is necessary to ensure that the various subplans developed by each of the DW staffing roles can be integrated into a cohesive and logical project plan for the DW. The latter characteristic suggests that a high level of detail for each proposed task in the plan be provided so as to ensure no misunderstanding or confusion. In addition, high detail implies that the project plan will be maintained in an up-to-date manner to include the

FIGURE 6-4 Example of Graphical Breakeven Analysis

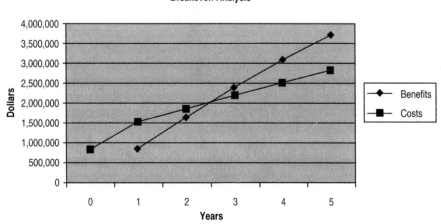

TABLE 6-8 Typical Staffing Roles Associated with a Data Warehouse Project

Staffing Role	Role Description
Project Sponsor	Business owner(s) of the project and/or those who bear the direct financial responsibility for the project.
Project Manager	Responsible for the day-to-day coordination of project activities and tasks. Will supervise all roles but will work closely with the Business Community Liaison.
Business Community Liaison	Works daily with the Project Manager as well as serves as the central communication channel regarding the project to the rest of the business community.
Business Systems Analyst	Responsible for leading the business requirements definition stage of the project. In addition, this role is responsible for the creation of the initial dimensional model for the project.
Data Modeler	Responsible for the detailed data analysis and development of the dimensional model for the DW.
DW Database Administrator (DBA)	Translates the dimensional model into a set of physical table structures. In addition, the DBA is responsible for determining initial aggregation, partitioning, and indexing strategies for the DW. Upon completion of the DW, the DBA will also be responsible for the day-to-day operational support of the database, ensuring data integrity, database availability, and DW performance.
Data Staging Designer	Responsible for the end-to-end design of the production process to extract, transform, and load the data in preparation for the DW.
End-User Application Developers	Responsible for the creation and maintenance of end-user applications associated with the DW. In addition, this role is generally responsible for loading the metadata for the data access tool.
DW Educator	Responsible for educating the business end users on the content and structure of the DW, as well as the various end-user applications and the data access tool.
Technical/Security Analyst	Responsible for the design of the technical infrastructure and security strategy for the DW.
Technical Support Specialist	Focus on issues related to mainframe systems software, client/server systems, and networking. In addition, this role serves as the primary support for the DW upon its completion.
Data Staging Programmer	Responsible for the programming of applications needed to automate data staging extraction, transformation, and load processes.
Data Steward	Responsible for gaining organizational consensus on common definitions for conformed DW dimensions and facts. In addition, this role is responsible for the ongoing maintenance of the DW data dictionary. Also referred to as the data administrator.
DW Quality Assurance Analyst	Responsible for ensuring that the data loaded into the DW are accurate.

TABLE 6-9   Typical Staffing Plan for DW User Requirements Phase

Requirement Definition Task	EU	BS	ISS	BD	PL	PM	SA	DM	DBA	DSD	DE	AD	TA	TS	DSP	DS	QA
Prepare interview team						1	2	2									
Select respondents	3	3	3	1	1												
Schedule interviews					2	1											
Conduct user kickoff	2	2	2	2	2	1	2	2									
Conduct interviews	2	2		2	2	5	1	5				5					
IS data discovery						5	1	1	2	2		5			2		
Analyze interviews					2	2	1										
Document findings	3			3	2	2	1	2									
Publish requirements	4	4	4	4	2	2	1	2	4	4	4	4	4	4	4	4	4
Revise project scope	3	3	3	2	1	2	2	2	2	2	5	2	5	5	2	5	5
User acceptance review	5	4	4	2	1	2	2	2	2	2	5	2	5	5	2	5	5

Legend	Description
EU	Business End Users
BS	Business Sponsor
ISS	IS Sponsor
BD	Business Driver
PL	Business Project Leader
PM	Project Manager
SA	Systems Analyst
DM	Data Modeler
DBA	Database Administrator
DSD	Data Staging Designer
DE	DW Educator
AD	Application Developer
TA	Technical/Security Analyst
TS	Technical Support Specialist
DSP	Data Staging Programmer
DS	Data Steward
QA	Quality Analyst
1	Primary responsibility for the task
2	Involved in the task
3	Provides input to the task
4	Informed of task results
5	Optional involvement in the task

latest iteration of all dependencies and task assignments. Although no specific template is available for developing a DW project plan, several guidelines as to its content can be offered:

- **Required resources.** All human, financial, and material resources should be clearly defined and tied to a specific task in the project plan.
- **Current estimated schedule.** A current estimate of the number of days for each stage in the project as well as the total estimated project duration.

- **Task commencement date.** The date the project, and each of its associated tasks, is scheduled to begin.
- **Current estimated completion date.** The date the project, and each of its associated tasks, is scheduled to be completed.
- **Project status.** The current status, often represented as a percentage of total effort, of the project and each of its associated tasks.
- **Task dependencies.** Clear and detailed identification of tasks that must be completed prior to the commencement of this task.
- **Late flags.** A mathematical calculation based on the difference between the expected completion date for both the project and its associated tasks and the current date. Normally expressed in terms of a positive or negative number of days. Positive numbers indicate project tasks that are ahead of schedule.

The single most important thing to remember regarding the project plan is that, as a living document, it will require multiple, sometimes daily, updates. It is the road map for the project and must always accurately reflect the current status of the project if it is to be of any value.

6.3: SPECIFYING THE ANALYSIS AND DESIGN TOOLS

Once the project plan is completed and approved and the gathering of business user requirements has begun, we can begin to focus on the logical modeling processes necessary to create an implementation-independent model of the proposed DW. Our intention here is to transform the legacy data resources throughout the organization into the final DW data structures. These models will also provide the basis for designing the data extraction and transformation strategies for the project, estimation of the overall size and administrative needs of the central DBMS, and the prototyping of end-user applications.

DIMENSIONAL MODELING APPROACH TO DW LOGICAL DESIGN

Through your studies in the field of information systems analysis and design, you probably recognize entity-relationship diagrams (ERD). These diagrams graphically depict the logical entities, relationships, and data structures in a relational data environment. Although the ERD approach could serve as a modeling tool for the DW, its several disadvantages make it less desirable in this domain. Instead, the logical design technique known as dimensional modeling is often used when building a DW. Dimensional modeling differs from the ERD approach in several important ways and, currently, is considered to be the only viable technique for effective design of a DW. To be sure we can make a clear distinction between the two techniques, however, it might be useful to provide a brief review of the ERD approach to data modeling. For those of you who are comfortable with your understanding of the approach, just skip down to the next section. For those of you who are not, our explanation will not take too long.

Entity-Relationship Modeling

Entity-relationship modeling (ERM) is a disciplined approach to structuring data such that the microscopic relationships among the data elements are revealed. The goal is to remove all redundancy in the data and to create a set of stable relationships that can be easily translated into a physical set of tables or databases. This technique now provides the mainstay of transactional systems designs because it stores transactions in simple and deterministic ways. Even complex lookups are controlled by a single-record key data element, and the use of indexed lookup is easily accomplished using a relational approach.

The real problem lies with the efficiency and effectiveness with which the ERM approach reaches its stated goals. In a typical organizational data structure, we find situations where a transaction as simple as taking an order can create dozens of tables linked together by a cacophony of spiderweb-like joins that are confusing at best. At the enterprise level, the ERM will contain literally hundreds of logical entities, and enterprise resource planning (ERP) installations can number in the thousands. This situation can bring even the most stalwart data query designers to their knees. As such, the ERM approach creates situations that are counter-intuitive and counterproductive to the concept of a DW:

- Business end users cannot be expected to remember or even fully understand the complexities of an enterprise-level ERM. Such a model is not easily navigated and offers no simple graphical interface to make the job easier.
- Generally speaking, end-user application software cannot readily query an ERM. A common example is the cost-based optimizer applications that attempt to query but are notorious for suggesting the wrong choices.
- The ERM approach tends to defeat the purpose of a DW, namely high performance and intuitive retrieval of relevant data.

To combat these problems and to facilitate other issues associated with DW design, the concept of dimensional modeling was developed.

Dimensional Modeling

Similar to ERM, dimensional modeling is a logical design technique to provide access to the data contained in the DW in a highly efficient, effective, and intuitive manner. The dimensional modeling approach differs significantly from the more conventional ERM technique.

Every dimensional model is composed of three basic elements. The first element is a central table containing multipart keys called the *fact table*. Surrounding the fact table are two or more smaller tables referred to as the *dimensional tables*. Each dimensional table contains a single-part primary key that directly corresponds to exactly one of the component elements of a multipart key in the fact table. Joining the dimensional tables to the fact table is a set of relationships referred to as a *star join*. Figure 6-5 illustrates a dimensional model for a typical retail sales process.

Note the many-to-one relationships between the fact table and each of the dimensional tables as illustrated in the figure. As the fact table contains a multipart key made up of two or more foreign keys, the relationship between it and any single dimensional table will always be many-to-one. Also, as shown in the figure, in addition to the multipart foreign keys, a typical fact table also contains one or more numerical facts that occur for the combination of keys that define each record.

ERM versus Dimensional Modeling

Certainly, the model illustrated in Figure 6-5 contains several characteristics reminiscent of an ERD, but it is clearly not an ERD. Ironically enough, the real difference between ER models and dimensional models lies in their relationship to one another.

The key to understanding this relationship is to realize that a single ERD can be broken down into multiple fact table diagrams (dimensional models). If we envision the ERD as a model that represents every possible business process and rule throughout the enterprise, we can quickly understand why it is so complex and unwieldy for data query purposes. The ERD

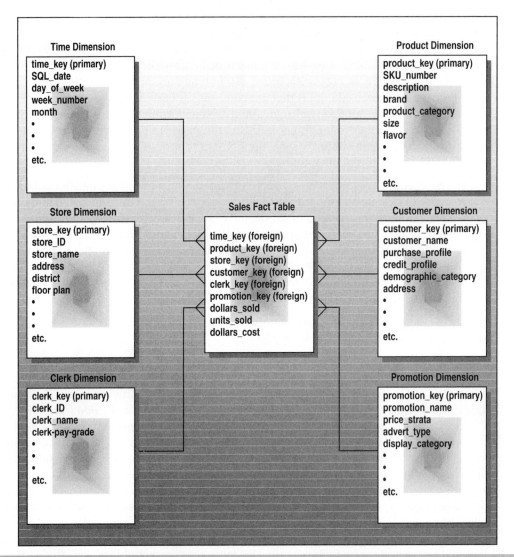

FIGURE 6-5 Dimensional Model for a Typical Retail Sales Process

Source: Adapted from Kimball, Reeves, Ross, and Thornthwaite. *The Data Warehouse Lifecycle Toolkit.* New York: John Wiley & Sons Publishing, 1998.

represents on one diagram multiple processes and business rules that never actually coexist in a single dataset at any consistent point in time. In contrast, the dimensional model represents a holistic characterization of a single business process. As such, in a DW environment where the data are organized into a set of star joins via dimensional modeling, a single fact table can be queried independently from all others with a simple query.

We can identify several additional advantages to the dimensional model that are lacking in the ERM approach. First, the dimensional model can be more readily thought of as a standardized and predictable framework. Therefore, a user interface can be constructed to allow the end user to browse the various dimensional tables associated with a relevant fact table for the purposes of establishing the constraints in the query and thus facilitating the design of query tools and report generators. This predictability in the framework also offers measurable advantages with regard to processing.

Another advantage to the star join schema is its graceful extension and scalability in accommodating unexpected new data elements and/or new design decisions. It allows new data rows to be easily added to existing tables without reloading the tables. Further, none of the query or reporting tools need to be reprogrammed to accommodate the new data. Finally, and probably most exciting, all old applications can continue to run without any changes and without yielding different results.

One final point regarding the differences between ERM and dimensional modeling approaches is that, despite its shortcomings, there is a place for the ERD in the DW. The ERD should be used in all legacy OLTP applications based upon relational technology. This approach ensures the highest levels of transaction performance and data integrity. In addition, the ERD may be quite useful in designing the data-staging activities associated with data cleaning and loading. Do not just focus on the dimensional model and forget the ERD. If used appropriately, each will serve to make the DW design stronger and more efficient.

DESIGNING A DW FACT TABLE

Even though the details associated with the design of a large-scale DW logical model are beyond the scope of this text, we can look at a typical fact table design process in order to better understand the steps associated with its design. In general terms, the logical design of a dimensional schema can be described in four basic steps: (1) choosing the data mart, (2) determining fact table granularity, (3) determining the dimensions, and (4) determining the facts. We will briefly discuss each of these steps in their logical sequence.

1. **Choosing the data mart.** Recall that the data mart is often viewed as a way to gain entry into the DWs and to make all the mistakes on a smaller scale. Further, vendors of data warehousing applications find it easier to deal directly with a small group of isolated users than with the IS department of an entire organization. When developing a fact table, the concept of a data mart can be broadened slightly to include any operational legacy source of data. Typically, these sources include elements such as purchase orders, sales, payments, and shipments. In some cases, legacy data may reside in multiple data marts, bringing an additional level of complexity to the problem. Once the source of data is identified as viable and accessible, however, the first step toward a fact table will be complete.

2. **Fact table granularity.** Data granularity refers to the smallest defined level of data to be used in the fact table. In other words, the degree of granularity determines exactly what constitutes a fact record in the table. This step, sometimes referred to as "declaring the grain," attempts to create the finest possible degree of granularity for the fact table. The finer the grain, the more robust the design will be. Examples of fine granularity records for a fact table might include a sales transaction, an ATM transaction, a daily sales product total, or even a single line item on an order. Generally speaking, sufficient granularity can be found at the transaction, snapshot, or line-item levels depending upon the nature of the data source.

3. **Fact table dimensions.** The first two steps in the process lead to a straightforward selection of the dimensions. In some cases, the chosen level of granularity dictates the dimensions for the table. In other cases, certain decisions or trade-offs may be required. Regardless of the situation,

however, the fact table must ultimately represent a set of simultaneous measurements at the specified level of granularity. For this reason, the dimensions can be thought of as those data elements that take on a single value in the context of the measurements set forth by the definition of the fact table. Further, the granularity of any single element in a dimensional table cannot be lower than the granularity of the records in the fact table. In other words, if the fact table granularity is specified at the month level, then the dimensions cannot be specified in days or weeks.

4. **Determining the facts.** At the final step in the process, the facts to be contained in the fact table are selected. In most cases, if the level of granularity is set at the transaction level, then the only useful fact would be the amount of the transaction. If the snapshot level is used, however, many more open-ended facts can be stored because any summary activity fact would be considered relevant at this level. Snapshot tables offer the most flexible extension of the facts contained in the fact table. Line-item fact tables can also contain several facts; a typical line item can be broken down into its subelements—quantities, gross totals, adjustments, net amounts, taxes, and so on.

The details associated with the development of fact tables for the DW are extensive. Further, a typical DW can be expected to contain hundreds, if not hundreds of thousands, of fact tables. As you can see, the development of the DW is an often tedious and lengthy process. During this stage, the designers and sponsors need to remind themselves of the long-term value to be achieved by a DW. Otherwise, it can become easy to wonder why you are performing these tedious and meticulous activities.

6.4: DW ARCHITECTURE SPECIFICATION AND DEVELOPMENT

The next phase in the DW project is the specification and design of the technical architecture associated with the DW. DW architecture describes the elements and services of the DW, and details how the components will fit together and how the system will grow over time. Whether ad hoc or planned, an architecture always evolves, but experience shows that planned architectures stand a better chance of succeeding. Regardless of the exact business requirements for the DW, a planned DW architecture must identify certain elements if it is to be useful in the design and construction of the DW. We will briefly outline each of these required architectural elements in the following sections.

COMMON SOURCES

The DW architecture must identify the best system to obtain each required dimension key and metric used in the anticipated DW environment. It involves determining the best source system in the business to obtain "Customer ID" information, for example. Once the source system is identified, the first incremental data mart team builds an extract and transformation process to populate its incremental data mart. This extraction process needs to be stored in a central repository where other teams can utilize it when they need the same information.

Many times, the different elements of the organization served by individual data marts cannot agree on a common source system. In this case, you must integrate these two sources into a common source for the various data marts in the organization.

COMMON DIMENSIONS

Every business looks at its activities in a variety of ways common to most user groups in the organization. Popular categorical examples include *customer, product, time, geography,* and *employee.* A primary goal of the DW architecture is to identify common business dimensions that are shared across multiple targeted user groups for multiple incremental data marts in the organization.

COMMON BUSINESS RULES

Business rules provide the algorithms and logic used to calculate metrics and derive classification and structure. Various business units commonly use a variety of ways to calculate standard business metrics such as "sales" or "net profit." It is the job of the DW design team during the formation of the enterprise architecture to identify as many common business rules as possible. It is also a necessity to identify all the different ways the business calculates the same metrics, classifications, and structure. If the designers fail to, or are unable to, gain consensus on these business rules, the DW will need individual columns identifying each method of calculation.

COMMON SEMANTICS

Semantic terms are what the business uses to label itself, its elements, its structure, its metrics, and its activities. As elsewhere in life, semantic differences between different elements of the organization lead to many challenges. When two different groups use the same term for two different entities or use two different terms for the same entity, confusion and frustration can result. Enterprise-wide consensus for semantic terms may be challenging to obtain, but certainly necessary.

COMMON METRICS

Organizations use a variety of methods, referred to as *metrics,* to measure the operations of the business. Common metrics include *units, dollars, hours,* and other measures of *output, throughput,* or *productivity.* Metrics are fundamentally what the business is about and how it measures itself.

The creation of the DW architecture is an absolute prerequisite for success, and its absence will guarantee long-term failure of the design team's efforts. It is most tempting when faced with the need for only a single incremental data mart solution to avoid or defer this step. An initial single solution, however, soon leads to a proliferation of "single solutions" that pop up across the landscape of the organization. Without a common enterprise-wide DW architecture to lay the groundwork for common sources, dimensions, metrics, semantics, and business rules, the business end users ultimately face multiple versions of the truth, mass confusion, and frustration about semantic differences and a lack of data mart integration.

Figure 6-6 illustrates a generic technical architecture configuration for a typical DW. The individual components can be found in your DW, but the exact nature of the components will differ depending on your business requirements and the overall complexity of your extraction and transformation processes.

DW ARCHITECTURE KEY COMPONENT AREAS

A complete DW architecture includes all data and technical elements. We can categorically break down the DW architecture into three broad areas. The first, data architecture, centers on business processes. The next area, infrastructure, includes hardware, networking and operating systems, and desktop machines. Finally, the technical area encompasses the decision-making

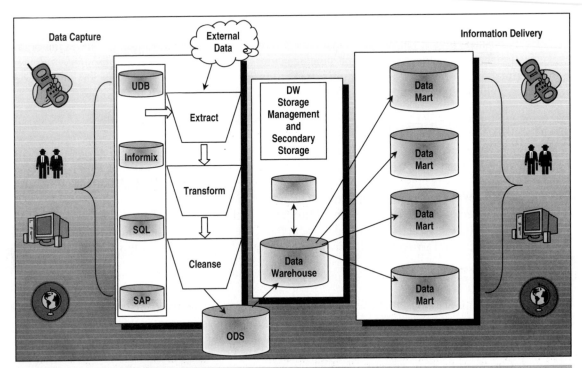

FIGURE 6-6   Generic Technical Architecture for a Typical Data Warehouse

technologies needed by the users, as well as their supporting structures. Each of these categorical areas is detailed in the following sections.

Data Architecture

As stated previously, the data architecture portion of the overall DW architecture is driven by business processes. For example, in a manufacturing environment, the data model might include orders, shipping, and billing. Each area draws on a different set of dimensions. However, where dimensions intersect in the data model, the definitions must be the same—the customer that buys is the same one that builds. Thus, data items should have a common structure and content and involve a single process to create and maintain.

As the designers work through the architecture and present data to the business end users, tool choices will be made, but many choices disappear as the requirements are set. For example, product capabilities are beginning to merge, such as MOLAP and ROLAP. As we discussed in Chapters 1 and 2, MOLAP is most efficient when the query or queries stay within the cube. It is fast and allows for flexible querying, within the confines of the cube. Its weaknesses are size (overall and within a dimension), design constraints (limited by the cube structure), and the need for a proprietary database. Nonetheless, as product capabilities continue to evolve in functionality, tool choice becomes an even greater contributor to overall DW success.

Infrastructure Architecture

Given the need for the required hardware platform and boxes, often the DW grows to become its own IS shop. Indeed, lots of "boxes and wires" accompany data warehousing, mostly for databases and application servers.

The issues with hardware and DBMS choices are size, scalability, and flexibility. In about 80 percent of data warehousing projects, businesses can get enough power to handle their needs.

In terms of the network, check the data sources, the warehouse staging area, and everything in between to ensure enough bandwidth to move data around. On the desktop, run the tools and actually get some data through them to determine if enough power is available for retrieval. Sometimes the problem is simply with the machine, and the desktops must be powerful enough to run current-generation access tools. Also, remember the need to implement a software distribution mechanism.

Technical Architecture

The technical architecture is driven by the metadata catalog. Most DW experts follow the idea that "everything should be metadata-driven." The services should draw the needed parameters from tables, rather than hard-coding them. An important component of technical architecture is the data-staging process, which covers five major areas:

1. **Extraction.** Data come from multiple sources and are of multiple types. Data compression and encryption handling must be considered at this area, if applicable.
2. **Transformation.** Data transformation includes surrogate key management, integration, denormalization, cleansing, conversion, aggregation, and auditing.
3. **Loading.** This is often done to multiple targets, with load optimization and support for the entire load cycle.
4. **Security.** This involves administrator access and data encryption policies.
5. **Job control.** This element includes job definition, job scheduling (time and event), monitoring, logging, exception handling, error handling, and notification.

The staging box needs to be able to extract data from multiple sources, so designers of the architecture must be specific when choosing key products. It must handle data compression and encryption, transformation, loading (possibly to multiple targets), and security (which is often considered a major challenge at the front end). In addition, the staging activities need to be automated. Many vendors' offerings do different things, so it is becoming common for organizations to use multiple products.

A system for monitoring DW use is valuable for capturing queries and tracking usage, and performance tuning can also be helpful. Performance optimization includes cost estimation through a "governor" tool and should include ad hoc query scheduling. Middleware can provide query management services. Tools for all of these and other related tasks are available for the front end, for server-based query management, and for data from multiple sources. Tools are also available for reporting, connectivity, and infrastructure management. Finally, the data access piece should include reporting services (such as publish and subscribe), a report library, a scheduler, and a distribution manager.

A Word About Metadata

Recall our discussion of metadata from Chapter 2. The standard definition of metadata is "data about data." Consider the creation and management of data via the DW in terms of the following sequence:

1. Warehouse model
2. Source definitions
3. Table definitions

4. Source-to-target maps
5. Map and transformation information
6. Physical information (table spaces, etc.)
7. Extracted data
8. Transformed data
9. Load statistics
10. Business descriptions
11. Query requests
12. The data itself
13. Query statistics

To demonstrate the importance of metadata in the architecture, of the steps listed, only three involve any "real" data—7, 8, and 12. All of the other steps involve metadata. Using this lens, it becomes easy to see that the whole DW process relies on the clear definition and accessibility of the metadata. For architecture definition, the major technical elements of a metadata catalog should include:

- **Business rules.** Definitions, derivations, related items, validation, and hierarchy information (versions, dates, etc.)
- **Movement/transformation information.** Source/destination information, as well as data definition language (DDL) (data types, names, etc.)
- **Operations information.** Data load job schedules, dependencies, notification, and reliability information (such as host redirects and load balancing)
- **Tool-specific information.** Graphic display information and special function support
- **Security rules.** Authentication and authorization

DEVELOPING A DW TECHNICAL ARCHITECTURE

When developing the DW technical architecture model, the architecture requirements document is typically drafted first. The architecture implications are listed next to each business requirement. These implications are then grouped according to architecture areas (remote access, staging, data access tools, etc.).

We must acknowledge and recognize that developing a DW architecture is difficult and, thus, a "just do it" approach is probably not a good solution. Numerous prescriptions for architecture development can be found, but a simple approach consisting of a four-layer process is often sufficient: (1) *business requirements,* (2) *technical architecture,* (3) *standards definition,* and (4) *application product development.*

As discussed earlier in this chapter, business requirements essentially drive the architecture, which would suggest the value, and necessity, of talking to business managers, analysts, and power users. From these interviews, major business issues, as well as indicators of business strategy, direction, frustrations, business processes, timing, availability, and performance expectations, can be derived. Document everything well and often!

From an IT perspective, talk to existing DW/DSS support staff, OLTP application groups, and database administrators (DBAs), as well as networking, operating system, and desktop support staff. Also speak with architecture and planning professionals. You want to get their opinions on data warehousing considerations from the IT viewpoint. Learn whether existing

TABLE 6-10 Benefits Typically Realized Through a Sound Data Warehouse Architecture	
Benefit	*Description*
Provides an organizing framework	The architecture draws the lines on the map in terms of what the individual components are, how they fit together, who owns what parts, and priorities.
Improves flexibility and maintenance	This permits quick addition of new data sources, offers interface standards, and allows plug and play. The model and metadata allow impact analysis and single-point changes.
Provides faster development and reuse	Warehouse developers are better able to understand the data warehouse process, database contents, and business rules more quickly.
Provides management and communications tool	Defines and communicates direction and scope to set expectations, identify roles and responsibilities, and communicate requirements to vendors.
Coordinates parallel efforts	Multiple, relatively independent efforts have a chance to converge successfully. Also, data marts without architecture become the stovepipes of tomorrow.

architecture documents, IT principles, standards statements, organizational power centers, and so on are available.

Few standards exist for data warehousing, but standards may be available for many of the components. Regardless of what standards they support, major data warehousing tools are metadata-driven. However, they seldom share metadata with each other and vary in terms of openness. The key here is to research and shop for tools carefully, and use the architecture as your guide.

How detailed does a DW architecture need to be? The question to ask is this: Is this enough information to allow a competent team to build a warehouse that meets the needs of the business? As for how long it will take, the architecture effort will grow exponentially as more people are added for its development (i.e., it becomes "techno-politically complex") and the more complex the resulting system needs to be (i.e., "functionally complex").

Like almost everything in data warehousing, an iterative process is best. So begin with the high-leverage, high-value aspects of the process. Then, use your success to make a case for additional phases. Table 6-10 summarizes the benefits associated with a sound DW architecture.

6.5: DW PROJECT SUCCESS FACTORS

By now, you probably understand that developing a sound architecture for the DW is considered the key to a successful DW initiative. You should also see that, like any other complex information system, the architecture of a DW must be a living document, which means that throughout its life it will, and should be expected to, change. As time moves forward and the DW becomes institutionalized in the organization, the velocity of change in the architecture document will slow, but it will probably never become static. As new requirements emerge, new architectures become necessary.

At this point, we have covered the basics. If your intention is to become conversant in DW issues, then you can congratulate yourself on a job well done. If you aspire to become an expert, then thousands of pages of information await you. In either case, the DW is rapidly becoming a standard fixture in the modern information-driven organization, and understanding its concepts and uses will become de facto literacy.

To that end, it seems like a good time to set forth a set of guidelines for DW project success. Such guidelines are intended to be prescriptive in nature but should be viewed as probably necessary but definitely not sufficient for a successful DW venture. Essentially, these guidelines, combined with strong business justification and a great deal of tenacity, will probably result in project success and a DW that grows daily in its value to the organization. Table 6-11 lists these success guidelines and briefly describes each.

TABLE 6-11 Guidelines for a Successful Data Warehouse Project

Have a strong project sponsor	Two sponsors are always better than one. Regardless, the business sponsor must be committed to the project and prepared to defend it with resources.
Generate user buy-in	Business user buy-in is as important as corporate sponsorship. The end users must see the value of the project as it directly relates to their needs.
Identify business needs	The project must be constructed to meet the business needs of the supporters. Clearly identify these needs and motivations before the project begins.
Start with a narrow scope	Do one or two things well and expand as successes become realized.
Understand the organizational culture	The organization has certain cultural norms and power relationships. The success of the DW will be dependent on how well it conforms to the existing cultural fabric.
Create clear requirements documents	Who will use the system? How will they use it? What are the criteria for measuring success? Remember, you cannot manage what you are not measuring, and you cannot measure what you have not defined.
Determine availability of necessary resources	Make an accurate assessment of the current and necessary resources with regard to their availability.
Define all data requirements	Create a clear enterprise-wide data architecture and define all necessary fact tables and dimensions.
Define all communications requirements	Where are the databases? How will they be accessed? What external databases must be accessed? Are the existing communication links sufficient, or will more bandwidth be required?
Use a best-of-breed approach to application selection	Realize that the best package for your DW may consist of several commercial applications. Each manufacturer will have a specialization. Use that specialization to create a package that best fits the business needs of the DW users.
Prototype	Prototype often during the requirements determination stages and use the business-user feedback to create a closer iteration to their expectations. Realize that in some ways, a DW is always a prototype for the next iteration.
Train and support	Be ready to train the users and to support their requests for more features, tools, and analysis.

6.6: CHAPTER SUMMARY

Because of its unique use and potential value to the organization, a DW can, in most cases, be thought of as any other complex information systems development effort. DW projects proceed through requirements determination, architecture specification, logical and physical modeling, implementation, and maintenance. The real key is to ensure strong justification for the project. This admonition should be applied to all information systems development efforts, but the enterprise nature of the DW makes it even more of a necessity. The more tangible the benefits, the more likely that the necessary buy-in from the business constituents will be realized.

Key Concepts

- The enterprise model of a firm consists of a number of separate models that, when properly integrated, provide a coherent picture of the enterprise. The various submodels may describe the enterprise in terms of strategy, organization, data, processes, or culture. Enterprise modeling helps determine the level of alignment between the business and its cadre of systems.

- A top-down approach to DW design is firmly based on the enterprise model itself. Such an approach implies a strategic rather than an operational perspective of the data.

- A bottom-up approach to DW design focuses more on making use of whatever existing data are available in the current operational systems.

- To be effective, integration must occur on three distinct axes: (1) horizontal, (2) vertical, and (3) enterprise.

- An organization's readiness for a DW can be assessed using five key factors:

  1. Strong management sponsorship

  2. Compelling business motivation

  3. Level and quality of IS/business partnership

  4. Analytic culture of the organization

  5. DW feasibility

- The first item on the agenda is the formal definition of the project scope. This establishes an agreed boundary for the project and defines not only what the project is, but equally important, what the project is not.

- Once project scope is successfully established and agreed to by all relevant parties, the process of making the business case for the project can begin. This exercise formally articulates the various justifications for the allocation of resources necessary to design, construct, and deliver the DW.

- Any DW project, regardless of size or scope, requires a number of different roles and skills to be successful.

- Similar to ERM, dimensional modeling is a logical design technique for providing access to the data contained in the DW in a highly efficient, effective, and intuitive manner. In other aspects, the dimensional modeling approach differs significantly from the more conventional ERM technique.

- Every DM is composed of three basic elements. The first element is a central table containing multipart keys called the fact table. Surrounding the fact table are two or more smaller tables referred to as the dimensional tables. Each dimensional table has a single-part primary key that directly corresponds to exactly one of the component elements of a multipart key in the fact table. Joining the dimensional tables to the fact table is a set of relationships referred to as a star join.

- Regardless of the exact business requirements for the DW, a planned DW architecture must identify certain elements if it is to be useful in the design and construction of the DW. These include: common sources, common dimensions, common business rules, common semantics, and common metrics.

- A complete DW architecture includes all data and technical elements.
- For architecture definition, the major technical elements of a metadata catalog should include:

  Business rules. Definitions, derivations, related items, validation, and hierarchy information (versions, dates, etc.)

  Movement/transformation information. Source/destination information, as well as DDL (data types, names, etc.)

  Operations information. Data load job schedules, dependencies, notification, and reliability information (such as host redirects and load balancing)

  Tool-specific information. Graphic display information and special function support

  Security rules. Authentication and authorization

Questions for Review

1. Describe the concept of an enterprise model and its importance to a successful DW project.
2. What are the two most important components of a fully specified enterprise model?
3. Describe the two basic approaches to designing an enterprise model. What are their relative advantages and disadvantages?
4. Compare and contrast horizontal, vertical, and enterprise integration.
5. What are the five organizational readiness factors for a DW?
6. What methods are available to address DW readiness shortfall?
7. Describe the process of defining the project scope for a DW. What are some of the important elements in this process?
8. What is scope creep?
9. What are the primary elements of an economic feasibility analysis?
10. Why are intangibles so important in constructing the business justification for a DW?
11. Describe the component elements in a fact table.
12. What are the four steps in developing a dimensional schema?
13. What are the key component areas of a DW architecture?
14. Identify and discuss the five areas associated with the data-staging process.
15. What major technical elements should be found in a metadata catalog?

For Further Discussion

1. Using the techniques discussed in this chapter, conduct a thorough feasibility analysis of the purchase of a new computer system for your personal use. Assume a 3-year analysis period and use a reasonable rate of return on your investment. Can you justify it from a feasibility analysis perspective? Does it indicate a positive NPV?
2. Contact a local organization's IT department and see whether you can arrange a time to discuss the various processes and activities they are involved in that relate to the development of a DW. What do these processes have in common? Are any of the processes outsourced? If so, what is the rationale for outsourcing these particular activities and not others? Could an organization conceivably outsource all DW activities and just manage the relationships?
3. Identify three intangible costs and three intangible benefits associated with a software development project. Create a logical approach to converting them to expected values. Be sure to clearly state the logic behind your surrogate measures.

7
THE FUTURE OF DATA MINING, WAREHOUSING, AND VISUALIZATION

Learning Objectives

◆ Understand the challenges to data warehousing over the next decade.

◆ Be aware of the trends in data warehousing, mining, and visualization.

◆ Appreciate the issues of privacy that must be addressed if DM is to become a pervasive and effective source of new knowledge.

◆ Understand the importance of moving toward a federated information environment.

◆ Be aware of the need for development of alternative methods of data storage.

◆ Understand the importance of the World Wide Web and the Internet in the development of large-scale DWs.

◆ Develop an awareness of the value of DM to future network intrusion detection systems.

◆ Familiarize yourself, via several scenarios, with the future applications of data visualization technologies.

> **DATA MINING MINICASE**

THE TRENDS TOWARD DATA, DISCOVERY, AND DECISIONS

Knowledge Discovery Nuggets (www.KDnuggets.com) is one of the leading sources of information on DM, Web mining, knowledge discovery, and decision support topics, including news, software, solutions, companies, jobs, courses, meetings, publications, and more. The Web site and its associated newsletter have been recognized as the premier e-newsletter for the DM and knowledge discovery community, reaching about 11,000 professionals.

The KDnuggets.com Web site is managed and operated by Gregory Piatetsky-Shapiro, who founded it in February 1997. Gregory also maintained an earlier version of this site at GTE Laboratories from 1994 to 1997.

One of the most useful services provided by KDnuggets.com is its regular membership polling function. From these polls, various trends can be identified, keeping professionals in the data warehousing and mining field abreast of the direction of the state-of-the-art in their industry. In this final case study, we will look at the results of several polls, with an eye toward identifying several relevant data warehousing, mining, and visualization trends.

A poll conducted on January 10, 2002, sought to answer the following question: What categories of data have you mined in during the year 2001? Figure 7-1 contains the results of this survey. As one might expect, analysis of Web content and click-stream data were two of the larger categories of mined data. What is of real interest, however, is the significant amount of text-based data that was mined. The advent of powerful text mining tools, such as Megaputer's TextAnalyst, has opened the door for highly sophisticated text mining endeavors. Also, as expected, time-series data also showed up as a significant focus of DM operations.

A second survey was conducted during the same period to determine the expected range of business domains in which DM would be applied in 2002. As can be seen by the results, shown in Figure 7-2, DM is becoming ubiquitous across a broad range of industries and business environments. Although banking and Web marketing were the leaders, several areas of growth, such as telecom and fraud detection (discussed later in this chapter), showed significant use of DM applications. As we begin to better understand the power and effectiveness of DM techniques, a greater variety of business contexts will begin to emerge as major players in the field.

Similar data were collected during midyear 2002. Note the differences in expectations at midyear 2002 (Figure 7-3) from those for 2002 in early 2001. Notice that many of the same business areas remain as leading areas for DM, but a much wider variety of business applications is beginning to emerge. The data suggest that DM is rapidly becoming a mainstay across most, if not eventually all, data-driven business environments.

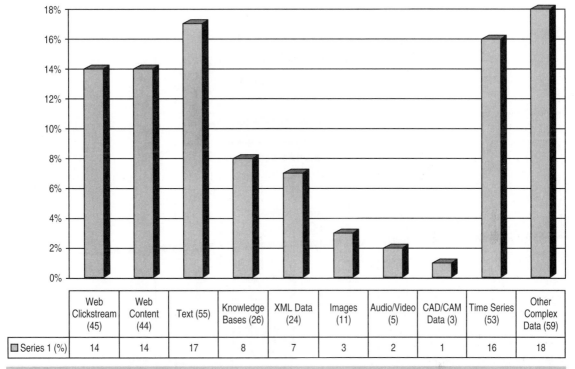

	Web Clickstream (45)	Web Content (44)	Text (55)	Knowledge Bases (26)	XML Data (24)	Images (11)	Audio/Video (5)	CAD/CAM Data (3)	Time Series (53)	Other Complex Data (59)
☐ Series 1 (%)	14	14	17	8	7	3	2	1	16	18

FIGURE 7-1 Types of Data Mined in 2001

INTRODUCTION

We have covered a great deal of ground in these brief chapters, but, as you have probably figured out by now, we have barely scratched the surface of these important topics in warehousing, mining, and visualization. To be sure, there are a number of facts that we know to be true. However, many more areas of understanding await our exploration and exploitation with regard to these topics. This text was intended to provide you with a solid starting foundation in your quest to understand and apply the techniques of data warehousing, mining, and visualization. In this final chapter, we will focus our attention on what lies ahead for these powerful business tools and what challenges exist that must be met if we are to advance our knowledge in this area.

Although the amount of available data has clearly been growing exponentially over the last few decades (in the next 10 years, we will generate as much codified data as has been generated in all the years before), only a few people are aware of the size or, more importantly, the potential of this growing ocean of data. This, in fact, is probably the single greatest challenge facing the data-driven organizations of tomorrow: *the ways and means for using all this data lag far behind the increase of available data.* A great deal of information is present; however, it can only be found through coincidence (e.g., Internet surfing); it is not explicitly available (e.g., nonintegrated company databases); and, in many cases, it is only accessible through the use of extensive

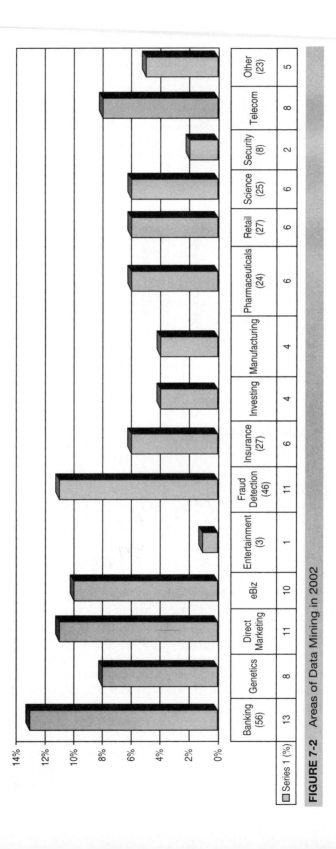

	Banking (56)	Genetics	Direct Marketing	eBiz	Entertainment (3)	Fraud Detection (46)	Insurance (27)	Investing	Manufacturing	Pharmaceuticals (24)	Retail (27)	Science (25)	Security (8)	Telecom	Other (23)
Series 1 (%)	13	8	11	10	1	11	6	4	4	6	6	6	2	8	5

FIGURE 7-2 Areas of Data Mining in 2002

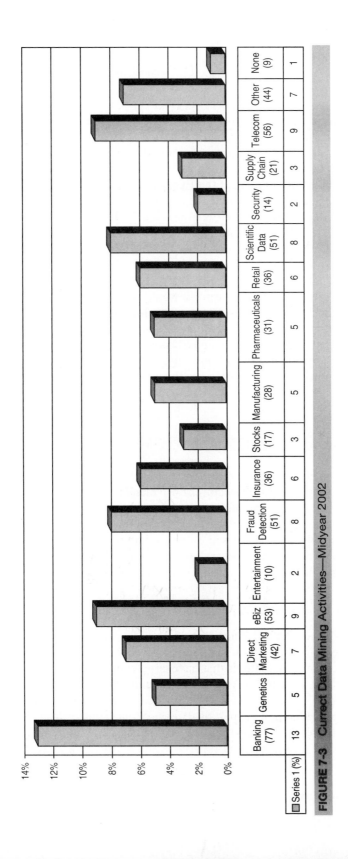

	Banking (77)	Genetics	Direct Marketing (42)	eBiz (53)	Entertainment (10)	Fraud Detection (51)	Insurance (36)	Stocks (17)	Manufacturing (28)	Pharmaceuticals (31)	Retail (36)	Scientific Data (51)	Security (14)	Supply Chain (21)	Telecom (56)	Other (44)	None (9)
Series 1 (%)	13	5	7	9	2	8	6	3	5	5	6	8	2	3	9	7	1

FIGURE 7-3 Current Data Mining Activities—Midyear 2002

processing power (e.g., astronomical, meteorological, and earth observation data). Consider the following facts:

- The best search engine on the Internet indexes only 16 percent of all sites. In 1999, the Internet contained over 15 terabytes of data.
- The quantity of data in GenBank, the international repository for genome sequences, doubles every 14 months.
- The "Large Hadron Collider" at the European Organization for Nuclear Research (CERN) will generate 20 terabytes of test data each day for at least the next 15 years.
- The wireless data market will grow from about 170 million subscribers worldwide this year to more than 1.3 billion in 2004.
- IBM estimates that the total amount of data on earth will increase from the current 3.2 million exabytes to 43 million exabytes by the year 2005.[1]

Given these rather startling statistics, it would seem that the good news is that we will have no problem finding enough data to mine and explore. The bad news, however, lies in our existing inability to store and manage the data we currently have, let alone that on the horizon. When added to the ever increasing value of knowledge, this leads to a clear demand for means of uncovering the information and knowledge hidden in the massive quantities of data. Data warehousing, mining, and visualization are the answer to this demand.

7.1: THE FUTURE OF DATA WAREHOUSING

It is both highly likely and highly desirable that as the DW becomes a mature part of an organization's decision support infrastructure, it will blend into the fabric of the organization and be as anonymous as the data communication network used to move data from place to place. In other words, once the problems currently associated with an inability to access corporate data are completely resolved, an increased effort to find new ways to use those data will emerge. This new focus will bring with it several new challenges. This final chapter identifies several of these challenges facing data warehousing in the future.

REGULATORY CONSTRAINTS

The power associated with the ability to analyze and extract information from large volumes of disparate data continues to spark legislation that seeks to protect individuals from abuse by government or commercial entities that have large volumes of data concerning those individuals. In response to escalating fears over covert and overt invasions of privacy, the ease with which external data sources can be accessed is measurably declining. This tightening of security calls for a concerted effort on the part of all users of data sources to craft a workable set of rules and guidelines that allow for the privacy of individuals while simultaneously facilitating the use of large datasets for meaningful analyses.

---

[1]An exabyte is 1,000,000,000,000,000,000 bytes, or 10^{18} bytes. For example, approximately 2 exabytes is the total volume of information generated worldwide annually.

STORAGE OF UNSTRUCTURED DATA

Currently, the modern DW is limited to storage of structured data in the form of records, fields, and databases. Unstructured data, such as multimedia, maps, graphs, pictures, sound, and video files, are rapidly increasing in importance throughout modern organizations. The need to store, retrieve, and combine these new data types will require a new and expanded DW architecture and interface. In the DW environment of tomorrow, a user may search for relationships between different types of products. The DW will contain not only structured data for such an analysis, but may also allow for the scanning and analysis of the contents of images and audio and video files to facilitate the establishment of such relationships. To bring this level of use and functionality to reality, vendors of DW applications and tools face a number of technological and practical challenges. Issues such as how to manage the storage and retrieval of unstructured data and how to search for specific data items must be addressed and resolved if the DW of tomorrow is to accommodate the technology and data being generated today.

THE WORLD WIDE WEB

As with everything else it comes into contact with, the World Wide Web will undoubtedly have a profound impact on data warehousing. The ability to access and transfer large numbers of data relatively easily and economically will make the Internet and the Web ideal vehicles to integrate external data into the DW environment. If this is to become a reality, however, a myriad of issues relating to data integrity, accuracy, and quality will have to be addressed and resolved. It is conceivable that third-party *infomediaries* will evolve whose sole purpose is to evaluate and rate the quality and integrity of external data sources. Such quality ratings could be used to determine the degree of value to be placed on the integration of a particular source of external data into the DW. Equally conceivable is the use of a quality rating to determine the price to be paid for access to such data; the higher the quality rating, the higher the price.

Historically, market and business forces have moved organizations inexorably toward a fate of multiple, nonintegrated business intelligence (BI) systems rather than the "ideal" monolithic, hub-and-spoke enterprise DW favored by various vested-interest vendors, theorists, and idealists, and as discussed in this and many other textbooks on the subject. Indeed, rather than the clean, pure world promised by the DW revolution, the typical organization of today has evolved into an ineffective nonintegrated architecture such as that shown in Figure 7-4.

The real problem is that businesses have paid close attention to what has been delivered to date. In the early days of the DW revolution, businesses were sold a vision of a single version of the truth, a cure for the silo data sources of the past with their multiple versions of the truth. Instead of the universal cure they were promised, they have been delivered more of the same, with silo DWs replacing silo OLTP-reporting systems. Businesses still have multiple versions of the truth, along with the honor of paying millions of dollars to achieve this state.

The other part of this dilemma that is painfully clear is that these same market and business forces that have led us to this place are not about to go away easily or without a hefty price tag. In contrast, these forces will be increasing, and no IT-led argument about the elegance or potential dollar savings of a long-term investment in the idealist vision of a single hub-and-spoke enterprise architecture is going to slow them down. As anyone who has spent any significant time in the corporate world knows, the only word in the previous sentence the business will hear is "long," which is counter to the quarter-to-quarter performance metrics most organizations live under. Ergo, we will continue for some time to witness the ongoing proliferation of

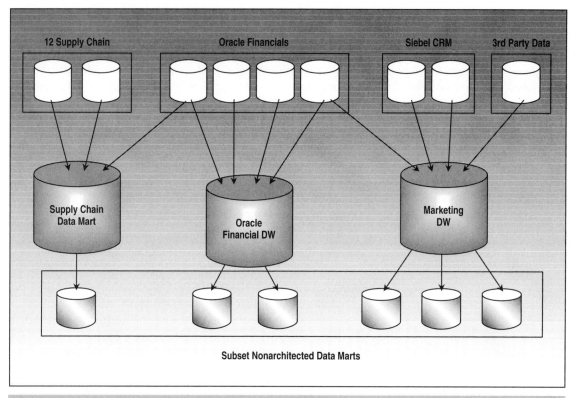

FIGURE 7-4 Typical Nonintegrated Information Architecture

nonarchitected data marts and nonintegrated, proprietary "favored son" ERP data warehouse/ analytical application systems.

To survive in the current and future world of low-cost, turnkey analytical applications and proprietary ERP DW systems, the transition to a federated architecture, one where the data warehouse can serve a variety of related constituencies, must be made. Figure 7-5 illustrates this necessary transition.

The importance of making the transition to a federated information environment cannot be understated. Such an environment is viable and sustainable for several important reasons. First, a federated information environment does not resist the power and momentum of the market and business forces driving nonarchitected/nonintegrated systems. Instead, a federated environment facilitates the integration of these systems, thereby avoiding the certain political death of opposing a powerful executive's tactical agenda.

Second, a federated environment reaches the goal of a single version of the truth. By sharing key metrics, measures, and dimensions across the entire range of business information systems, it allows each system to manifest a consistent reflection of key business indicators and measures while simultaneously allowing each system to maintain proprietary measures within its own captive environment. An example of this might be the simultaneous existence of corporate net sales versus marketing net sales versus finance net sales.

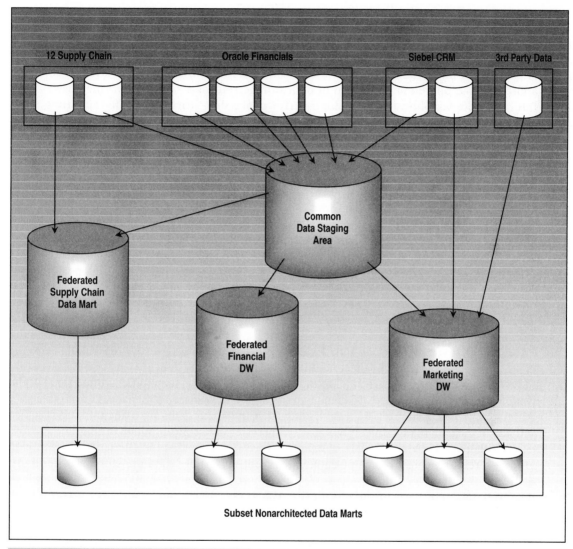

FIGURE 7-5 Federated Integrated Information Architecture

Finally, the federated approach increases business information flexibility. By creating an architecture that can accommodate the shifting needs and priorities of the business, members of the business information team are viewed as the key players in responding to quick changes in competitive or regulatory contexts. Rather than being the obstructionist team hiding behind the shield of a one-size-fits-all, hub-and-spoke architecture, the DW architects can quickly and successfully accommodate custom, turnkey, and proprietary systems.

7.2: ALTERNATIVE STORAGE AND THE DATA WAREHOUSE

A closer look into the future to see what is in store for data warehousing when it comes to addressing the burgeoning problem of data storage returns a rather surprising answer—the future of data warehousing is *not* high-performance disk storage, despite the strong track record of disk storage for the past 20 years. Instead, high-performance disk storage will play only a secondary role in the future of data warehousing. The real future of data warehousing is in an array of storage media collectively known as *alternative storage.*

ALTERNATIVE STORAGE

Alternative storage consists of two forms of storage: *near-line storage* and/or *secondary storage.* Near-line storage is siloed tape storage where siloed cartridges of tape are archived, accessed, and managed robotically. The technology for siloed tape storage has been around for a long time, and it is both a proven and mature technology. In contrast, secondary storage is a form of disk storage that is slower, significantly less expensive, and less cached than high-performance storage. Common secondary storage media include CD-ROM, digital tape, and even a floppy diskette. Table 7-1 summarizes the speed and capacity specifications for various near-line and secondary data storage media. Figure 7-6 contains several pictures of a typical near-line tape storage silo.

Alternative storage fits well with the DW environment for a variety of reasons. Perhaps the most fundamental reason why there is such a good fit is that DW data are very stable. The nature of DW data is that the data are put into the warehouse in a time-stamped, snapshot mode. If the warehouse needs to be aware of a change to the data, a new snapshot is made. The old snapshot of data remains undisturbed. With this storage method, no updates are made into the DW. The stability of the data fits very nicely with the "write once" data concept found in near-line storage.

Another reason why DW data fit on alternative storage is that the queries that operate on DW data require long streams of data, and, oftentimes, those data are stored sequentially. Unlike a job stream for online processing where there is constant demand for different units of data from different parts of the disk device, DW processing is fundamentally different. Both near-line and secondary storage fit this job stream model very nicely.

Yet another very important reason for alternative storage is the need to store an indeterminately large volume of records in the DW. Because DWs store detailed and historical data, they contain far more data than their online, OLTP counterpart. The ability to store far more data on near-line and/or secondary storage is a very important reason why high-performance disk storage is not the future of data warehousing. Not only can much greater volumes of data be stored in alternative storage, but those massive volumes can be stored much less expensively than on high-performance disk storage. It is estimated that the cost savings associated with using alternative storage will be realized as an order of magnitude less than high-performance disk storage.

There is still another powerful reason why high-performance disk storage is not the future of data warehousing. Ironically, and much to the chagrin of the high-performance vendors, performance gets better when data are moved to near-line or secondary storage. The reason for this improvement is because of the phenomenon in data warehousing called *dormant data.* Dormant data are data that are seldom or never used. In the early days of a DW, when the warehouse is new and small, there is little or no dormant data. However, as the DW matures, the volumes of data rise and the patterns of usage of the data begin to stabilize. Soon, only a

TABLE 7-1 Speed and Capacity of Various Near-Line and Secondary Storage Media

Device	Capacity	Data Access Speed	Media Lifetime	Write Once (WO) or Write Many (WM)
DAT DDS2	4–8 Gbyte	510 Kbyte/s	10–25 Yrs	WM
DAT DDS3	12–24 Gbyte	1 Mbyte/s	10–25 Yrs	WM
CD-ROM	640 Mbyte	X times 1.5 Mbits/s to Read	10 Yrs Plus	WO
CD-RW	640 Mbyte	X times 1.5 Mbits/s to Read	10 Yrs Plus	WM
Exabyte	20–40 Gbyte	3–6 Mbyte/s	10–25 Yrs	WM
DLT	35 Gbyte	5 Mbyte/s	30 Yrs	WM
DVD	up to 15 Gbyte	Not Known	Not Known	WO
DTF	42 Gbyte	12 Mbyte/s	10–25 Yrs	WM
Data D3	50 Gbyte	12 Mbyte/s	10–25 Yrs	WM
DVD-RAM	up to 3 Gbyte	Not Known	Not Known	WM
Magneto-optical	2.6–5.6 Gbyte	Not Known	Not Known	WM

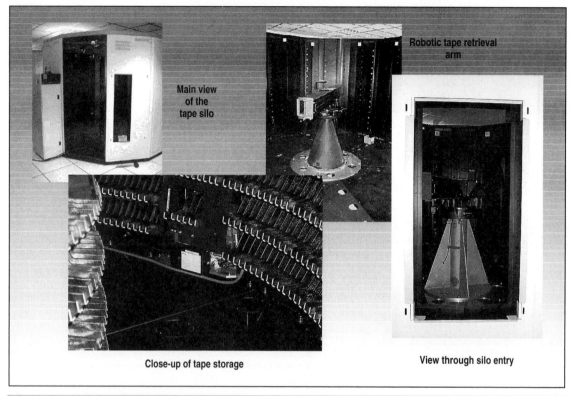

Main view
of the
tape silo

Robotic tape retrieval
arm

Close-up of tape storage

View through silo entry

FIGURE 7-6 Typical Near-Line Tape Storage Silo

fraction of the DW is being used. At this point, the dormant data can be moved to alternative storage. Thus, performance for the remaining actively used data picks up dramatically. If dormant data are left on high-performance disk storage, the dormant data tend to "get in the way" of query processing. Data required for the query are hidden by the masses of data that are not regularly needed. By moving dormant data to alternative storage, however, performance is greatly enhanced.

Finally, the greatest advantage of selecting alternative storage as the basis for the data in the DW environment is that the designer can choose the lowest level of granularity desired for the DW. When high-performance disk storage is the only storage medium, the designer is restricted as to how much detailed data can be placed in the DW. The telecommunications designer must aggregate or summarize detailed call-level data. The bank designer must add together checking and ATM activity into a monthly aggregate record. The retailing executive must summarize POS data to the store level and/or to the daily level. In short, placing the DW on disk storage forces a compromise. However, when the bulk of the data in the warehouse are stored on alternative storage, the designer can afford to store data at the lowest level of detail that exists. In doing so, the DW ends up with a great deal more functionality than if it were stored on high-performance disk storage.

MAKING ALTERNATIVE STORAGE WORK

In order to make the alternative storage architecture perform at the optimal level, two types of software are needed. The first type of software is that of the *activity monitor*. The activity monitor sits between the DW DBMS server and the users and collects information about the activity that is occurring inside the DW. Once collected, the DW administrator is in a position to be able to know what data are and are not being used in the actively used portion of the DW. With that knowledge, the DW administrator is able to precisely determine what data belong in actively used storage and what data belong in alternative storage. Figure 7-7 contains examples of information derived from a typical network activity monitor.

FIGURE 7-7 Various Information Screens from a Typical Activity Monitor Application

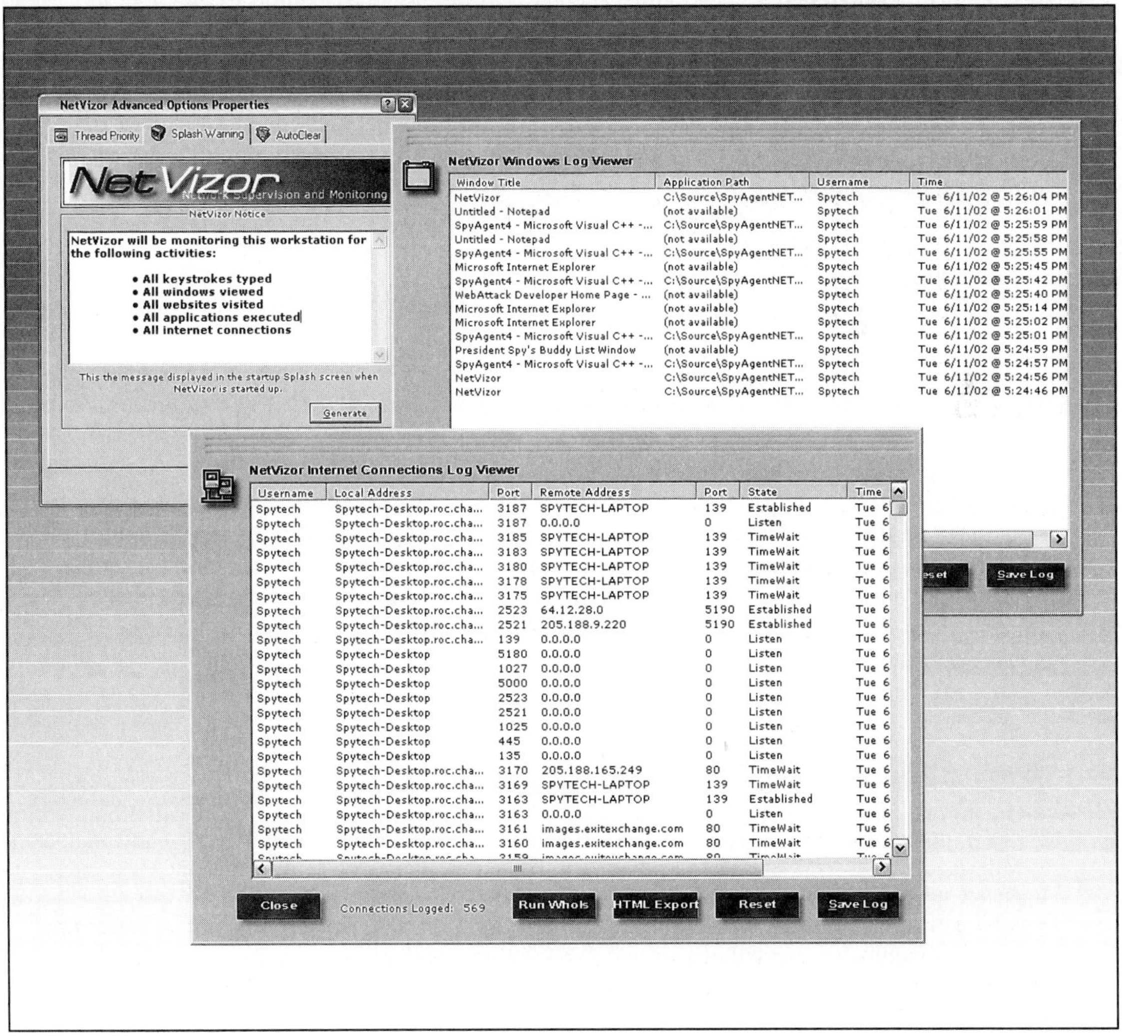

The second type of software that is needed for the DW environment that operates on alternative storage is the *cross media storage manager*. The job of the cross media storage manager is to manage the traffic between the actively used storage and alternative storage. The traffic can be managed by actually moving data to and from one component and the other, or it can be used to satisfy query processing where the data reside in either actively used storage or alternative storage.

The alternative storage solution for data warehousing is compelling. For warehouses that will grow to any size at all, alternative storage is not an option—it is a necessity. What then are the obstacles to the success and adoption of alternative storage? The primary obstacle to alternative storage is a familiar one to those who have been around the information processing community a while. "Well, we didn't used to do it that way before. . . ." is the primary reason why people do not immediately adopt alternative storage. In addition, we must consider the pressure from vendors of high-performance storage. The vendors have made so much money for so long selling high-performance disk storage that it seems as if OLTP online processing is the only available option. The very success of the high-performance disk vendors traps them into thinking that their world will remain static forever. The high-performance disk vendors may wish to stick their heads in the sand and pretend that the world is not changing, but the fact is that the genie is out of the bottle and it will not be coming back again. Alternative storage is the future of data warehousing.

7.3: TRENDS IN DATA WAREHOUSING

Traditionally, corporate DWs have been accessed by only a few business analysts; some explorers, but mostly farmers. The DWs could be used to glean a wealth of knowledge from historical information and empower companies to act on what they have learned, to acquire and keep more profitable customers, to introduce new products and services, and to improve competitive positioning in various marketplaces. However, the recent growth in Web use and advances in e-business applications have pushed the DW from the back office to the front lines of the organization—from internal use by a few people to all employees and every customer.

This move to the forefront of the organization has resulted in the identification of several trends in corporate DWs. Table 7-2 contains a brief listing of several of the more relevant trends in warehousing.

TABLE 7-2   Trends in Data Warehousing

- One-to-one customer interaction and learning relationships with customers require capturing customer information from every enterprise system and using this information to intelligently interact with customers in "real time" by any channel of communication, such as Web mail and call centers. This requirement demands *massive scalability* for data volume as well as for performance.
- The number and types of users have increased significantly. Enterprise applications are generating data very rapidly, which is doubling in size every 9 to 12 months.
- The time available for collecting, integrating, analyzing, and acting is shrinking rapidly, and around-the-clock access is becoming the norm.
- Fast implementation, continuous scalability, and ease of management, which result in lower project risk and total cost of ownership (TCO), are becoming more important.

Today's DWs must be accessible to customers, suppliers, partners, and employees throughout the enterprise. They must also be able to process information requests and deliver results in real time. The sometimes esoteric nature of past DW implementations is being superseded by online data resources that are used by hundreds or thousands of concurrent users on a 24/7 basis—a rather sharp contrast to the previous access patterns of a limited number of analysts during traditional business hours.

Predictably, enterprise-wide operational and transactional systems generate enormous amounts of data that must be collected, integrated, managed, and analyzed in a timely manner in order to gain the intelligence required for making critical business decisions, optimizing processes, increasing productivity, and fostering meaningful customer interactions. These days, terabyte-size DWs are becoming increasingly common, with many companies having plans for petabyte-size systems.[2]

Making the situation more complex are decision-cycle times encompassing operational data collection systems, BI analysis, and responsive actions that have shrunk from a quarter, to a month, to a day, to a few minutes.

Compounding the complexity problem for IT managers who design, deploy, and manage leading-edge DWs is the wide spectrum of users, each with different information and knowledge requirements, who query the databases. Queries involve varying levels of length and complexity, and many of them are ad hoc.

As a result, DWs have evolved into multitier, complex architectures carrying higher levels of risk. Many companies are tempted to compromise on the DW project scope and benefits so that it fits within existing IT budgets and infrastructure. This approach always leads to unsuccessful design and deployment in the competitive Web-based business environment that neither demands, nor allows for, compromise. Given that near-term budget constraints are a reality, however, the smart approach is to start small but plan, and be prepared for, fast and enormous growth.

EMERGING DW TRENDS IN THE NEW MILLENNIUM

The growth of the Web has reset expectations for end users' access to corporate data. Broad new communities of end users with diverse needs are now putting pressure on IT to deliver high-performance access to corporate information over the Web.

In the future, typical end users will need to perform more sophisticated data analysis than they currently perform. This will result in the need to provide users with a more user-friendly method to answer questions that are typically statistical nature. As such, organizations will need to demystify statistical analysis and make it less intimidating.

In addition, companies will need to provide easy-to-use, Web-enabled analysis applications to all decision makers throughout the enterprise—from sales to marketing to finance and human resources. These new Web-enabled applications must go beyond simple query capabilities and move to the next level of answering sophisticated questions, be they statistical, data mining, or modeling, in a Web-based, point-and-click data analysis environment. Traditional statistical tools have been difficult to use and are not geared at business end users. These traditional tools are targeted at expert users, thereby distancing business managers from critical decision support techniques such as the ability to do trend analysis.

---

[2]A petabyte is equal to 2^{50} (1,125,899,906,842,624) bytes. A petabyte is equal to 1,024 terabytes. In contrast, a terabyte is equal to 240^{40} (1,099,511,627,776) bytes. This is approximately 1 trillion bytes.

In sharp contrast, by providing data analysis tools through an easy-to-use graphical user interface, end users can analyze and interpret the results of their own business data. For example, a sales manager will be able to use these tools to more accurately forecast sales based on current and past sales figures, as well as perform correlation analysis to look into the future. Marketing managers will better relate the impact of marketing campaigns to company sales, and e-commerce managers will use data analysis to identify shared characteristics of the company's most profitable online customers.

In the future, more organizations will build Web information applications operating in conjunction with data warehouses/marts. A Web information system captures and integrates business information stored in the data warehouses/marts, groupware systems, and Web servers. This information will be available via Web browsers. As Web use increases, we also foresee significant growth in the use of tools that enable users to subscribe to the information they need and to have it delivered to them from a Web information store at predefined intervals.

One cautionary note, however, is that working with multiple vendors and investing limited IT resources to integrate disparate software products could negate the cost and time benefits of bringing data warehouses/marts to the Web. Consequently, there will be a need for single vendors and service organizations, serving as infomediaries, with tightly integrated, high-performance solutions for deploying DWs to the Web.

The future of data warehousing is clearly bright, but it is not without significant challenges. In the remaining sections of this last chapter, we will turn our attention to the future trends and associated challenges with the close companions of the modern DW: DM and data visualization.

7.4: THE FUTURE OF DM

Similar to the future of data warehousing, as promising as the field may be, DM also has its pitfalls. To begin, the quality of the data can make or break the DM effort. An organization can provide state-of-the-art algorithms and technology, but if the data do not possess the necessary integrity and granularity, the algorithms can lead an organization in the wrong direction. Oftentimes, the data are a proxy for something else that is likely to be linked to a purchase decision. For example, an address may be associated with wealth or income. However, if the data are not a good proxy or insufficient (e.g., a person at a wealth-indicating address is a nanny, butler, or gardener), DM can give false results or can lead to gross misinterpretation.

As we have seen throughout this text, in order to mine their information, companies first have to integrate, extract, transform, and cleanse their data to serve a purpose for which it was never intended. Handling massive amounts of data, ensuring accuracy, and integrating data gathered from different entry points is both a time-intensive and costly endeavor—particularly for old-line companies with legacy systems from different parts of the business that have to be made to communicate with one another.

Moreover, to obtain value from DM, organizations must be able to change their mode of operation and maintain that effort. In the case of supermarket loyalty cards, for instance, the commitment has to be one that will endure because of the enormous amount of mailing and chronicling that is required by the company. If the company lets the loyalty program languish, customers may start wondering why information about their purchases is being collected. The company will then be in a bind, because loyalty programs are also hard to end. Customers who have been choosing to fly on a particular airline to accumulate a given number of miles will not appreciate it if the program is curtailed or changed before they reap the rewards.

WALKING THE TIGHTROPE BETWEEN PERSONALIZATION AND PRIVACY

Perhaps the most important challenge to the future of DM is the ever-growing concern over privacy. The public's awareness of how private firms acquire and handle data has increased, particularly since the early 1990s when public uproar forced Equifax and Lotus Development Corporation to cancel the sale of their Lotus MarketPlace: Households—a series of disks containing the names, addresses, buying habits, and income information of about 120 million Americans (Culnan 1991):

> On April 10, 1990, Lotus Development Corporation proudly announced its plans to release the Lotus MarketPlace: Households. According to the trade press, MarketPlace was expected to revolutionize the list industry by making names, addresses, demographic and prior purchase behavior data for 120 million U.S. consumers available on a CD-ROM. The product was a joint venture between Equifax, one of the country's largest credit bureaus, and Lotus, a major player in the computer software industry. Equifax supplied the data from its Consumer Marketing Database while Lotus developed the software for the Macintosh desktop computer. A second version of MarketPlace for the IBM PC was on the drawing board. On January 23, 1991, Equifax and Lotus issued a joint press release stating that they were canceling the project. The statement indicated that the decision resulted from consumer concerns and "the substantial, unexpected additional costs required to fully address consumer privacy issues." (Culnan 1991, www.cpsr.org/conferences/cfp91/culnan.html)

Companies that use DM for target marketing are often walking a tightrope between personalization and respect for privacy. The actions companies have taken to know their customers better and use this information have, in some cases, backfired. In its attempt to start a "friends and family" program in the United Kingdom, British Telecom mailed its customers a "five favorite calls" list with the most frequently dialed numbers in each account. According to several media reports, this program was the direct cause of a broken marriage when an unsuspecting wife realized she didn't recognize the most frequently dialed number from their home. The errant husband told the publication that he was considering suing BT for having blown the whistle on his carefully concealed 20-year love affair (Culnan, 1991).

Going beyond the potential backlash of the market, privacy advocates and the Federal Trade Commission (FTC) have been pushing for stricter rules similar to those applied in European Union countries. At a minimum, the guidelines proposed by the FTC state that companies must disclose their information practices before collecting any personal information and that consumers should have a choice as to whether and how personal information may be used. Also, the FTC states that consumers should be able to view and contest the accuracy and completeness of the data collected about them. Since early 2002, virtually every credit card issuer has formulated guidelines and informed each of its customers with regard to a formal privacy policy intended to protect individual information.

Unfortunately, however, the implementation of these guidelines in DM is not always straightforward and can be quite costly to companies. Firms would have to let customers know that they are using billing and account information (to name a couple of categories) for DM purposes. Yet, companies often do not know what they are going to do with this information until the DM process reveals patterns in the data. Moreover, providing customers with access to the data in an intelligible form can be costly and cumbersome, and it can raise the very privacy concerns it is designed to appease. For example, how does a company guarantee that the person who requests to review and correct their personal information is really the person whose data were collected? Further, if a company guarantees that it will not share the data with others, what happens to the data when a company is bought or goes into bankruptcy and has to sell its assets? Are the data contained within the DW a company asset that can be sold to another organization without notifying every potentially affected individual?

In many ways, technology is outpacing the ability of our legal system to handle the ethical and property issues that arise. DM is pushing the definition of privacy from individuals' claims over determining what information about them is communicated to others to include determining what information is *created* by others.

Yet another facet of this problem lies with the technology itself. The technology that renders data useful as a source of information is the same technology that makes it a valuable commodity that can be sold. Defining which information is personal and owned exclusively by the individual and which can be owned by companies—as well as the guidelines for what can be done with the different types of information—remains a significant challenge for the future.

As the rules are laid out and the technology becomes more widespread, DM could have an impact on the efficiency with which companies cater to the preferences of individual customers, in the same way that it has been improving the efficiency with which loans are evaluated, fraud is detected, and NBA coaches formulate their strategies. Better target marketing and customer segmentation can reduce costs for companies and offer customers products they are more likely to buy, reducing the amount of junk mail. However, there can still be winners and losers, as those who turn out to be in the least-profitable segment for a company will see their options reduced—as those bank customers whose late fees are not forgiven can attest.

To further exacerbate the problem, current DM models are not fail-safe. For all the talk of prediction, companies cannot impel customers to buy their products; they can only try to pitch their best offer. In many ways, this is not so different from the old-time corner grocer who could greet you by name and tell you that the apples you like so much are especially juicy and ripe this week. And for you, just for you, he will cut you a special deal. In the end, selling is still more of an art than a science, and the odds of you getting no more junk mail in the near future are quite slim.

Privacy. It is a loaded issue. In recent years, privacy concerns have taken on a more significant role in American society as merchants, insurance companies, and government agencies amass warehouses containing personal data. The concerns that people have over the collection of these data will naturally extend to any analytic capabilities applied to the data. Users of DM should begin to think about how their use of this technology will be impacted by legal issues related to privacy.

Consider the recent uproar over CVS drugstores and their use of Elensys, a Massachusetts direct marketing company that sends reminders to customers who have not renewed their prescriptions. After receiving criticism over what was considered to be a violation of privacy of their customer's medical records, CVS terminated its agreement with Elensys. Although there was no direct mention of DM during the controversy, recent Senate hearings on medical privacy legislation included discussions of Elensys and the use of DM for marketing activities. If and when this legislation is enacted, it could very well contain one of the first legal limitations on the use of DM technology. The following excerpt from *The Washington Post* tells the whole story.

COMPANY THAT VIOLATED PRIVACY CHANGES NAME

Two years after Elensys Care Services Inc. ran into an explosion of disapproval over its use of confidential prescription records, the Massachusetts database management company has taken an unusual approach to public relations, *The Washington Post* reported.

It went away.

According to the *Post*, Elensys dropped its old name, without issuing a press release, and, in state documents filed last fall, quietly became Adheris Inc. The company still helps drug stores to remind patients to take medication on time. It has the same executives, the same address at a Woburn, MA, office park, the same telephone number. But gone is the name that came to symbolize the growing unease about personal privacy, after people in the Washington region learned that CVS, Giant and other pharmacies were sending personal medical information to Elensys without their permission.

At the time, Elensys used the data to identify customers who had not refilled prescriptions and to send personalized letters urging them to do so. Elensys also sent out materials about drugs, on behalf of manufacturers who paid a fee, to customers with particular ailments.

So fierce was the backlash from customers that CVS and Giant quickly apologized publicly and cut ties to the company. Several customers went after Elensys and its partners in a class-action lawsuit for breaching their privacy. The name "Elensys" is routinely cited during Capitol Hill discussions about privacy, data mining, and data ownership.

(*Source: Washington Post*, May 2, 2000.)

Stories such as this reveal only the tip of the iceberg. A cursory search of the Internet will yield a wide variety of sites describing U.S., Canadian, and European policy decisions that could directly or indirectly impact the use of DM technology by database marketing organizations. Although currently the United States takes a much more laissez-faire approach to privacy than its Canadian and European counterparts, these policies are facing challenges. As far back as 1998, the European Union's Directive on Data Protection barred the movement of personal data to countries that do not have sufficient data privacy laws in place. Industry groups argue that voluntary controls currently in place in the United States are sufficient; however, privacy advocates argue that any controls must be backed by legislation. Whether or not voluntary measures will suffice is still an open question, but recent comments by EU officials have been critical of this voluntary approach.

Although broadly written use statements are regularly being added to customer agreements to allow DM, privacy advocates question whether or not these waivers are truly meaningful to consumers. As DM is based on the extraction of unknown patterns from a database, those performing DM do not know, and cannot know, at the outset what personal data will be of value or what relationships will emerge. Therefore, identifying a primary purpose at the beginning of the process, and then restricting one's use of the data to that purpose are, in fact, the antithesis of a DM exercise.

Although this debate rages on with no end in sight, we are beginning to see some standards and guidelines emerge that may, at least, begin the process of formulating agreeable legislation for all involved parties. Basically, these standards allow the customer to elect one of three possible scenarios for their data:

1. Do not allow any DM of my data
2. Allow DM of my data only for internal use
3. Allow DM for both internal and external uses

The important fact to take away from this discussion and from your understanding of the power of DM is that these collisions between DM and privacy are just the beginning. Over the next few years, we can expect to see an increased level of scrutiny of DM in terms of its impact on privacy. The sheer amount of data that is collected about individuals, coupled with powerful new technologies such as DM, will generate a great deal of concern from consumers. Unless this concern is effectively addressed, expect to see continued and more aggressive legal challenges to the use of DM technology.

THE CONCEPT OF INFORMATION AS A NATURAL RESOURCE

The need to protect and manage personal information has been likened to the management of a country's natural resources and coveted monuments. Personal information is a resource, exploited commercially but valued as an element of human dignity and enjoyment of one's private life. It is, therefore, to be protected and managed, not unlike the protection and management of other resources. As with early efforts to protect the environment in the absence of legislation, privacy protection currently relies on ancient common law principles that continue to adapt to new technological challenges to personal integrity, happiness, and freedom. These principles have now found legislative expression in various statutes relating to environmental protection. Information, however, has some unique qualities in need of special regulatory and judicial attention. Despite the concerted efforts of legislators to adapt the ancient common law principles to modern times, technology has created situations for which our forefathers had no possible concept and, therefore, no possible perspective on a solution. New technology requires new laws and new definitions of old, long-standing concepts such as privacy.

Looking ahead, consumers will not only want goods and services, but they will also increasingly want assurances that the information they provide to a business is, from a privacy perspective, protected. To deal with this need, a shared responsibility for the management of personal information will be essential, involving government, the business community, and consumers. Only through shared responsibility, sustained by the business community through a culture of privacy and strengthened by the voice of consumers, can personal information become a protected, managed, and valued resource (see Figure 7-8).

THE CURSE OF LARGE DATASETS

By now, you should realize, and agree, that it is relatively easy to generate a large dataset on just about anything. Consider a commercial enterprise that wants to know more about the people to whom it sells products. It believes there are at least five factors that influence customer behavior. These might be age, occupation, marital status, number of children, and social status. The company sets out to develop a formula that relates these factors to each other, hoping for a simple procedure for assessing potential clients.

If, on average, each of the five factors has 10 possible values (i.e., age might be categorized into brackets such as 21–25, 26–30, and so on), then the total number of possible combinations is relatively small. However, as we all know, potentially thousands of factors may influence customer behavior. Let's say there are 1,000, each with 10 possible values. The total number of possible values is, therefore, $10^{1,000}$ (10 followed by 1,000 zeroes). This phenomenon is often called the *curse of dimensionality;* as the number of dimensions within a database grows, so too will the curse.

Another challenge, discussed previously in Chapters 1 and 2, is to achieve the ideal of *scalability,* which holds that if a database doubles in size then it should only take twice as long to mine it using the same-sized computer. The problem is, however, that scientists are finding that this linear effect does not always apply and that the time needed to run an algorithm can actually increase exponentially as the database grows.

FIGURE 7-8   Concept of Personal and Corporate Information as a National Resource

7.5: USING DM TO PROTECT PRIVACY

In today's world, where nearly every company is dependent on the Internet, it is not surprising that problems associated with network intrusion detection have grown so rapidly. Although there may still be some argument as to the best way to protect a company's networks (i.e., firewalls, patches, intrusion detection, training, etc.), it is certain that some form of intrusion detection system (IDS) will likely maintain an important role in providing for a secure network architecture.

That being said, what can an IDS do? For the analyst who sits down in front of an IDS, the ideal system would identify all intrusions (or attempted intrusions) and take or recommend the necessary actions to stop an attack.

Unfortunately, the IDS marketplace is still quite young, and a "silver bullet" solution to detect all attacks does not appear to be on the horizon or even plausible. So what is the next step for intrusion detection? A strong case could be made for the use of DM techniques to improve the current state of intrusion detection.

HOW DO CURRENT IDSs DETECT INTRUSIONS?

In order for us to determine how DM can help advance intrusion detection, it is important to understand how current IDSs work to identify an intrusion. There are two different approaches to intrusion detection: *misuse detection* and *anomaly detection*. Misuse detection is the ability to identify intrusions based on a known pattern for the malicious activity. These known patterns are referred to as *signatures*. The second approach, anomaly detection, is the attempt to identify malicious traffic based on deviations from established normal network traffic patterns. Most, if not all, IDSs that can be purchased today are based on misuse detection. Current IDS products come with a large set of signatures that have been identified as unique to a particular vulnerability or exploit. Most IDS vendors also provide regular signature updates in an attempt to keep pace with the rapid appearance of new vulnerabilities and exploits.

SHORTFALLS WITH CURRENT IDSs

Although the ability to develop and use signatures to detect attacks is a useful and viable approach, this approach does have shortfalls that should be addressed.

Variants

As stated previously, signatures are developed in response to new vulnerabilities or exploits that have been posted or released. For a signature to be successful, it must be unique enough to only alert on malicious traffic with virtually no false alerts on valid network traffic. The difficulty here is that *exploit code,* the basic code engine used by the hacker to attempt to penetrate a system weakness, can often be easily changed. It is not uncommon for an exploit tool to be released and then have its defaults changed shortly thereafter by the hacker community. This changes the basic signature and, unless the IDS is updated quickly, the IDS can miss this new type of hack.

False Positives

Just like the various correlations that can result from an explorer approach to DM, a common complaint in network intrusion detection is the number of *false positives* an IDS will generate. Developing unique signatures is a difficult task, and oftentimes vendors will err on the side of alerting too often rather than not enough. It is much more difficult to pick out a valid intrusion attempt if a signature also alerts regularly on valid network activity. The major problem arising from this is how much can be filtered out without potentially missing an attack.

False Negatives

In contrast to the problems associated with false positive reporting, *false negatives* are also an issue. This situation occurs when an IDS does not generate an alert when an intrusion is actually taking place. Simply put, if a signature has not been written for a particular hack, there is an extremely high chance that the IDS will not detect it.

Data Overload

Another aspect of IDS that does not relate directly to misuse detection but is also extremely important is related to the volume of data an analyst can effectively and efficiently analyze. We know from our discussion earlier in this chapter that this problem is both pervasive and growing rapidly. Depending on the intrusion detection tools employed by a company and its size, logs could literally reach millions of records per day. To effectively analyze such a volume of data would require an army of intrusion detection analysts and a cadre of sophisticated IDS applications.

What Are We Looking For?

The SANS (System Administration, Networking, and Security) Institute was established in 1989 as a cooperative research and education organization. The SANS Institute enables more than 156,000 security professionals, auditors, system administrators, and network administrators to share the lessons they are learning and find solutions to the challenges they face. At the heart of SANS are the many security practitioners in government agencies, corporations, and universities around the world who invest hundreds of hours each year in research and teaching to help the entire information security community.

Recently, the SANS Institute and the National Infrastructure Protection Center (NIPC) released a document summarizing the top 20 most critical Internet security vulnerabilities. The list segments threats into three categories: (1) general vulnerabilities, (2) Windows vulnerabilities, and (3) Unix vulnerabilities.

The SANS/NIPC top 20 list is valuable because the majority of successful attacks on computer systems via the Internet can be traced to the exploitation of security flaws on this list. For instance, system compromises in the Solar Sunrise Pentagon hacking incident and the easy and rapid spread of the Code Red and NIMDA worms can be traced to exploitation of unpatched vulnerabilities on this list.

HOW CAN DM HELP?

DM can help improve intrusion detection by adding a greater level of focus to anomaly detection. By identifying bounds for valid network activity, DM can aid analysts in distinguishing attack activity from common everyday traffic on the network.

Variants

Because anomaly detection is not based on predefined signatures, concern over variants in the code of an exploit is not as great as if we are looking for abnormal activity versus a unique signature. An example might be a Remote Procedure Call (RPC) buffer overflow exploit whose code has been modified slightly to evade an IDS using signatures. With anomaly detection, the activity would be flagged because the destination machine has never seen an RPC connection attempt and the source IP was never seen connecting to the network.

False Positives

With regard to false positives, some work has been conducted to determine if DM can be used to identify recurring sequences of alarms in order to help identify valid network activity that can be filtered out.

False Negatives

By attempting to establish patterns for normal activity and identifying that activity that lies outside identified bounds, attacks for which signatures have not been developed might be detected. An extremely simple example of how this would work would be to take a Web server and develop a profile of the network activity seen to and from the system. Let's say the Web server is locked down and only connections to Ports 80 and 443 are ever seen to the server. Thus, whenever a connection to a port other than 80 or 443 is seen, the IDS should identify that activity as an anomaly. Although this example is quite simple, it could be extended to profiling not only individual hosts, but entire networks, users, traffic based on days of the week or hours in a day, and so on.

Data Overload

The area where DM is sure to play a vital role is that of data reduction. Current DM algorithms are able to identify or extract data that are the most relevant and provide analysts with different "views" of the data to aid in their analysis.

CHALLENGES TO INTRUSION DETECTION DM

As we have seen, DM has been evolving in sophistication for years. However, the use of DM in intrusion detection is a relatively new concept. Thus, there will likely be obstacles in developing an effective DM intrusion detection solution.

One obstacle is that even though the concept of DM has been around for some time, the amount of data to be analyzed and its complexity is increasing dramatically. As stated earlier, a company may collect millions of records per day that must be analyzed for malicious activity. With such a large amount of data, one can guess that DM will become quite computationally expensive. Unfortunately, for some, processing power or memory is not always cheap or available. Of course, some may argue that an analyst only needs samples of the data in order to generate profiles; however, others argue that analyzing anything, especially network traffic, without all the data could lead to false conclusions.

Another obstacle will be in tailoring DM algorithms and processes to fit intrusion detection. An effort to identify how the data need to be looked at in order to provide us with a better picture is surely integral in providing accurate and effective results.

7.6: TRENDS AFFECTING THE FUTURE OF DM

In this section, we will briefly identify four trends that promise to have a fundamental impact on DM.

DATA TRENDS

Perhaps the most fundamental external trend in DM is the explosion of digital data during the past two decades. During this period, the amount of data has grown between 6 to 10 orders of magnitude, with much of these data accessible via public networks. During this same period, the number of scientists, engineers, and other analysts available to analyze these data has remained relatively constant. The number of new Ph.D.'s in statistics graduating each year has remained relatively constant during this period. Only two conclusions are possible: Either most of the data are destined to be written and never read, or techniques such as DM must be developed that can automate, in part, the analysis of these data, filter irrelevant information, and extract meaningful knowledge.

HARDWARE TRENDS

DM requires numerically and statistically intensive computations on large datasets. The increasing memory and processing speed of workstations enables the mining of datasets that were too large to be mined just a few years ago using current algorithms and techniques. In addition, the commoditization of high-performance computing through high-performance workstation clusters now allows analysts to analyze DM problems that were accessible using only the largest supercomputers of a few years ago.

NETWORK TRENDS

The next-generation Internet will connect sites at speeds in excess of 155 MBits/sec. This is over 100 times faster than the connectivity provided by current networks. With this type of connectivity, it will become possible to correlate distributed datasets using current algorithms and techniques. In addition, new protocols, algorithms, and languages are being developed to facilitate distributed DM using current and next-generation networks.

BUSINESS TRENDS

Today, businesses must be more profitable, react more quickly, and offer higher-quality services than ever before, and do it all using fewer people and at lower cost. With these types of expectations and constraints, DM is becoming a fundamental technology, enabling businesses to more accurately predict opportunities and risks generated by their customers and their customers' transactions.

A POSSIBLE SCENARIO FOR THE FUTURE OF DATA MINING

What does the future have in store for DM? In the end, much of what is called DM will likely end up as standard tools built into database or DW software products. As justification for this statement, we can use common spell-checking software as an example. Look back 20 years to the infancy of computer word processing. Many companies manufactured and sold spell-checking software. Users would usually buy a spell checker as a separate piece of software for use with whatever word processor they might have. Sometimes the spell checker was not able to understand a particular word processor's file format. Some spell checkers even required users to save their documents as ASCII files before it would check the spelling. In that case, users had to manually make corrections in the original document. Eventually, spell checkers became more user friendly and understood every possible document format. Functionality also increased. The future of spell checking probably looked quite prosperous.

So, where are all the spell-checking companies today? Where is the spell-checking software? If you look at your local computer store, you will not find much there. Instead, you will find that your new word processor comes with a built-in spell checker. As word processor software increased in sophistication and functionality, it was a natural progression to include spell checking into the standard system.

The future of DM may very well parallel the history of spell checking. The functionality of database marketing products will continue to integrate with relational database products and with key decision support system application environments. Such software will stress the business problem rather than the technology and present the process to the user in a friendly and intuitive manner. Database exploration will start to lose some of its hype and begin to provide real value to users. The larger RDBMS and DW companies have already expressed an interest in integrating DM into their database products. In the end, this new market and its business opportunities will drive mainstream database companies to providing an integrated data warehousing and mining solution. Ten years from now there may be only a few independent DM companies left in the market. The real survivors will likely be the ones with the foresight to develop a strong relationship with the mainstream database industry.

We cannot possibly explore all of the future possibilities and challenges for DM in this short chapter or even in a single text. The ever-changing business environment makes prediction difficult, but the message remains clear: DM is going to be the tool that revolutionizes the way organizations conduct their business and view their customers.

In our final look toward the future, we will turn our attention to the most likely approach to mining the data of tomorrow, data visualization.

7.7: THE FUTURE OF DATA VISUALIZATION

It is easy to argue that one needs larger disk farms, higher I/O bandwidth, and better visualization software and devices. The memory size and computation rate of emerging multi-teraflops architectures and the I/O bandwidth of earth observation satellites demonstrates this need. However, this line of reasoning is inherently abstract, giving one little feel for the magnitude and urgency of the need. To accomplish this, we need to focus on the impact of data visualization in a variety of contexts and extrapolate its power and impact to other areas of business endeavor.

To advance one of several examples, the quality of visualizing and data handling tools will, in part, determine the reliability of our nation's nuclear stockpile and whether or not the United States needs to resume underground testing. Also, in many areas of science, our ability to manipulate and understand very large datasets will dictate the pace of progress. The visualization of scientific data is a major component of computational science and engineering and is critical to understanding the results of large-scale scientific simulation. This is true also in areas such as pharmaceutical design, where science can have a huge impact on quality of life. Finally, one can point to medical and battlefield applications where visualization directly impacts life and death decisions. Progress in visualization can have enormous benefits, both in economically quantifiable ways and in subtler, but equally important, ones. Conversely, failure to make rapid progress will have a severe negative impact on a large number of activities critical to our society.

In the following sections, we will explore the future of data visualization via a series of short of vignettes, suggesting the potential impact of breakthroughs in graphics, visualization, and data manipulation. It is not easy to assess this impact. As with ARPANET, the precursor to the Internet, the greatest benefits may be entirely unforeseen. However, these simple vignettes suggest at least some of the real and tangible developments and benefits that data visualization could bring in the near future.

WEAPON PERFORMANCE AND SAFETY SIMULATION

To illustrate the role that data visualization will play in the U.S. government's evaluation of its nuclear stockpile, we consider a hypothetical scenario in 2004, examining the information flow within design and engineering teams at various nuclear laboratories and highlighting the contributions of data visualization technologies.

In the spring of 2004, we posit the detection of an anomaly in a nuclear warhead (referred to as "XYZ" in this scenario) as part of a routine inspection at a warhead construction plant performed as part of a surveillance program. It is clear from the context of the anomaly that it does not represent a manufacturing defect, but is a result of aging materials in the weapon. It is also clear from the examination of the device that the anomaly exhibits three-dimensional characteristics. Following the initial detection of the change, the particular device is examined via industrial-computed tomography and then disassembled and explored in detail. A complete product model of the weapon is generated and sent to the design teams at the laboratories. The model represents repair and replacement components, their intended functionality, experimentally measured "as-built" tolerances, and the observed anomaly that is being analyzed, as well as existing information from the original CAD/CAM model. As the process unfolds and more devices are tested, it becomes clear that approximately 10 percent of the deployed XYZ warheads exhibit similar anomalies. The model is updated to reflect the variations from the different devices, reflecting as many shared components and subassemblies as possible, but with distinct versions to account for differences. The questions faced by the Department of Energy are:

- Does this anomaly impact or change the safety, reliability, or performance of warhead XYZ?
- If so, what actions should be taken to maintain the safety, reliability, and performance of warhead XYZ?

Figure 7-9 contains a visualization of a simulated warhead impact that could be used to test the XYZ warhead and answer the questions regarding safety and reliability.

MEDICAL TRAUMA TREATMENT

At 3:00 A.M. on a cold February night, an unrestrained occupant in a motor vehicle accident with falling blood pressure and a tense abdomen was brought to the emergency room of County Medical, a 100-bed hospital in a rural county in the Midwest. The emergency room staff, a nurse, a paramedic, and a physician instituted immediate trauma protocol measures based on the mechanism of injury and the patient's status. In assessing the potential for intra-abdominal injuries, a *paracentesis* (introducing a needle through the abdominal wall to determine presence and composition of fluid in the abdominal cavity) was performed that revealed blood in the peritoneal cavity. At that point, Central Memorial Hospital, the major regional

FIGURE 7-9   Visualization of a Simulated Warhead Impact

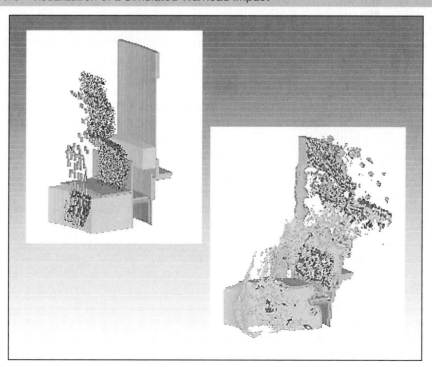

center for a multistate area of the Midwest, was contacted, and discussion ensued with their chief trauma surgeon.

An ice storm had essentially paralyzed the region; no helicopters were available, and ambulances were unable to cross interstate freeways because of fallen power lines. The family physician on duty, despite training including Advanced Cardiac Life Support (ACLS), Advanced Trauma Life Support (ATLS), and Pediatric Advanced Life Support (PALS), felt overwhelmed by the clinical situation combined with the fact that there were also other seriously needy patients in the emergency room. He requested assistance in stabilizing the accident victim. With time delay and imperfect communications, the trauma center directed the physician to stabilize the patient's airway and develop an access point for intravenous resuscitation, and instructed the physician to contact the nearest surgeon. In the interaction, a number of key elements of basic trauma protocol had been forgotten. The patient's bladder was never catheterized, nor was the patient's back ever checked or stabilized because of the numerous tasks necessary. Before the initial protocol could be administered, the patient died in the emergency room from internal bleeding.

PROJECTED TECHNICAL CAPABILITIES BY 2004

By 2004, we envision data visualization and communication technologies to have progressed such that a dynamic, real-time, 3D scene of an important facility (such as an operating theater or an emergency room) can be captured via multiple video cameras strategically positioned on the walls of the room. The image streams from these cameras can be combined by several techniques to form a dynamically changing 3D video stream of information. This dynamic 3D dataset could be sent to a distant specialist, such as a trauma surgeon, who can observe the scene in a variety of ways: conventional monitor, a Cave (the most immersive virtual reality environment—a small room, typically, a 1,000-square-foot space with surfaces on which head-tracked stereo graphical images are projected, allowing the user to move freely in the scene), or panoramic wide-screen display. The most natural way, as shown in Figure 7-10, may be for a user to wear a miniaturized, lightweight, head-mounted display (HMD) that enables the user to observe and explore the scene by simply walking around as if actually present. A similar system could be used to capture the movements and gestures of the distant specialist so that the local physicians can see and hear the specialist merged into their own scene through their own HMDs. In order for the telepresence system to be medically useful, bandwidth and computational power will be sufficient to transmit the high-resolution imagery and 3D scenery to all clinicians in adequate detail, both of the whole scene and of specific areas of interest.

MEDICAL TRAUMA SCENARIO REVISITED IN 2004

When the patient arrives in the emergency room at County Medical, the on-call physician begins trauma protocols and assessment. He quickly realizes that the patient may have injuries with which he has little prior experience in treating. The patient is moved to the telepresence operating room (TOR), and the on-call trauma staff at the Central Memorial trauma center are notified. A few moments later the virtual presence of the trauma surgeon enters the TOR, which is visible to the emergency room physician, the nurse, and the EMT through their lightweight, augmented-reality HMDs. The trauma surgeon sees the entire TOR, including the patient and physician, through her head-mounted display. The two clinicians recognize each other from 2 months earlier when the trauma surgeon taught the Advanced Trauma Life Support course that the emergency room physician took via this same telepresence facility (See Figure 7-11).

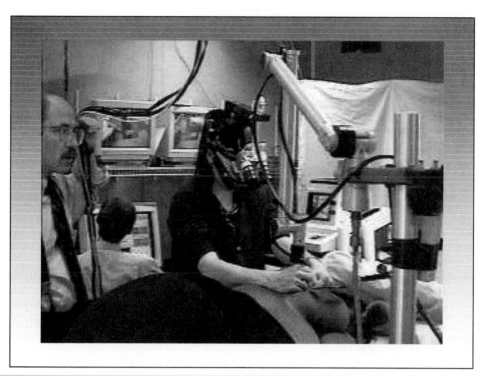

FIGURE 7-10 Augmented-Reality Headset Worn by Surgeon
The surgeon simultaneously sees the patient and the potential tumor inside the patient, displayed by the computer using live, real-time, ultrasound data.

FIGURE 7-11 Example of Surgery Being Conducted Via a Telepresence Facility

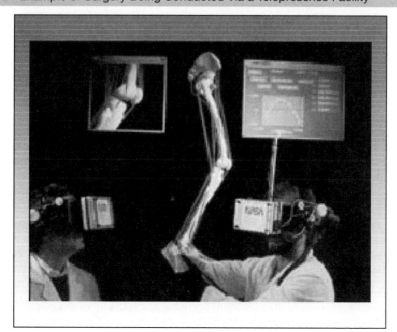

For the next half hour, the entire team works as if the trauma surgeon were present in the room but has not yet been able to scrub into the surgery; the surgeon can advise, but cannot perform procedures herself. The trauma surgeon notices that a number of key elements of basic trauma protocol have been forgotten. The patient's bladder has not been catheterized, nor has the patient's back been checked and/or stabilized. After these two elements are completed, the trauma surgeon suggests an ultrasound examination to the local physician to determine the extent of internal bleeding.

The ultrasound procedure reveals such significant internal bleeding that the patient may bleed to death before arriving at the trauma center. Under the trauma surgeon's careful guidance, the emergency physician opens the patient's abdomen, finds the lacerated artery, performs a rudimentary repair, and closes the abdominal wall. During the next several hours, before the patient can be evacuated to the trauma center, the emergency staff keep the patient stabilized while the trauma surgeon periodically checks in. Six hours later, the weather has cleared and the patient is sufficiently stable to withstand transport to the trauma center. There, the trauma surgeon, by now intimately familiar with the case, reevaluates the patient and performs definitive surgical procedures.

The trauma surgeon later requests permission from the patient to use portions of the 3D data stream in her next Advanced Trauma Life Support course. In this teaching lesson, students learn while fully immersed in the scenarios from their local telepresence TOR suites.

7.8: COMPONENTS OF FUTURE VISUALIZATION APPLICATIONS

The data visualization environment links the critical components—the people, the computer platforms, the display devices, and the storage systems—and enables the smooth flow and transformation of data among the components. The type of research enabled by data visualization, as illustrated by the previous scenarios, is not unique to any particular field or organization. Many fields conduct research projects that require multidisciplinary, geographically separated groups; interweaving results from complex simulations with observed data; and manipulation of huge, multifaceted data collections. In other words, scientific and engineering advances, particularly in the study of complex phenomena, are increasingly dependent on new approaches to computing and communications that blur the boundaries between the realm of bits and numbers in the computer, the realm of graphics and images, and the realm of acquired human knowledge. Figure 7-12 contains a conceptual mapping of the information architecture necessary to support real-time access of large datasets for effective visualization endeavors.

Many advances in a number of technologies will be needed to create the data visualization environment of the future. As the simulations carried out on the multi-teraflop computers of the future will generate vast amounts of data, networks will require much higher bandwidth, and data archives will need to scale to much larger capacity—hundreds of petabytes—and support much faster I/O than ever before. The data expected from large-scale simulation codes and other large sources of scientific and technical data over the next few years vastly exceed today's data management and visualization capabilities in both quantity and complexity. Moreover, current systems and software are completely inadequate for this volume of data. New intelligent file systems and data management software for thousands of coupled storage devices will be needed to allow interactive visualization of 100-terabyte datasets from multipetabyte

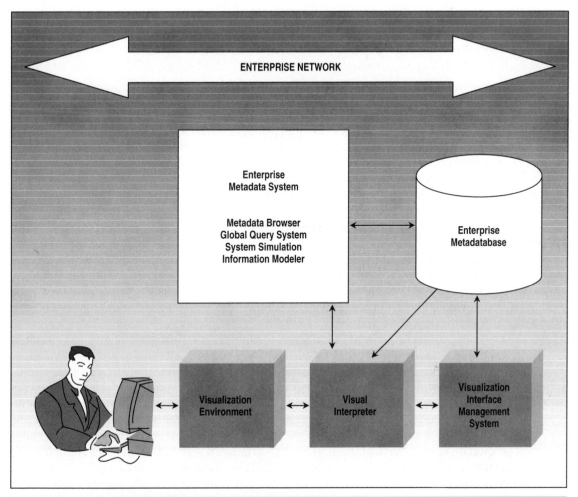

FIGURE 7-12 Conceptual Mapping of an Information Architecture Necessary to Support Real-Time Access of Large Datasets for Effective Visualization

archives. Data exploration of petabyte databases will require both technology development and altered work patterns for research scientists and engineers. In addition, visualization systems will need to manipulate and display terabyte-scale datasets, in some cases, with high interactivity. *Telecollaboration* and *virtual prototyping* will require networks to incorporate Quality of Service (QOS) not yet available. The complexity and size of the simulation results will require automated capabilities for extracting quantitative information from massive datasets and using 3D visualizations to compare the results of different codes and to compare code results to experimental results. Current graphics and visualization technology cannot cope with the volume or complexity of the data produced by the simulations that will be carried out on the teraflops computer platforms in the next 2 to 4 years.

In order to have the technologies to create the desired data visualization environment, rigorous, interdisciplinary research and development programs, aimed at significantly improving the ability to see and understand output from large data sources, must be established. Such programs should be composed of both small- and large-scale research and development focused on the interaction of data management and data visualization technologies.

7.9: CHAPTER SUMMARY

As we have seen in this final chapter, the future of data warehousing, mining, and visualization is both promising and challenging. Probably the single greatest challenge lies with the multitude of complex decisions associated with data storage and retrieval. The structure of the DW will be crucial to its ability to grow and scale up to new and more effective levels of query and analysis. Once this challenge is met, however, the tools are already in place to explore and exploit the data in ways previously unimaginable.

One short note: In lieu of the usual end-of-chapter questions and concepts, much of which would not be applicable to our discussion in this chapter, I have included hopefully useful tools in your quest to understand the warehouse and its mining operations as appendices at the end of this chapter. Appendix A is a fairly comprehensive glossary of data warehousing terminology. Appendix B is a list of data warehousing information resources that can be accessed via the World Wide Web. These listings are my personal favorites with regard to thoroughness of coverage, and I hope they serve you well.

Thus ends our exploration of the foundations of data warehousing, mining, and visualization. As I said in the beginning, our best effort here will only slightly scratch the surface of understanding. Hopefully, however, the material contained in this text will have accomplished two additional goals. First, it is my hope that you have gained a new appreciation for the power of these new technologies and for the myriad of contexts in which they can prove invaluable. Second, I hope that this text has served to whet your appetite for additional exploration and learning in this valuable technological area. The future will need many types of knowledge workers, but none more so than those who possess the skills and understanding to find new and strategically valuable patterns in the vast stores of data that will be sitting quietly in the corporate data warehouse. When we learn how to fully exploit the data we already possess, new worlds and opportunities for technical and social advancement will begin to emerge. The future is an exciting place to be. I hope to see you there.

References

Culnan, M. J. (1991). *The Lessons of the Lotus Marketplace: Implications for Computer Privacy in the 1990s*. Retrieved September 1, 2002, from www.cpsr.org/conferences/cfp91/culnan.html.

(May 2, 2002). The Twenty Most Critical Internet Vulnerabilities: The Experts' Consensus, V2.405. Retrieved September 1, 2002, from www.sans.org/top20.htm.

GLOSSARY OF DATA WAREHOUSING TERMINOLOGY[1]

access—the operation of seeking, reading, or writing data on a storage unit.

access method—a technique used to transfer a physical record from or to a mass storage device.

access pattern—the general sequence in which the data structure is accessed (e.g., from tuple to tuple, from record to record, from segment to segment, etc.).

access time—the time interval between the instant an instruction initiates a request for data and the instant the first of the data satisfying the request is delivered. Note that there is a difference—sometimes large—between the time data are first delivered and the time when *all* the data are delivered.

accuracy—a qualitative assessment of freedom from error or a quantitative measure of the magnitude of error expressed as a function of relative error.

active data dictionary—a data dictionary that is the sole source for an application program insofar as metadata is concerned.

activity ratio—the fraction of records in a database that have activity or are otherwise accessed in a given period of time or in a given batch run.

ad hoc processing—one time only casual access and manipulation of data on parameters never before used.

address—an identification (e.g., number, name, storage location, byte offset, etc.) for a location where data are stored.

addressing—the means of assigning data to storage locations and locating the data upon subsequent retrieval on the basis of the key of the data.

after image—the snapshot of data placed on a log upon completion of a transaction.

agent of change—a motivating force large enough to not be denied, usually aging of systems, changes in technology, radical changes in requirements, and so on.

algorithm—a set of statements organized to solve a problem in a finite number of steps.

alias—an alternative label used to refer to a data element.

alphabetic—a representation of data using only upper and/or lowercase letters.

alphanumeric—a representation of data using numbers, and/or letters, and punctuation.

analytical processing—the use of the computer to produce an analysis for management decision making, usually involving trend analysis, drill down analysis, demographic analysis, profiling, and so on.

ANSI—American National Standards Institute

anticipatory staging—the technique of moving blocks of data from one storage device to another with a shorter access time in anticipation of their being needed by a program in execution or a program soon to go into execution.

API—Application Program Interface—the common set of parameters needed to connect the communications between programs.

application—a group of algorithms and data interlinked to support an organizational requirement.

application blocking of data—the grouping of multiple occurrences of data controlled at the application level into the same physical unit of storage.

---

[1]Glossary entries adapted from www.billinmon.com//library/glossary.asp (2002).

application database—a collection of data organized to support a specific application.

archival database—a collection of data containing data of a historical nature. As a rule, archival data cannot be updated. Each unit of archival data is relevant to a moment in time, now passed.

area—in network databases, a named collection of records that can contain occurrences of one or more record types. A record type can occur in more than one area.

artifact—a design technique used to represent referential integrity in the DSS environment.

artificial intelligence—AI—the capability of a system to perform functions typically associated with human intelligence and reasoning.

association—a relationship between two entities that is represented in a data model.

associative storage—(1) a storage device whose records are identified by a specific part of their contents rather than their name or physical position in the database; (2) content-addressable memory. See also parallel search storage.

atomic—(1) data stored in a data warehouse; (2) the lowest level of process analysis.

atomic database—a database made up of primarily atomic data; an enterprise data warehouse; a DSS foundation database.

atomic-level data—data with the lowest level of granularity. Atomic-level data reside in a data warehouse and are time variant (i.e., accurate as of some moment in time, now passed).

atomicity—the property in which a group of actions is invisible to other actions executing concurrently to yield the effect of serial execution. It is recoverable with successful completion (i.e., commit) or total backout (i.e., rollback) of previous changes associated with that group.

attribute—a property that can assume values for entities or relationships. Entities can be assigned several attributes (e.g., a tuple in a relationship consists of values). Some systems also allow relationships to have attributes as well.

audit trail—data that are available to trace activity, usually update activity.

availability—a measure of the reliability of a system indicating the fraction of time when the system is up and available divided by the amount of time the system should be up and available. Note that there is a difference between a piece of hardware being available and the systems running on the hardware also being available.

B-tree—a binary storage structure and access method that maintains order in a database by continually dividing possible choices into two equal parts and reestablishing pointers to the respective sets but not allowing more than two levels of difference to exist concurrently.

back-end processor—a database machine or an intelligent disk controller.

back up—to restore the database to its state as of some previous moment in time.

backup—a file serving as a basis for the activity of backing up a database. Usually a snapshot of a database as of some previous moment in time.

backward recovery—a recovery technique that restores a database to an earlier state by applying before images.

base relation—a relation that is not derivable from other relations in the database.

batch—computer environment in which programs (usually long-running, sequentially oriented ones) access data exclusively and user interaction is not allowed while the activity is occurring.

batch environment—a sequentially dominated mode of processing. In batch, input is collected and stored for future, later processing. Once collected, the batch input is transacted sequentially against one or more databases.

batch window—the time at which the online system is available for batch or sequential processing. The batch window occurs during nonpeak processing hours.

before image—a snapshot of a record prior to update, usually placed on an activity log.

bill of materials—a listing of the parts used in a manufacturing process along with the relation of one product to another insofar as assembly of the final product is concerned. The bill of materials is a classical recursive structure.

binary element—a constituent element of data that takes either of two values or states—either true or false or 1 or 0.

binary search—a dichotomizing search with steps in which the sets of remaining items are partitioned into two equal parts.

bind—(1) to assign a value to a data element, variable, or parameter; (2) the attachment of a data definition to a program prior to the execution of the program.

binding time—the moment in time when the data description known to the dictionary is assigned to or bound to the procedural code.

bit—(b)inary digi(t)—the lowest level of storage; a bit can be in a 1 state or a 0 state.

bit map—a specialized form of an index indicating the existence or nonexistence of a condition for a group of blocks or records. Bit maps are expensive to build and maintain but provide very fast comparison and access facilities.

block—(1) a basic unit of structuring storage; (2) the physical unit of transport and storage. A block usually contains one or more records (or contains the space for one or more records). In some DBMSs, a block is called a page.

block splitting—the data management activity in which a filled block is written into two unfilled blocks, leaving space for future insertions and updates in the two partially filled blocks.

blocking—the combining of two or more physical records so that they are physically colocated together. The result of their physical colocation is that they can be accessed and fetched by a single execution of a machine instruction.

buffer—an area of storage that holds data temporarily in main memory while data are being transmitted, received, read, or written. A buffer is often used to compensate for the differences in the timing of transmission and execution of devices. Buffers are used in terminals, peripheral devices, storage units, and CPUs.

bus—the hardware connection that allows data to flow from one component to another (e.g., from the CPU to the line printer).

byte—a basic unit of storage made up of 8 bits.

C—a programming language.

cache—a buffer usually built and maintained at the device level. Retrieving data out of a cache is much quicker than retrieving data from a cylinder.

call—to invoke the execution of a module.

canonical model—a data model that represents the inherent structure of data without regard to either individual use or hardware or software implementation.

cardinality (of a relation)—the number of tuples (i.e., rows) in a relation. See also degree (of a relation).

CASE—Computer Aided Software Engineering

catalog—a directory of all files available to the computer.

chain—an organization in which records or other items of data are strung together.

chain list—a list in which the items cannot be located in sequence but in which each item contains an identifier (i.e., pointer) for the finding of the next item.

channel—a subsystem for input and output to and from the computer. Data from storage units, for example, flow into the computer by way of a channel.

character—a member of the standard set of elements used to represent data in the database.

character type—the characters that can represent the value of an attribute.

checkpoint—an identified snapshot of the database or a point at which the transactions against the database have been frozen.

checkpoint/restart—a means of restarting a program at some point other than the beginning, for example, when a failure or interruption has occurred. N checkpoints may be used at intervals throughout an application program. At each of those points, sufficient information is stored to permit the program to be restored to the moment in time the checkpoint was taken.

child—a unit of data existing in a 1:n relationship with another unit of data called a parent, where the parent must exist before the child can exist, but the parent can exist even if no child unit of data exists.

CICS—Customer Information Control System—an IBM teleprocessing monitor.

circular file (queue)—an organization of data in which a finite number of units of data are allocated. Data are then loaded into those units. Upon reaching the end of the allocated units, new data are written over older data at the start of the queue. Sometimes called a "wrap around" queue.

claimed block—a second or subsequent physical block of data designated to store table data when the originally allocated block has run out of space.

class (of entities)—all possible entities held by a given proposition.

cluster—(1) in Teradata, a group of physical devices controlled by the same AMP; (2) in DB2 and Oracle, the practice of physically colocating data in the same block based on the content of data.

cluster key—the key around which data are clustered in a block (DB2/Oracle).

coalesce—to combine two or more sets of items into any single set.

code—(1) to represent data or a computer program in a form that can be accepted by a data processor; (2) to transform data so that it cannot be understood by anyone who does not have the algorithm used to decode the data prior to presentation (sometimes called "encode").

collision—the event that occurs when two or more records of data are assigned the same physical location. Collisions are associated with randomizers or hashers.

column—a vertical table in which values are selected from the same domain. A row is made up of one or more columns.

command—(1) the specification of an activity by the programmer; (2) the actual execution of the specification.

commit—a condition raised by the programmer signaling to the DBMS that all update activity done by the program be executed against a database. Prior to the commit, all update activity can be rolled back or cancelled with no ill effects on the contents of the database.

commit protocol—an algorithm to ensure that a transaction is successfully completed.

commonality of data—similar or identical data that occur in different applications or systems. The recognition and management of commonality of data is one of the foundations of conceptual and physical database design.

communication network—the collection of transmission facilities, network processors, and so on, that provides for data movement among terminals and information processors.

compaction—a technique for reducing the number of bits required to represent data without losing the content of the data. With compaction, repetitive data are represented very concisely.

component—a data item or array of data items whose component type defines a collection of occurrences with the same data type.

compound index—an index over multiple columns.

concatenate—to link or connect two strings of characters, generally for the purpose of using them as a single value.

conceptual schema—a consistent collection of data structures expressing the data needs of the organization. This schema is a comprehensive, base level, and logical description of the environment in which an organization exists, free of physical structure and application system considerations.

concurrent operations—activities executed simultaneously or during the same time interval.

condensation—the process of reducing the volume of data managed without reducing the logical consistency of the data. Condensation is essentially different than compaction.

connect—to forge a relationship between two entities, particularly in a network system.

connector—a symbol used to indicate that one occurrence of data has a relationship with another occurrence of data. Connectors are used in conceptual database design and can be implemented hierarchically, relationally, in an inverted fashion, or by a network.

content addressable memory—main storage that can be addressed by the contents of the data in the memory, as opposed to conventional location addressable memory.

contention—the condition that occurs when two or more programs try to access the same data at the same time.

continuous time-span data—data organized so that a continuous definition of data over a span of time is represented by one or more records.

control character—a character whose occurrence in a particular context initiates, modifies, or stops an operation.

control database—a utilitarian database containing data not directly related to the application being built. Typical control databases are audit databases, terminal databases, security databases, and so on.

cooperative processing—the ability to distribute resources (e.g., programs, files, and databases) across the network.

coordinator—the two-phase commit protocol defines one database management system as coordinator for the commit process. The coordinator is responsible for communicating with the other database manager involved in a unit of work.

corporate information warehouse—CIF—the architectural framework that houses the ODS, data warehouse, data marts, I/T interface, and the operational environment. The CIF is held together logically by metadata and physically by a network such as the Internet.

CPU—central processing unit

CPU-bound—the state of processing in which the computer can produce no more output because the CPU portion of the processor is being used at

100 percent capacity. When the computer is CPU-bound, typically, the memory and storage processing units are less than 100 percent utilized. With modern DBMS, it is much more likely that the computer be I/O-bound rather than CPU-bound.

CUA—Common User Access—specifies how the user interface is to be constructed.

current value data—data whose accuracy is valid as of the moment of execution. As opposed to time-variant data.

cursor—(1) an indicator that designates a current position on a screen; (2) a system facility that allows the programmer to thumb from one record to the next when the system has retrieved a set of records.

cursor stability—an option that allows data to move under the cursor. Once the program is through using the data examined by the cursor, it is released. As opposed to repeatable read.

cylinder—the area of storage of DASD that can be read without the movement of the arm. The term originated with disk files, in which a cylinder consisted of one track on each disk surface so that each of these tracks could have a read/write head positioned over it simultaneously.

DASD—see direct access storage device.

data—a recording of facts, concepts, or instructions on a storage medium for communication, retrieval, and processing by automatic means and presentation as information that is understandable by human beings.

data administrator—DA—the individual or organization responsible for the specification, acquisition, and maintenance of data management software and the design, validation, and security of files or databases. The data model and the data dictionary are classically the charge of the DA.

data aggregate—a collection of data items.

data definition—the specification of the data entities, their attributes, and their relationships in a coherent database structure to create a schema.

data definition language—DDL (also called a data description language)—the language used to define the database schema and additional data features that allow the DBMS to generate and manage the internal tables, indexes, buffers, and storage necessary for database processing.

data description language—see data definition language.

data dictionary—a software tool for recording the definition of data, the relationship of one category of data to another, the attributes and keys of groups of data, and so forth.

data-driven development—the approach to development that centers around identifying the commonality of data through a data model and building programs that have a broader scope than the immediate application. Data-driven development differs from classical application-oriented development.

data-driven process—a process whose resource consumption depends on the data on which it operates. For example, a hierarchical root has a dependent. For one occurrence, there are two dependents for the root. For another occurrence of the root, there are 1,000 occurrences of the dependent. The same program that accesses the root and all its dependents will use very different amounts of resources when operating against the two roots although the code will be exactly the same.

data element—(1) an attribute of an entity; (2) a uniquely named and well-defined category of data that consists of data items and that is included in a record of an activity.

data engineering—the planning and building of data structures according to accepted mathematical models, on the basis of the inherent characteristics of the data itself, and independent of hardware and software systems. See also information engineering.

data independence—the property of being able to modify the overall logical and physical structure of data without changing any of the application code supporting the data.

data item—a discrete representation having the properties that define the data element to which it belongs. See also data element.

data item set—DIS—a grouping of data items, each of which directly relates to the key of the grouping of data in which the data items reside. The data item set is found in the mid-level model.

data mart—a department-specific data warehouse. There are two types of data marts: independent and dependent. An independent data mart is fed data directly from the legacy environment. A dependent data mart is fed data from the enterprise data warehouse. In the long run, dependent data marts are architecturally much more stable than independent data marts.

data model—(1) the logical data structures, including operations and constraints provided by a DBMS for effective database processing; (2) the system used for the representation of data (e.g., the ERD or relational model).

data record—an identifiable set of data values treated as a unit, an occurrence of a schema in a database, or a collection of atomic data items describing a specific object, event, or tuple.

data security—the protection of the data in a database against unauthorized disclosure, alteration, or destruction. There are different levels of security.

data storage description language—DSDL—a language to define the organization of stored data in terms of an operating system and device-independent storage environment. See also device media control language.

data structure—a logical relationship among data elements that is designed to support specific data manipulation functions (e.g., trees, lists, and tables).

data type—the definition of a set of representable values that is primitive and without meaningful logical subdivision.

data view—see user view. The structure of the data that is seen by the user when interacting with the data warehouse. This is normally documented via some form of logical model such as an entity-relationship diagram.

data volatility—the rate of change of the content of data.

data warehouse—DW—a collection of integrated subject-oriented databases designed to support the DSS function where each unit of data is relevant to some moment in time. The data warehouse contains atomic data and lightly summarized data. A data warehouse is a subject-oriented, integrated, nonvolatile, time-variant collection of data designed to support management DSS needs

data warehouse administrator—DWA—the organization function designed to create and maintain the data warehouse. The DWA combines several disciplines, such as the DA, DBA, EMN user, etc.

database—a collection of interrelated data stored (often with controlled, limited redundancy) according to a schema. A database can serve a single or multiple applications.

database administrator—DBA—the organizational function charged with the day-to-day monitoring and care of the databases. The DBA function is more closely associated with physical database design than the DA is.

database key—a unique value that exists for each record in a database. The value is often indexed, although it can be randomized or hashed.

database machine—a dedicated-purpose computer that provides data access and management through total control of the access method, physical storage, and data organization. Often called a "back-end processor." It usually manages data in parallel.

database management system—DBMS—a computer-based software system used to establish and manage data.

database record—a physical root and all of its dependents (in IMS).

dataset—a named collection of logically related data items arranged in a prescribed manner and described by control information to which the programming system has access.

DB/DC—database/data communications.

DBMS language interface (DB I/O module)—software that applications invoke in order to access a database. The module, in turn, has direct access to the DBMS. Standards enforcement and standard error checking are often features of an I/O module.

deadlock—see deadly embrace.

deadly embrace—the event that occurs when transaction A desires to access data currently protected by transaction B, while at the same time transaction B desires to access data that is currently being protected by transaction A. The deadly embrace condition is a serious impediment to performance.

decision support system—DSS—a system used to support managerial decisions. DSS typically involves the analysis of many units of data in a heuristic fashion. As a rule, DSS processing does not involve the update of data.

decompaction—the opposite of compaction; once data are stored in a compacted form, the data must be decompacted to be used.

decryption—the opposite of encryption; once data are stored in an encrypted fashion, the data must be decrypted to be used.

degree (of a relation)—the number of attributes or columns of a relation. See also cardinality (of a relation).

delimiter—a flag, symbol, or convention used to mark the boundaries of a record, field, or other unit of storage.

demand staging—the movement of blocks of data from one storage device to another device with a shorter access time when programs request the blocks and the blocks are not already in the faster-access storage.

denormalization—the technique of placing normalized data in a physical location that optimizes the performance of the system.

derived data—data whose existence depends on two or more occurrences of a major subject of the enterprise.

derived data element—a data element that is not necessarily stored but that can be generated when needed (e.g., age given current date and date of birth).

derived relation—a relation that can be obtained from previously defined relations by applying some sequence of retrieval and derivation operator (e.g., a table that is the join of others plus some projections

design review—the quality assurance process in which all aspects of a system are reviewed publicly prior to the striking of code.

device media control language—DMCL—a language used to define the mapping of the data onto the physical storage media. See also data storage description language.

dimension table—the table that is joined to a fact table in a star join. The dimension table is the structure that represents then nonpopulous occurrences of data in a data mart.

direct access—retrieval or storage of data by reference to its location on a volume. The access mechanism goes directly to the data in question, as is generally required with online use of data. Also called random access or hashed access.

direct access storage device—DASD—a data storage unit on which data can be accessed directly without having to progress through a serial file such as a magnetic tape file. A disk unit is a direct access storage device.

directory—a table specifying the relationships between items of data; sometimes a table or index giving the addresses of data.

distributed catalog—a distributed catalog is needed to achieve site autonomy. The catalog at each site maintains information about objects in the local databases. The distributed catalog keeps information on replicated and distributed tables stored at that site and information on remote tables located at another site that cannot be accessed locally.

distributed database—a database controlled by a central DBMS but in which the storage devices are geographically dispersed or not attached to the same processor. See also parallel I/O.

distributed data warehouse—when more than one enterprise data warehouse is built, the combination is called a distributed data warehouse.

distributed environment—a set of related data processing systems where each system has its own capacity to operate autonomously but also has some applications that execute at multiple sites. Some of the systems may be connected with teleprocessing links into a network in which each system is a node.

distributed free space—space left empty at intervals in a data layout to permit insertion of new data.

distributed metadata—metadata that resides at different architectural entities, such as data marts, enterprise data warehouses, ODSs, and so on.

distributed request—a transaction across multiple nodes.

distributed unit of work—the work done by a transaction that operates against multiple nodes.

division—an operation that partitions a relation on the basis of the contents of data found in the relation.

domain—the set of legal values from which actual values are derived for an attribute or a data element.

dormant data—data loaded into a data warehouse that have a future probability of access of zero.

download—the stripping of data from one database to another based on the content of data found in the first database.

drill down analysis—a type of analysis where examination of a summary number leads to the exploration of the components of the sum.

dual database—the practice of separating high-performance, transaction-oriented data from decision support data.

dual database management systems—the practice of using multiple database management systems to control different aspects of the database environment.

dumb terminal—a device used to interact directly with the end user when all processing is done on a remote computer. A dumb terminal gathers data and displays data.

dynamic SQL—SQL statements that are prepared and executed within a program while the program is executing. In dynamic SQL, the SQL source is contained in host-language variables rather than being coded into the application program.

dynamic storage allocation—a technique in which the storage areas assigned to computer programs are determined during processing.

dynamic subset of data—a subset of data selected by a program and operated on only by the program that is released once the program ceases execution.

EDI—Electronic Data Interchange

EIS—Executive Information Systems—systems designed for top executives that feature drill down capabilities and trend analysis.

embedded pointer—a record pointer (i.e., a means of internally linking related records) that is not available to an external index or directory. Embedded pointers are used to reduce search time; however, they do have maintenance overhead.

encoding—a shortening or abbreviation of the physical representation of a data value (e.g., male = M, female = F).

encryption—the transformation of data from a recognizable form to a form unrecognizable without the algorithm used for the encryption. Encryption is usually done for the purposes of security.

enterprise—the generic term for the company, corporation, agency, or business unit. Usually associated with data modeling.

enterprise data warehouse—a data warehouse holding the most atomic data the corporation has. Two or more enterprise data warehouses may be combined in order to create a distributed data warehouse.

entity—a person, place, or item of interest to the data modeler at the highest level of abstraction.

entity-relationship-attribute model—ERA model—a data model that defines entities, the relationship between the entities, and the attributes that have values to describe the properties of entities and/or relationships.

entity-relationship diagram—ERD—a high-level data model; the schematic showing all of the entities within the scope of integration and the direct relationship between those entities.

event—a signal that an activity of significance has occurred. An event is noted by the information system.

event discrete data—data relating to the measurement or description of an event.

expert system—a system that captures and automates the usage of human experience and intelligence.

explorer—a DSS end user who operates on a random basis looking at large amounts of detailed data for patterns, associations, and other previously unnoticed relationships.

extent—(1) a list of unsigned integers that specifies an array; (2) a physical unit of disk storage attached to a dataset after the initial allocation of data has been made.

external data—(1) data originating from other than the operational systems of a corporation; (2) data residing outside the central processing complex.

external schema—a logical description of a user's method of organizing and structuring data. Some attributes or relationships can be omitted from the corresponding conceptual schema or can be renamed or otherwise transformed.

extract—the process of selecting data from one environment and transporting the data to another environment.

fact table—the central component of the star join. The structure where the vast majority of the occurrences of data in the data mart reside.

farmer—a DSS user who repetitively looks at small amounts of data and who often finds what he or she is looking for.

field—See data item.

file—a set of related records treated as a unit and stored under a single logical file name.

first in first out—FIFO—a fundamental ordering of processing in a queue.

first in last out—FILO—a standard order of processing in a stack.

flag—an indicator or character that signals the occurrence of some condition.

flat file—a collection of records containing no data aggregates, nested repeated data items, or groups of data items.

floppy disk—a device for storing data on a personal computer.

foreign key—an attribute that is not a primary key in a relational system but whose values are the values of the primary key of another relation.

format—the arrangement or layout of data in or on a data medium or in a program definition.

forward recovery—a recovery technique that restores a database by reapplying all transactions using a before image from a specified point in time to a copy of the database taken at that moment in time.

fourth-generation language—language or technology designed to allow the end user unfettered access to data.

functional decomposition—the division of operations into hierarchical functions (i.e., activities) that form the basis for procedures.

gigabyte—a measurement of data between a megabyte and a terabyte; 10×10^9 bytes of data.

global data warehouse—a data warehouse that is distributed around the world. In a global data warehouse, the system of record resides in the local site.

granularity—the level of detail contained in a unit of data. The more detail there is, the lower the level of granularity. The less detail there is, the higher the level of granularity.

graphic—a symbol produced on a screen representing an object or a process in the real world.

hash—to convert the value of the key of a record into a location on DASD.

hash total—a total of the values of one or more fields used for the purposes of auditing and control.

header record (header table)—a record containing common, constant, or identifying information for a group of records that follow.

heuristic—the mode of analysis in which the next step is determined by the results of the current step of analysis. Used for decision support processing.

hierarchical model—a data model providing a tree structure for relating data elements or groups of data elements. Each node in the structure represents a group of data elements or a record type. There can be only one root node at the start of the hierarchical structure.

hit—an occurrence of data that satisfies some search criteria.

hit ratio—a measure of the number of records in a file expected to be accessed in a given run. Usually expressed as a percentage (the number of input transactions divided by the number of records in the file multiplied by 100).

homonyms—identical names that refer to different attributes.

horizontal distribution—the splitting of a table across different sites by rows. With horizontal distribution, rows of a single table reside at different sites in a distributed database network.

host—the processor receiving and processing a transaction.

IEEE—Institute of Electrical and Electronics Engineers

image copy—a procedure in which a database is physically copied to another medium for the purposes of backup.

IMS—Information Management System—an operational DBMS by IBM.

index—the portion of the storage structure maintained to provide efficient access to a record when its index key item is known.

index chains—chains of data within an index.

index point—a hardware reference mark on a disk or drum that is used for timing purposes.

index sequential access method—ISAM—a file structure and access method in which records can be processed sequentially (e.g., in order or by key) or by directly looking up their locations on a table, thus making it unnecessary to process previously inserted records.

indirect addressing—any method of specifying or locating a record through calculation (e.g., locating a record through the scan of an index).

information—data that human beings assimilate and evaluate to solve a problem or make a decision.

information center—the organizational unit charged with identifying and accessing information needed in DSS processing.

information engineering—IE—the discipline of creating data-driven development environments.

input/output—I/O—the means by which data are stored and/or retrieved on DASD. I/O is measured in milliseconds (i.e., mechanical speeds), whereas computer processing is measured in nanoseconds (i.e., electronic speeds).

instance—a set of values representing a specific entity belonging to a particular entity type. A single value is also the instance of a data item.

integration/transformation program—I/T program—a program designed to convert and move data from the legacy environment to the data warehouse environment. Such programs are notoriously unstable and require constant maintenance.

integrity—the property of a database that ensures that the data contained in the database are as accurate and consistent as possible.

intelligent database—a database that contains shared logic as well as shared data and automatically invokes that logic when the data are accessed. Logic, constraints, and controls relating to the use of the data are represented in an intelligent data model.

interactive—a mode of processing that combines some of the characteristics of online transaction processing and batch processing. In interactive processing, the end user interacts with data over which the user has exclusive control. In addition, the end user can initiate background activity to be run against the data.

interleaved data—data from different tables mixed into a simple table space where there is commonality of physical colocation based on a common key value.

internal schema—the schema that describes logical structures of the data and the physical media over which physical storage is mapped.

Internet—a network that connects many public users.

interpretive—a mode of data manipulation in which the commands to the DBMS are translated as the user enters them (as opposed to the programmed mode of process manipulation).

intersection data—data that are associated with the junction of two or more record types or entities, but which have no meaning when disassociated from any records or entities forming the junction.

intranet—a network that connects many private users.

inverted file—a file structure that uses an inverted index, where entries are grouped according to the content of the key being referenced. Inverted files provide for the fast, spontaneous searching of files.

inverted index—an index structure organized by means of a nonunique key to speed the search for data by content.

inverted list—a list organized around a secondary index instead of around a primary key.

I/O—input/output operation—I/O operations are the key to system performance because they operate at mechanical speeds, not at electronic speeds.

I/O bound—the point after which no more processing can be done because the I/O subsystem is saturated.

"is a type of"—an analytical tool used in abstracting data during the process of conceptual database design (e.g., a cocker spaniel is a type of dog).

ISAM—see index sequential access method.

ISDN—Integrated Services Digital Network—telecommunications technology that enables companies to transfer data and voice through the same phone line.

ISO—International Standards Organization

item—see data item.

item type—a classification of an item according to its domain, generally in a gross sense.

iterative analysis—the mode of processing in which the next step of processing depends on the results obtained by the existing step; heuristic processing.

JAD—joint application design—an organization of people, usually end users, used to create and refine application system requirements.

join—an operation that takes two relations as operands and produces a new relation by concatenating the tuples and matching the corresponding columns when a stated condition holds between the two.

judgment sample—a sample of data where data are accepted or rejected for the sample based on one or more parameters.

junction—from the network environment, an occurrence of data that has two or more parent segments. For example, an order for supplies must have a supplier parent and a part parent.

justify—to adjust the value representation in a character field to the right or to the left, ignoring any blanks that are encountered.

keeplist—a sequence of database keys maintained by the DBMS for the duration of the session.

key—a data item or combination of data items used to identify or locate a record instance (or other similar data groupings). See also primary key, secondary key.

key compression—a technique for reducing the number of bits in keys; used to make indexes occupy less space.

label—a set of symbols used to identify or describe an item, record, message, or file. Occasionally, a label may be the same as the address of the record in storage.

language—a set of characters, conventions, and rules used to convey information and consisting of syntax and semantics.

latency—the time taken by a DASD device to position the read arm over the physical storage medium. For general purposes, average latency time is used.

least frequently used—LFU—a replacement strategy in which new data must replace existing data in an area of storage; the least frequently used items are replaced.

least recently used—LRU—a replacement strategy in which new data must replace existing data in an area of storage; the least recently used items are replaced.

legacy environment—the transaction-oriented, application-based environment.

level of abstraction—the level of abstraction appropriate to a dimension; the level of abstraction that is appropriate is entirely dependent on the ultimate user of the system.

line—the hardware by which data flow to or from the processor. Lines typically go to terminals, printers, and other processors.

line polling—the activity of the teleprocessing monitor in which different lines are queried to determine whether they have data and/or transactions that need to be transmitted.

line time—the length of time required for a transaction to go from either the terminal to the processor or the processor to the terminal. Typically, line time is the single largest component of online response time.

linkage—the ability to relate one unit of data to another.

linked list—set of records in which each record contains a pointer to the next record on the list. See also chain.

list—an ordered set of data items.

living sample—a representative database typically used for heuristic statistical analytical processing in place of a large database. Periodically, the very large database is selectively stripped of data so that the resulting living sample database represents a cross section of the very large database as of some moment in time.

load—to insert data values into a database that was previously empty.

local transaction—in a distributed DBMS, a transaction that requires reference only to data that are stored at the site where the transaction originated.

locality of processing—the design of a distributed database so that remote access of data is eliminated or reduced substantively.

lockup—the event that occurs when update is performed against a database record and the transaction has not yet reached a commit point. The online transaction needs to prevent other transactions from accessing the data while update is occurring.

log—a journal of activity.

logging—the automatic recording of data with regard to the access of the data, the updates to the data, and so on.

logical representation—a data view or description that does not depend on a physical storage device or a computer program.

loss of identity—when data are brought in from an external source and the identity of the external source is discarded, loss of identity occurs. This is a common practice with microprocessor data.

machine learning—the ability of a machine to improve its performance automatically based on past performance.

magnetic tape—(1) the storage medium most closely associated with sequential processing; (2) a large ribbon on which magnetic images are stored and retrieved.

main storage database—MSDB—a database that resides entirely in main storage. Such databases are very fast to access but require special handling at the time of update. Another limitation is that they can only manage small amounts of data.

master file—a file that holds the system of record for a given set of data (usually bound by an application).

maximum transaction arrival rate—MTAR—the rate of arrival of transactions at the moment of peak period processing.

megabyte—a measurement of data; 10×10^6 bytes of data.

message—(1) the data input by the user in the online environment that is used to drive a transaction; (2) the output of a transaction.

metadata—(1) data about data; (2) the description of the structure, content, keys, indexes, and so on, of data.

metalanguage—a language used to specify other languages.

microprocessor—a small processor serving the needs of a single user.

migration—the process by which frequently used items of data are moved to more readily accessible areas of storage and infrequently used items of data are moved to less readily accessible areas of storage.

MIPS—million instructions per second—the standard measurement of processor speed for minicomputers and mainframe computers.

mode of operation—a classification for systems that execute in a similar fashion and share distinctive operational characteristics.

multilist organization—a chained file organization in which the chains are divided into fragments and each fragment is indexed. This organization of data permits faster access to the data.

multiple key retrieval—requires searches of data on the basis of the values of several key fields (some or all of which are secondary keys).

natural forms—first normal form: data that have been organized into two-dimensional flat files without repeating groups. Second normal form: data that functionally depend on the entire candidate key. Third normal form: data that have had all transitive dependencies on data items other than the candidate key removed. Fourth normal form: data whose candidate key is related to all data items in the record and that contains no more than one nontrivial, multivalued dependency on the candidate key.

natural join—a join in which the redundant logic components generated by the join are removed.

natural language—a language generally spoken, whose rules are based on current usage and not explicitly defined by a grammar.

navigate—to steer a course through a database, from record to record, by means of an algorithm that examines the content of data.

network—a computer network consists of a collection of circuits, data switching elements, and computing systems. The switching devices in the network are called communication processors. A network provides a configuration for computer systems and communication facilities within which data can be stored and accessed and within which DBMS can operate.

network model—a data model that provides data relationships on the basis of records and groups of records (i.e., sets) in which one record is designated as the set owner and a single member record can belong to one or more sets.

nine's complement—transformation of a numeric field calculated by subtracting the initial value from a file consisting of all nines.

node—a point in the network where data are switched.

nonprocedural language—syntax that directs the computer as to what to do, not how to do it. Typical nonprocedural languages include RAMIS, FOCUS, NOMAD, and SQL.

normalize—to decompose complex data structures into natural structures.

NT—an operating system built by Microsoft.

null—an item or record for which no value currently exists and possibly may never exist.

numeric—a representation using only numbers and the decimal point.

occurrence—see instance.

offset pointer—an indirect pointer. An offset pointer exists inside a block and the index points to the offset. If data must be moved, only the offset pointer in the block must be altered; the index entry remains untouched.

online storage—storage devices and storage medium where data can be accessed in a direct fashion.

operating system—software that enables a computer to supervise its own operations and automatically call in programs, routines, languages, and data as needed for continuous operation throughout the execution of different types of jobs.

operational data—data used to support the daily processes of an organization.

operational data store—ODS—the form of the data warehouse in the operational environment. Operational data stores can be updated, provide rapid and consistent response time, and contain only a limited amount of historical data.

operations—the department charged with the running of the computer.

optical disk—a storage medium that uses lasers as opposed to magnetic devices. Optical disk is typically write only, is much less expensive per byte than magnetic storage, and is highly reliable.

order—to place items in an arrangement specified by such rules as numeric or alphabetic order. See also sort.

overflow—(1) the condition in which a record or a segment cannot be stored in its home address because the address is already occupied. In this case, the data are placed in another location referred to as overflow; (2) the area of DASD where data are sent when the overflow condition is triggered.

ownership—the responsibility for update of operational data.

padding—a technique used to fill a field, record, or block with default data (e.g., blanks or zeros).

page—(1) a basic unit of data on DASD; (2) a basic unit of storage in main memory.

page fault—a program interruption that occurs when a page that is referred to is not in main memory and must be read from external storage.

page fixed—the state in which programs or data cannot be removed from main storage. Only a limited amount of storage can be page fixed.

paging—in virtual storage systems, the technique of making memory appear to be larger than it really is by transferring blocks (pages) of data or programs into external memory.

parallel data organization—an arrangement of data in which the data are spread over independent storage devices and managed independently.

parallel I/O—the process of accessing or storing data on multiple physical data devices.

parallel search storage—a storage device in which one or more parts of all storage locations are queried simultaneously for a certain condition or under certain parameters. See also associative storage.

parameter—an elementary data value used as a criteria for qualification, usually in searches of data or in the control of modules.

parent—a unit of data in a 1:n relationship with another unit of data called a child, where the parent can exist independently, but the child cannot exist unless there is a parent.

parsing—the algorithm that translates syntax into meaningful machine instructions. Parsing determines the meaning of statements issued in the data manipulation language.

partition—a segmentation technique in which data are divided into physically different units. Partitioning can be done at the application or the system level.

path length—the number of instructions executed for a given program or instruction.

peak period—the time when the most transactions arrive at the computer with the expectation of execution.

performance—the length of time from the moment a request is issued until the first of the results of the request are received.

periodic discrete data—a measurement or description of data taken at a regular time interval.

physical representation—(1) the representation and storage of data on a medium such as magnetic storage; (2) the description of data that depends on such physical factors as length of elements, records, pointers, and so on.

pipes—vehicles for passing data from one application to another.

plex or network structure—a relationship between records or other groupings of data in which a child record can have more than one parent record.

plug compatible manufacturer—PCM—a manufacturer of equipment that functionally is identical to that of another manufacturer (usually IBM).

pointer—the address of a record or other groupings of data contained in another record so that a program may access the former record when it has retrieved the latter record. The address can be absolute, relative, or symbolic, and hence the pointer is referred to as absolute, relative, or symbolic.

pools—the buffers made available to the online controller.

populate—to place occurrences of data values in a previously empty database. See also load.

precision—the degree of discrimination with which a quantity is stated. For example, a three-digit numeral discriminates among 1,000 possibilities, from 000 to 999.

precompilation—the processing of source text prior to compilation. In an SQL environment, SQL statements are replaced with statements that will be recognized by the host language compiler.

prefix data—data in a segment or a record used exclusively for system control, usually unavailable to the user.

primary key—an attribute that contains values that uniquely identify the record in which the key exists.

primitive data—data whose existence depends on only a single occurrence of a major subject area of the enterprise.

privacy—the prevention of unauthorized access and manipulation of data.

privilege descriptor—a persistent object used by a DBMS to enforce constraints on operations.

problems database—the component of a DSS application where previously defined decision parameters are stored. A problems database is consulted to review characteristics of past decisions and to determine ways to meet current decision-making needs.

processor—the hardware at the center of execution of computer programs. Generally speaking, processors are divided into three categories: mainframes, minicomputers, and microcomputers.

processor cycles—the hardware's internal cycles that drive the computer (e.g., initiate I/O, perform logic, move data, perform arithmetic functions, etc.).

production environment—the environment where operational, high-performance processing is run.

program area—the portion of main memory in which application programs are executed.

progressive overflow—a method of handling overflow in a randomly organized file that does not require the use of pointers. An overflow record is stored in the first available space and is retrieved by a forward serial search from the home address.

projection—an operation that takes one relation as an operand and returns a second relation that consists of only the selected attributes or columns, with duplicate rows eliminated.

proposition—a statement about entities that asserts or denies that some condition holds for those entities.

protocol—the call format used by a teleprocessing monitor.

purge data—the data on or after which a storage area may be overwritten. Used in conjunction with a file label, it is a means of protecting file data until an agreed-upon release date is reached.

query language—a language that enables an end user to interact directly with a DBMS to retrieve and possibly modify data managed under the DBMS.

record—an aggregation of values of data organized by their relation to a common key.

record-at-a-time processing—the access of data a record at a time, a tuple at a time, and so on.

recovery—the restoration of the database to an original position or condition, often after major damage to the physical medium.

redundancy—the practice of storing more than one occurrence of data. In the case where data can be updated, redundancy poses serious problems. In the case where data are not updated, redundancy is often a valuable and necessary design tool.

referential integrity—the facility of a DBMS to ensure the validity of a predefined relationship.

reorganization—the process of unloading data in a poorly organized state and reloading the data in a well-organized state. In some DBMSs, reorganization is used to restructure data. Reorganization is often called "reorg" or an "unload/reload" process.

repeating groups—a collection of data that can occur several times within a given record.

rolling summary—a form of storing archival data where the most recent data have the lowest level of detail stored and the older data have higher levels of detail stored.

scope of integration—the formal definition of the boundaries of the system being modeled.

SDLC—system development life cycle—the classical operational system development life cycle that typically includes requirements gathering, analysis, design, programming, testing, integration, and implementation. Sometimes called a "waterfall" development life cycle.

secondary key—a nonunique attribute used to identify a class of records in a database.

sequential file—a file in which records are ordered according to the values of one or more key fields. The records can be processed in this sequence starting from the first record in the file, continuing to the last record in the file.

serial file—a sequential file in which the records are physically adjacent in sequential order.

set-at-a-time processing—access of data by groups, each member of which satisfies some selection criteria.

snapshot—a database dump or the archiving of data as of some moment in time.

snowflake structure—the grouping together of two or more star joins.

star join—a denormalized form of organizing data optimized for access by a group of people, usually a department. Star joins are usually associated with data marts. Star joins were popularized by Ralph Kimball.

storage hierarchy—storage units linked to form a storage subsystem in which some units are fast to access and consume small amounts of storage, but which are expensive, and other units are slow to access and are large, but are inexpensive to store.

subject database—a database organized around a major subject of the corporation. Classical subject databases are for customer, transaction, product, part, vendor, and so on.

system log—an audit trail of relevant system events (e.g., transaction entries, database changes, etc.).

system of record—the definitive and singular source of operational data or metadata. If data element ABC has a value of 25 in a database record but a value of 45 in the system of record, by definition the first value must be incorrect. The system of record is useful for the management of redundancy of data. For metadata, at any one moment in time, each unit of metadata is owned by one and only one organizational unit.

table—a relation that consists of a set of columns with a heading and a set of rows (i.e., tuples).

terabyte—a measurement of a large amount of data; 10×10^{12} bytes.

time stamping—the practice of tagging each record with some moment in time, usually when the record was created or when the record was passed from one environment to another.

time-variant data—data whose accuracy is relevant to a moment in time. The three common forms of time-variant data are continuous time-span data, event discrete data, and periodic discrete data. See also current value data.

transaction processing—the activity of executing many short, fast-running programs, providing the end user with consistent response times of 2 to 3 seconds.

transition data—data possessing both primitive and derived characteristics; usually very sensitive to the running of the business. Typical transition data include interest rates for a bank, policy rates for an insurance company, and retail sale prices for a manufacturer/distributor.

trend analysis—the process of looking at homogeneous data over a period of time.

true archival data—data at the lowest level of granularity in the current level detail database.

update—to change, add, delete, or replace values in all or selected entries, groups, or attributes stored in a database.

user—a person or process issuing commands or messages and receiving stimuli from the information system.

Zachman framework—a specification for organizing blueprints for information systems popularized by the great John Zachman.

APPENDIX 7B
DATA WAREHOUSE WEB RESOURCES

BILLINMON.COM (WWW.BILLINMON.COM)

Bill Inmon, one of the leaders in data warehousing, produces this Web site. The site includes a library with data models, articles, white papers, book reviews, a bibliography, and a glossary of DW terms. A "resource center" provides links to data warehousing industries, solution companies, DM software vendors, and product reviews. Visitors can also access a speakers bureau and a description of Inmon's Corporate Information Factory, which revolves around a DW and incorporates data marts, exploration warehouses, near-line storage, and operational data stores.

RALPH KIMBALL ASSOCIATES (WWW.RKIMBALL.COM)

Ralph Kimball, the father of data warehousing, is a leading proponent of the dimensional approach to designing large DWs. He teaches data warehousing design skills and helps selected clients with specific DW designs. The site includes links to Kimball's data warehousing classes and consulting services, his articles in *Intelligent Enterprise* (formerly *DBMS Magazine*), and a review of his book, *The Data Warehouse Toolkit*.

STANFORD DATA WAREHOUSING PUBLICATIONS (WWW-DB.STANFORD.EDU/WAREHOUSING/PUBLICATIONS.HTML)

This site offers a list of publications compiled as part of Stanford University's data warehousing project. The list is organized by subjects such as extracting source data, warehouse consistency, warehouse maintenance, physical and logical design, query processing, warehouse recovery, and data mining. Files are only available in PostScript format, but viewer guidance is provided.

THE DATA WAREHOUSING INFORMATION CENTER (WWW.DWINFOCENTER.ORG)

The goal of this site is to help visitors learn about data warehousing and decision support systems by providing links to vendors supplying end-user data retrieval and analysis tools, system infrastructure tools, and tools directed at specific industries and functions. Links point to data warehousing and decision support publications (articles, white papers, books, technical evaluations, periodicals, and other nonvendor sources of information) and service providers (consultants, trainers, conference organizers).

THE DATA ADMINISTRATION NEWSLETTER (TDAN) (WWW.TDAN.COM/EDATT1_TOCF.HTM)

Robert Seiner maintains this online publication and updates it on a quarterly basis. Articles typically have a business spin, focusing on such issues as metadata management, DWs, repositories, and data modeling. Among the other services offered by the site are book reviews, conference lists, and vendor and product lists.

DM REVIEW (WWW.DMREVIEW.COM)

The DM Review Web site offers content from *DM Review* magazine as well as online-only articles, resource lists, discussion forums, issue archives, etc. *DM Review* focuses on data warehousing and related topics such as metadata management. Frequent contributors include such industry leaders as Bill Inmon, Clive Finkelstein, and Larry English.

INTELLIGENT ENTERPRISE (WWW.INTELLIGENTENTERPRISE.COM)

Intelligent Enterprise's mission is to serve "as the key technical resource for cross-functional teams providing detailed analyses of the products, trends, and strategies that help accelerate the creation of the enterprise's information infrastructure." This publication resulted from *DBMS's* merger with its sister publication, *Database Programming & Design*. All current content is available online, and article archives (nonsearchable) provide access to past issues. Online "communities" offer focused information and interactive forums in the areas of customer relationship management, enterprise application integration, enterprise resource planning, and knowledge management.

DATAWAREHOUSING.COM (WWW.DATAWAREHOUSING.COM)

Operated by DataMirror Software, this searchable site is dedicated to "documenting all data warehousing-related information on the Internet." It includes links to software companies and consultants, a directory of relevant sites, and a list of papers and articles submitted to the site by the data warehousing community. Additionally, DataWarehousing.com hosts data warehouse-specific list servers and newsgroups.

DATAWAREHOUSE.COM (WWW.DATAWAREHOUSE.COM)

DataWarehouse.com bills itself as "the data warehouse community." The site offers discussion forums, live chats, e-seminars, articles, trade show information, and more. Membership (free) allows visitors to post to discussion boards and personalize the site, among other things.

DATA WAREHOUSE INSTITUTE (WWW.DW-INSTITUTE.COM)

The Data Warehousing Institute (TDWI) is a member-based organization whose goal is to educate decision makers and information professionals on data warehousing strategies and technologies. This site serves as a clearinghouse for case studies, white papers, and data warehousing events and conferences worldwide. Membership includes a subscription to the quarterly *Journal of Data Warehousing*.

UNIVERSITY OF NEBRASKA DATA WAREHOUSE (NULOOK; WWW.NULOOK.UNEB.EDU/INDEX.HTML)

This site is the public access point for the University of Nebraska's DW, known as "nulook." The warehouse contains financial, payroll, personnel, budget, and student data that are periodically extracted from the university's administrative computing systems. Supporting information includes online reports and queries, the data dictionary and data models, view definitions, data elements, procedures, training and support, contact information, and the nulook user group proceedings. The site has additional links to white papers and briefings on data warehousing and Web technology, resources, and a glossary of DW and related terms.

INDEX